Giuseppe Pace

Mushrooms of the World

With 20 photographs and 634 full color illustrations of species and varieties

FIREFLY BOOKS

A FIREFLY BOOK

This edition published by Firefly Books Ltd. 1998

Cataloguing in Publication Data
Pace, Giuseppe
Mushrooms of the World
Translation of: L'Atlante dei Funghi
Includes index
ISBN 1-55209-212-7
1. Mushrooms - Identification. 2. Mushrooms. I. Title
QK617.P3213 I998   579.6   C98-930634-8

Published in Canada in 1998
by Firefly Books Ltd.
3680 Victoria Park Avenue
Willowdale, Ontario, Canada M2H 3K1

Published in the United States in 1998
by Firefly Books (U.S.) Inc.
P.O. Box 1338, Ellicott Station
Buffalo, New York, USA 14205

Printed and bound in Spain by Artes Gráficas Toledo, S.A.
9 8 7 6 5 4 3 2 1
D.L. TO: 196 - 1998

Above: *Volvaria bombycina*. For a description of the species see page 41.
Opposite title page: a typical natural environment where mushrooms may be found, in the Abruzzo National Park, Italy.

Preface

This book is addressed to the amateur naturalist. Professional mycologists have their treatises, but this book is not a treatise. Therefore not all the known fungi are described here, but only the most common and the more easily identifiable species. It is our purpose to take the amateur naturalist by the hand and lead him up to the threshold of scientific mycology, letting him remain an amateur, that is, someone whose learning, interests and pleasures are continuously renewed. For this reason we will not hesitate to repeat ourselves when we think it helpful to make easy and painless the learning process and its consolidation.

In the first part of this book, the identification section, we describe about 1,000 species and varieties of mushrooms and other fungi from Europe, America, Africa, and Asia, from the Middle East to the Far East. About 400 of these species and varieties are only briefly described, whereas the rest have been dealt with in a more detailed form and are illustrated in 300 color plates.

In the second part of the book, after some general information on the biology of fungi and on their alimentary properties, there are some directions that should help the reader identify the principal and most common genera of fair-sized fungi. Then there is a list of the scientific names of genera and species, properly accented and explained. The etymological meanings of these names often emphasize important morphological characteristics, thus becoming a valid mnemonic help in the identification of the genus and species of the fungi. Regarding the tonic accent of words, it is well known how much uncertainty there is, even among the specialists, about the syllable on which the emphasis should fall, especially for words of Greek derivation. Perhaps this will be the first occasion, for some of our readers, to become acquainted with many Latin and Greek words. Actually this will help them understand the meaning of other scientific terms, even outside the mycological field.

All the color illustrations in this work were prepared by the painter Laura Rosano Maggiora; this gives the book a certain unity and adds an undisputed artistic value to it. The illustrations have been based on the best-known mycological iconographies and on original color photographs. Why were the photographs not directly reproduced? The reason is that very often in color pictures certain details, which are important for the identification of the genus and of the species, are either out of focus, altered in color, or not visible at all. The photographs, reproducing the individual features, sometimes fail to show the general features typical of a given species, which are important for its proper identification; but color drawings can do this. For these reasons, even the modern mycologists sometimes prefer to use drawings, in spite of the availability of complete photographic files. However, photographs will be found in the last part of this book, both of rare species of special interest for the professional mycologist, and of species that all amateurs should know and that have already been illustrated in the identification section.

The Swedish botanist Carolus Linnaeus introduced the system of binomial nomenclature for the designation of the species of plants and animals; hence, every species is designated with a Latin name, the first part indicating the genus and the second part the species. However, you must keep in mind that sometimes the same species is classified by one author under one genus and under another genus by another. This explains why some speak of Tricholoma rutilans *(Quelet, 1872) and others of* Tricholomopsis rutilans *(Singer, 1939). In this, as in many other cases, the specific denominations, in our example* rutilans, *are more stable than the generic denominations,* Tricholoma *and* Tricholomopsis. *For this reason, in the index we have chosen to give precedence to the species denominations. In some cases, to avoid confusion, we thought it necessary to have the species denomination followed by the name, in parenthesis, of the author who described it.*

Genera and species follow each other according to a systematic order, except when typographical necessities have required slight changes. In the identification section the species are illustrated smaller than life size and we have given their respective dimensions in centimeters (cm) in the descriptions, near the words cap, *or* stem. *We wish to note here that mycologists often refer to the base of the stem to mean the part we ordinarily call the foot (the term* base *was used by the translators); and refer to the width of the lamellae to indicate the dimension we call height (the translators have used the terms* broad *and* narrow *to allow the reader an easier comparison with American and English books on fungi); they use the term* hygrophanous *to indicate a species with a particular type of sensitivity to atmospheric humidity, which makes it become generally darker, or rarely lighter; they use the term* amyloidal *to indicate those spores that, in the presence of iodine, turn violet, just as starch does. The color of the spores given in the description of the various species is their color en masse; when seen through the microscope, the color can be different, usually paler. A mass of spores large enough to identify the color can be obtained by laying the cap of a mature specimen on a piece of white paper for a few hours in a place shielded from air currents. The lamellae (gills), or the tubules, or, generally, the part called hymenium, should face the paper; sometimes it will be useful to cut the stem of the mushroom so that the spore-bearing parts will be nearer to the paper and the spores will be collected in a closer, denser mass. When the time and place of growth of some species is not indicated, it is implied that such species grow at times and places common for most fungi: from summer to autumn, in woods of conifers or of latifoliate trees. When a species is said to be edible, the following conditions are implied: the specimens to be used for alimentary purposes must be not too ripe, completely healthy (not even slightly spoiled), properly cleaned and cooked; other conditions will be given as required.*

If this work of ours contributes something to making family vacations more enjoyable, creating more careful observers, friends and protectors of nature, and permitting everybody, especially young people, to discover, even in these modest organisms, the fungi, the inexhaustible cleverness of our Creator, we will feel well rewarded.

Giuseppe Pace

Looking for Mushrooms

It might be true that "he who sleeps late does not catch any fish," but "he who sleeps late does not find mushrooms" is not true at all. During the mushroom season, between summer and fall, the professional collectors don't wait for the sun to come up: they leave their villages when it is still dark and hurry along the trails to be the first to arrive, with the first light, to the mushroom-gathering places that they know so well. Sometimes it is a race. On other occasions it is less urgent; this happens when the professionals have come to a friendly agreement on the division of various areas or when they have formed an association both for the search and for the sale of the mushrooms.

The amateur who starts looking for mushrooms in those early hours before dawn probably comes back from such an adventure tired and disappointed, soaked with dew, but with an empty basket, or sometimes with a full one but with mushrooms very different from those that he sees filling up the baskets of the professionals, the ones that he really likes. It is perfectly useless to try to compete against the professionals in such an uneven game. On the contrary, it is often convenient not to start looking for mushrooms until the sun has evaporated the dew and dried somewhat the more viscid mushrooms. Even in the afternoon you can still find many different species of mushrooms in the woods and in the meadows, species overlooked by the professionals, who sometimes don't know their value or think that they are not good commercially.

Unfortunately there are still people who, after finding a mushroom, either pull it out, perhaps throwing it away a few minutes later, or try to destroy it; they cannot leave it, intact, in its place. What foolishness! And how damaging, sometimes, for all the vegetation around! It is worthwhile, sometimes, to start looking for mushrooms early in the morning, if only to be ahead of such people and to miss seeing along the footpaths and in the woods so many fragments of magnificent, ruined mushrooms. It is not true that if you sleep late you will not be able to find good mushrooms anymore. The professionals, in fact, pay attention only to those three or four species that the markets demand, but the amateurs have a greater choice: they can gather many different species of mushrooms for the kitchen; they can collect for their studies some samples of all the species of mushrooms that they can find.

For study purposes all the species are interesting, including the poisonous mushrooms (toadstools) and the very tiny ones. For kitchen purposes one must exclude and avoid rigorously all those species that one is not absolutely sure of being edible and tasty. It is also advisable not to collect mushrooms that have been in rain for days and days even though they seem to be of excellent quality: they would be tasteless and indigestible. With few exceptions, which will be indicated later, one should also avoid mushrooms that have been frozen in cold weather. Sometimes people fill up their baskets with everything they find, but the result of such a practice is merely to take home an unnecessarily large quantity of stuff that will be good only for the garbage can. Often the mushrooms will be too old and full of maggots. For the kitchen, one should collect only unripe samples, or at least not too ripe. But do not fall into the opposite trap and collect samples that are too unripe. Do not collect samples that have just appeared: you can go back later when they will have grown to a sufficient size. For studying, one should collect samples of various ages. Generally, there is no need for a long and difficult search; mushrooms often grow in groups that include ripe, half-developed, and just emerged samples. A question often asked is how to collect the mushrooms. Does one pull them out of the soil or does one cut them at the base with a knife? Either system is good for the mushrooms with lamellae, provided one digs all around the base of the stalk so as to collect the volva if there is one wrapped around the base. Otherwise, the volva could remain overlooked in the soil, and a sample of some deadly *amanita* collected without the volva wrapped around the base of the stalk could be mistaken for an innocent *psalliota*. Many deplorable accidents are actually due to carelessness of this type. There is no need to use a knife to collect specimens of *Cantharellus*; but it is better to cut at the base with a sharp knife the lignicolous mushrooms: the *Pleurotus*, the *Polyporales*, the *Armillaria mella* (page 110) and similar species. It is also convenient to use a knife to cut the *Hydnum repandum* (page 214); by doing so you will be able to collect more of these specimens, perhaps two or three times, later in the season, for they grow in the same place near the base, if left under the soil.

Immediately after you collect the mushrooms for kitchen use, clean them of dirt, sand, and vegetables residues; also eliminate any bruised parts, tubules, and lamellae if they are flaccid, part of the stalk if fibrous, and all the stalk from the *lepiotas* of large size. But mushrooms to be used for study should not be cleaned; everything on them is an object for study, just as much as the mushrooms are. Therefore in collecting mushrooms to be used for studies one should keep some soil around the base if they are soil-growing species, or wood fragments if they are lignicolous species. This can make the research easier, faster, and more accurate. The mushrooms should then be placed, either one by one or in small groups, into numbered collection containers, such as plastic bags or boxes; the containers should then be placed into a basket carefully so as not to squash them.

The collector should immediately write down in a notebook, under the appropriate number, all those observations that might be useful for the identification of the collected samples. One should not be afraid to record even minute details: sometimes the starting point for a fast and accurate identification is just one minute detail. One should specify the date and time of collecting each sample, the weather on the day it was collected, whether it was fair, dry, windy, rainy, cold, and the climatic conditions of the season or of the days before the sample was collected. One should specify the locality where the mushroom was picked up, and its height above sea level; the exact place where it was growing, meadow, glade, or woods; if the meadow is cool, humid, or dry; if the woods are thick and shady or thin and sunny; what trees are found in the woods; if the mushroom was growing in the soil or on a tree. It would also be convenient to specify immediately the odor and taste of the mushroom; one should not be afraid to taste a morsel of it, which, however, should not be swallowed, but spit out, especially if one suspects one is handling a dangerous species such as the *Amanita phalloides* (page 26–27) and similar ones.

Immediately after picking them, the mushrooms to be used in the kitchen should be placed in the basket with the stalks turned up. By doing so, the little worms that might eventually be inside will start moving toward the base of the stalk; on the following day it is sufficient to cut the base away to get rid of many undesirable guests.

As soon as one gets home, it is necessary to complete the cleaning of the mushrooms. Often the first thing one does is to put them into water: this is a mistake. To clean the mushrooms one should use a small brush, not a very hard one, and a small pointed knife. The mushrooms should be sectioned lengthwise from the cap to the base; thus one can see if there still are clandestine guests to expel; if there should be too many of them, the only thing to do is to throw the mushrooms into the garbage can. Some worms in a few hours can destroy mushrooms that, at the time of picking, appeared perfectly healthy.

Some of the species of the genus *Boletus* and the unripe *Gomphidius* have a very sticky cap cuticle; this has to be taken off. The *Polyporus confluens* (page 205) has a bitter cuticle; one should cut it away with a potato peeler. The cap of the large size *lepiotas* is often covered with warts that should be taken off with a vigorous brushing, using a rather stiff brush. The cuticle of other mushrooms is tasty and nice smelling; to take it off would ruin the good qualities of the mushrooms.

If you have more mushrooms than you need immediately, dry some of them or find some way to preserve them. For immediate consumption, one should choose the most delicate and mature specimens. Fresh mushrooms should be rinsed, very quickly, only a few minutes before starting your preparations for a meal, paying attention that they do not imbibe too much water; they should be dried immediately after rinsing, first with a slightly damp towel and then with a dry one.

On this page top and opposite top: *Mutinus caninus* (Hudson) and *Calvatia lilacina* (Henn.).
Opposite centre and bottom: *Psathyrella stipatissima* and *Lepiota haematosperma* (Boud.).
On this page left: *Boletus edulis*.
On this page above: *Cortinarius orellanus* (Fries).

Mushrooms and Their Habitat

Habitat is a Latin word meaning "he dwells"; here we will use this word to indicate the locality where the mushroom grows and the time of production of the fruiting bodies. The temperate zones are certainly the most suitable for mushrooms; several thousand species of large and small dimensions are found in these zones. The main factor in determining the temperature of the earth is the radiation from the sun, which warms up the air, water, and soil. Since most of the fungal mycelium grow under the soil surface, the growth and development of the mushrooms will depend more upon the soil temperature than on that of the air. And since the darker and moister a soil is, the higher the quantity of heat absorbed, it is easy to understand why dark and moist soils are more suitable for the growth of mushrooms than those of clear color and with scarce water reserves. The professional collectors know not only the places, but also the weather and the times most favorable for the growth of the mushrooms; thus, they welcome the rains with great pleasure, especially those during the summer and the beginning of autumn, followed by a few sunny days and mild nights without winds. The growth of the fungal mycelium requires water. On the contrary, the fruiting bodies start forming when the conditions for the growth of the mycelium become unfavorable, when the availability of water, the solvent for the nutrients needed for growth, is decreasing. It is as if the mycelium, feeling itself near death or a period of idleness, musters all the reserves stored during the good season to produce the fruiting bodies, which in turn will produce the spores, necessary for the continuation of the species.

What about the fairy rings (witches' rings, in Italian)? The mycelium of some mushrooms can continue to grow in the soil for many years, sometimes for centuries, expanding into concentric rings of larger and larger diameter, as the waves produced by a stone thrown into a pond. The fruiting bodies are formed on the new, peripheric mycelium, while the old one decomposes. Thus the mushrooms come to the surface disposed in rings: this is the reason for the formation of the fairy rings. And it has been through the study of these rings, not at all bewitched, that we were able to find out that the mycelium of some mushrooms can live for a very long time. The old decomposed mycelium is a good fertilizer for grass; one can be quite sure that, at the proper time of the year, mushrooms such as the Meadows mushroom (*Psalliota*) will be found along the periphery of those circular spots where the grass, after mowing, grows greener and more vigorous than in the surrounding areas.

Most mushrooms belong to species that form their fruiting bodies in summer and in autumn. But there are some spring species, such as the *Morchellae* and a few winter species. *Collybia velutipes* (page 90) grows in dense clusters, from December to March on trees, as a very damaging parasite, or saprophytically on dead logs and tree stumps. The stems of this mushroom are coriaceous and somewhat bitter, but the caps can be really delicious if cooked for a long time and with the proper seasoning. Another excellent winter species is the *Hygrophorus marzuolus* (page 171). The snow protects the mycelium and, sometimes, the fruiting bodies already above the surface of the soil but dormant under the snow. This is the reason why, in Tuscany, they call them dormant mushrooms. As soon as the snow melts, they appear scattered everywhere in groups, sometimes quite numerous. This species is largely diffuse in woods of conifers, beeches, oaks, and chestnuts, either in the plains or in the mountains. But, if the winter has been cold and without snow, it is perfectly useless to go in search of these mushrooms: the frost, penetrated deeply into the soil, has either destroyed the mycelium or, at least, prevented it from growing.

As there are mushrooms relatively resistant to cold, so there are various species of the genus *Tylostoma*, which can endure the bright sun and the aridity of the desert. Others instead will not grow unless the mycelium is continuously submerged in water.

The professional collectors do not like the wind, which, they say, can drive the mushrooms off. Actually, a few days of persistent winds are sufficient to dry up the ground to such an extent that the mycelium of several species will stop growing or forming fruiting bodies.

It is said that mushrooms can grow overnight. For some species of the genus *Coprinus* a few hours can be sufficient to sprout from the ground or manure, to grow, to ripen and to dissolve away; but other species of mushrooms, especially the lignicolous ones, can continue to grow and develop for days and weeks; others will do so for seasons or even for years, even though they will be dormant during the coldest periods. Sometimes the growth of certain mushrooms can be quite a sensational affair. Once under a portico with a concrete pavement, facing a large courtyard, there was a loud noise, as of an exploding firecracker, and people saw the concrete splitting and several *psalliotas*, in a compact and compressed mass, emerging from the crevice. On another occasion Dr. Carlo Luciani, a well-known mycologist and experienced collector, found two fine *boletuses* near the trunk of a chestnut. He made sure that there were no more of them around at the time, but a few hours later, in exactly the same spot, he found a third one, of quite large dimensions.

Most of the mushrooms of interest to us find their preferred

Left: *Stropharia inuncta*.
Below: *Sclerangium polyrrhizon* (Lev.).
Bottom left and right: *Limacella roseofloccosa*
(Hora) and *Sebacina Laciniata* (Bres.).

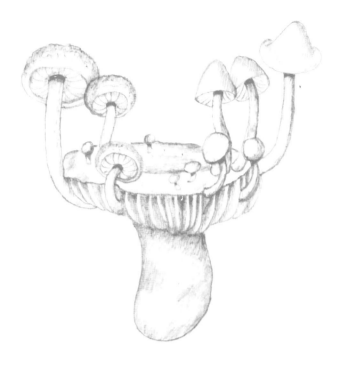

habitat in the woods. But not all woods are good for all the mushrooms: some species will not grow at all unless that particular species of higher plants with which they are associated, either as symbionts or in some other fashion, is available. For instance, *Boletus granulatus* (see page 193) requires young pines, and it succeeds in taking enough nutrients from them to be able to "fruit" as many as five times a year; *Boletus luteus* (page 192) also requires pines, but only those trees that are ten years or older; *Boletus elegans* (page 191), *Boletus viscidus* (page 191) and *Boletus cavipes* (page 199) need larches, and *Boletus aereus* (page 180), found in woods of latifoliate trees, cannot live in those of conifers. On the contrary, *Amanita phalloides* (page 26–27), a species that should be well known because it is deadly poisonous and common, grows in coniferous woods, in the plains, in the hills, in the mountains. *Amanita caesarea* (page 17) grows in woods of latifoliate trees, but not in all of them: only in those of oaks and chestnuts; however, in Mexico and Japan, it grows in pine woods. In the woods we also find those mushrooms that grow on live or dead tree trunks, on decaying stumps, on leaves, on pine cones, and even on other mushrooms, such as *Boletus parasiticus* (see page 277), growing on *Scleroderma aurantium*.

Still in the woods, in the places where the charcoalmakers build their kilns to make charcoal, or in the areas destroyed by fire, certain species of *Cantharellus* thrive. Several species of *Pesiza* grow, in autumn, on the beaten and naked ground of trails in the woods.

Some species of *Hygrophorus* and *Psalliota* grow in the woods, others in the meadows. *Clitocybe geotropa* (see page 113), of very good quality, and *Melanoleuca grammopodia* (page 109), somewhat indigestible, unless parboiled, grow in the grass of the meadows in groups often arranged in large circles. In the gràss, along the trails, grows *Marasmius oreades* (page 91), a species very much in demand and rightly so. *Boletus strobilaceus* (see page 200) prefers the soft soil displaced by moles. Various species of *Coprinus* grow near

decaying materials, manure, plaster rubbish, sewer discharges. *Volvaria gloiocephala* (page 40) grows either in open meadows, or on decaying materials, especially on heaps of decaying straw, covered or not by a light layer of soft soil. *Stropharia Ferrii* (page 55) grows on rotten branches and leaves. Some species of *Morchella* grow, after the first spring thunderstorms, on the soil displaced by digging operations. All the species of the genus *Morchella* require abundant water, plenty of light, and a warm temperature. They prefer sandy grounds facing east.

Various species of *Morchella, Volvaria, Coprinus,* and *Peziza* grow in uncultivated soils. On the contrary, on cultivated soils, especially if fertilized with chemical fertilizers, one will find very few mushrooms. The salty sprays from the sea do not provide a good habitat for most mushrooms; however, *Psalliota Bernardi, Bovista plumbea* (page 231), and *Geaster nanus* (page 232) thrive on the sandy dunes along the seashore. However, *Coprinus atramentarius* (page 50) and some species of the genus *Psalliota* thrive in meadows and in vegetable gardens fertilized with manure.

Hypogeous mushrooms grow buried underground. Several hundred species are known. Among them there are the much-sought-after *Tuber magnatum* (see page 240), which grows in woods of oak, poplar, willow, hazelnut, beech, almost exclusively in a few regions in North Italy; and *Tuber melanosporum,* also very much in demand, which grows in thin woods of oak, holm oak, beech, hornbeam, if the soil is limy.

Some mushrooms change slightly in shape, color, and flavor, depending on the species of the host plant, the latitude, or the altitude at which they grow. For instance, *Armillaria nellea* (see page 110) is honey yellow when growing on mulberry trees, cinnamon yellow on poplars, with olivaceous shades on oaks, olivaceous brown on robinias, reddish brown and with distinctly bitterish flavor when growing on conifers. *Cantharellus cibarius* (see page 225) is an early species, about medium size and bright colored when growing in oak woods; in beech woods it grows three weeks later, is larger and paler than those growing in oak woods; in hornbeam woods it is even later, is smaller and grows in small tufts; and finally, later in the season, it can be found in fir woods, squat, fleshy, discolored, and with a bitterish flavor. In relation to latitude and altitude, *Boletus edulis* (see page 177) has no rivals; it is found from one side of the ocean to the other, from the plains to the mountains. *Polyporus ovinus* (page 204) and *Tricholoma pardinum* (page 98) grow on the mountains in the south and in the plains in the north. All other conditions being equal, going from warm regions to colder ones, the diffusion of *Amanita caesarea* (page 17) decreases just as much as that of *Amanita muscaria* (page 18–19) increases. In the temperate regions, between 2,000 and 3,000 meters, even the alpine species, about 2,000 of them, cease growing. Considering the numerous variations to which mushrooms are subject, the finding of a specimen which, at first sight, seems very different from the typical form described in the books, does not mean that one has discovered a new species or variety; the amateur collectors who so easily convince themselves that they have discovered a new species should use a little more caution; often their new species is nothing else than an oddly shaped specimen of a species known for a long time.

What we have written above about the mushroom habitat is only a small and simple exemplification; if we had to deal with this subject in any depth, a treatise would be required, and its size would not be small.

Top: *Mutinus elegans* (Mont.).
Above left: fairy ring of *Tricholoma populinum*.
Above: *Coprinus niveus*.
Left: *Lepiota meleagroides* (Huissm.).

Top: *Boletus granulatus*.
Above: *Pluteus cinereofuscus* (J. Lange).
Right: *Tremella mesenteria*.
Opposite: *Sarcoscypha coccinea*.

Part One
The Identification of Mushrooms
and Other Fungi

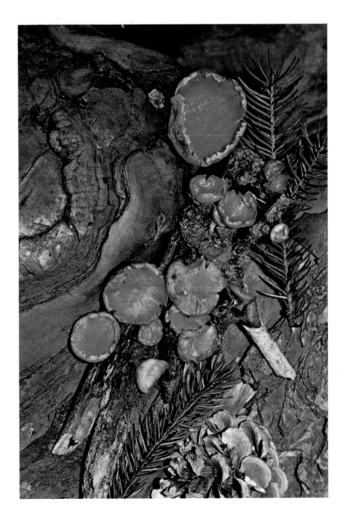

Acknowledgments

The authors gratefully acknowledge the help contributed by several people in the preparation of this book, and in particular:

Prof. Beniamino Peyronel, President Emeritus of the Faculty of Agriculture of the University of Torino
Prof. Agostino Archeni
Prof. Antonio Bettin, of the Mycological Group Ferrovieri di Verona
Dr. Carlo Luciano Alessio of the Mycological Group FIAT, Torino
Dr. Eng. Ernesto Rebaudengo, of the Ceva Mycological Group
Prof. Giulio Pace
Prof. Giuseppe Pace
Maestro Giulio Chiapasco, of the Boves Mycological Group
Painter Laura Rosano Maggiora
Prof. Pietro Chasseur
Mr. Umberto Nonis, of the FIAT (Torino) Mycological Group, to whom we owe, among other things, the finding, the photographs, and the identification of the following, particularly interesting, species: Aleuria olivacea, Calvatia Lilacina, Coprinus niveus, Lepiota haematosperma, Limacella roseofloccosa, Mitrula Rhemii, Sebacinia laciniata, Sclerangium polyrrhizon, Stropharia inuncta.
The firm Interfungo di Casazza, Bergamo, which gave permission to photograph their cultivations of meadow mushrooms.
The Japanese firm Nihon Kyoto Kabushikigaisya, which made available the photographs of the mushroom cultivations of Shiitake.

American Publishers' Note

The following table of metric system equivalences is given here for the convenience of American readers.

unit	abbreviation	approximate U.S. value
centimeter	cm	0.39 inch
gram	gm	0.035 ounce
milligram	mg	0.015 grain
kilometer	km	0.62 mile

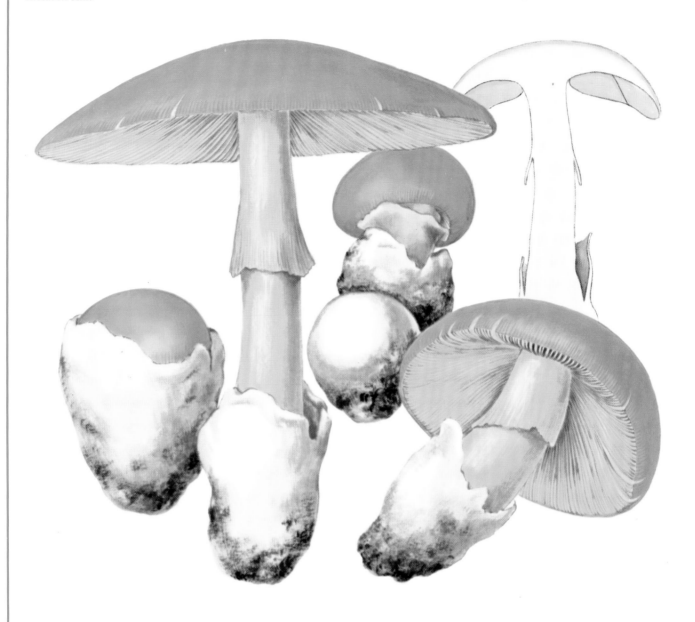

AMANITA CAESAREA (Caesar's mushroom)

Cap ovoid or hemispheric, then convex, finally expanded and sometimes somewhat depressed, 8–18 cm; margin striated by light grooves in the direction of the gills; color orange or red orange; rarely yellow, tending to orange or faded yellow; cuticle usually without remains of the universal veil, smooth, shining, somewhat viscid in humid weather, easily separable from the cap. **Stem** cylindric, thick, slightly bulbous at the base; yellow, stuffed at first, then soon hollow. **Ring** large, pendulous, kiltlike; yellow; sometimes striate from the top down. **Volva** large, white, lobate, free from the base and enwrapping it. **Flesh** firm, white, yellow under the cuticle of the cap. **Odor** light and delicate. **Flavor** pleasant. **Gills** close, broad, free from the stem, yellow. Intermediate gills with posterior end truncate, almost at right angles: this characteristic is found in several species of *Amanita*. **Spores** white, tending to yellowish. It grows in wood clearings, preferring chestnut and oak woods of warm and warm temperate regions; in Central America and in Japan it is found, somewhat smaller, under pines in the mountains. **Edible**, excellent either cooked or raw, in salads; it can be preserved in oil or exsiccated.

Similar to *Amanita caesarea* is the *Amanita calyptroderma*: **edible**, cap 10–30 cm, orange or yellow, covered by one or two large, white pieces of the universal veil; large, white volva; stem squat, cream color, as are the ring and the gills; grows in North America, in autumn, under oaks and conifers.

AMANITA MUSCARIA
Description on page 19.

AMANITA FLAVOCONIA (1)
Cap, warts, ring, and part of the stem chrome yellow; found in North America; **not advisable** for eating.

AMANITA MUSCARIA form FORMOSA (2)
Cap orange yellow with scarce yellowish warts; **poisonous**.

AMANITA MUSCARIA faded and yellowed (3)

AMANITA MUSCARIA variety AUREOLA (4)
Characterized by the cap, 3–7 cm, free from warts from the beginning; **poisonous**.

AMANITA MUSCARIA variety REGALIS (5)
Sturdy and bulky. Cap liver brown with yellow warts; **poisonous**.

Persistent rain can wash off the pigment from the cap of the *Amanita muscaria* and deposit it on the gills, on the stem and ring, which from white become yellow, whereas the cap's color fades, as in the specimen number 3 of the drawings below, which can almost be mistaken for an *Amanita caesarea* (see page 17).
Some people use *Amanita muscaria* for various purposes, and even as food, after first treating it. Let us not imitate them! Once, sprinkled with milk, it was used to kill flies. It is in fact poisonous, more or less dangerous even though not deadly.

AMANITA PANTHERINA (Panther Amanita) (1)
Cap 6–12 cm, fuliginous brown, ochraceous brown, oliveaceous brown, or grayish brown, darker toward the center; sometimes very faded; covered with white, small, numerous, nonpersistent warts; margin striate in the direction of the gills. **Stem** generally long, slightly tapering upward; bulbous base with a conspicuous, flat, steplike margin; white or whitish, glabrous, striate on top near the gills; at first stuffed, then hollow. **Ring** membranous, large, with an often halved, white, striate, evanescent margin. **Volva** wrapped around the bulbous base, white; just over the bulb, around the stem, there are two or three remains of volva, like flocculous rings, more or less slanted and whole. **Flesh** friable, not very thick, moist, white. **Odor** mild. **Flavor** mild. **Gills** close, broad, free from the stem, white. **Spores** white. Found in woods and bushy clearings. **Poisonous**.
The variety *abietum* grows in the mountains, in coniferous woods, especially fir; it is **poisonous**, darker, sturdier, bigger, fleshier, without striae along the cap's margin, with few but large warts.
Similar to *A. pantherina* is *Amanita brunnescens*: **poisonous**, typical of North America, frequently found under oak trees; dark grayish brown, but whitish when old.

AMANITA MUSCARIA (Fly mushroom)

Cap globular, then hemispheric, finally expanded, 8–20 cm; vermilion red or carmine red, with numerous whitish, polygonal, soft warts; yellow tending to orange and with few yellowish warts in the form *formosa*; liver brown with yellow warts in the variety *regalis*; pinkish in the form *rosans*; margin smooth, then striate in the direction of the gills; cuticle viscid in humid weather, otherwise dry and glossy; easily detachable from the cap; with white warts, then yellowish or faded; sometimes rain and wind can disperse all the warts; in this case it might be mistaken for *Amanita caesarea* (page 17), which rarely has on its cap the remains of the volva. **Stem** cylindrical, slender, with bulbous base; white, soon hollow. **Ring** large, soft, white with yellow margin; at times with vertical striae; then it narrows, becomes membranous and whitish; sometimes the rain stains it yellow with the pigment washed off from the cap. **Volva** white, adhering to the base of the stem, fragmented in bulky scales, arranged into belts. **Flesh** a little hard but friable; white; red under the cuticle of the cap when this is red. **Odor** mild. **Flavor** agreeable. **Gills** close, broad, narrower toward the stem, free, interspaced with intermediate gills; white, but sometimes tending to lemon yellow. **Spores** white. It grows in autumn, in woods, especially under birches, firs, and larches, where the light is brighter. **Poisonous**.

AMANITA SPISSA (1)

Cap fuliginous gray, brown, or olivaceous brown, often darker at the center; covered with soft grayish or brownish but never white warts; hemispheric, then convex, 6–15 cm; thin, even margin, that is, without striae. **Stem** thick, covered with squamules; with the bulbous base without a conspicuous margin and sometimes extending into a root-shaped appendix; white or pale gray, with darker stripes made by fine scales or hairs; striate vertically in the part above the ring. **Ring** large, white, vertically striate. **Volva** not very distinguishable from the base of the stem, which it enwraps with tenuous remains. **Flesh** thick, firm, moist, white. **Odor** mild, radishlike. **Flavor** mild. **Gills** close, broad, of different length (unequal), free from the stem, but sometimes decurrent on it by a thin thread; white. **Spores** white. It grows in woods, especially under oaks and pines. **Edible**, but to be avoided by the inexperienced collector because it is easily mistaken for *Amanita pantherina* (page 18), which presents a bulbous base with a steplike margin and is **poisonous**.

AMANITA SPISSA variety VALIDA (2)

Smaller than the typical form, of various colors, with warts that become black thorns when dried; **suspect**.

AMANITA SPISSA variety EXCELSA (3)

Cap cinereous, long; base buried in the ground; odor of green apples; **edible**, of poor quality.

AMANITA RUBESCENS (Blusher)

Cap 5–15 cm, Marsala wine colored, brown, or almost rosy; sometimes faded, even whitish, slightly colored only at the center; sometimes also yellowish or greenish; with white, or slightly reddish or faded warts, which are small and in small groups; margin even without striae. **Stem** generally stout, a shade paler than the cap; white or striate above the ring; soon becoming reddish at the base; bulbous base with series of scales, remnants of the volva, but not very prominent. **Ring** large, pendulous, striate, white or rosy or yellowish. **Flesh** white; slowly becoming light vinous-red when exposed to air, especially the flesh of the stem. No particular **odor**. **Flavor** at first pleasant, then slightly acrid. **Gills** close, broad, linked to the stem by a short thread or free; white, becoming spotted with red where bruised. **Spores** white. From spring to autumn, in coniferous and latifoliate woods. **Edible**, but with caution: raw, it is toxic, but properly cooked it is excellent.

What some authors call *Amanita pseudorubescens* is only an *A. rubescens* grown in particularly dry weather; it has violet brown cap, stem covered with pointed warts, and violet gray ring.

Related to *A. rubescens* is *Amanita annulosulphurea*, of smaller size, with a sulfur yellow ring; **edible with caution**, as *Amanita rubescens*.

rubescens Am.

AMANITA or ASPIDELLA ECHINOCEPHALA (1)

Cap 7–20 cm, from white to brownish, with pointed, globose, or flattened warts, adhering to the cuticle, but soon easily removable; margin lacking warts, but with pendulous remains of the partial veil; totally decorticable. **Stem** stout, rather fibrous, base deeply buried; white; the lower half covered with brownish scales; slight remains of the volva. **Ring** white, pendulous, very high on the stem, vertically striate. **Flesh** of the cap firm, rather granulose, white in dry weather, ash blue when humid; stem's flesh fibrous, slightly greenish, becoming slowly yellowish when bruised. **Odor** of the cap mild; of the stem aromatic but disgusting. **Flavor** pleasant. **Gills** close, thin, broad, free or connected to the stem by a tooth; white or shaded with yellow or green; intermediate gills rounded, not truncated; edges finely fimbriate, white. **Spores** white or tinged with green. It grows on dry, calcareous soil, where it is sunny and warm; or even a few yards out of the woods, where there is little or no grass. **Suspect.**

AMANITA or ASPIDELLA VITTADINI (2)

Similar to *A. echinocephala*, but more slender and rather thin; pointed warts, especially numerous toward the center of the cap; it is a Mediterranean species; **suspect.**

AMANITA OVOIDEA

Cap ovoid, then convex, finally expanded, 10–30 cm, white smooth, moist, lucid; thick margin without grooves; festooned with the soft, evanescent remains of the partial veil; cuticle easily removable. **Stem** stout, cylindrical, flocculose or farinaceous, stuffed. **Ring** white, soft, ephemeral, or farinose and longer lived. **Volva** large, thick, often with a lobate margin; persistent; yellowish or whitish, darker in the form *proxima*, which presents also a more resistant ring and smaller carpophore. **Flesh** very thick, white. **Odor** mild or not very pleasant. **Flavor** agreeable. **Gills** close, broad, free from the stem; white, then tending to cream. **Spores** white. It grows in groups, in thin woods of warm temperate regions, especially on calcareous soil, where it forms crevices. **Edible,** cooked or raw: the gills are tasty, the flesh of the cap is rather tasteless.

Also with white caps, at least initially, are: *Amanita lepiotoides,* **edibility not verified**, cap white, then ochraceous or purple, 6–12 cm, margin striate, volva brownish, gills and flesh white, then reddish; and *Amanita ponderosa,* **edibility not verified**, cap 10–13 cm, white, then reddish ocher, margin striate only in ripe age, ring inconsistent, volva large, dark, sometimes double, flesh white, then pinkish, finally brownish.

AMANITA SOLITARIA form PELLITA (1)

Cap white, with rather large white, then grayish, finally ochraceous warts, easily washed off by rain and wind; globose, then convex, finally expanded, 6–18 cm; moist; margin even, festooned with large remains of the partial veil. **Stem** white, stout, nearly cylindrical; with mealy white, easily removable scales; slightly bulbous base, covered with belts of white scales, remains of the volva; rootlike appendix. **Ring** white, of mealy and creamy consistency at the same time; fimbriate, fragile, soon washed off in inclement weather. **Flesh** tender, thick, white. **Odor** mild. **Flavor** pleasant. **Gills** close, white, with flocculose edges; first reaching to the stem, then free. **Spores** white. Contrary to what its name indicates, it often grows in groups, on calcareous soil, in thin latifoliate woods and in meadows. **Edible**, but the cuticle should be removed from the cap because of its disagreeable flavor.

AMANITA SOLITARIA form STROBILIFORMIS (2)

Cap white, but soon cinereous, ochraceous in the center, adorned with feltlike warts, shaped like truncated pyramids, arranged in a rather regular pattern. **Ring** pendulous, vertically striate, white. **Base** of the stem bulbous with distinct margin; white, then soon ochraceous. It grows solitary or in groups, in thin woods of latifoliate or coniferous trees, especially under oaks. **Edible**.

porphyria Am.

1

2

AMANITA PORPHYRIA (1)

Cap 4–8 cm, expanded and slanted on the stem; of various colors, from gray to brown, generally with an amethystine shade, darker toward the center where sometimes it is slightly umbonate; no warts, but at times one or two large, membranous, cinereous remains of the universal veil; with radiating fibrils; even margin. **Stem** generally tall and thin, but sometimes rather thick; white and striate above the ring; whitish or yellowish or more or less the same color as the cap in the part beneath the ring, and with irregular, darker streaks, more or less evident; fibrous toward the base; becoming brownish when bruised; stuffed, then soon hollow. **Base** bulbous gradually less evident; either covered with a thin, white volva, with a lobed margin detached from the base, a constant characteristic of *Amanita pseudoporphyria* (2); or with a steplike margin and covered with gray, adhering volva. **Ring** disklike, then pendulous, petticoat-like; white and striate above, tending to the color of the cap underneath; finally reduced to a violet brownish rag adhering to the middle of the stem. **Flesh** white, violet under the cuticle; rather friable. Turnip **odor**. **Flavor** mild, then rather acrid. **Gills** close, free or almost free from the stem, with numerous intermediate lamellae; whitish. **Spores** white. It grows in coniferous woods, especially under pine trees, but also in latifoliate woods. Both *Amanita porphyria* and *Amanita pseudoporphyria* **are not edible** because of the smell and flavor, which are not improved by cooking.

AMANITA JUNQUILLEA

Cap yellowish or whitish or even ochraceous, then at the center often tending to purple; slightly viscid, bright; with floccose whitish warts, either small, or larger and less numerous; sometimes completely glabrous; hemispheric, slightly campanulate, then expanded, 5–11 cm; thin margin with regular, well-defined, long grooves in the direction of the lamellae. **Stem** white, fibrillar; now tall, now stout; at times with a bulbous, globose base, or with the base slightly thickened, or even thin; fragile, stuffed, then hollow. **Ring** white, caducous, sometimes no longer evident in old specimens. **Volva** often with a margin forming a well-defined step around the base of the stem to which it adheres; at times whole, sometimes broken here and there; at times forming one or more rings around the lower part of the stem. **Flesh** tender, friable, white; yellowish under the cuticle. **Odor** mild. **Flavor** mild. **Gills** close, broad in the middle, unequal, free; white. **Spores** white. It grows from spring to the beginning of winter, especially on sandy soil, in woods of pines, oaks, chestnuts. **Edible with caution**: eaten in abundance it is harmful. Similar species: *Amanita vernalis*, **edible**, thicker than *A. junquillea*, faded yellow, almost white; *Amanita Eliae,* **edible**, with a bulbous base extending rootlike; *Amanita Amici*, **suspect**, creamy colored, then yellowish with brownish center; in warm temperate regions.

AMANITA CITRINA

Cap hemispheric or conical, then plane, 6–12 cm; but umbonate in the variety *glabra*; slightly viscid; glossy; lemon yellow or greenish yellow, but white in the variety *alba*; warts scattered, large, irregular, whitish, then brownish, always brownish in the variety *mappa*, almost completely absent in the var. *glabra*; even margin. **Stem** cylindrical, with a bulblike base, spheric or compressed; stuffed, then soon hollow; white, tinted with yellow; above the ring it often shows the striae imprinted by the gills, earlier adhering to the stem. **Ring** yellowish; striate on the surface which was in contact with the gills; thin, fimbriate; larger in the variety *mappa*. **Volva** adhering to the base with which it forms a bulb with even, flattened margin; whitish, here and there cracked and brownish, especially in the variety *glabra*. **Flesh** white, slightly yellow under the cuticle. Turniplike **odor**, but mild in the variety *glabra*. **Flavor** soon slightly acrid. **Gills** close, broad, unequal, free from the stem, whitish. **Spores** white. It is found in coniferous or latifoliate woods, especially under birches, beeches, and oaks, on sandy soil. **To be avoided**, because of the disgusting flavor and because it is easily mistaken for *Amanita phalloides* (see page 27), **which is deadly**. It can be also mistaken for *Amanita junquillea* (page 25): **edible**, which however has the cap's margin striate and does not have either the turniplike odor or the acrid flavor.

AMANITA PHALLOIDES
Description on page 27.

AMANITA PHALLOIDES variety CITRINA (1)

AMANITA PHALLOIDES variety UMBRINA (2)

AMANITA PHALLOIDES variety ALBA (3)

Amanita phalloides, when it is yellow, can be confused with *Amanita junquillea* (see page 25) and with *Amanita citrina*, which however have a volva tightly adhering to the base of the stem. When the *A. phalloides* loses the ring and is of white or slate gray color, it can be confused with species of the genus *Volvaria* (see pages 40 and 41), which lack the ring and have the volva at the base of the stem, but have rosy gills. If the *A. phalloides* loses its volva, sometimes remaining unnoticed in the ground, and it is of white, grayish, or brownish color, it can be mistaken for *Lepiota naucina* (page 38), with white or rosy gills, or for some of the *Psalliota* (pages 43–49), with white gills changing in time to rosy and then tobacco color. When it appears without volva and without ring, and is of green color, it lis likely to be confused with some species of *Russula* (pages 148, 149, 152, 153, 155) and of *Tricholoma* (page 101); if it is white, it can be confused with *Tricholoma columbetta* (page 102) and with *Melanoleuca cnista* (page 106). Finally, when still very young and egg shaped, it can be mistaken for *Amanita caesarea* (page 17), which however, when cut, does not appear internally white but yellowish; or for some *Lycoperdon* (pages 228–231), which, when cut, appears internally uniform; whereas in all species of the *Amanita* the future cap, stem, and gills are already recognizable.

AMANITA PHALLOIDES (Poison amanita)

Cap 4–15 cm, of various shades of green in the var. *viridis* and *virescens*, slate gray in the var. *umbrina*, yellowish in the variety *citrina*, white with yellowish or greenish or cinereous shades at the center in the variety *alba*; almost always presenting darker, radiating fibrils; even margin. **Stem** flocculose, with whitish or greenish streaks; rarely smooth and white. **Ring** white; sometimes lacking in older specimens. **Volva** white, large, with lobes detached from the base of the stem. **Flesh** white; it does not change color when exposed to air. **Odor** of clover hay, then slightly disgusting. **Flavor** insignificant or even agreeable: it is not dangerous to taste it, if one is careful to spit it out without swallowing any fragment. **Gills** white, sometimes with greenish shades; free or almost free from the stem; close, broad, unequal. **Spores** white. It grows in all kinds of woods, but especially in latifoliate woods, from spring to early winter, but particularly in summer and autumn. **Deadly**, even cooked and desiccated; the lethal dose is 20 grams of fresh mushroom; the symptoms can sometimes appear as late as two days after eating the mushroom; in case of poisoning, give the patient a teaspoon of salt dissolved in water every thirty minutes, and take him immediately to a hospital.

AMANITA VERNA (spring amanita)

Cap 3–10 cm, white or slightly ochraceous at the center; glabrous, viscid in humid weather, but fibrillar, sericeous, glossy in dry weather; thin, even margin. **Stem** tall, thin, white, with or without streaks, striate above the ring; farinose from the ring to the base, but not flocculose; stuffed, then hollow; bulbous, ovoid base. **Ring** close to the stem, white. **Volva** white, membranous, thin, tapering and enveloping the bulbous base. **Flesh** tender, white. **Odor** mild, but disgusting in old specimens. **Flavor** slightly acrid: do not swallow any fragment of the mushroom. **Gills** close, with numerous intermediate lamellae; free from the stem; white. **Spores** white. It grows from spring to autumn, in coniferous or latifoliate woods. **Deadly** like the *phalloides* (pages 26–27). It is likely to be confused with all the mushrooms with which *Amanita phalloides* can also be mistaken, that is: *Lepiota naucina* (page 38), which does not have a volva and can have rosy gills; white varieties of *Psalliota* (pages 43–49), lacking volva, with rosy, then tobacco colored gills; and with the following mushrooms, white or whitish, lacking volva and ring: *Tricholoma columbetta* (page 102) white with yelllow, pink, green, violet, rust colored spots; *Tricholoma album* (page 102), acrid-bitter; *Melanoleuca cnista* (page 106), which however has gills annexed to the stem and decurrent on it.

AMANITA VIROSA (Destroying Angel) (1)

Cap white, often with rosy ochraceous shades at the center; slightly viscid in humid weather; fibrillar, glossy in dry weather; globose, then cone or bell shaped, finally expanded, but almost never totally, 4–10 cm; always cuspidate; margin smooth, often with pendulous remains of the partial veil; cuticle easily removable from the cap. **Stem** slender, tapering upward, bulbous, white, with a fibrous-lanate surface, torn in several places; stuffed with a fibrous pith, then hollow. **Ring** malformed, thin, cottony, fragile, white, transient. **Volva** white, membranous, enveloping the bulbous base and narrowing above it. **Flesh** soft, thin, white. **Odor** none or yeastlike or even rather disgusting. **Flavor** disgusting: do not swallow when tasting a fragment of the mushroom. **Gills** rather close, with numerous intermediate lamellae; free from the stem; white with velvety edges. **Spores** white. It grows from spring to autumn, in humid and sandy woods, of conifers but especially of latifoliate trees; luckily it is rare. **Deadly**, as *phalloides* (see pages 26–27).

AMANITA BISPORIGERA (2)

Similar to *virosa*; stem smooth or only slightly striate, volva asymmetric, enveloping the bulbous base, which is oval; odorless and tasteless; grows in oak woods, in North America; **deadly**.

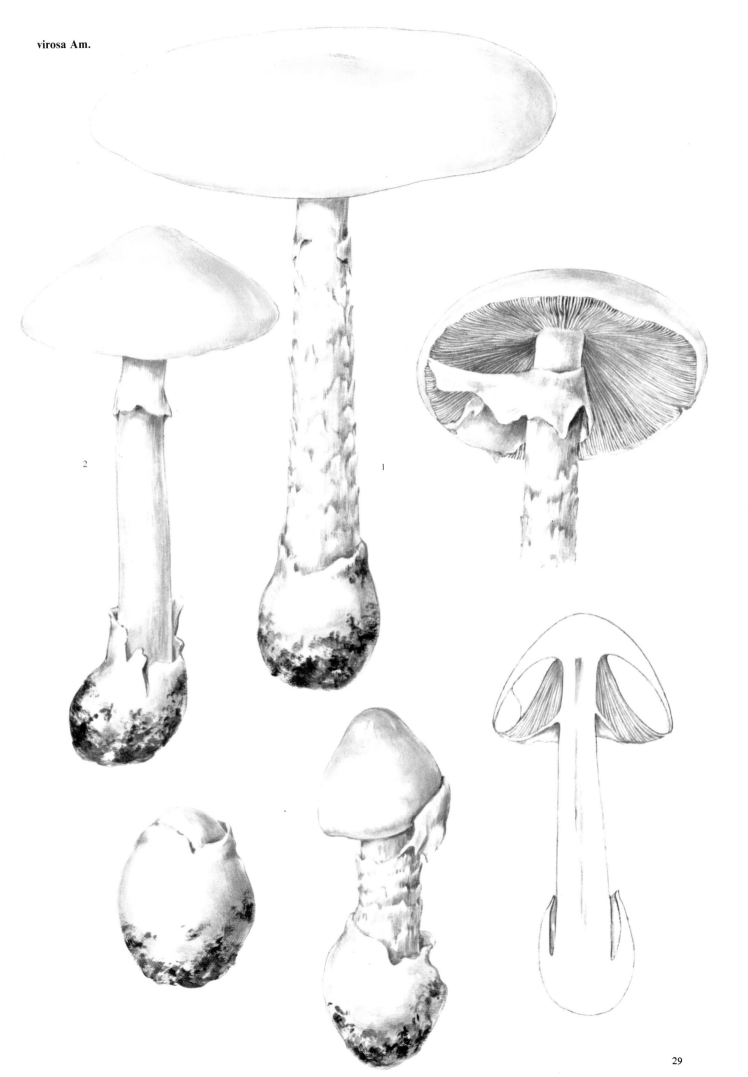

virosa Am.

2

1

AMANITOPSIS or AMANITA VAGINATA var. LIVIDO-PALLESCENS

Cap whitish or yellowish gray, with membranous, large, whitish, transient warts, lacking sometimes in older specimens; hemispheric, with the margin sulcate in the direction of the gills; then expanded, 10–20 cm, also depressed, with more accentuated grooves at the margin. **Stem** rather stout, tapering upward; thickened base; initially wrapped in a white sheath; then the sheath divides into several scales that cover the stem with pale ocher or olivaceous yellow markings. **Volva** white, large, membranous, with pointed lobes. **Flesh** thick, white. **Odor** none. **Flavor** mild. **Gills** white, tending to cream, narrowing at the stem and free from it; equal. **Spores** white. It grows at the edge of woods or along forest paths. **Edible with caution**: raw, it is toxic, but cooked it is excellent.

We want to mention here two more white *Amanitopsis*: *Amanitopsis nivalis*, typical of the Scottish highlands, probably corresponding to *Amanitopsis vaginata* var. *nivea* (page 33), **edible with caution**, which grows in the Alps; *Amanitopsis oreina*, of no alimentary interest, small, cap 3–4 cm, whitish, stem 3–4 cm, with a thick volva wrapping around more than half of it; in the Alps, up to 3,000 meters; for this reason it is called, *oreina*, which means highlander. The lack of the ring distinguishes the white *Amanitopsis* from the deadly white *Amanita* (pages 28–29).

AMANITOPSIS or AMANITA INAURATA

Cap 8–12 cm, fuliginous brown, reddish brown, yellowish brown, olivaceous brown, or grayish brown; lighter at the margin; margin initially striate in the direction of the gills, then channeled, and with a few cracks; with thick, mealy-flocculose gray warts, which become gradually smaller and finally blackish. **Stem** tall, twice the diameter of the cap, thicker at the base; white or hazel yellow, without ring; instead there are stripes formed by brownish or grayish flocci, spread along the entire stem, becoming smaller upward. **Volva** white, then gray; thick, farinose, fragile, soon reduced to circular, short-lived fragments. **Flesh** white. **Odor** none. **Flavor** mild. **Gills** close, free and remote from the stem; white, tending to creamy or gray. **Spores** white. It grows in woods, especially in the mountains. **Edible**. In the same group: *Amanitopsis strangulata* (Strangulated amanitopsis), **edible**, cap 8–22 cm, color from yellow to brown, volva very big, lobed, cinereous, grows in the mountains, in clearings, in the moss, on sandy soil; and *Amanitopsis malleata*, **probably edible**, smaller than the previous species, with gibbous cap as if it had been hammered, grows in the grass, in the meadows, edging oak woods.

inaurata Am.

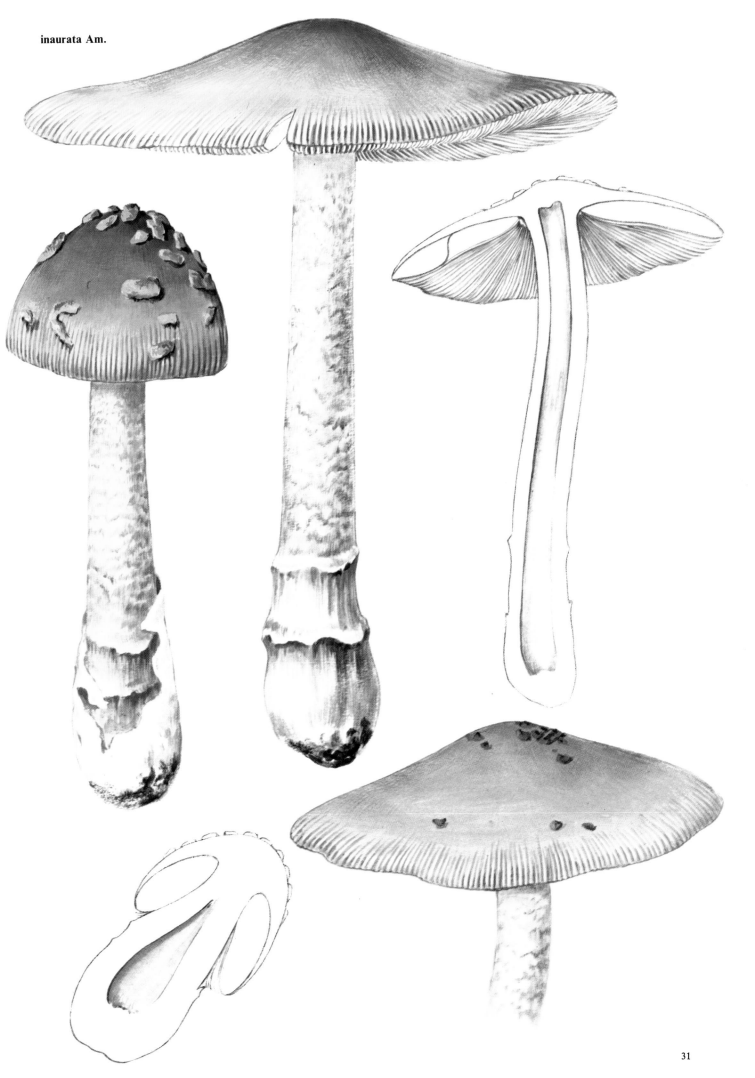

AMANITOPSIS or AMANITA UMBRINOLUTEA

Cap first conical, then expanded, 4–10 cm, often umbonate; the center is brown, whereas the margin is light cinereous hazel and sulcate; the grooves often terminate at the edge of a narrow, circular region, dark, fuliginous; sometimes, however, the cap is yellowish or greenish yellow. **Stem** slender, cylindrical, tapering upward; thickened base; white, generally marked by fuliginous squamules, tinged with orange; no ring. **Volva** tall, large, deep, consistent, white with creamy or rosy shades, and more intensely colored internally. **Flesh** thin, fragile. **Odor** slight. **Flavor** agreeable. **Gills** rather close, very broad, free from the stem, white. **Spores** white. It grows especially under fir trees, but also in meadows. **Edible**, of good quality. Remarks: *Amanitopsis* has volva but not a ring; *Amanita* has both volva and ring; *Aspidella* has volva, ring, and pointed warts on the cap; *Limacella* has ring, no volva, and cuticle of the cap is viscous. These are mushrooms with the cap easily separable from the stem, with the universal veil persistent, sometimes in the shape of a volva wrapping the base of the stem and more or less adhering to the same, with the partial veil persistent at times as a ring, with the gills free and the spores white.

LIMACELLA GUTTATA

Cap 5–12 cm, creamy or rosy or reddish creamy color; darker at the center and slightly tinted with yellow; mucilaginous, then dry and lucid. **Stem** cylindrical, stout; base with scales, thickened or bulbous, often buried in the ground; fibrillar, slightly lighter than the cap, white in the part above the ring; stuffed. **Ring** large, thin, remaining expanded for a long time; both the ring and the stem above the ring exude dewy droplets in humid weather. **Flesh** thick, fragile, fibrous, white or with reddish shades; yellowish at the base. **Odor** strongly of flour. **Flavor** mild. **Gills** very close, broad, free from the stem; often with dewy droplets, white or whitish. **Spores** white. It is found in humid woods, especially beech and fir woods. The variety *Fischeri,* found in North America, is paler than the typical form. **Edible**.

Limacella illinita, **edible**, cap 4–8 cm, hazel color, then white, with only the umbo hazel; glossy, completely covered by a gelatinous, colorless, transparent coat; grows under conifers, after a period of rain. *Limacella glioderma*, **edible**, cap 2–5 cm, rosy hazel, yellow gills. *Limacella irrorata*, **edibility unknown**, cap 2–7 cm, besprinkled with clear, glutinous, pale, evanescent droplets; stem with flocculose sheath; in sunny, even stony, grounds.

AMANITOPSIS (Amanita) VAGINATA

Cap campanulate, then expanded 3–10 cm, umbonate, more rarely with a small depression at the center, moist, glossy; margin initially striate in the direction of the gills, then grooved, finally with the gills standing out like the teeth of a circular saw; white in the variety *nivea* or *alba*, cinereous in the variety *grisea*; silvery in the variety *argentea*; plumbeous in the variety *plumbea*; orange in the former variety *crocea*, which is now considered by the mycologists to be a different species; brownish red and rather thin in the variety *fulva*; violaceous-plumbeous and with the edge of the gills marked by blackish dots in the variety *punctata*. Sometimes a part of the universal veil remains adhering to the cap like a large, thick, whitish wart. **Stem** slender, cylindrical, rather narrower at the top; white or the same color as the cap but paler, or with streaks of that color; soft, hollow. **Volva** tall, detached from the base of the stem, with lobed margin. **Odor** mild. **Flavor** insignificant. **Gills** sometimes very close, sometimes less; generally broad; sometimes free, sometimes adnexed; white or whitish. **Spores** white. It grows from late spring to midautumn, in woods and meadows, but the variety *fulba* grows normally on decaying trunks of chestnuts. **Edible with caution**; raw it is harmful, cooked it is excellent. (From left: *nivea, punctata, grisea, plumbea, fulva, crocea.*)

LEPIOTA UMBONATA (1)

Cap campanulate, whitish tending to ocher, especially at the center; with whitish remains of the two veils hanging from the margin; then expanded, 6–13 cm, and considerably umbonate, whereas the cuticle, by now yellowish brown, but reddish brown at the center, breaks, starting at the margin, into small, fugaceous squamules, so that the margin, soon without them, appears whitish, fibrillar, sericeous, frayed, and scatteredly fissured in the direction of the gills. **Stem** set into a socket in the cap and easily disconnectable; tall, thin, fibrillar; whitish above the ring; hazel, with brownish squamules or granules from the ring to the base; hollow; globose, bulblike base, brownish. **Ring** large, with several layers, soft; soon dry, movable, evanescent; white above, yellowish brown and granular beneath. **Flesh** fragile, thin, white, it remains white even when exposed to air. **Odor** slight. **Flavor** of hazelnuts. **Gills** close, broad, thin, remote; white, then rosy cream. **Spores** white. It grows under latifoliate trees, in groups. **Edible**, of good quality.

LEPIOTA PUELLARIS (2)

Similar to *Lepiota procera* (page 35), but smaller; cap often hemispheric, 4–15 cm, with not very prominent central umbo; stem lacking scales; flesh white, becoming slightly rosy, but not red, when exposed to air; grows in groups, at the end of summer, in coniferous woods and also in meadows; **edible**, of good quality.

LEPIOTA PROCERA (Parasol mushroom)

Cap spheroid or campanulate; then convex or plane, 10–25 cm, with a large, smooth umbo at the center; upper cuticle as a coarse felt, brownish, fragmented in scales that become smaller toward the margin; subcuticle whitish or yellowish brown, sericeous, fibrillar, finely desquamating, fimbriate at the margin. **Stem** slender, bulbous at the base; hard, fibrous, hollow; set into a socket in the cap and easily disconnectable; whitish with brownish zebra markings, but entirely brownish and velvety, as the cap, in the variety *fuliginosa*. **Ring** large, doughnut-like, multilayered with a lacerated margin; movable. **Flesh**: the cap, soft; the stem, fibrous; white, changing to rosy when exposed to air, but to reddish in the variety *permixta*. **Odor** pleasant; of broth in the older specimens. **Flavor** of hazelnuts. **Gills** close, broad, remote; white or tinted with pink, then yellowish; the edges becomes brownish when bruised. **Spores** white. It grows, sometimes from spring, on even rocky ground, in sunny clearings of latifoliate or mixed woods, but preferably in meadows and among the stubble of grainfields. **Edible**, excellent; use only the cap of older specimens; it is edible also when dried naturally on the ground; in this case pick up only the caps leaving the stems in the soil; before cooking keep them immersed in warm water; then they can be prepared, breaded like veal cutlets.

procera Lep.

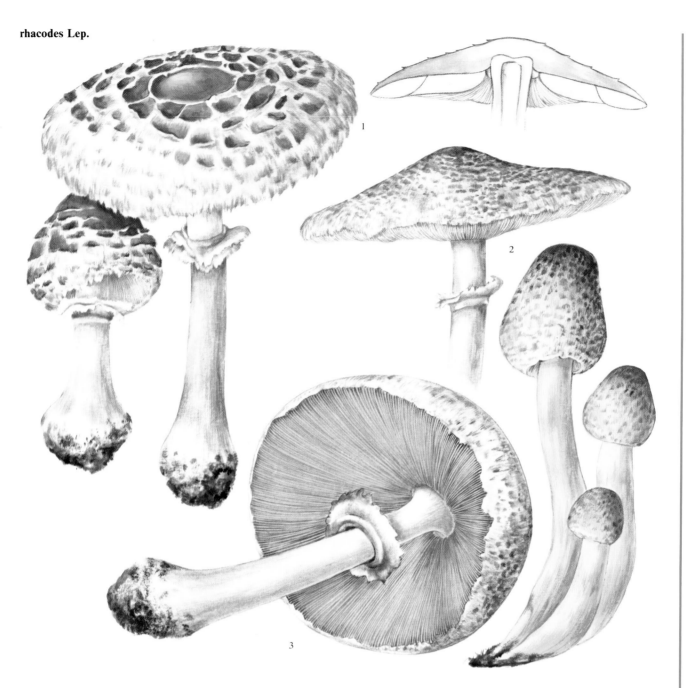

LEPIOTA RHACODES (1)

Cap at first ovoid, brown, with fimbriate margin; then expanded, 5–15 cm, with the cuticle fragmenting into large, coarse scales, and exposing the paler, fibrillar subcuticular surface; but at the center, slightly umbonate, the cuticle remains whole and brown. **Stem** disconnectable from the cap, stout, hard, fibrous, hollow; white, then grayish; with bulbous base, very big in the variety *hortensis* (page 37, specimen 2). **Ring** large, frayed, movable; whitish. **Flesh** soft, white, changing to saffron yellow, then reddish, finally brownish when exposed to air. **Odor** soft. **Flavor** slight, not particularly pleasant. **Gills** close, broad, unequal, remote from the stem; white with pinkish edges; when bruised or upon ripening they become reddish, then fuliginous. **Spores** white. It grows in cultivated fields, or in coniferous or latifoliate woods. **Edible**.

LEPIOTA BADHAMII or AMERICANA (2, with section)

Less scaly than *L. rhacodes*; both internally and externally becoming yellow, then reddish, at the slightest touch; base fusiform and radicating; spores ochraceous-creamy color; on wooden debris; **poisonous** when raw, **edible** well cooked.

LEPIOTA MOLYBDITES (3, lying down)

Without umbo; cuticle soft and smooth; ripe gills greenish as the spores; **edible with caution**: not everybody can tolerate it. Also with greenish gills is *Lepiota Morgani*, **poisonous**, whose cap can reach, and even surpass, 40 cm in diameter; typical of North America.

LEPIOTA EXCORIATA (1)

Cap 5–15 cm, often with central umbo, more or less prominent; cuticle gray, ochraceous, or brownish, darker at the center; the specimens shown here have a particularly intense coloring; with the expansion and the development of the cap, the cuticle breaks along the margin, exposing the paler, sericeous, shining subcuticular surface. **Stem** whitish on top, more colored in the middle; fibrous, soon hollow; base thickened, almost bulbous, generally darker than the stem, but initially covered with a white down. **Flesh** white, unchanging in contact with air. **Odor** mild. **Flavor** sometimes slightly acrid. **Gills** close, thin, very broad, free from the stem; white, then whitish. **Spores** white or slightly ochraceous. It grows in summer, but especially in autumn, in untilled or cultivated fields, in pastures and along paths, rarely in the woods. **Edible**, excellent: the caps naturally dried on the ground must be first regenerated in warm water and then cooked with the proper seasoning.

LEPIOTA RHACODES var. HORTENSIS (2)

Cap 5–15 cm, conical, with cinereous or brownish cuticle, which covers, like a hood, the white, fibrous subcuticle; with frayed margin; stem flasklike, whitish, with brownish or blackish variegations; huge basal bulb, blackish brown; ring disklike, white, soft above, cinereous or brownish on the lower margin. It grows in tufts, rarely singly, in open, even rocky, grounds, but also in coniferous or latifoliate woods. **Edible**.

LEPIOTA ACUTESQUAMOSA

Cap at first globular, brownish, pubescent; then expanded, 5–12 cm, umbonate, covered with evanescent thorns, denser at the center, even more numerous in the variety *furcata*. **Stem** stout, soon hollow; rosy white, striate above the ring; brownish beneath the ring to the base. Bulbous base, often bearing thorns like the cap. **Ring** large, hanging down like a petticoat, persistent, with the surface toward the gills whitish, smooth, and that toward the stem darker and often bearing few thorns. **Flesh** soft, fragile, white. **Odor** disgusting. **Flavor** acidulous, disgusting. **Gills** close, unequal; in the variety *furcata* irregularly bifurcate; white, then cream with reddish iridescence, often dotted with brown; free from the stem. **Spores** white. It grows on sandy soil and on plant debris, in humid but sunny recesses, in woods especially of conifers, in meadows, in vineyards. **Not edible**: the odor itself advises against its use.

We remember here: *Lepiota hystrix*, **not edible**, cap 4–5 cm, covered with brown, conical, persistent thorn, as the stem; gills not bifurcate, yellow, edges borded with black; brown dew on the stem just under the cap. *Lepiota echinata*, **not edible**, cap 1–4 cm, fuliginous, granular, without thorns; stem carmine rose, furfuraceous; gills vinous red; growing in spring and summer, on rich humic soil.

LEPIOTA HELVEOLA (2)

Cap 2–6 cm, often umbonate; margin soon fissured; upper cuticle brownish, soon whole only at the center, elsewhere fragmented into squamules, over the paler subcuticle. Once collected, the mushroom acquires a rosy iridescence, then becomes reddish ocher. **Stem** the same color as the cap, sericeous, slightly streaked at the base; hollow. **Ring** fugaceous. Flesh white or pinkish, becoming rosy when exposed to air like the flesh of *Lepiota brunneoincarnata*, **poisonous**, and of *Lepiota subincarnata*, **poisonous**. **Odor** slight: sweet when numerous specimens are stored together in a closed space. **Gills** close, broad, free from the stem; whitish, then cream colored. **Spores** white. It grows in the grass, in clearings, in parks. **Poisonous**, perhaps deadly.

LEPIOTA CRISTATA (1)

Similar to *L. helveola*, but it does not become rosy when collected; conspicuous and brown umbo, fruity but disgusting odor; **not edible**.

Also to be avoided: *Lepiota felina*, with distinct, brown umbo, odorless; *Lepiota fuscovinacea*, vinous red tending to brown, with a fibrillar, velvety stem; *Lepiota clypeolaria*, even though it can be considered **edible**; cap yellowish brown, stem with woolly brownish sheath, pleasant odor; stem with yellow scales in the variety *metulaespora*, with brown ring in the variety *latispora*, with white cap in the mountainous variety *alba*.

LEPIOTA NAUCINA (1)

Cap white, changing to slightly cinereous or yellowish; globular, then hemispheric or campanulate, finally expanded, 4–10 cm; sometimes cuspidate, sometimes rather depressed; cuticle dry, sericeous, smooth or finely granular; after a long drought it cracks up into several polygonal squamules. **Stem** rather slender, robust, with thickened and sometimes curved base; same color as the cap and easily disconnectable from it; fibrous, soon hollow. **Ring** white, narrow, fragile, lacerated, soon appressed to the stem, sometimes lacking in older specimens. **Flesh** thick, tender, white, then tinged with yellow; but the base of the stem and old specimens are yellowish brown. **Odor** slight. **Flavor** agreeable. **Gills** close, broad, thin, free from the stem; white then rosy, finally gray amethystine. **Spores** white, then pinkish. It grows from spring to autumn, in grassy places. **Edible**, of good quality. Do not confuse it with the white species of *Amanita* (page 28).

LEPIOTA (*naucina* variety) CARNEIFOLIA (2)

Cinereous, then reddish, gills flesh pink; **edible**.

LEPIOTA (*naucina* variety) DENSIFOLIA (3, incomplete)

Gills very close; **edible**. Similar to the above-mentioned species: *Lepiota holoserica*, **edible**, white and shiny as silk; *Lepiota cinerascens*, **edible**, white, tending to cinereous, but with white gills.

naucina Lep.

VOLVARIA GLOIOCEPHALA

Cap campanulate, then plane, 8–12 cm, often umbonate; margin rather striate in the direction of the gills in the ripe specimens; otherwise smooth; grayish or fuliginous gray or also whitish with a darker center; white in the variety *speciosa* (in the figure: specimen lying down); cuticle glabrous; viscid in humid weather; shining in dry weather; partly removable, very thin. **Stem** slender, white, or tinged with the color of the cap; glabrous. **Volva** white, cottony, soft, lobed, very often tall, large; sometimes sticking to the base of the stem; easily compressible onto the base of the stem, which it enwraps so that it is not distinguishable from it. Sometimes it remains adhering to the cap, sometimes it remains in the ground. **Flesh** soft, white. **Odor** slight, but very distinctly of turnip. **Flavor** slight, watery. **Gills** close, broad, thin, free from the stem; white, then rosy, finally rosy brownish: by this characteristic one can avoid confusing this mushroom with the deadly *Amanita*. Intermediate gills at times rounded, at times abruptly terminating at right angles, as in various species of *Amanita*. **Spores** ochraceous pink. It grows on soft, loose soil rich in decomposing organic substances: manure, straw, sawdust; along paths, in vegetable gardens, under hedges; in cool, humid, shady places; in the cool season. **Edible**, but not particularly pleasant.

CYSTODERMA AMIANTHINUM (1)
Cap 3–5 cm, white, ochraceous, or tending to orange; usually umbonate; with radiating creases in the variety *rugosoreticulatum*; covered with darker flocci and granules, especially at the center. **Stem** tall, cylindrical, thin; yellowish above the ring; from the ring to the base brownish ocher and covered with flocci or granules as the cap. **Ring** stretching toward the gills, flocculose, fragile, fugaceous. **Flesh** scarce, fragile, yellowish, gradually darker toward the base. **Odor** strongly of mold. **Flavor** mild. **Gills** not very close, annexed to the stem, white or yellowish. **Spores** white. It grows in woods or on moors. **Edible**, but of little interest.

CYSTODERMA CARCHARIAS (2)
Slightly bigger than the previous species; cap amethystine, rosy, or ochraceous pink, with slightly darker flocci or granules; festooned margin; gills close; stem wrapped by a granular sheath; odor disagreeable, flavor mild; grows under conifers; **edible**.

CYSTODERMA CINNABARINUM (3)
Orange red; flesh thick, fragile, white; **of no alimentary interest**.

CYSTODERMA GRANULOSUM (4)
Cap brownish, very granular; **no alimentary interest**. Similar to the previous species and equally **of no alimentary interest**: *Cystoderma fallax*, ocher, not too granular; *Cystoderma Ambrosii*, white; *Cystoderma haematites*, violaceous red, stouter than the others.

VOLVARIA BOMBYCINA (Silky Volvaria)

Cap ovoid, then convex, 5–20 cm, generally umbonate; white, but yellowish in the form *Potronis*; fibrillous, shining; then ochraceous, covered with darker fibrils and scales. **Stem** sturdy, slender, often rather curved, thickened base, sometimes even bulbous; white, smooth, stuffed. **Volva** large and tall, brownish, then squamose. **Flesh** tender, white. **Odor** of wood. **Flavor** pleasant. **Gills** close, free from the stem; whitish, then rosy, finally brownish. **Spores** ochraceous pink. It grows on the decomposing wood of latifoliate trees, especially in the hollow of trees, and can grow again in the same place in the same season. **Edible**, very good: the woody smell disappears during cooking. The small *Volvaria marinella* grows on rotten wood, in moss, in coniferous woods; it is **of no alimentary interest**: cap 2–4 cm, covered with delicate felt, cinereous yellow, but blackish at the center; odor of pelargonium. Also **of no interest from the alimentary standpoint** are *Volvaria pubipes*, cap 2–4 cm, white, volva white; *Volvaria pusilla*, cap 1–3 cm, white, growing in the summer, in gardens and along paths, seldom in woods; *Volvaria plumulosa*, cap 2–4 cm, conical, sericeous-pubescent, cinereous-ochraceous color, darker at the center, volva dark. Similar to *V. gloiocephala* (page 40) is *Volvaria media*: **edible**; cap viscid, ivory white, then dry and sericeous; smooth margin; stem white, hollow; volva rosy ocher; growing in the woods, in spring.

PLUTEUS CERVINUS

Cap 6–24 cm, often umbonate, viscid in humid weather; fibrillar and radially fissured in dry weather; brown, cinereous brown, or fuliginous, darker at the center. **Stem** easily detachable from the cap; stiff, stuffed; whitish with brownish fibrils sometimes standing out in relief. **Flesh** tender, fragile, white. **Odor** mild of turnip. **Flavor** delicate. **Gills** free from the stem, with abrupt intermediate lamellae; whitish, then rosy, finally amethystine brown with brownish edges. **Spores** rosy ocher. It grows on rotting wood or coniferous or latifoliate trees, or on sawdust where it can grow to enormous size. **Edible**, of poor quality.

Similar to the above-mentioned species are *Pluteus magnus*, **edible**, distinguishable from *P. cervinus* only by microscopic analysis; *Pluteus nigroflocculosus*, **edible**, cap 6–12 cm, gills' edges soon brownish; growing specifically on conifers; *Pluteus patricius*, **edible**, grayish, with brown, evanescent squamules; *Pluteus murinus*, **edible**: stem fibrillar, brown gray as is the cap. Without alimentary interest: *Pluteus salicinus*: cap 3–6 cm, gray, growing on latifoliate trees; *Pluteus cinereo-fuscus*: growing on humus, under latifoliate trees; *Pluteus nanus*: cap 2–4 cm, fuliginous brown, stem yellowish, growing on humus or live trees; *Pluteus plautus*: cap 2–4 cm, entirely fuliginous brown, growing on humus; *Pluteus coccineus*: cap 2–6 cm, red, margin orange, stem yellow, growing on latifoliate trees.

VOLVARIA VOLVACEA (1)

Cap 5–14 cm, ochraceous gray, faded at the margin, umbonate at the center; dry; covered with regularly grouped, fuliginous fibrils, darker in the variety *nigricans* (3). **Stem** tapering upward, often with a rather bulbous base; fibrillar, white; pruinose on top, flocculose the rest, but soon glabrous. **Volva** with lobed margin, externally whitish or grayish, fuliginous in the variety *nigricans*. **Flesh** tender, white or slightly brownish. **Odor** slight. **Flavor** mild, but then sometimes slightly bitterish. **Gills** somewhat close, thin, broad, free from the stem; rosy, then rusty. **Spores** ochraceous pink. It grows in summer on rotting wood, and throughout the year in hothouses on organic substances. **Edible**.

VOLVARIA LOVEIANA (2)

Cap hemispheric, then convex, 3–5 cm, white tending to cinereous or blue green; fibrillar, lanate, slightly viscid in humid weather. **Stem** cylindric, often curved, with slightly bulbous base; fibrillar, white. **Volva** large, thick, soft, white. **Flesh** white. **Odor** mild. **Flavor** mild. **Gills** close, thin, white then rosy. **Spores** rosy. It grows in late autumn, sometimes in clusters, on *Clitocybe nebularis* (page 114), on *Clitocybe clavipes* (page 114), and on some decomposing *Tricholoma*; rare species, therefore it is not easy to establish its edibility; anyway it is **of no interest** from a nutritive and culinary standpoint.

PSALLIOTA (Agaricus) BISPORA

Cap globular, or hemispheric, then convex and finally completely expanded, flat, 5–10 cm; white, pinkish, grayish, or brownish; almost always brownish in ripe age; in some varieties and forms the cap is covered with fibrils or squamules more or less deep colored; where bruised it becomes reddish brown; the unripe specimens have the margin adorned with a thick, soft, denticulate, white, fugaceous fringe. **Stem** squat, easily separable from the cap; at first stuffed with pith, then hollow; white, but above the ring it can be rosy in unripe specimens, and brownish in ripe specimens; flocculose beneath the ring. **Ring** somewhat thick, soft, white, the surface that was in contact with the gills more or less striate. **Flesh** thick and firm, especially in young specimens; white; exposed to air the flesh of unripe specimens becomes decisively reddish, that of the ripe ones becomes brownish. **Odor** mild. **Flavor** agreeable. **Gills** close, free; pinkish in unripe specimens, blackish brown in ripe ones. **Spores** cocoa colored. It grows in manured soils, along road embankments; not found in places dense with trees; largely cultivated in almost every country in the world and sold at all seasons. **Edible**, excellent, cooked or raw, in salads, or preserved in oil.

PSALLIOTA (Agaricus) BISPORA
See the description on page 43. Some other varieties are illustrated below.

PSALLIOTA BISPORA var. HORTENSIS brown (1)
Edible.

PSALLIOTA BISPORA var. HORTENSIS blonde (2)
Edible.

PSALLIOTA BISPORA var. BITORQUIS (3)
With two rings, the more external of the two ascending from the base of the stem like a thin, adhering volva; **edible**. Also *Psalliota subperonata*: **edible**; has two rings; the cap is, however, yellowish brown, covered with brown scales; it grows on straw, or along paths, and it can easily reach sizes notably greater than those of *bitorquis*.

PSALLIOTA RADICATA (4)
Base of the stem rather thickened or even bulbous; with a rootlike appendix penetrating few centimeters in the ground, but easily breakable when collecting the mushroom, remaining therefore in the soil and going unnoticed. Cap ordinarily white, but in the specimens growing on a hard and compact ground it can be more or less fuliginous and squamose. Odor of carbolic acid, accentuated by cooking. It grows in the country, in meadows and gardens, but also in towns along dirt roads. **Poisonous**: it causes gastrointestinal disorders.

PSALLIOTA (Agaricus) SILVATICA (Wood Psalliota)
Cap 7–15 cm, covered with yellowish brown or reddish brown, almost triangular, fibrillar scales adhering to the lighter and fibrillar surface. **Stem** slender in the specimens from latifoliate woods, slightly stouter in the specimens from coniferous woods; bulbous base; soon hollow; white on top, whitish and squamose from the ring down; soon grayish and brownish. **Ring** thin, large; with the surface toward the gills smooth, and the surface toward the stem floccose; white, then brownish; often lacerated; fugaceous. **Flesh** tender; white tinged with red; in contact with air it becomes spotted with reddish; upon ripening it becomes brownish. **Odor** acidulous. **Flavor** agreeable. **Gills** close, narrow, free from the stem; pinkish, then gray pink, finally violaceous brown. **Spores** cocoa colored. It grows in woods. **Edible**, of good quality, even raw, while still unripe.

Similar to *P. silvatica*, but with the center of the cap darker, purple brown or vinous brown, is *Psalliota subrutilascens*, **edible with caution**, because it is harmful to some people; it grows during rainy autumns, under conifers, in North America and the Far East. Also found in North America and the Far East, even outside the woods, is *Psalliota placomyces*, **not advisable**: cap white with numerous grayish brownish squamules; stem covered from the ring to the base with plaques initially very conspicuous.

PSALLIOTA (Agaricus) CAMPESTRIS (Meadow mushroom) (1)

Cap globose or hemispheric; this shape persists for a long time before expanding more or less completely, 5–15 cm; the margin extends beyond the gills; in the typical form, sometimes named variety *alba*, it is silky white; at other times whitish or yellowish brown or brownish; sometimes covered with brownish scales; where bruised it becomes yellowish. **Stem** thick; rarely somewhat slender; of various shapes; white, sometimes slightly rosy; base often thinning, fusiform; other times thickened **Ring** thin, simple, fragile, with fringed margin; evanescent, white. **Flesh** rather thick, firm; white; sometimes the flesh under the cuticle and that of the stem becomes pinkish in contact with air. **Odor** mild. **Flavor** agreeable. **Gills** rather close, free from the stem; in unripe specimens delicate rosy color; in full maturity, blackish brown. **Spores** cocoa color. It grows in large groups, often forming fairy rings, in manured grounds, even along road embankments, but very rarely in woods; it appears a first time in late spring, then again at the end of the summer, when the weather is warm and dry, after a period of humid weather. **Edible**, excellent, even raw.

PSALLIOTA COMTULA (2)

Similar to *P. campestris*, but smaller; slight almond odor; found in meadows and in fields fertilized with organic manure substances; **edible**.

PSALLIOTA (Agaricus) ARVENSIS (1)

Cap 6–16 cm, with flocculose and festooned margin; white, hazel at the center; becoming yellowish when bruised or upon ripening. **Stem** thick, white or with yellow spots; sericeous, smooth, sometimes bulbous, enwrapped by an adhering membrane. Two-layered **ring**: the upper layer thin, white then yellowish; the lower thicker, often star shaped, soft, whitish. **Flesh** white: becoming yellow when exposed to air or upon ripening. **Odor** of anise. **Flavor** pleasant. **Gills** close, narrow, free; whitish, then pinkish, then tobacco with lighter edges. **Spores** cocoa color. It grows in groups, on grassy and sunny grounds and in clearings of coniferous woods. **Edible**, excellent, also raw in salads.

PSALLIOTA NIVESCENS (2)

Cap very fleshy, white, cracked at the center by the wind; almond smell; **edible**, excellent, even raw. Bigger than the previous ones, and equally **edible** are *Psalliota crocodilina*, which grows along the Pacific Coast, in North America; and *Psalliota villatica*: cap 15–35 cm, with sparse, hazel squamules along the margin, flesh becoming slowly pinkish when exposed to air; growing in mountain pastures. *Psalliota Bernardi* is, on the contrary, **indigestible**: cap hemispheric, 10–25 cm, with coarse, ochraceous scales; soon creviced; stem thick, covered by a coarse sheath from the base to the ring; flesh becoming reddish, then grayish, when exposed to air; odor brackish; growing along Mediterranean marshy coasts.

PSALLIOTA (Agaricus) HAEMORRHOIDARIA (Bleeding mushroom)

Cap spheroid or cylindroid, then expanded 5–12 cm; deep brown and almost smooth at the center; faded brown at the margin with delicate, whitish fringes; the rest fibrillar and covered with brown scales. **Stem** white and smooth above the ring; covered with brownish scales and flocci below the ring; becoming spotted with red when touched; at first stuffed with pith, then hollow. Base sometimes rather bulbous, deeply planted in the ground. **Ring** thin, large, with denticulate margin; white and striate the upper surface, brownish the lower. **Flesh** white, changing immediately to carmine red when exposed to air, especially in the lower part of the cap, where the gills are, and in the upper section of the stem. **Odor** acidulous. **Flavor** pleasant. **Gills** close, free or slightly connected to the stem; pinkish, then brownish violet. **Spores** purplish brown tending to purple. It grows in late summer, in groups, in the clearings of oak and beech woods, but more frequently in pine woods. **Edible**, of good quality. In the lower right-hand corner are illustrated specimens of the variety *silvaticoides*, **edible**, very similar to *Psalliota silvatica* (page 44), but with a thicker stem and fleshier cap; moreover the gills are broader in the middle and pointed near the margin; the flesh of *silvaticoides* in contact with air becomes totally and deeply reddish, whereas in *Psalliota silvatica* it shows only lightly colored reddish spots.

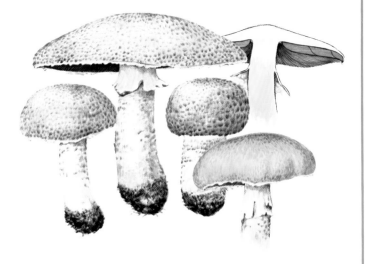

PSALLIOTA (Agaricus) AUGUSTA

Cap globose, compressed, or truncate cone-shaped, then expanded 10–24 cm; brownish or yellowish; soon covered with fibrillar, brownish scales, with a whitish or yellowish background under them. The cuticle, scraped, becomes instantly yellow. **Stem** thick, often thicker at the base, deeply planted into the soil; white; in unripe specimens it is slightly pinkish above the ring; bruised it turns dark yellow; smooth and shining above the ring, whereas below it, it is flocculose or squamose. **Ring** white tinged with yellow; large, kiltlike, thin, flaccid, smooth, often lacerated; margin adorned with white, then yellowish brown flocci or squamules. **Flesh** white; exposed to air it does not become red, but it often assumes a light yellowish shade, especially at the base; finally it becomes brownish. **Odor** of almonds. **Flavor** agreeable. **Gills** close, narrow, free; pallid, then pinkish, finally blackish brown. **Spores** cocoa color to purple. It grows in groups, in coniferous or latifoliate woods. **Edible**, of good quality. The specimen in the upper right-hand side of the picture is the variety *perrara*, **edible**, typical of fir woods. *Psalliota vaporaria* also grows in fir woods, as well as in richly manured pastures; **edible** when young, smaller than *perrara*, lighter golden or tobacco color, with bulbous base.

PSALLIOTA (Agaricus) SILVICOLA (1)

Cap 5–12 cm, smooth, dry, satiny; white, then yellowish. **Stem** slender, stiff; stuffed, but soon hollow; white, sometimes with cinereous-amethystine shades above the ring; then completely yellowish or lightly cinereous; rather bulbous at the base. **Ring** large, flaccid, thick, flocculose on the side toward the stem; evanescent; white, then yellowish or brownish. **Flesh** thin, tender, white or tinged with reddish hues, especially in the stem. **Odor** of anise. **Flavor** agreeable. **Gills** very close, white then pinkish, finally cocoa colored; free from the stem; pointed near the cap's margin. **Spores** cocoa colored. It grows in sunny clearings, especially in coniferous woods, in groups of two or three specimens. **Edible**, excellent also raw.

PSALLIOTA (variety *silvicola*) ABRUPTIBULBA (2)

This is similar to the previous species, but with distinctly bulbous base, often covered with a thick layer of conifer needles; **edible**. The following three small psalliotas, also growing in woods, are equally **edible**: *Psalliota semota*, cap 2–5 cm, white, sericeous, with minute fibers that become reddish with age; *Psalliota rubella* form *pallens*, cap 2–4 cm, with fibers lighter than in *P. semota*; and *Psalliota amethystina*, cap 2–5 cm, of a more decidedly vinous color.

PSALLIOTA (Agaricus) XANTHODERMA (1)

Any part of this mushroom when bruised becomes immediately yellow and later brown. **Cap** campanulate depressed, or rather cylindrical, then expanded 5–12 cm, but often still slightly depressed at the center; white or tinged with ocher, especially at the center; becoming grayish with age; cuticle sericeous, smooth, with a tendency to lacerate radially; festooned margin. **Stem** cylindrical, slender, often with a somewhat bulbous base; sericeous, smooth; white, becoming blackish on top and brown at the base with age; stuffed, then hollow. **Ring** white, with vertical striae impressed by the gills; yellow flocci along the margin. **Flesh** white, slightly yellow in the stem, distinctly yellow at the base; exposed to air it becomes all yellow, but more rapidly and intensely at the periphery; then it becomes ochraceous pink and, with age, blackish. **Odor** of ink or iodine. **Flavor** disgusting. **Gills** close, free from the stem, with serrate and faded edges; white, then pink, finally brown. **Spores** cocoa colored. It grows in groups, in latifoliate woods, in meadows and in gardens. **Not edible**: it causes stomach disorders in particularly sensitive people.

PSALLIOTA XANTHODERMA var. MELEAGRIS (2)

Cap covered with squamules that make it appear fuliginous, especially at the center, in the typical variety; but gray in the variety *meleagris* form *grisea*. **Not edible**, as *P. xanthoderma*.

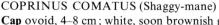

COPRINUS ATRAMENTARIUS (Ink coprinus)

Cap ovoid, then campanulate, 3–6 cm, soon with radial striae, grooves and crevices; whitish, then cinereous or yellowish; tinged with purple when the gills ripen. **Stem** cylindric, white; soon fibrillar, sericeous, and a little darker; hard, fibrous, hollow. **Ring** soft, whitish, appressed, evanescent. **Flesh** cinereous white, thin; however the mushroom gives the impression of being heavy. **Odor** and **flavor** agreeable. **Gills** very close, broad, free from the stem; whitish, then, beginning at the marginal portion of the cap, the color changes to brownish, violaceous, black; finally the gills dissolve into a dense, black liquid that drips at the base of the mushroom (deliquescent gills). **Spores** black. It grows throughout the year, except in the coldest months, in dense clusters, in cool, shady, grassy ground, manured with organic fertilizers; often also in parks and gardens, under fruit trees. **Edible with caution**: only when young and eaten as soon as collected, avoiding the use of alcohol in the meantime; otherwise it can cause palpitations of the heart, perspiration, chilled limbs, and other symptoms of illness, which however soon disappear without consequence. *Coprinus fuscescens*, **edible with caution**, is considered a more gracile form of *atramentarius*. *Coprinus insignis* differs from *astramentarius* only for a few microscopic peculiarities; **edible with caution** as the previous species.

COPRINUS COMATUS (Shaggy-mane)

Cap ovoid, 4–8 cm; white, soon brownish gray at the center, whereas the cuticle cracks into filamentous scales, the margin turning upward and splitting. **Stem** cylindrical, slender, white, sericeous, hollow. **Ring** white, thin, movable, evanescent. **Flesh** thin, watery. **Odor** mild. **Flavor** pleasant. **Gills** first white, appressed as the pages of a closed book; thin and very broad; then less close, free, pinkish; then violaceous, finally deliquescent. **Spores** black. It grows from spring to autumn, in loose or sandy soil, rich with organic fertilizers or calcareous substances. **Edible**, delicate, only if young; must be eaten as soon as collected, because it spoils quickly; it can be first boiled in water, in this way it will keep for a while and it can be prepared and cooked later on. Similar to *C. comatus* are *Coprinus ovatus*, **edible**: more delicate, cap spheroid, gills ripening slower; *Coprinus vošoustii* or *clavatus*, **edibility uncertain**: the summit of the cap bears a brownish felt disk with radiating splits; it grows in well-manured soil. Small Coprinii **of no alimentary interest** are *Coprinus niveus*, cap 1–3 cm, conical, white, mealy, growing on manure; *Coprinus silvaticus*, gray, growing in clusters, in woods; *Coprinus domesticus*, cap gray, covered with a coating decomposing into granular scales, growing in tufts; *Coprinus Hansenii*, ochraceous, delicate looking.

comatus Copr.

COPRINUS MICACEUS (Glistening Coprinus) (1)
Cap globular, ochraceous, cuspidate, with micaceous scales; margin uneven; then expanded 2–5 cm, with deep, radiating grooves and covered with granules. **Stem** cylindrical, smooth, sericeous, white, hollow. **Flesh** thin, whitish. **Odor** agreeable. **Flavor** mild. **Gills** close, narrow, free from the stem; whitish, then brown, finally black and mushy. **Spores** fuliginous. It grows in clusters, in all kinds of grounds, from spring to autumn. **Of no alimentary interest**; but harmful when its consumption is accompanied by alcoholic beverages. A similar species is *Coprinus radians*, of **no alimentary interest**, which grows singly on walls or on rotting wood.

COPRINUS PICACEUS (2)
Cap oval and covered by a white veil; then campanulate, 4–8 cm, fuliginous, with few sparse, whitish remains of the veil; radiating striae and grooves. **Stem** tall, bulbous base; white, fragile, hollow. **Flesh** thin. **Odor** disgusting. **Flavor** mild. **Gills** close, free, white, then pinkish, finally black and mushy. **Spores** black. It grows singly, in latifoliate woods. **Edible**.

COPRINUS DISSEMINATUS (3)
Cap 0·5–1·5 cm, white, whitish, or ochraceous; unlike other species of *Coprinus*, its gills do not dissolve into a slimy fluid; grows from spring to autumn, in dense clusters of hundreds of specimens, on latifoliate trunks, in humid woods; very pretty but **not very interesting** from an alimentary standpoint.

DROSOPHILA (Psathyrella) CANDOLLEANA (1)
Cap globose, ochraceous; then plane 2–7 cm, with a lighter and festooned margin; humidity enhances the colors, dry weather wrinkles the cuticle. **Stem** cylindrical, tall, slightly curved, white, slightly furfuraceous on top; fragile, hollow; rarely with filamentous ring. **Flesh** thin, fragile, white. **Odor** mild. **Flavor** agreeable. **Gills** close, thin, adhering to the stem; white, then covered with purplish brown powder: the **spores** en masse, whereas the edges appear white. It grows in clusters, from spring to autumn, in the ground and on wood, in humid and shady places. **Edible**, tasty.

DROSOPHILA HYDROPHILA (2)
Cap 2–5 cm, brown and with diaphanous margin when humid; ochraceous and with wrinkled cuticle in dry weather; the color of the flesh follows that of the cap; in groups or tufts, from spring, on tree trunks or tree stumps, or near them; **edible**: it seems that it can decrease the sugar content of the blood in the same way that insulin can. Similar to the previous *Drosophilae* are *Psilocybe sarcocephala*, **edible**, bigger than *Drosophila candolleana*, thicker, faded ocher color when dry, fuliginous brown in humid weather; *Psilocybe spadicea*, **harmless**, similar to *sarcocephala* but with fleshier cap of a brighter brown color, tending to red, like ripe, fresh dates.

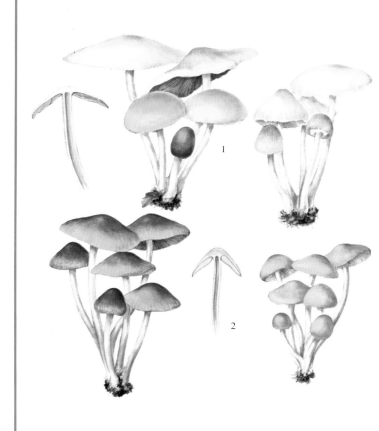

LACRYMARIA VELUTINA (Lange)

Cap 3–12 cm, often umbonate; ochraceous, reddish ocher, or cinereous ocher; now with uniform color, now with reddish center; covered with lanate, cinereous fibrils not separable from the cuticle; finally glabrous; margin with filamentous remains of the partial veil (cortina). **Stem** cylindric, sturdy, fibrillar, pubescent (hairy); white or with ochraceous stains; speckled with granules in the section above the ring; hard, hollow. **Cortina** abundant, white; soon appressed around the stem and blackish. **Flesh** hard, fragile, thick, white or slightly ochraceous. **Gills** not too close, but with numerous intermediate gills toward the margin of the cap; rounded near the stem to which they are slightly adhering; brownish with black spots; then uniformly blackish brown with light edges; when the weather is humid they ooze dewy droplets. **Spores** blackish cocoa. It grows in clearings of latifoliate woods, solitary or in small clusters. **Edible**, of good quality. This species is also known as *Lacrymaria lacrymabunda*, *Geophila lacrymabunda*, *Hypholoma lacrymabundum*; but, notwithstanding the name, it is not to be confused with *Psathyrella lacrymabunda* (Fries) of distinctly different appearance: cap whitish, then brownish; scaly cuticle; gills rarely exuding dewy droplets and never as abundantly as in *Lacrymaria velutina*; growing in small tufts, on stumps and dead roots; rare species; **edibility unknown**.

PANAEOLUS PAPILIONACEUS (1)

Cap campanulate or hemispheric, then slightly more open, 2–4 cm; first brownish pink, viscid; then dry, lucid, white tinged with pink, but still a little brownish at the center, where it easily cracks; margin extending over the gills. **Stem** thin, tall, stiff, same color as the cap, hollow. **Flesh** thin. **Odor** and **flavor** mild. **Gills** attached to the stem, broad, yellowish brown, then olivaceous with darker stains. **Spores** black. It grows from spring to autumn, on manure or in manured grounds. **Not edible**.

Growing under the same conditions, and equally **non-edible** are: *Panaeolus subbalteatus* (2), ocher tinged with pink, with brownish or blackish radiating striae; *Panaeolus sphinctrinus* (3), cinereous or olivaceous gray or fuliginous, with festooned margin; it is sometimes hallucinogenic; *Panaeolus campanulatus* (4), pinkish brown or reddish brown; *Panaeolus semiovatus*, cap 1–6 cm, conical, deep brown, shining. Similar to *Panaeolus* is *Psilocybe uda*, **of no alimentary interest**: cap 1–3 cm, brownish, not too sensitive to humidity, margin even; stem fibrous, tenacious; gills white, then violaceous brown, like the spores; growing in the moss, in humid places.

STROPHARIA (Geophila) CORONILLA (1)
Cap 2–5 cm, yellow or pinkish ocher; often umbonate; paler and festooned margin; glabrous, somewhat fibrillar; viscid in humid weather. **Stem** rather short, white; glabrous, fibrillar, sericeous, stuffed, pithy. **Ring** with pinkish striae; fragile, ephemeral. **Flesh** thick, white. **Odor** mild. **Flavor** mild. **Gills** annexed to the stem, amethystine, then brown with lighter edges. **Spores** fuliginous violet. It grows from spring to autumn, in pastures and clearings. **Edible.**

STROPHARIA MELASPERMA (2)
Cap white; gills gray then black, like the ripened spores; ring thick, denticulate, evanescent; flavor agreeable; in well manured grounds; **not edible.**

STROPHARIA UMBONATESCENS (3)
Similar to *Stropharia semiglobata*, but with white cap and with rather prominent umbo. It grows in the mountains; **not edible.**

STROPHARIA SEMIGLOBATA (Hemispheric Stropharia) (4)
Cap 1–4 cm, yellowish or greenish, paler along the margin; glabrous, viscous in humid weather; shining in dry weather. **Stem** thin, glabrous, viscous near the ring, paler than the cap, soon hollow. **Ring** thin, viscid, reddish, then black; evanescent. **Flesh** pallid. **Odor** and **flavor** mild. **Gills** broad, decurrent on the stem by a thread; whitish, then violaceous gray with lighter edges. **Spores** blackish violet. It grows where manure is present. **Not edible.**

STROPHARIA (Geophila) AERUGINOSA

Cap 3–9 cm, exceptionally 12; often umbonate; green or blue green, becoming yellow with age or after being picked; viscid, with rare, evanescent squamules; festooned margin. **Stem** lighter than the cap; covered with soft, lighter squamules. **Ring** frayed, fugaceous; white or stained black by the ripe spores. **Flesh** white, tinged with green. **Odor** of radish. **Flavor** disgusting. **Gills** annexed to the stem; amethystine, then violaceous brown; darker spots; lighter edges. **Spores** violaceous brown. It grows in ground rich in organic substances. **Harmless.** We want to mention here the following *Strophariae*: *Stropharia albocyanea*, **not edible**, smaller than *aeruginosa* and gracile; *Stropharria Hornemannii,* **not edible**, bigger than *aeruginosa*, cap yellowish brown, flavor disagreeable; growing under conifers, also in the Far East; *Stropharia ambigua*, **not edible**, bigger still, cap yellowish brown, stem tall and covered with white flocci from the·base to the ring; gills white, then purplish brown, growing in spring and autumn, in North America. But a very good **edible** species is the large *Stropharia Ferrii*, whose cap can reach up to 25 centimeters in diameter; yellow to brick red; gills violaceous; it can be found in all kinds of ground, on leaves, weeds, and twigs.

HYPHOLOMA (Nematoloma) FASCICULARE

Cap 2–7 cm, not umbonate; lemon yellow or sulfur yellow, then orange yellow; more deeply colored at the center; smooth, sericeous, not viscid. **Stem** cylindrical, slender, curved; yellow, darker at the base; fibrillar, sericeous; tenacious, hollow. **Cortina** filamentous, yellowish, stretched from the margin of the cap to the apex of the stem; but only in unripe specimens; soon disappearing, forming a pseudoring on the stem soon made brownish or fuliginous by the spores. **Flesh** thin, especially near the cap's margin, sulfur yellow, but reddish under the cuticle; it tends to become reddish. **Odor** disagreeable. **Flavor** very bitter. **Gills** very close, narrow, annexed to the stem or free; yellow or yellowish, then olivaceous, finally covered by a blackish violet powder: the ripe **spores**. It grows throughout the year, except in freezing weather, in tufts of numerous specimens, on dead or live wood, on the surface or into the ground. **Not edible**, if for anything else, because of its bitter taste. A similar species is *Hypholoma squamosum*, with the cap spotted with triangular squamules, stem bearing a blackish ring, scaly from the ring to the base, growing solitary or in tufts, in woods, in grassy places, on wooden debris; **edibility unknown**, but of no interest from an alimentary standpoint.

HYPHOLOMA (Nematoloma) SUBLATERITIUM

Cap 4–9 cm, but much bigger in the variety *permagnum*; glabrous, soon dry; orange red or brick red, with lighter and festooned margin. **Stem** stout, often curved, fibrillar; yellowish, but reddish brown at the base; sometimes with filamentous pseudo-ring; soon hollow. **Cortina** whitish, stretched from the cap's margin to the stem, but only in unripe specimens; soon appressed to the stem or completely disappearing; in the form *pomposum* it forms a large and permanent ring. **Flesh** firm, white, then yellowish; the stem reddish. **Odor** mild. **Flavor** bitterish or bitter. **Gills** close, narrow, annexed to the stem by a tooth; whitish, then yellowish, finally olivaceous or fuliginous violet, with undulate and yellowish edges. **Spores** fuliginous violet. It grows in autumn, in tufts, on old stumps. **Not edible**; but the variety growing in North America, slightly or not at all bitter, is **edible**. Similar to the previous *Hypholoma*, and also **not edible**: *Hypholoma epixanthum*, cap yellowish, center reddish, margin covered by the white and cottony remains of the veil; bitter and fetid; grows in the mountains, on pine and beech stumps; *Hypholoma radicosum*, cinereous, stem with ring and darker zones, radicating base; growing solitary on coniferous stumps.

HYPHOLOMA CAPNOIDES

Cap 3–8 cm, umbonate or gibbous; margin hazel, tinged with yellow, sharpened and somewhat eroded; center brownish; orange yellow between the center and the margin; on the whole of a rather dirty color; dry in dry weather, it becomes somewhat viscid in humid weather and slightly more colored, especially at the margin. **Stem** thin, slender, smooth; in unripe specimens it can still bear tenuous remains of the cortina; from the top down whitish, then brown and tawny at the base; hollow. **Cortina** whitish, covering the gills in unripe specimens, soon disappearing. **Flesh** whitish or tinged with yellow. **Odor** mild. **Flavor** mild or bitterish. **Gills** close, adnate (attached to the stem), cinereous, then blue gray. **Spores** violaceous black. It grows throughout the year, except when it is freezing weather, on stumps of latifoliate trees or conifers, but especially on pine and fir, in large tufts. **Edible**: it is advisable to boil it a few minutes in water, then drain it, before cooking it. It can sometimes be confused with *Hypholoma fasciculare* (page 55) and with *Hypholoma sublateritium*, both **not edible**, which have yellow or greenish gills, whereas *capnoides* has no trace of yellow or green in the gills. If in doubt, however. a little taste of the specimens in question can solve the problem: *capnoides*, as we already said, has mild or only slightly bitter flavor, whereas *sublateritium* often, and *fasciculare* always, are very bitter.

capnoides Hyph.

FLAMMULA (Gymnopilus) PENETRANS (1)

Cap plane-convex, 5–10 cm, sometimes depressed, sometimes umbonate; smooth, glabrous, dry; orange yellow, center tending to red, margin tending to yellow; rarely uniformly colored. **Stem** cylindric, sometimes undulate; fibrous; whitish or yellowish, then of the color of the cap; firm, stuffed, then hollow. **Cortina** tenuous, fugaceous; but conspicuous and appressed around the stem, ringlike, in the form *hybrida* (lower right-hand corner). **Flesh** tender, whitish, then yellowish; stem rusty. **Odor** now mild, now strong. **Flavor** very bitter. **Gills** rather close, annexed or sometimes slightly decurrent along the stem; yellow, then orange, finally rusty, with lighter, flocculose edges. **Spores** rust colored. It grows on rotting, exposed or buried wood, in coniferous woods, especially pine; solitary, sometimes in small tufts. **Not edible**.

FLAMMULA SAPINEA (2)

Similar to *penetrans*; with the cuticle of the cap fibrillar-lanate, soon cracked, and with often compressed stem; bitter and **not edible**. Generally smaller is *Flammula gummosa* (3), **harmless**, cap greenish yellow, covered with very fine squamules, then brownish and glabrous; stem squamous-pubescent, hollow and elastic as if made of rubber; growing in tufts, rotting stumps, and wood debris.

PHOLIOTA SQUARROSA (1)

Cap hemispheric, then expanded, 5–12 cm; ocher or slightly orange; with coarse, rusty scales; dry; festooned margin. **Stem** stout, scaly as the cap, but whitish and smooth above the ring; stuffed, then hollow. **Ring** filamentous, white and smooth above, brownish and scaly below. **Flesh** tenacious, yellowish; yellowish and hard that of the stem. **Odor** mild or of garlic. **Flavor** of turnip. **Gills** close, adhering to the stem; yellowish, then ochraceous. **Spores** ochraceous. It grows in autumn, in dense tufts, at the base of dead tree trunks. **Edible**, but of mediocre quality; parboiling necessary. Similar to the previous species, lignicolous, **edible**, mediocre: *Pholiota subsquarrosa*, cap dry, lemon yellow, with thin, appressed scales; *Pholiota squarrosoides* (Sharp-scale Pholiota), whitish, with numerous, small, pyramidal scales.

PHOLIOTA ADIPOSA (Fat Pholiota) (2)

Cap 8–16 cm, yellow, tending now to saffron, now to golden yellow, brown or rusty scales, disappearing with age and finally reduced to brownish granules; growing preferably on beech trees; **edible**, but mediocre.

PHOLIOTA AURIVELLA (3)

Cap orange yellow, lighter along the margin, rusty at the center; brownish scales; viscid only in humid weather; stem fibrillar but not squamose; growing in small tufts, in the crevices of trunks of latifoliate trees; **edible** of poor quality.

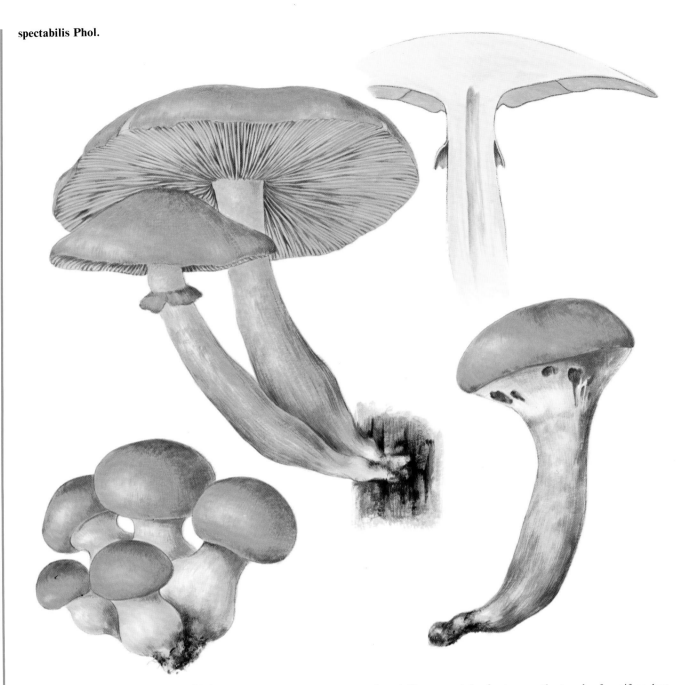

PHOLIOTA SPECTABILIS (Gillet)

Cap hemispheric, then convex and also expanded 8–15 cm; golden yellow, apricot yellow, orange, or reddish; smooth initially, then covered with very fine squamules or sericeous fibrils, brownish or reddish brown. **Stem** tall, thick, generally swollen in the middle, and with pointed base; golden yellow; pruinose above the ring, fibrillar and squamose from the ring to the base. **Ring** membranous, same color as the stem. **Flesh** yellow. **Odor** mild. **Flavor** slightly or distinctly bitter. **Gills** close, thin, not very broad; eroded near the stem and decurrent along it by a tooth; yellow then rusty. **Spores** rust colored. It grows at the foot or on the trunk of conifers, but mostly of old latifoliate trees; sometimes solitary, more often in tufts of few specimens with confluent bases. **Not edible**, at least when it is distinctly bitter. Smaller, cap 3–9 cm, lignicolous, bitterish, and with **no alimentary interest**: *Pholiota flammans*, entirely golden yellow, on spruces, in the mountains; *Pholiota astragalina*, cap red, smooth, stem yellow, on conifers; *Pholiota lucifera*, cap lemon yellow, scaly, on wooden debris; *Pholiota alnicola*, cap greenish yellow, smooth, on alders and birches; *Pholiota carbonaria*, brownish, not bitter, in groups, on burned grounds.

mutabilis Phol.

PHOLIOTA (Hygrophana) MUTABILIS

Cap not too fleshy, convex, then plane, 3–8 cm, umbonate; thin, even margin; surface glabrous, smooth; in dry weather or when old, ocher yellow, often slightly darker at the center; in humid weather it absorbs water and, at least when still unripe, it becomes cinnamon colored, starting from the margin. **Stem** cylindrical, gracile, curved; same color as the cap, gradually darker toward the base where it is fuliginous brown; light just under the cap; from the ring to the base first covered with brown squamules, then fibrillar and vertically sulcate; tenacious, soon hollow. **Ring** membranous, brown, ephemeral. **Flesh** whitish, but of the color of the cap in humid weather. **Odor** mild. **Flavor** mild. **Gills** close, thin, whitish, then yellowish, finally rusty. **Spores** rust colored. It grows throughout the year, but especially in summer, in tufts, on stumps of latifoliate trees. **Edible**, of good quality when not too old, and only the caps: the stem is too tough to eat. Similar to *Pholiota mutabilis*, only smaller, is *Galera marginata*, **harmless**, growing singly on coniferous, rarely on latifoliate, wood; odor and flavor of flour.

PHOLIOTA DESTRUENS

Cap hemispheric, then convex 6–20 cm, generally umbonate; margin tightly involute, then explanate and festooned; whitish or yellowish or brownish; covered with coarse, woolly, irregular scales, white, then brownish. **Stem** thick, sometimes eccentric with respect to the cap; slightly lighter than the cap; fibrillar; from the ring down flocculose; firm, stuffed; base thickened, rootlike, brownish. **Ring**, same color as the cap or slightly lighter; flocculose, striate; frayed margin; transient. **Flesh** thick, firm; white, yellowish at the base of the stem. **Odor** somewhat disagreeable. **Flavor** sometimes sweetish, sometimes bitter. **Gills** close, broad, thick; whitish, then brownish with lighter edges; more or less broadly attached to the stem. **Spores** ochraceous. It grows solitary or in tufts, especially on poplars but also on other felled latifoliate trees, rarely on living trees. **Not edible**, or at least not advisable. We mention here one other species, bitter, lignicolous, more frequent in North America: *Pleurotus* or *Rhodotus palmatus*, **not edible**, cap 2–8 cm, apricot color; thick cuticle, soon cracked; stem thin, curved, eccentric, pinkish white, darker at the base; gills free, whitish, then slightly paler than the cap; flesh elastic, acidulous, then bitter; growing from June to October, in groups, on dead wood of latifoliate trees.

ROZITES (Pholiota) CAPERATA

Cap ovoid, then campanulate, finally expanded and also plane, 5–15 cm, sometimes umbonate; soon radially corrugated, but often not as far as the margin; margin soon creased and here and there radially fissured, but only tardily striate or sulcate in the direction of the gills; ochraceous, more intense when the air is humid (1, the small specimen); often faded (2, specimen with atypical cap, grown between two rocks, in the shade); cuticle furfuraceous, transient along the margin, but persistent at the center. **Stem** thick, fibrous, stuffed; cylindrical, slightly thickened at the base; white and flocculose above the ring, whitish, with sericeous, silvery or amethystine striae from the ring to the base. Unripe specimens present a thin, more or less whole, sheath, appressed, amethystine, yellowish, or whitish, which sometimes reaches from the base halfway up to the stem. **Ring** soft, white with a yellowish or amethystine zone; evanescent, therefore sometimes lacking in the older specimens. **Flesh** yellowish, rather soft and fragile. **Odor** mild. **Flavor** pleasant. **Gills** close, medium height, becoming suddenly narrow near the stem, to which they are often attached only by a tip; yellowish, then ochraceous, with lighter and uneven edges. **Spores** ochraceous. It grows among mosses and huckleberries, but also among rocks, in gravel and dry grounds, in woods especially of pine and fir, sometimes also in latifoliate woods. **Edible**, good; it can be preserved dried or in oil.

PHAEOLEPIOTA AUREA (Maire)

Cap hemispheric, then convex, finally expanded, 5–15 cm, with umbo at the center, but often not too prominent; initially rather moist and covered with branlike particles formed by very minute squamules and by granules, cinnamon colored; then it becomes dry, velvety and darker, brownish; margin smooth, rolled toward the gills and with granular remains of the universal veil; sometimes cracked here and there in the direction of the gills. **Stem** stout, thick, cylindrical, generally tall; covered, from the base to the ring, with a sheath of the same tissue as that of the cap's cuticle, velvety-granular, cinnamon colored; white or slightly ochraceous, pruinose above the ring. **Ring** formed by the upper margin of the sheath that covers the stem; for long time adhering to the cap's margin, then funnel shaped; membranous, furfuraceous, golden brown. **Flesh** whitish, exposed to air or upon aging it becomes yellowish, but that of the stem is reddish. **Odor** strong. **Flavor** strong and disgusting. **Gills** close, unequal, annexed to the stem, often rounded near the stem, therefore adhering to it only by a tooth; ochraceous, then rust colored. **Spores** ochraceous. It grows in autumn, in latifoliate, but especially in fir woods, on the bare ground near the roots, or among mosses and nettles. **Edible**, although mediocre; therefore not to be confused with *Pholiota spectabilis* (Gillet) (page 59), which is, however, smaller than *Phaeolepiota aurea*, has no sheath around the stem, and is bitter and lignicolous.

AGROCYBE DURA (1)

Cap whitish, 3–9 cm; sometimes slightly umbonate; margin festooned, then fissured; cuticle strewn with fine powder; in dry weather it cracks, starting from the center, in many polygonal scales. **Stem** cylindrical, but turbinate and wrinkled in the variety *obconipes*; white and smooth, but with dark scales and radicating base, in the variety *squamulosipes* (these varieties, *squamulosipes* and *obconipes* are probably only forms). **Ring** membranous, whitish. **Flesh** thick, tough, white. **Odor** of flour. **Flavor** bitterish. **Gills** rather close, broad, rounded near the stem and adhering to it; white, then cinereous-amethystine, finally brownish. **Spores** fuliginous ocher. It grows in meadows, parks, and gardens. **Edible**, of poor quality.

AGROCYBE PALUDOSA (2)

Cap 2–4 cm, ochraceous or brownish; stem cylindrical, tall, thin, undulate, hollow; with small, disklike ring, but evanescent, and therefore often disappearing in older specimens; gills broad, annexed, ochraceous; growing in moist ground; **of no interest** from the alimentary standpoint.

AGROCYBE ERESIA (3)

Cap 3–8 cm, fuliginous brown, sometimes slightly umbonate, always with distinct radial grooves at the margin. **Stem** thick, base dark as the cap and becoming lighter upward; vertically striate near the gills. **Ring** membranous, white, vertically striate. **Flesh** thick, cinereous. **Gills** whitish, then brown. It grows on loose soil, often under poplars. **Edible**.

AGROCYBE PRAECOX

Cap whitish or faded grayish hazel color, with cream colored margin; brownish ocher in humid weather, deeper at the center; hemispheric or campanulate, then plane, 3–8 cm; sometimes with festooned margin; cuticle glabrous, pruinose, shining; but rugose and opaque in dry weather. **Stem** generally thin and slender; rarely somewhat thick, often with thickened or also bulbous base; fibrillar, whitish; brownish at the base; stuffed, then hollow; fibrous. **Ring** membranous, very thin, large, situated very high on the stem, soon appressed around the stem; whitish, then covered with rusty brown powder. **Flesh** thick at the center; soft, fragile, pale ocher, then whitish. **Odor** of flour. **Flavor** unpleasant and sometimes bitterish. **Gills** close, thin, broad, semioval near the stem, annexed; pallid, then amethystine gray, finally fuliginous brown or cinnamon. **Spores** fuliginous or brownish gray. It grows from April to July, in grassy places near latifoliate trees. **Edible**. It is sometimes mistaken for *Agrocybe dura* (page 63), **edible**, which however is generally thicker, with the cap's cuticle cracked, and the flesh of the cap quite tougher.

There are atypical specimens of *Agrocybe praecox* that can be confused with specimens of *Agrocybe aegerita*, **edible**, which is lignicolous, not terricolous.

PHOLIOTA (Agrocybe) AEGERITA

Cap hemispheric, then plane 3–14 cm, finally concave; generally brown in unripe specimens; then fading to whitish; in some varieties and forms it appears brown in spring and white in autumn; the cuticle, smooth and sericeous, soon cracks; in persistent dry weather it cleaves. **Stem** slender, rarely stout; curved, thinner toward the base; whitish, then hazelnut colored, more or less faded; in specimens grown in the shade it can be white as the cap. **Ring** large, white; soon reduced to a skimpy, brownish shred. **Flesh**, tender that of the cap; fibrous that of the stem; white, then ochraceous. **Odor** pleasant. **Flavor** of hazelnuts. **Gills** close, thin, broad; annexed to the stem, or eroded near it and decurrent by a thin, paler thread; whitish, then ochraceous, finally tobacco; sometimes with paler and undulate edges. **Spores** brownish or fuliginous. It grows from spring to the beginning of winter, on the trunks of poplars and other latifoliate trees. **Edible**, of good quality, easily cultivated on disks of poplar wood, rubbed with the ripe gills of the mushroom; then the disks are placed on the ground, covered with a light layer of dirt and kept moderately humid: the first carpophores appear at the end of ten months and fructification continues, in season, until all the wood has been consumed.

HEBELOMA CRUSTULINIFORME (1)

Cap 5–15 cm, cream colored or ochraceous or rosy ocher, darker at the center; slightly viscid. **Stem** firm, cylindric, sometimes with a bulbous base; whitish, very fibrous; furfuraceous or flocculose on top. **Flesh** whitish. **Odor** of turnip. **Flavor** disgustingly bitter. **Gills** rather close, narrow especially near the stem; with denticulate edges; whitish, exuding moisture droplets in humid weather; then ochraceouscinerous with paler edges. **Spores** fuliginous ocher. It grows in groups, under latifoliate trees, especially poplars and birches; on swampy grounds it is more gracilent; in high mountains it is smaller, 2–3 cm, with gills not crowded and hollow stem, and is called *Hebeloma alpinum*. **Not edible**. A similar species is *Hebeloma fragile*, **not edible**, growing in groups in the grass, under poplars: turnip odor, cap 8–12 cm, which, like the stem, is whitish and very fragile.

HEBELOMA SINAPIZANS (2)

Cap 6–16 cm, color ranging from cream to reddish brown; from the ceiling of the stem's cavity hangs a sort of stalactite, characteristic of this mushroom; gills not exuding moisture droplets; turnip odor, bitter taste, spores tobacco colored. **Poisonous**: it causes gastrointestinal disorders. A similar species is *Hebeloma birrum*, **not edible**: cap 6–10 cm, ochraceous tinged with red, margin radially striate; stem thick, shaped like an upside-down club; slightly paler than the cap, with fibrous, rumpled cuticle with filamentous granules; odor of turnip but pleasant; bitter taste; growing under conifers.

CORTINARIUS (Myxacium) ELATIOR

Cap campanulate, yellowish or ochraceous or brown, tinged with violaceous or olivaceous hues; then plane, 5–12 cm, umbonate or gibbous; margin soon with deep, radial grooves; in humid weather it is shining, viscid or even sticky. **Stem** tall, slightly thickened in the middle; fibrillar, viscid in humid weather; rather striate or also rugose on top; whitish with hazy violaceous spots; fragile, hollow; tapering base, deeply buried into the ground. **Cortina** glutinous, stretched from the margin of the cap to the stem, but only in unripe specimens. **Flesh** rather thin, soft, fragile; whitish or yellowish. **Odor** mild. **Flavor** mild. **Gills** not too close, rather thick, very broad; connected to each other by fine veins; vertically rugose; with undulate edges; adhering to the stem; whitish, then violaceous, finally rust colored. **Spores** rust colored. It grows in latifoliate woods, especially under beeches. **Edible**.

The genus *Cortinarius* is divided into the following subgenera: *Myxacium*, cortina glutinous, viscous cap and stem. *Phlegmacium*, cortina glutinous, cap viscous, stem not viscous. *Inoloma*, cortina filamentous, cap fibrillar or velvety or flocculose, not too sensitive to humidity; stem thick, gills neither yellow nor red. *Dermocybe*, like *Inoloma*, but with thin stem, and yellow or olivaceous or red gills. *Telamonia*, cortina filamentous, cap glabrous and with white fibrils, more or less sensitive to humidity; stem with flocculose veil or with fibrillar rings. *Hydrocybe*, like *Dermocybe*, but sensitive to humidity, and with glabrous stem. These subgenera terms are a more precise terminology, but little used.

HEBELOMA RADICOSUM

Cap convex, umbonate, with involute and festooned margin; then somewhat expanded, 7–17 cm, whitish, ochraceous, or brownish, never of a distinct and clean color; cuticle smooth, viscid, with large, thin, generally darker scales, adhering to the cuticle and blending with it. **Stem** fusiform, stuffed, whitish and farinaceous above the ring; whitish from the ring down but covered with brownish gray scales, arranged as superimposed and irregular rings; base buried in the ground by means of a radiciform appendix which is sometimes longer than the stem, straight, tough, pointed, sometimes darker, sometimes paler than the stem. **Ring** thin, fragile, rather distant from the cap, whitish, then brownish. **Flesh** thick, firm, white. **Odor** of bitter almonds exhaled by the gills. **Flavor** mild. **Gills** rather close, slightly rounded toward the stem to which they adhere; fairly broad, whitish, then grayish ocher and finally brownish, with paler edges. **Spores** tobacco colored. It grows in latifoliate woods, especially around very old stumps, but also in meadows. **Edible**, of poor quality. The following, small *Hebeloma* are **not edible**: *Hebeloma hiemale*, 3–4 cm, cream color, bitterish, autumnal; *Hebeloma helatum*, 2–6 cm, white, brownish at the center, stem tall, gills amethystine, turnip odor, growing under conifers; *Hebeloma sacchariolens*, 2–5 cm, white at the margin, brown at the center, odor of burnt sugar.

radicosum Heb.

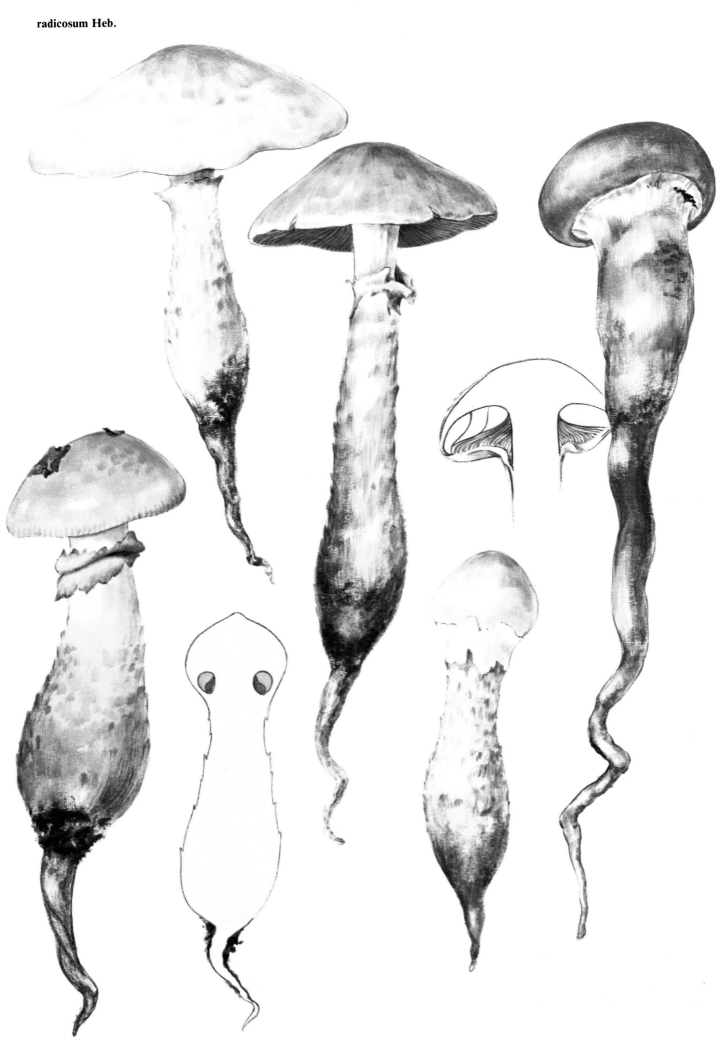

CORTINARIUS (Myxacium) COLLINITUS (1)
Cap 3–12 cm, rather cuspidate, glutinous; orange brown or olivaceous brown, with lighter margin. **Stem** tall, cylindrical, stout; white, striate, pruinose on top; the rest is covered with annular plaques, white or ochraceous, on brownish and fibrous background; swollen and gelatinous in dry weather; long base, buried in the ground. **Cortina** glutinous, white. **Flesh** thick, firm, whitish or ocher. **Odor** mild. **Flavor** sapid. **Gills** whitish, then amethystine, covered with a rust colored powder: the **spores**. In groups, in fairy rings, in the moss, under conifers. **Edible**. Similar to the above is *Cortinarius trivialis,* **edible** of poor quality: cap ochraceous or argillaceous; gills cinereous, then cinnamon color; growing especially under willows.

CORTINARIUS (Inoloma) PHOLIDEUS (2)
Cap 4–8 cm, not viscous, but velvety and squamose; stem thin, with annular plaques formed by scales; gills amethystine, then rusty; **of no alimentary interest**.

CORTINARIUS (Myxacium) MUCIFLUUS (3)
Cap 3–7 cm, thin, with striate margin; stem soft, spongy, white tending to pinkish; under latifoliate trees; **edible**. Similar to this is *Cortinarius mucosus*, **edible**: cap orange, stem white, but coeruleous in the variety *coeruleipes*; under spruces, autumnal. With violet stem and brown violet cap is *Cortinarius salor*: sparse, violaceous, then rusty gills; growing under beeches.

CORTINARIUS (Phlegmacium) PRAESTANS

Cap globose, then hemispheric, finally convex, 5–30 cm; viscid in humid weather; reddish brown or leather brown, often with violet shades; then faded brown; with sparse, sericeous, violaceous gray plaques, remains of the universal veil; margin flocculose, then glabrous, but radially striate; finally deeply sulcate. **Stem** thick, thickened at the base, which is pointed; stuffed; white, with zones amethystine and then ochraceous, more evident at the base. **Cortina** white or with pale blue shades; filamentous; stretched from the margin of the cap to the stem; then appressed on the stem in a brownish, annular zone. **Flesh** abundant, firm; whitish, yellowish under the cap's cuticle, the stem amethystine white. **Odor** pleasant. **Flavor** sapid. **Gills** fairly close, broad, rather thick; sometimes eroded near the stem, sometimes slightly decurrent along it; at first amethystine white, then brownish. **Spores** rust colored. In summer and in autumn, in woods, especially birch and oak woods, in groups, in rings; sometimes partly buried. **Edible**, good. Similar, tough smaller, is *Cortinarius cumatile*, **edible** of good quality: cap 6–10 cm, violet cinereous or bluish cinereous; stem white and thick, base thick, cortina filamentous, amethystine white; flesh firm, white, odorless, tasty; gills annexed to the stem, whitish, then ochraceous.

CORTINARIUS (Phlegmacium) PURPURASCENS (1, and sections at the bottom)

Cap 7–14 cm, convex; fibrillar; slightly viscid; violaceous brown, faded in dry weather; with darker spots in humid weather; margin rolled toward the gills, then rather explanate. **Stem** thick; base bulbous with clear-cut margin; fibrillar, bluish, violaceous when bruised. **Cortina** soon filamentous, moist, violaceous; evanescent; soon only a slight, brownish trace around the stem. **Flesh** thick, violaceous, the stem darker; discoloring with age; becoming slightly more purpureous in contact with air. **Odor** slight but characteristic. **Flavor** agreeable. **Gills** rather close, thin, somewhat broad; semioval or eroded near the stem; purpureous violet, then cinnamon brown. **Spores** rusty ocher. It grows in autumn, in coniferous woods. **Edible**. Another mushroom also grows in coniferous woods, with cap, gills, and flesh more or less violaceous in humid weather but rusty in dry weather: *Cortinarius muricinus*, **not edible**, with odor of burnt fingernails.

CORTINARIUS PURPURASCENS form LARGUSOIDES (2)

Cap large, 8–16 cm, chestnut color with violaceous margin; stem cylindrical; base not bulbous but only slightly thickened; bluish flesh; growing in latifoliate woods. **Edible**.

CORTINARIUS (Phlegmacium) MULTIFORMIS (1)
Cap 5–10 cm, viscid only in humid weather; ochraceous, darker at the center; fibrillar and furfuraceous. **Stem** not viscid, cylindrical, thick, whitish, then yellowish; base thickened, even bulbous, brownish. **Cortina** soon filamentous, white. **Flesh** white; ochraceous under the cap's cuticle, yellowish in the stem, brownish at the base. **Odor** mild. **Flavor** agreeable. **Gills** close, semioval near the stem, free or almost free; with uneven edges; white, then ochraceous. **Spores** rust colored. It grows in groups, in woods; but under conifers in the variety *napus*, which is more colored. **Edible**.

COERINARIUS (Phlegmacium) VARIUS (2)
Cap 5–12 cm, orange at the center, yellow along the margin; gills violaceous, then rusty; grows in autumn, in groups, under conifers; **edible**, of good quality.
Other *cortinarii* with cap viscid in humid weather and stem not viscid: *Cortinarius fulmineus*, **edible**; reddish brown, sericeous, fibrillar, with the edges of the gills uneven. *Cortinarius aurantio-turbinatus*, **of no alimentary interest**; entirely yellow, under beeches. *Cortinarius elegantior*, **edible**, yellowish with brownish cap; growing in the mountains, under conifers. *Cortinarius delibutus*, **edible**: yellow, with amethystine gills; growing especially under beeches, birches, oaks, and firs. *Cortinarius calochrous*, **harmless**; yellowish, stem white, gills amethystine; under beech trees.

CORTINARIUS (Phlegmacium) LARGUS
Cap amethystine white or cinereous amethystine, then pale ocher; hemispheric, then convex or expanded, 9–15 cm; often cuspidate; smooth, viscid in humid weather, soon dry and sericeous. **Stem** tall and thick, not very hard, with the base thickened but not bulbous; amethystine on top, same color as the cap below the cortina; stuffed. **Cortina** soon filamentous, sericeous, white, evanescent. **Flesh** tender, amethystine, then white. **Odor** very mild. **Flavor** mild. **Gills** close, rather broad, eroded near the stem; with finely serrate edges; amethystine, then hazel color. **Spores** reddish brown. It grows in latifoliate woods. **Edible**. *Cortinarius variicolor* (*top right*), considered by some as edible of good quality, by others of poor quality, with disgusting soil odor, different from *largus* because of its shining, brown cap, firm flesh and stiff stem, growing in the mountains under conifers; it is different from the smaller specimens, 5–10 cm, of *C. praestans* (page 69), because it does not have remains of the veil on the cap. *Cortinarius caerulescens* (page 71) can be of the same color as *largus* when young, but has bulbous base, slightly bitterish flesh, and grows also under conifers, whereas *C. largus* grows only under latifoliate trees, has mild flavor, and the base is only slightly thickened, never bulbous. From the standpoint of edibility it is not dangerous to confuse these mushrooms since they are equally **edible**.

caerulescens Cort.

CORTINARIUS (Phlegmacium) CAERULESCENS (2)
Cap violet blue, cinereous blue, or pale violet; soon becoming ochraceous, starting from the center, then brownish; convex, then expanded. 5–10 cm; often umbonate; margin rolled toward the gills, and of a faded color; cuticle viscid, easily detachable from the cap. **Stem** thick, sericeous, with tenuous brownish remains of the veil; amethystine, then ochraceous; base bulbous with clear-cut margin, woolly, whitish. **Cortina** soon filamentous, violaceous white, evanescent. **Flesh** thick; the cap white; the stem violaceous; the base ochraceous. **Odor** mild. **Flavor** mild at first taste, then bitterish. **Gills** close, thin, eroded near the stem; initially amethystine, then covered by a rusty ocher powder: the

spores. It grows in coniferous or latifoliate woods. **Edible**, rather sapid.

CORTINARIUS SODAGNITUS (Henry) (1, specimen with tall stem)
Gracilent, violet, gills always amethystine. **Edibility unknown**.

CORTINARIUS CAESIO-CYANEUS (Britz) (3)
Blue gray, gills whitish, then amethystine. **Edibility unknown**.

CORTINARIUS DIBAPHUS (Fries) (4)
Stem violet, gills for long time whitish. **Edibility unknown**.

CORTINARIUS (Phlegmacium) CYANOPUS (1)

Cap 4–10 cm, brownish gray, darker at the center, faded at the margin; but olivaceous yellow or cream colored in the variety *amoenolens* (3); margin involute, then slightly explanate and undulate; viscid in humid weather. **Stem** stout, fibrillar, bluish violet; base ochraceous and bulbous in unripe specimens. **Cortina** abundant, bluish violet, soon appressed on the stem and brownish. **Flesh** thick, firm, whitish or tinged with blue; the flesh of the stem bluish violet. **Odor** agreeable; fruitlike in the variety *amoenolens*. **Flavor** agreeable, but the viscid cuticle is bitter. **Gills** rather close, eroded near the stem, with undulate edges; bluish violet, finally rusty. **Spores** rusty. It grows in latifoliate woods. **Harmless**.

CORTINARIUS (Phlegmacium) GLAUCOPUS (2)

Cap 5–12 cm, viscid in humid weather; yellowish ocher, reddish ocher, or olivaceous brown; then rusty brown; margin greenish, then yellowish, undulate, corrugated. **Stem** bluish with violet or blue green shades; then brownish or pale olivaceous; base bulbous, compressed. **Cortina** amethystine with olivaceous shades. **Flesh** of the cap cream colored, then yellowish; the base ochraceous. **Odor** mild. **Flavor** mild. **Gills** rather close, eroded near the stem; amethystine, then grayish, finally brownish. **Spores** rust colored. It grows in the mountains, under conifers. **Harmless**.

CORTINARIUS (Inoloma) TRAGANUS

At first the cap and the stem are like two little spheres, one upon the other, covered with the universal veil, and of a pale blue-amethystine color; then the **cap** unfolds slightly, 5–13 cm, but still with the margin rolled down toward the gills; finally becoming irregular; cuticle pale blue-amethystine, dry sericeous, then ochraceous and cracked into small squamules. **Stem** solid, pear shaped; same color as the cap, but whitish and woolly at the base. **Cortina** pale cinereous blue, soon disappearing, leaving few brownish more or less complete belts on the stem. **Flesh**: the cap faded ocher; the stem of a more intense color and tending to yellow; rather cinereous when imbibed with water. **Odor** goatlike. **Flavor** agreeable. **Gills** rather sparse, broad, annexed to the stem; yellowish ocher, then brownish. **Spores** cinnamon brown. It grows in woods, especially fir. **Not edible**; but a few specimens fried a long time in butter until mummified will give sauces a very tasty flavor and aroma. Distinguishable from *Cortinarius violaceous* (page 77), **edible**, which has the cap dry, velvety, dark violet, the flesh violaceous with cedar wood odor, and grows in latifoliate woods.

traganus Cort.

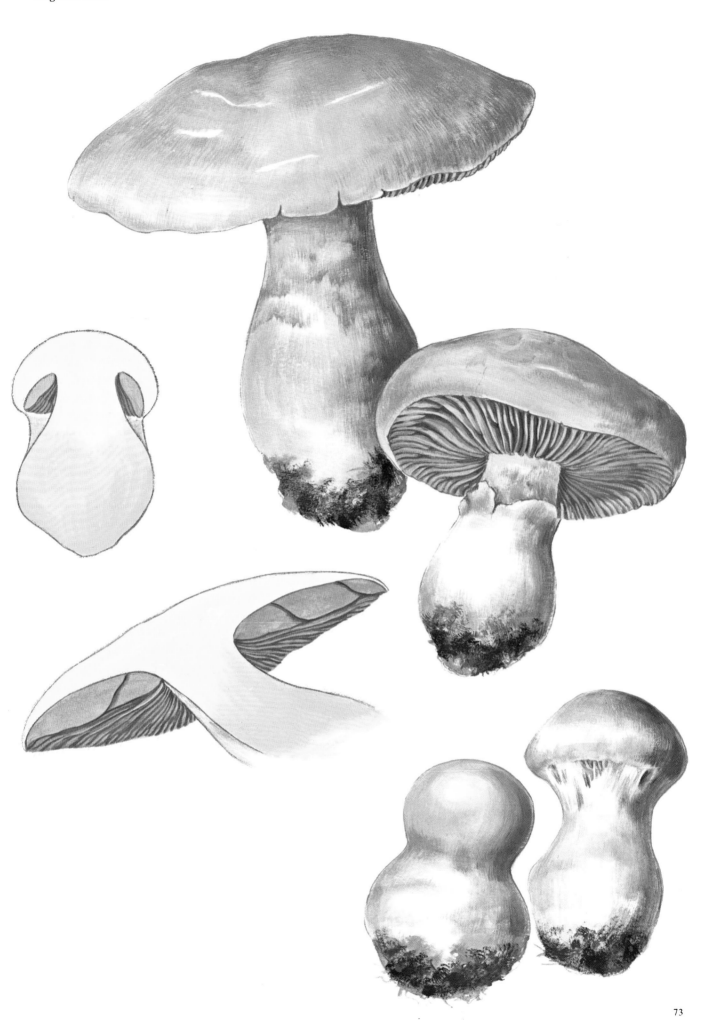

CORTINARIUS (Inoloma) ALBOVIOLACEUS (1)

Cap oval, then convex, finally expanded, 3–8 cm; with promi-nent umbo at the center; margin thin, slightly undulate, then radially fissured; amethystine white, fading with age; dry, sericeous, fibrillar, shining. **Stem** tall, sometimes curved, thickened at the base, which sometimes presents a mem-branous hoselike sheath; same color as the cap; fragile, stuffed, fibrous, spongy. **Cortina** white, then rusty; transient. **Flesh** tender, violaceous, fading with age, starting from the cap. **Odor** mild. **Flavor** mild. **Gills** not too close, rather broad, annexed to the stem; cinereous-amethystine, then rusty gray, finally rusty brown with white and serrate edges.

Spores rusty ocher. It grows in latifoliate woods especially oak and beech woods. **Edible.**

CORTINARIUS (Inoloma) ANOMALUS (2)

Cap hemispheric, then plane-convex, 2–7 cm; ochraceous or brown, often with amethystine hues along the margin; dry. **Stem** rather gracile, often thickened at the base; white, covered with brownish filaments, but glabrous and amethyst-ine on top, then whitish or brownish and glabrous. **Flesh** white, amethystine in the upper part of the stem, then brown-ish. **Odor** slight, of camphor. It grows in latifoliate or coni-ferous woods, especially under pines and birches. **Edible.**

CORTINARIUS (Dermocybe) ORELLANUS (1)

Cap 3–8 cm, often umbonate; brown tending to pink, orange, or red; dry, sericeous, fibrillar or with hairy scales which are sometimes olivaceous; margin thin, often lobate, undulate, fissured. **Stem** sometimes thickened in the middle; yellow or slightly paler than the cap; with fibrillar, reddish striae, darker at the base. **Cortina** yellowish, evanescent. **Flesh** yellowish, slightly pinkish under the cap's cuticle; juicy. **Odor** of turnip. **Flavor** acidulous. **Gills** rather sparse, broad, somewhat thick; annexed to the stem; sometimes eroded near it; yellowish orange, then of the same color as the cap, but with pinkish iridescence; sometimes wrinkled. **Spores** rust colored. It grows in the mountains and in the plains, under latifoliate trees, especially birch and oak, and under conifers, especially pine. **Deadly**: the symptoms of the poisoning appear late, even fifteen days after eating the mushroom: it causes a poisoning similar to that of *Amanita phalloides*, but with some slight differences.

To be avoided because they are easily mistaken for *orellanus*: *Cortinarius phoeniceus* (2), with gills red, then rusty; *Cortinarius cinnabarinus* (3), vermilion red, with gills of more intense color, found only in beech woods. Similar to the latter is *Cortinarius sanguineus*, which grows under conifers; *Cortinarius bolaris* (4): whitish or ochraceous, with bright red scales and cinnamon colored gills.

CORTINARIUS (Dermocybe) CINNAMOMEUS (1)

Cap olivaceous yellow, reddish brown, or ochraceous brown, but olivaceous brown in the specimens growing in swampy grounds; soon expanded, 3–6 cm, gibbous or also depressed and yet with a more or less prominent central umbo; margin undulate; cuticle dry, sericeous, fibrillar. **Stem** tall, thin, cylindrical; a bit lighter than the cap; fibrillar; sometimes with remains of the cortina; soon hollow. **Flesh** thin; the cap pallid; the stem olivaceous yellow. **Odor** of turnip. **Flavor** mild. **Gills** not too close, rather broad, eroded near the stem; yellowish, then olivaceous brown; orange yellow in the variety *croceus* (2). *Spores* rusty brown. It grows in woods, in humid recesses. **Suspect**.

The following *cortinarii* are similar to *C. cinnamomeus* and are to be avoided, as well as all those of modest sizes, and of ocher, brown, or reddish color, because they are likely to be confused with *C. orellanus*, which is deadly: *Cortinarius semisanguineus* (3), gills initially vermilion, finally brown like the spores that cover them but still vermilion if observed at an angle; *Cortinarius venetus*, smaller, paler, more olivaceous than *C. cinnamomeus*; the variety *montanus* grows in tufts under firs; *Cortinarius zinziberatus*, with no turnip odor, growing in tufts, in spring; *Cortinarius malicorius*, cap velvety, orange or cinnamon, margin yellow, stem yellow, typical of coniferous woods.

CORTINARIUS (Inoloma) VIOLACEUS

Cap 6–14 cm, sometimes umbonate, sometimes depressed; dry, covered with violet velvet. **Stem** first pear shaped, bigger than the cap; then tall with thickened base; of the same color as the cap; first velvety, then fibrillar; stuffed, spongy; then hollow. **Cortina** lanate, violet; soon disappearing without leaving any trace. **Flesh** tender, soft, soon flaccid; pale violet, marbled with whitish variegations. **Odor** of cedar wood. **Flavor** mild. **Gills** rather apart; soon broad; often connected by fine veins; rounded near the stem and adhering to it; initially violet, then rusty. **Spores** rust colored. It grows in humid latifoliate woods. **Edible**. Also *Cortinarius corrugatus*, **edible**, presents initially violet gills: but it differs from *violaceus* in its cap, rugose, faded ocher or reddish ocher, and its stem, tall and stout, whitish or of the same color as the cap; it grows in North America. *Cortinarius praestans* (page 69), **edible**, of imposing appearance, sometimes gigantic, is also violaceous or violaceous brown, with corrugated but viscid cap. *Cortinarius largus* (page 70), **edible**, is much paler than *C. violaceus*, soon becoming ochraceous, it is not velvety but somewhat viscid. *Cortinarius traganus* (page 72), **not edible**, is lighter than *C. violaceus*, not viscid but smooth, and only tardily squamose and ochraceous.

CORTINARIUS (Telamonia) ARMILLATUS

Cap campanulate, moist; then plane-convex, 5–12 cm, dry; with radiating fibrils and squamules; reddish brown or yellowish brown. **Stem** rather tall and slender, cylindric, thickened at the base, which is sometimes slightly curved; brownish; soon hollow starting from the base. **Armillae**, three or four, like slanted belts around the stem; of a vermilion red color; sometimes reduced to few faded scales. **Cortina** yellowish or faded. Flesh thick at the center of the cap, thin at the margin; brownish. **Gills** rather apart from each other; whitish, then cinnamon colored, with paler edges. **Spores** cinnamon colored. It grows on peat soil, often among bilberries, in groups, in birch woods. **Edible**. Related species are: *Cortinarius hinnuleus*, cap 2–6 cm, cuspidate, dark brown in humid weather, pale ocher in dry; gills sparse, broad, not annexed, of cinnamon color; stem thick, thinner at the base, with white ring and white filamentous remains of the cortina; flesh yellowish with a disgusting odor of soil; growing in woods and meadows; **not edible**. *Cortinarius brunneus*, cap 4–8 cm, cuspidate, fleshy, reddish brown or blackish brown, paler in dry weather, with the margin covered with fibrils or white flocci; stem thick, blackish, with white fibrils, and white, flocculose ring; gills blackish red; flesh tender, slowly becoming brown; growing near conifers; **harmless**.

CORTINARIUS (Telamonia) TORVUS (1)
Cap violet brown, sericeous, with faded margin; then red brown or brown with sericeous fibrils, and rather faded in dry weather; then lacking fibers; hemispheric, then convex, finally expanded, 4–10 cm, often cuspidate. **Stem** stout, even squat, sometimes curved, thickened at the base which is covered with white down; sericeous or violaceous on top; with a thick, white sheath that terminates with an annular, membranous, and persistent cuff; then the sheath dissolves into oblique, faded, flocculose streaks. **Cortina** evanescent, disappearing without leaving any trace. **Flesh** thick, firm, whitish, marbled with amethystine, here and there reddish, then brownish. **Odor** more or less distinct of fruit or camphor, but disgusting; this makes it possible to distinguish this mushroom from the smaller specimens of *Cortinarius praestans* (page 69). **Flavor** mild. **Gills** rather sparse, broad, thick, sometimes with vertical creases; eroded near the stem; violaceous, then rust colored. **Spores** rusty. It grows in latifoliate woods, especially under beeches, rarely under conifers. **Edible**, of poor quality.

CORTINARIUS (Telamonia) SCUTULATUS (2)
Similar to the previous species, but smaller; initially rather bulky, becoming then gradually thinner; cap 3–5 cm, violet; stem tall, thin, with a sheath ending in several cuffs, as a multiple ring; flesh amethystine; **edible**, of poor quality.

LEUCOCORTINARIUS BULBIGER
Cap cream colored, ocher, or reddish, always paler at the margin; hemispheric, then convex and also plane, 5–10 cm, but cuspidate or gibbous; margin undulate, often fissured, usually adorned with the remains of the veil which are white and flocculose, then brownish and fibro-membranous, sometimes also present on the rest of the cap; cuticle dry, slightly scabrous. **Stem** thick, stout, flocculose; white, then the same color as the cap; base bulbous, flattened, with the margin forming a clear-cut step, covered initially with white down. **Cortina** abundant, white, woolly filamentous. **Ring** filamentous, white, soon reduced to few brownish fibers. **Flesh** firm; the cap white, the stem brownish and then yellowish. **Odor** mild. **Flavor** mild. **Gills** big, eroded near the stem; white, then of the same color as the cap, often with speckled edges. **Spores** white. It grows in groups, under conifers, in sandy grounds. **Edible.** Also *Cortinarius odorifer*, **not edible**, grows under conifers and presents a clear-cut bulbous base; but it has viscid cap, yellowish flesh with anise odor, ochraceous spores. *Ripartites tricholoma*, the only species of the genus *Ripartites*, is between *Cortinarius* and *Inocybe*: cap depressed, 2–4 cm, whitish with white cilia at the margin; stem thin, white, here and there reddish; gills close, decurrent, ochraceous; growing in autumn, under beeches and conifers; the variety *helomorfa*, slightly bigger and less hairy, grows under firs.

INOCYBE PATOUILLARDI (1)
Once gathered this mushroom tends to become vermilion. **Cap** 3–7 cm, white then yellowish, finally brownish; cuspidate or umbonate; with radial fibers; dry, sericeous; fissured margin. **Stem** thick, fibrillar, white, with reddish spots; pruinose and granular the upper part; stuffed. **Cortina** tenuous and evanescent. **Flesh** firm, fibrous, white; exposed to air, bruised, or with aging, it becomes reddish. **Odor** slightly pungent. **Flavor** mild. **Gills** close, unequal, broad; eroded near the stem; free or almost free; white or pinkish, then olivaceous brown or rusty, with irregular, flocculose, white edges. **Spores** rusty ocher. It grows in groups, in spring and summer, under latifoliate trees, especially linden trees. **Poisonous.** Equally **poisonous** are: *Inocybe fibrosa*, cap straw colored; thick stem, bulbous base; flesh white, tough, fibrous; gills white, then chocolate brown, with white and uneven edges; growing in sandy fields, close to conifers; *Inocybe geophylla*: smaller and thinner than the latter, with ocher gills; white; violet in the variety *violacea*, reddish in the variety *lateritia*.

INOCYBE JURANA (2)
Once picked it becomes carmine colored. **Cap** 2–10 cm, brown gray, covered in the center by squamules and in the rest by long, radial, reddish fibrils here and there detached; reddish base; rosy flesh; tobacco colored spores; **to be avoided** because it is very similar to poisonous species.

INOCYBE FASTIGIATA (1)
Cap 3–9 cm, campanulate, then expanded, umbonate; with radiating fibers; margin upturned, lobate, soon fissured; on dry grounds it is white or whitish, otherwise ochraceous, brownish, or olivaceous; slightly reddish at the center. **Stem** cylindric, rather tall, often thickened at the base; whitish, fibrillar, sericeous; white and pruinose the upper part; stuffed, but soon hollow. **Flesh** fibrous, white. **Odor** of bread, but disgusting. **Flavor** mild. **Gills** close, narrow, free or almost free from the stem; yellowish white tinged with green; then olivaceous brown with white and flocculose edges. **Spores** brownish. It grows in woods, in parks, under hedges. **Poisonous**.

INOCYBE PIRIODORA (2)
Cap 3–10 cm, reddish ocher, fibrillar and squamose especially the center; stem rather tall; flesh white, becoming reddish when exposed to air; jasmine odor. **To be avoided**: easily confused with toxic species.

INOCYBE CORYDALINA (3)
Cap 3–6 cm, white, then hazel, sometimes with squamose and slightly greenish umbo; thick stem; flesh white, reddish when exposed to air; nauseating odor; **poisonous**.

INOCYBE BONGARDII (4)
Cap 3–6 cm, hazel, fibrous, squamose; stem tall, violaceous gray; flesh white, becoming carrot colored when exposed to air; odor of pears; **to be avoided**: easily mistaken for toxic species.

INOCYBE MACULATA (1)
Cap sometimes faded hazel, more often brown, darker at the center; sometimes with whitish spots, remnants of the universal veil; conical, with lobate margin here and there attached to the stem; then becoming expanded, 2–8 cm; cuticle formed by radial fibers, showing under them the paler surface. **Stem** tall, fibrous, whitish; then of the same color as the cap; white and farinaceous the upper part; base bulbous and downy. **Flesh** thin, fibrous, white; the flesh of the base becomes easily rosy. **Odor** same as *Boletus edulis*. **Flavor** mild. **Gills** close, broad, thick in the ripe specimens; adhering to the stem little or not at all; whitish or cinereous; then olivaceous brown; edges faded and uneven. **Spores** brown. It grows solitary or in groups, in grassy fields or on bare grounds, rarely in shady woods. **Poisonous**.

INOCYBE ASTEROSPORA (2)
Cap 3–6 cm, gibbous, pallid, with brown, radial fibers; gills whitish then brown; bulbous base; **poisonous**.

INOCYBE NAPIPES (3)
Cap 3–5 cm, tobacco colored; glabrous, soon fibrillar; base bulbous, compressed; growing on peat soil, especially under birches. **Poisonous**: dangerous.

INOCYBE SQUAMATA (4)
Cap 3–7 cm, yellowish, with brown radial fibers and brown scales on the central umbo; fissured margin; thick stem. **Suspect**.

INOCYBE GODEYI (5)
Cap 2–5 cm, white, then cream, finally reddish; clearly outlined bulbous base; fruitish odor. **Poisonous**.

maculata Inoc.

1

5

3

2

4

ENTOLOMA (Rhodophyllus) LIVIDUM

Cap cinereous or ochraceous with plumbeous shades and whitish spots; darker at the center, paler at the margin; convex, then plane 6–20 cm, uneven, often umbonate at the center; glabrous, with fine, sericeous, radial striae; slightly viscid in humid weather; dry and shining in dry weather; margin involute, pruinose; then explanate, undulate, and often fissured. **Stem** thick, sometimes slightly eccentric; often thickened at the base, which can be somewhat curved; sometimes with a longitudinal groove; the upper part is covered with powder and then with granules; white, then yellowish; hard, stuffed, medullate, soon spongy. **Flesh** tough, fragile, white; sometimes with yellowish erosions. **Odor** of flour, soon nauseating. **Flavor** sapid. **Gills** sparse, but crowded near the margin by several intermediate lamellae; eroded toward the stem and adhering to it; broad, with uneven edges; initially yellowish, then rosy ochraceous, becoming gradually darker, with yellow shades where the surface is not yet covered by the spores. **Spores** rusty pink. It grows under latifoliate trees, especially oaks, beeches, and robinias, rarely under conifers; in large groups, often forming fairy rings; in summer and in autumn, but not in spring. **Poisonous**, rarely deadly. It is likely to be confused with *Clitocybe nebularis* (page 114), **edible**, growing in late summer and in autumn, but with gills close, decurrent, and whitish.

ENTOLOMA (Rhodophyllus) RHODOPOLIUM (1)

Cap 2–12 cm, gibbous; margin involute, then explanate and undulate; grayish brown, with diaphanous margin in humid weather; hazel, fibrillar, sericeous, shining, with opaque margin in dry weather. **Stem** slender, cylindrical, whitish or tending to cinereous; glabrous, pruinose in the upper part; stuffed, soon spongy, then hollow. **Flesh** fragile, thin, white. Soft **odor** and **flavor**. **Gills** sparse, broad, rounded toward the stem and annexed to it; with uneven edges; white, then hazel pink. **Spores** yellowish pink. It grows in latifoliate woods, especially beech woods, in the mountains, rarely in the plains. **Poisonous**: it causes intestinal trouble.

ENTOLOMA NIDOROSUM (2)

Almost identical for shape and color to *E. rhodopolium*, from which it can sometimes be distinguished only by its odor of burnt flesh; often, however, it is more delicate-looking, and in dry weather it can appear faded, as in the two specimens illustrated here; the stem is stuffed, and grows under bushes, in very humid recesses. **Poisonous** like *E. rhodopolium*.

ENTOLOMA LIVIDOALBUM (Kühner-Romagnesi) (3)

Bigger than the above-described species, with firm flesh persistently smelling of flour; **to be avoided**, as the smaller *E. sordidum*, with odor of flour, *E. nitidum*, blue, under conifers, *E. scabiosum*, blue, squamose, with flocculose stem, in the heaths, *E. medium*, grayish violet, growing in meadows and woods.

ENTOLOMA (Rhodophyllus) CLYPEATUM (1, 2)
Cap 4–10 cm, umbonate; grayish or brownish; fibrillar, sericeous, shining; but faded, viscid, diaphanous at the margin in humid weather. **Stem** whitish, pruinose in the upper part; with yellowish fibrils; soon hollow. **Flesh** thin, whitish. **Odor** and **flavor** of flour. **Gills** eroded near the stem; whitish, then pinkish, covered with rosy yellow powder: the **spores**. It grows in spring and summer, in grassy and shady places. **Edible**. Similar and also in spring: *Entoloma sepium*, **edible**, whitish, with reddish fibers on the stem and reddish erosions in the flesh, growing along hedges of thornbushes; *Entoloma aprile* (Britz), **not edible**, very sensitive to humidity, oily in humid weather, stem soon hollow, gills cinereous, flesh fragile; under elms and hornbeans. Similar to the preceding species, but autumnal and growing in meadows, is *Entoloma prunuloides*, **edible**, not too sensitive to humidity. with fleshy and umbonate cap.

ENTOLOMA NIPHOIDES (3)
White, in spring, **poisonous**. Similar to it is *Entoloma Saundersi*, **better avoided**, growing often in tufts, with pale cap and thick stem.

NOLANEA (Rhodophyllus) PASQUA (4)
Cap campanulate, 2–5 cm, grayish; stem grayish, thin, pruinose, with a longitudinal groove; hollow; gills almost free from the stem, cinereous tending to violaceous; growing in spring and autumn, in alpine pastures. **Poisonous**.

NOLANEA MAMMOSA (5)
Similar to *pasqua*, equally **poisonous**; growing under the same conditions: cap brownish; stem tall, thin, fragile; rancid odor. Slightly smaller is *Nolanea proletaria*, **better avoided**, cuspidate, watery, with odor of watermelon; growing in the moss.

XERULA (Collybia) LONGIPES

Cap 4–7 cm, umbonate; basically brown; but fuliginous in the variety *fusca* (the darker specimens, at right); cuticle covered with very fine hair, paler than the bottom surface, particularly dense along the margin. **Stem** tall, sometimes very tall; cylindrical, generally very regular, tapering a little toward the cap; at times though, rather irregular, as that of the specimens illustrated here; often with longitudinal grooves, at times twisted, especially toward the base; all covered with felt; of the same color as the cap, except the upper part, which is paler; fibrous, tenacious. Base thickened, with a rootlike appendix, sometimes very long and deeply buried. **Flesh** thin, white, coriaceous. **Odor** of hazelnuts. **Flavor** soft. **Gills** sparse, broad, thick, rounded toward the stem and not, or only very little, adhering to it; elastic; white, then whitish or cream. **Spores** white. It grows in humid recesses of latifoliate woods, especially oak, feeding on buried, rotting wood. **Edible**, of good quality if fresh and well cooked; discard the stems.

Bigger and squatter than *longipes* and of a more cheerful color is *Xerula umbonata*, **edibility unknown**: cap of a beautiful orange brown color, with prominent umbo at the center, which distinguishes it; growing in the woods of Northern California.

MUCIDULA MUCIDA (1)

Cap hemispheric, then convex, 3–8 cm, thin at the margin; cinereous, then lighter, also white, with cinereous or olivaceous shades at the center; translucent; cuticle rugose, covered with a thick layer of viscid mucilage. **Stem** thin, stiff, curved; white, flocculose; slightly striate in the upper part; stuffed, fibrous. **Ring** large, thin, striate, white. **Flesh** thin, soft, white. **Odor** delicate. **Flavor** mild. **Gills** sparse, broad, rounded toward the stem, white, soft mucilaginous; finally pulverulent. **Spores** white. It grows in tufts or singly, on weak beeches or on dead branches of beech trees; rarely on other plants. **Edible**.

MUCIDULA RADICATA (2)

Cap convex, then expanded 4–10 cm, often uneven, also depressed, and yet still with umbo at the center; sometimes shriveled, wrinkled; viscous in humid weather; whitish or yellowish or brownish or also rather fuliginous. **Stem** very tall, tapered; glabrous; soon with longitudinal grooves; thickened at the base, which extends in a rootlike appendix, very long and tenacious; paler than the cap; with spots or stripes here and there; stiff, fragile, fibrous, hollow. **Flesh** thin, whitish. **Odor** slight. **Flavor** mild. **Gills** rather sparse, broad, rounded toward the stem and annexed to it; white, sometimes with brown edges. **Spores** white. It grows from spring to autumn, on rotting wood more or less buried into the ground in woods, especially beech woods. **Edible**.

mucida Muc.

COLLYBIA FUSIPES

Cap hemispheric or campanulate, then convex 4–10 cm, irregular, sometimes umbonate; margin involute, then explanate, undulate, and often fissured; reddish brown, then fading and with blackish spots; cuticle dry, shining. **Stem** fusiform, often misshapen and curved; with deep, longitudinal grooves; of the same color as the cap, lighter in the upper part, blackish at the base; elastic, tenacious, stuffed, fibrous, then hollow. **Flesh** whitish, thin, elastic. **Odor** slight. **Flavor** mild. **Gills** sparse, broad, thick, with undulate edges; almost free, connected together, ringlike, around the stem; whitish tinged with reddish; then grayish with brownish spots. **Spores** white. It grows in tufts, in spring and in summer, on trunks and on stumps of latifoliate trees. **Edible, but with caution**: keep in mind that where it grows, this mushroom can remain apparently unspoiled for over a month, but then it is no longer edible: it could cause serious intestinal trouble; only the caps of unripe specimens, very carefully cooked, can be eaten.

Similar is *Collybia rancidas,* **edibility uncertain**: cap 3–5 cm, gray or blackish, not too sensitive to humidity, with whitish down, then glabrous; stem paler than the cap, slender, with longitudinal grooves, base pubescent and radicating; gills free or almost free, gray; odor of rancid flour; autumnal, growing near stumps of latifoliate or coniferous trees.

COLLYBIA (Rhodocollybia) MACULATA

Cap 6–12 cm, white, soon with reddish or brownish spots; glabrous, smooth; thin margin. **Stem** tall, cylindric, rather curved, often with swollen and radicating base; of the same color as the cap; fibrous, sometimes twisted; hard, soon hollow. **Flesh** white. **Odor** mild. **Flavor** bitter. **Gills** close, very narrow, free from the stem; with denticulate edges; white, then with rusty stains. **Spores** white or yellowish rosy. It grows in autumn, in woods, in fairy rings. **Not edible,** bitter. Similar, though stouter, is *Collybia leucocephala*, **to be avoided**, with yellow spots and odor of flour. Other autumnal species: *Collybia inolens*, **edible**: cap 3–6 cm, cuspidate, smooth; gray, brownish gray, or olivaceous gray when moist; when dry it is paler and sericeous; margin lobate and undulate; stem gray, furfuraceous in the upper part, cottony at the base; hard, hollow; odorless; under conifers. *Collybia coracina*, **edible**: cap 2–4 cm, depressed, smooth; dark olivaceous gray when moist; paler when dry; stem gray, with cottony base, cartilagineous, hollow; odor of rancid flour; in groups under conifers. *Collybia atrata*, **of no alimentary interest**: cap 2–4 cm, soon depressed, with undulate and radially sulcate margin; fuliginous brown and viscid when moist; paler and shining when dry; smooth; stem brown, short, smooth, cartilagineous, hollow; odor and flavor of flour, but disgusting; growing in tufts, in grassy places at the edge of the woods, often on burned grounds.

COLLYBIA (Tricholomopsis) PLATYPHYLLA

Cap fuliginous, grayish brown, gray, cinereous, or whitish; with brown or blackish radial fibers, initially forming a continuous surface which then cracks exposing here and there the white flesh; convex, then plane, 5–15 cm, sometimes slightly umbonate; moist. **Stem** thick, cylindrical, fibrillar, whitish; hard, stuffed, fibrous, soon hollow; with some mycelium cords at the base, sometimes a few meters long; fragile, whitish. **Flesh** thin, fibrous, white. **Odor** delicate. **Flavor** bitterish. **Gills** rather sparse, very broad; semi-oval near the stem, to which they adhere little or not at all; white, then cream or ochraceous, with flocculose and sometimes brown edges. **Spores** white. It grows solitary or in groups, also in rings, on old latifoliate stumps or at the foot of the trees. **Edible, but not advisable**: it is not poisonous, but fibrous and bitter. The mushrooms of the genus *Tricholomopsis* are of remarkable sizes, fleshy, thick; the cap's tissue is confluent with the stem's, so that the two cannot be easily separated; furthermore the gills are not decurrent, with even, or at least not serrate, edges; they are lignicolous. These same characteristics are found in *C. platyphylla*, which, although presenting a thin fleshed cap, should be considered more naturally as belonging to the genus *Tricholomopsis* than to *Collybia*, together with *Tricholomopsis rutilans* (page 97) and with *Tricholomopsis edodes* (page 126).

COLLYBIA BUTYRACEA (1)

Cap 4–9 cm, umbonate; reddish brown or violet brown or gray brown or greenish brown, darker at the center; fading with age and in dry weather; smooth, moist, shining, glabrous. **Stem** conical, of the same color as the cap, paler near the gills, darker and with reddish hues near the base; striate; spongy and white internally; soon reduced to a cartilaginous, fibrous, shriveled crust; base swollen, wrapped in white cottony down, covered with decayed leaves and coniferous needles. **Flesh** of the cap soft, flaccid, watery, fragile; of the same color as the cap but paler; even paler in dry weather. **Odor** rancid. **Flavor** mild. **Gills** close, almost free from the stem and easily detachable from it; with rather uneven edges, at least in the more vividly colored forms. **Spores** white, slightly tinged with pink. It is found in woods, especially coniferous woods, on needles or on rotten leaves; it grows thick and colored (as in the illustrated specimens), when the season is favorable; faded and meager, almost like *Collybia asema*, when the season is dry. **Edible**.

COLLYBIA ASEMA (2)

Smaller than *butyracea*, considered by some authors only as a variety of the same; cap thin, umbonate, with margin striate in humid weather, cinereous; gills with even edges; growing in mixed woods. **Edible**.

MARASMIUS BRESADOLAE or COLLYBIA ACERVATA (Fries)

Cap convex, then expanded, 2–8 cm, generally cuspidate, but sometimes depressed or irregularly curled up; smooth or slightly rugose; with the margin slightly striate and also slightly knobby in older specimens; reddish brown in humid weather, deeper at the center, transparent, so that the gills show through; fading in dry weather or with age. **Stem** tall, glabrous; flared toward the gills; bright purple brown, lighter on top, with the base enwrapped in cottony down; tenacious, hollow, fibrous. **Flesh** thin, whitish or tending to brownish; dark and tough the flesh of the stem. **Odor** agreeable. **Flavor** mild. **Gills** not too close, thin, slightly or not adhering to the stem; sinuous, with undulate edges; whitish, then tending to brown. **Spores** white. It grows in dense tufts, in woods, on remains of decaying plants. **Edible**, although not too fleshy.

A similar species is *Collybia familia*, **edible**, growing in large tufts on decaying coniferous stumps, in North America; cap pallid, olivaceous gray, or whitish; stem whitish and sericeous. Almost identical to *Collybia acervata* (Fries), but with specific microscopic differences, according to some authors, is *Marasmius acervatus* (Fries), **edible**; gills sometimes closer than in *Collybia acervata*, and shorter stem; growing in the mountains, under firs.

COLLYBIA DRYOPHILA (1, two groups)

Cap 2–5 cm, glabrous, smooth; whitish or cinereous or brownish or orange, often paler at the margin, which in humid weather becomes diaphanous; in dry weather and with age it fades. **Stem** tall, thin, cylindrical; of the same color as the cap; glabrous, tenacious, hollow. **Flesh** thin, white; slightly cinereous or yellowish in humid weather. **Odor** agreeable. **Flavor** mild. **Gills** close, thin, narrow, adhering to the stem by a small tooth; white tending to yellow; but yellow in the variety *funicularis* (3), growing only in spring. **Spores** white. It grows in small groups, from spring to autumn, in woods, in meadows, after rain, in the ground or on wood debris. **Edible**, but uninteresting, especially because often infested by insects.

COLLYBIA DISTORTA (2)

Cap brown tending to orange; fading with age; campanulate, then somewhat expanded, 5–10 cm; sometimes oddly curled up; glabrous, smooth. **Stem** somewhat short, with longitudinal grooves, often twisted; base finely pubescent; whitish, then ochraceous. **Flesh** rather firm, white. **Odor** soft, slightly disgusting. **Flavor** mild. **Gills** very close, narrow, rounded near the stem and adhering to it; with uneven edges; whitish, then with brown spots. **Spores** white. It grows in autumn, in woods, in tufts. **Edible**, but not too interesting. A related species is *Collybia maculata* (page 86), which is however paler and does not have a twisted stem.

velutipes Col.

COLLYBIA VELUTIPES

Cap convex, then plane, 2–8 cm, rather gibbous, with striate margin; cuticle smooth, moist, viscid; honey colored, paler at the margin, brighter, tending to reddish brown at the center; becoming faded in dry weather; the variety *lactea* has cream white cap with even lighter margin. **Stem** sometimes short, sometimes slender; curved, sometimes eccentric; initially stuffed with pith, then hollow; fibrous; reddish yellow just below the cap; velvety blackish brown the rest of its length. Base compressed, ending in a rootlike appendix. **Flesh** of the cap soft but tenacious, cream colored; the stem fibrous and yellowish. **Odor** slight, of fruit. **Flavor** mild. **Gills** somewhat sparse, broad, sharpening toward the cap's margin. **Spores** white. It grows from late autumn to spring, in tufts, on latifoliate wood, dead or live. **Edible**, tasty even when gathered frozen under the snow. Only the caps are to be eaten; throw away the stems. Boil the caps in water for five minutes, then cook them for longer time with the proper seasoning. Growing in winter and spring: *Collybia tenacella*, **not edible** because it is bitter, found on pine and spruce cones: cap 1–3 cm, ranging from white to gray brown, the latter color typical of the variety *grisea*; and growing on spruce cones, *Collybia esculenta*, **edible**, bitterish, darker than *tenacella* and with gray gills.

MARASMIUS OREADES

Cap convex, more or less campanulate, then plane, 2–7 cm, with or without central umbo; in humid weather the margin appears striate in the direction of the gills; ocher, deeper at the center; fading in dry weather. **Stem** tall, thin, cylindrical, equal; sometimes somewhat curved in older specimens; of the same color as the cap, or slightly lighter; cottony at the base; elastic, tenacious, stuffed. **Flesh** thin, elastic, rather tough; whitish. **Odor** agreeable. **Flavor** pleasant. **Gills** rather sparse, broad, somewhat thick, free from the stem; whitish, then ochraceous. **Spores** white. It grows from spring to autumn, along trails, in the grass, in sandy grounds; in groups, in rings. **Edible**, of excellent quality; it dries out easily and it is edible even when collected dried; in this case it has to be regenerated in lukewarm water before cooking it; often the stem is too tough and should be discarded. Similar to *oreades*, but tender and fragile is *Marasmius collinus*; **not edible**, since it can cause intestinal trouble. Similar to *oreades* and **edible** are *Marasmius globularis*, grayish or amethystine, with radial grooves along the margin, brown and curved at the stem's base, growing in the woods, also in the mountains; and *Marasmius confluens*, with close, rosy white gills; growing in grouped tufts, in rows or circles, in wood clearings.

MARASMIUS SCORODONIUS (1, two groups)

Cap 1–4 cm, ranging from brown to ocher. **Stem** tall, thin; brown toward the base. **Flesh** whitish. **Odor** and **flavor** of garlic. **Gills** sparse, narrow. **Spores** white. In warm and rainy seasons, on plant debris, in groups. **Edible**: it can be used instead of garlic, either fresh or dried. Also with garlic odor, but **of no alimentary interest**, are *Marasmius alliaceus*, conic cap, black stem; *Marasmius prasiosmus*, cap hemispheric, enlarged base; *Marasmius perforans*, small, with black velvety stem, and growing throughout the year, each single specimen on a pine needle; easily distinguishable from *M. androsaceus*, which has neither a velvety stem nor garlic smell.

MARASMIUS PERONATUS (2, 3)

Cap 3–6 cm, slightly rugose, ochraceous, with striate margin; base of the stem villose; flesh tough, acrid; gills whitish, then reddish; on plant debris. **Not edible**, or only in small doses, like pepper. Similar to it is *Marasmius fusco-purpurens*, **of no alimentary interest**, chocolate colored, mild flavor.

MARASMIUS ROTULA (4)

Cap convex, 0.5–1.5 cm, umbilicate, with radial grooves and filiform stem; gills sparse, attached to a circular collar around the stem; on wood debris; **of no alimentary interest**.

MARASMIUS CONIGENUS (5)

Cap 1–3 cm, brown; stem long, brown, velvety; flesh tough; gills close; on buried pinecones; **of no alimentary interest**.

MYCENA PURA (1)

Cap violaceous pinkish or rosy or ochraceous or blue green, with yellowish or tawny umbo; also white tinged with pink or blue green or violaceous shades, especially in dry weather; conical, then expanded, 2–7 cm, but the variety *rosea* can reach 10–12 cm; umbonate; margin striate in humid weather. **Stem** slender, cylindric, with thickened and woolly base; of the same color as the cap or whitish; more often amethystine, when the cap is ochraceous; with dark, radial fibers; hollow as a pipe. **Flesh** fragile, thin, white, with touches of the cap's color. **Odor** and **flavor** mild of radish. **Gills** rather sparse, broad, eroded near the stem, connected by little veins; whitish tinged with the cap's colors. **Spores** white. It grows sometimes in large groups forming fairy rings, in woods, in the moss, and among dead leaves. **Edible**, but not recommended because generally tasteless. Similar to *M. pura* is *Mycena pelianthina*, **not edible** because of strong and disgusting radish odor: the color ranges from yellowish to violaceous, deeper in humid weather; characterized by violaceous gray gills with uneven, dark violet edges. Related to the previous species is *Mycena overholtzii*, **not edible**: cap gray or brown; stem white, with soft and white down on its lower part; it grows in the Rocky Mountains on coniferous wood in very pretty tufts, as soon as the snow disappears.

MYCENA GALERICULATA (1)
Cap 2–5 cm, color from ocher to fuliginous; umbonate, with striate margin. Stem thin, smooth, with pubescent base. Flesh white. Odor agreeable of flour. Gills close, annexed to the stem, white. Spores white.

MYCENA POLYGRAMMA (2)
Similar to the above, but with sparser gills, free or almost free. Stem with vertical striae.

MYCENA INCLINATA (3)
Cap gray or brown, umbonate, margin striate. Stem gracile, shiny white, then golden in the middle and brownish at the base; fragile, hollow. Flesh elastic, with odor and flavor of rancid tallow. *Mycena flavipes*, which sometimes has a rosy cap, has ammonia odor.

MYCENA TINTINNABULUM (4)
Cap fuliginous, mucilaginous; short stem; found in winter, cespitose.

MYCENA HAEMATOPUS (5)
Exudes a red latex.

MYCENA SANGUINOLENTA (6)
Exudes red latex; smaller than *haematopus*.

MYCENA GALOPUS (7)
Exudes a milky white latex.

MYCENA EPIPTERYGIA (8)
Cap covered with a gelatinous pellicle, removable with just a single pull.

These *Mycenae* grow on stumps or on plant debris and have **no alimentary interest**.

TRICHOLOMA (Armillaria) MATSUTAKE (1)
Cap yellowish, ochraceous, or brown, hemispheric, fibrillar, with the margin involute and connected by the veil to the stem; then somewhat expanded, 8–18 cm, more or less cuspidate, margin festooned, cuticle cracked at the center; then plane, often irregular, creviced especially at the center and on a circular band near the margin; the paler, subcuticular layer or even the white flesh is visible between the crevices; finally the whole cap becomes dark brown. **Stem** tall, thick, sometimes a little curved; white in the upper part, ochraceous and squamose from the ring to the base. **Ring** membranous, irregular, white. **Flesh** thick, firm, white. **Odor** sweet, characteristic. **Flavor** agreeable. **Gills** rather close, thick, narrow; eroded near the stem and sometimes free; white. **Spores** white. It grows in groups, under red pine, in Japan, after summer and autumn rains. **Edible**, sought after. The following edible species are considered by some mycologists identical to *T. matsutake: Tricholoma caligatum* (2), brown tending to violet; *Tricholoma ponderosum* (3, prostrate), growing under conifers in the mountains, but also along the seashore, under pines. Similar to the preceding species are *Tricholoma subannulatum*, **edible** only after parboiling because it is bitter: cap 5–20 cm, chestnut color, sericeous; growing in groups, under conifers; and *Tricholoma robustum* var. *focale*, not bitter, **edible** in small quantity: cap 4–8 cm, orange red, cracked and squamose; growing especially under pines.

TRICHOLOMA ALBOBRUNNEUM

Cap conical, with thin margin rolled toward the gills; then convex, finally plane 6–12 cm, sometimes umbonate or rather irregular; with thin, crowded, radial fibers; viscid in humid weather; ochraceous, brown, or reddish brown, darker at the center; cuticle easily removable; sometimes the margin of ripe specimens is distinctly striate in the direction of the gills. **Stem** thick, cylindric, with the base thickened and sometimes prolonging into a pointed appendix; fibrillar and brown or reddish brown from the base up to two-thirds of its length; the upper part white. These delimitations of color are sometimes uncertain, but sometimes so clear-cut as to simulate a ring. **Flesh** very firm, snow white. **Odor** of flour and soap. **Flavor** often, but not always, bitter and slightly acrid. **Gills** close, thin, broad, eroded near the stem, with undulate, uneven edges; white, tinged with cream; then with brownish stains. **Spores** white. It grows in rings, in coniferous woods, in the mountains, rarely in the plains. **Not advisable**, because it is indigestible; however some consider it edible when parboiled in water, drained, and carefully cooked in the proper sauce. *Tricholoma flavobrunneum*, **edible**, of poor quality and not advisable, is similar to *albobrunneum*, but with yellow stem, gills, and flesh; found under latifoliate trees, especially oaks and birches.

TRICHOLOMA AURANTIUM

Cap convex, then plane 6–12 cm, more or less cuspidate or depressed; margin rolled toward the gills; cuticle viscous, mucilaginous in humid weather; easily removable from the cap; orange tending to yellow or brown, paler along the margin, deeper at the center; covered with darker, slightly viscid squamules, more evident at the center. **Stem** thick, stuffed, but finally hollow; whitish and farinaceous in the upper part; brownish at the base; in the middle part adorned with a series of undulate and irregularly interrupted belts, formed by fibrous tufts of the same color as the cap; the upper belt is sometimes very conspicuous and simulates a ring. **Flesh** firm, whitish; the stem slightly reddish. **Odor** of watermelon or of flour, not too agreeable. **Flavor** bitter. **Gills** rather broad, eroded toward the stem, free or almost free; they can also appear decurrent on the stem; white, with reddish spots along the edges; then grayish. **Spores** white. It grows in late autumn, but occasionally in summer too, in groups, under conifers; **Not advisable**: it is not toxic, but even after parboiling and careful cooking, it often remains bitter and uneatable. Similar to *T. aurantium* is *Tricholoma Salero*, **not edible** because it is bitter: cap 4–14 cm, chestnut or reddish brown; stem with reddish fibrillar striping in the lower half.

aurantium Tric.

TRICHOLOMOPSIS RUTILANS (1)

Cap hemispheric, then convex; finally expanded, 5–18 cm, sometimes umbonate; cuticle covered with a velvetlike substance, at first dark red, then brown, uniform at the center but broken toward the margin into squamules, gradually smaller and sparser, among which one can see the yellow background; margin thin, for some time rolled toward the gills. **Stem** cylindrical, firm, elastic, stuffed, then hollow; yellow with red squamules, as the cap, especially on the upper part. **Flesh** firm, yellowish. **Odor** mild. **Flavor** mild. **Gills** rather close, thin, annexed to the stem, sometimes eroded near it; yellow with slightly flocculose edges. **Spores** white. It grows on stumps and decaying coniferous wood. **Edible**, of poor quality and indigestible.

TRICHOLOMOPSIS RUTILANS var. VARIEGATA (2)

Smaller than the typical form, paler, with the gills' edges non flocculose; also **edible**, of poor quality and indigestible. Similar to *Tricholomopsis rutilans*, but bigger, is *Tricholomopsis decora*, **edible**, golden yellow with brown squamules; grows in the mountains, under fir trees. Similar to *T. decora* is *Tricholomopsis ornata*, **edible**, cespitose, with yellow gills slightly decurrent at maturation.

The genus *Tricholomopsis* is different from the genus *Tricholoma* because it is lignicolous, and from the genus *Armillariella* for the presence of non-decurrent gills. It is a genus with a few species; perhaps also *Collybia platyphylla* (page 87) and *Cortinellus edodes* (page 126), differently named by different authors, should be classified in this genus.

TRICHOLOMA USTALE (1)
Cap 4–9 cm, viscid, chestnut color, lighter at the margin which is often lobate and undulate. **Stem** unequal, firm, pruinose, white, then with reddish fibers, velvety brown, darker at the base; always white in the upper part. **Flesh** bulky, white tending to reddish. **Odor** of flour, then of paint. **Flavor** bitter, disgusting. **Gills** tapering and uncinate toward the stem; whitish, with reddish spots. **Spores** white. It grows in humid ravines, under latifoliate trees, rarely under conifers. **Not edible**; slightly toxic.

TRICHOLOMA POPULINUM (2)
Cap 7–12 cm, light brown with darker spots; cuticle removable for a third of the radius. **Gills** removable in lumps; white. **Stem** white then brownish; fibrous; base bulbous, spongy. **Flesh** snow white. **Odor** of flour. **Flavor** also of flour or bitterish. In groups, almost cespitose, found in sandy grounds along the roots of poplars. **Not recommended**, but not toxic; preserved in oil it becomes **edible**, excellent. Easily mistaken for *Tricholoma ustaloides*, **not advisable**, which has redder cap; flesh with a strong and persistent floury smell.

TRICHOLOMA PESSUNDATUM (3)
Cap 6–12 cm, chestnut brown; stem speckled with small, plushy, reddish tufts; odor of cucumber; flavor of flour, not bitter; under conifers; **not edible**. It is likely to be confused with *Tricholoma montanum* (4), **poisonous**, which also grows under conifers and tastes of flour but is somewhat bitter.

TRICHOLOMA ACERBUM
Cap pale ocher, rosy ocher, or reddish ocher; darker at the center; hemispheric, then expanded 7–12 cm; margin thin, tightly rolled toward the gills, radially sulcate and covered with yellow down, viscid; then somewhat explanate and still radially sulcate; cuticle sericeous, dry; **Stem** stout, white or with shades of the same color as the cap; the upper section covered with yellowish velvet, which then gathers into evanescent flocci or granules. **Flesh** firm, thick, white. **Odor** soft. **Flavor** mild, sour, acrid, or bitterish. **Gills** close, eroded near the stem; white or cream; reddish where bruised. **Spores** white. It grows in latifoliate woods, especially under beeches and oaks. It is considered edible, but of poor quality; after a precautionary parboiling; it seems, however, to be slightly toxic and therefore **not advisable**. In the places where *Tricholoma acerbum* grows, also grows *Tricholoma pseudoacerbum* or *tricolor*, **edible**: cap 15–30 cm; gills sulfur yellow or with greenish shades; then yellow with darker spots; when heat-dried it becomes purplish brown; flesh not bitter; stem without flocci. *Tricholoma radotinense* (Pilat-Charvat), **not edible**, because it is bitter even after cooking, with the upper part of the stem covered with a yellowish powder; grows under firs in Czeckoslovakia; although it is very similar to *T. acerbum* it can be distinguished from it by the smooth cap's margin without radial grooves, by the dingier ochraceous color, and by the flesh that becomes pinkish when exposed to air.

TRICHOLOMA PARDINUM

Cap campanulate with involute margin; then convex, 6–20 cm, gibbous, with lobate margin, often uneven and fissured; cuticle easily removable, cinereous or ochraceous; plushy, uniform, and darker at the center; entirely darker in unripe specimens; then cracked along zones more or less concentric, into fibrillar squamules, grayish or fuliginous, gathered in more or less triangular tufts, sparse toward the margin, and among which one can see the lighter subcuticle. **Stem** thick, often unequal; striate and pubescent; stuffed, fibrous; the upper part white and farinaceous; the middle part with minute fibers or very fine brownish squamules; the base, often thickened, brownish more or less faded. **Flesh** thick, firm; thin near the margin of the cap; the flesh of the cap white, then cinereous; the base of the stem yellowish. **Odor** soft of flour, not persistent. **Flavor** mild. **Gills** close, broad, eroded near the stem, free or almost free; with slightly serrate edges; exuding droplets when unripe; whitish, sometimes with blue green hues; then yellowish with olivaceous shades; finally faded. **Spores** white. It grows only in the mountains, rarely in certain areas, abundantly in others, in groups, often in rings, under firs and beeches. **Poisonous**, the more attractive for size and odor, the more dangerous: it causes acute gastroenteritis. Similar to *T. pardinum* are *Tricholoma hordum*, **to be avoided**, less stout than *pardinum*, with gray gills spotted with blackish brown; *Tricholoma venenatum*, **poisonous**, paler than *T. pardinum* or even white and somewhat brown only when fully ripe; found in copses, in North America.

TRICHOLOMA TERREUM (1)

Cap 4–7 cm, umbonate, with thin, often fissured margin; cuticle cinereous, desquamating into pubescent, sericeous, grayish or brownish squamules. **Stem** white with cinereous shades, cylindric; hollow at the top. **Flesh** thin, fragile, tending to cinereous. **Odor** mild. **Flavor** mild; bitter when the mushroom is old. **Gills** sparse, broad, thick, eroded near the stem; white, then cinereous; with serrate edges; fragile. **Spores** yellowish white. It grows in groups, almost cespitose, also in winter, especially under conifers. **Edible**, good when still unripe; it can be preserved in oil or dried. It is likely to be confused with *Tricholoma groanense,* **poisonous**, which smells of bedbugs, and grows in the heaths of Lombardy, locally called "groane."

TRICHOLOMA VIRGATUM (2)

Cap 4–8 cm, umbonate, cinereous, or with rosy or violaceous shades, darker at the center; with dark, sericeous fibrils; stem tall, white, smooth, stuffed; flavor acrid; growing especially under beeches and firs; **not edible**. It is likely to be confused with *Tricholoma sciodes*, **not edible**, which, however, has a non-umbonate cap, brownish gills' edges, and is bitter.

TRICHOLOMA SCALPTURATUM or ARGYRACEUM

Color from cinereous to brownish; desquamate along the margin; gills close, thin, becoming spotted with yellow; flesh white becoming spotted with yellow with age; odor of flour; **edible**. Many authors differentiate *argyraceum* from *scalpturatum* and consider the latter a species and *argyraceum* a variety of it.

1

2

3

2

3

TRICHOLOMA EQUESTRE

Cap 5–12 cm, with more or less prominent umbo; removable cuticle; sulfur yellow or olivaceous yellow; reddish at the center because covered by very minute squamules, rust colored; however it is smooth and slightly viscid, especially when unripe. **Stem** stout, thickened at the base; stuffed, fibrillar; sulfur yellow with olivaceous or brownish zones. **Flesh** thick at the center, thin at the margin; whitish; yellowish under the cap's cuticle and at the base of the stem. **Odor** slight. **Flavor** agreeable. **Gills** close, eroded near the stem, free or almost free; with undulate edges; bright, persistent sulfur yellow color. **Spores** white. It grows in autumn, under conifers, especially pines; rarely under latifoliate trees. **Edible**, of good quality.

Related to *Tricholoma terreum* (page 99) and growing in humid woods are *Tricholoma orirubens*, **edible**, cap 5–8 cm, flesh and gills tending to become reddish, with some green spots at the base of the stem, odor and flavor of flour, autumnal, growing mostly in the mountains; *Tricholoma atrosquamosum*, **edible**, thick, cap 4–8 cm, with dark and crowded squamules at the center, often with the edges of the gills brown, odor agreeable of pepper; *Tricholoma squarrulosum*, **edible**, different from the latter for having the stem covered with fuliginous squamules; and *Tricholoma cingulatum*, **edible**, cap 3–6 cm, rather thin, with cottony ring around the stem, growing in moist ground, especially under willows.

TRICHOLOMA VACCINUM (1)

Cap convex, 5–8 cm, umbonate, brownish, covered with plushy, pubescent, reddish brown scales; margin thin, woolly, rolled and pressed against the gills, therefore for some time striate. **Stem** cylindrical, soon hollow; whitish, fibrillar, with brown hues; wrapped by the fibrillar, brownish veil, a remnant of the cortina that encloses the whole mushroom; white and pruinose in the upper part. **Flesh** thin; thick only at the center; firm, white, with zones tending to reddish. **Odor** slight of flour. **Flavor** mild, or acidulous or also bitterish. **Gills** rather sparse, thick, eroded near the stem; with uneven edges; whitish becoming spotted with reddish. **Spores** white. It grows in tufts or groups, especially in coniferous woods, particularly pine and spruce; rarely in latifoliate woods; mostly in the mountains, rarely in the plains. **Edible**, but of poor quality.

TRICHOLOMA IMBRICATUM (2)

Similar to the previous species: cap 6–12 cm, ochraceous, squamose-fibrillar, but sometimes almost smooth; flesh white, not changing to reddish; flavor mild; in late autumn, both in the mountains and in the plains, under pines and larches; **edible**. *Tricholoma psammopus*, **not edible**, with lanate-squamose cap, dry, 3–7 cm, tawny red; stem with rusty granules; bitter; growing under conifers, especially larches.

TRICHOLOMA PORTENTOSUM

Cap with fine radial striae changing from violet to black, over a gray or ocher amethystine background with yellowish or olivaceous shades; convex, then irregularly expanded, 5–14 cm, with central umbo more intensely colored, almost black; margin thin, undulate, soon radially fissured; cuticle viscid, smooth. **Stem** cylindric, thick, firm, sometimes unequal, sometimes with the base extending into a rootlike appendix; fibrillar, whitish with yellowish or greenish gray hues; rarely with squamules on the upper part; stuffed with pith. **Flesh** thick at the center, thin at the margin; fragile; white, with scattered yellowish spots; violet or black under the cap's cuticle. **Odor** mild of flour. **Flavor** of flour. **Gills** rather sparse and thick, quite broad; semioval or eroded near the stem; whitish, then yellowish or tinged with green. **Spores** white. It grows in autumn, also in latifoliate woods, under birches and other plants, but especially in coniferous woods; singly or in groups of several specimens forming rings. **Edible**, of good quality. Sometimes the cap of *Tricholoma portentosum* seems similar to that of *Amanita phalloides* (pages 26–27); it is worthwhile to remind the inexperienced and the absentminded that *A. phalloides* has a ring around the stem and a volva around the base of the stem, with no characteristic odor and flavor, whereas *T. portentosum* is without ring or volva, and smells and tastes of flour.

TRICHOLOMA SEIUNCTUM (1)

Cap hemispheric, then expanded 5–15 cm; finally depressed; but with the margin almost always turned downward; humid, viscid; olivaceous yellow or lemon yellow, lighter at the margin, darker at the center, with or without blackish, radial fibrils. **Stem** thick, often undulate, white with yellowish or olivaceous spots; stuffed. **Flesh** firm, white, slightly more colored under the cuticle. **Odor** of flour. **Flavor** at first mild, then bitterish. **Gills** somewhat sparse, broad, eroded near the stem, adhering to the stem only by a tooth, or completely free from it; white, with cinereous-amethystine edges; with the external part, near the cap's margin, lemon yellow. **Spores** white. It grows in woods. **Not edible**, because even when it is cooked and well seasoned, it is disgusting, nauseating, and causes vomiting.

TRICHOLOMA SEIUNCTUM var. SQUAMULIFERUM (2, lying down)

Cap olivaceous brown or greenish brown, covered with filamentous squamules; margin fissured in the direction of the gills at maturation; gills whitish, then yellowish or grayish; odor of fruit and flavor of flour; growing in spruce woods; **edibility unknown**.

Sometimes the cap of *Tricholoma seiunctum* appears similar to that of *Amanita phalloides* (pages 26–27), which however presents a ring around the stem and a volva around the base.

TRICHOLOMA COLUMBETTA (1)

Cap ovoid or campanulate, then plane 5–10 cm, with or without central umbo; margin thin, involute toward the gills; then explanate, undulate, and sometimes lobate and fissured in the direction of the gills; rather viscid; then fibrillar, sericeous, lucid, as if it were satin; white, sometimes with few yellow, green, blue, violet, rusty, or rosy spots. **Stem** slender, often tapering toward the base; more rarely, thickened at the base; base generally bluish or greenish, rarely rosy; fragile, stuffed, fibrous. **Flesh** firm, white. **Odor** none or mild or pleasant. **Flavor** mild or agreeable. **Gills** rather close, thin, eroded near the stem; with slightly serrate edges; white. **Spores** white. It grows in woods, in groups. **Edible**, of good quality.

TRICHOLOMA ALBUM (2)

Cap convex, 3–9 cm, often cuspidate or with a large and low umbo at the center; initially white or whitish; then slightly tinged with cream or hazel shades, deeper at the center; at first lanate, especially at the margin; then glabrous and dry. **Stem** cylindric, sometimes thickened at the base; white with reddish or brownish bands. **Flesh** firm, white. **Odor** rather disgusting; sweet in the variety *lascivum*. **Flavor** bitter and acrid. **Gills** rather sparse, thick, eroded near the stem, somewhat close in the variety *lascivum*; whitish tending to cream. **Spores** white. It grows in woods, especially beech and birch. **Not edible** in the typical form; the variety *lascivum* **edible with caution**.

TRICHOLOMA SAPONACEUM (1)

This is a mushroom of very varied appearance, because of its size, ranging from 5 to 15 centimeters in diameter, and of the color of the cap and of the stem. **Cap** convex, then plane, often misshapen, with undulate margin; cuticle glabrous; in dry weather cracked into several squamules; greenish gray, olivaceous green, brown, fuliginous brown, or also pallid or whitish; dark olive green in the variety *atrovirens* (3); always slightly darker at the center. **Stem** firm, of variable shape, sometimes pointed at the base; fusiform in the form *napipes* (bottom center); white, then with greenish or reddish bands; covered with darker squamules and flocci in the variety *squamosum* (2). **Flesh** thick, whitish, slowly but distinctly changing to reddish when exposed to air. **Odor** of mild laundry soap. **Flavor** bitterish. **Gills** rather sparse, thin, eroded near the stem; white to whitish with green shades; then speckled with reddish. **Spores** white. It grows in groups, in all kinds of grounds. **Edible**, but of poor quality. Similar to *T. saponaceum* and characterized by flesh that becomes rapidly and distinctly red: *Tricholoma lavedanum*, **not advisable**, grows especially in the mountains, in warm temperate regions, under conifers; *Tricholoma sudum*, **poisonous**: it causes gastroenteritis; often with the margin of the cap radially wrinkled, and with odor of rancid flour.

1

2

3

TRICHOLOMA SULPHUREUM (1)

Cap sulfur yellow, often slightly brown at the center; convex, then plane, 3–9 cm; with light central umbo or, vice versa, slightly depressed; sericeous, glabrous, dry. **Stem** cylindrical, generally slender; rarely short and squat; striate lengthwise; of the same color as the cap; fibrous, stuffed, then hollow. **Flesh** rather thin, fibrous, of the same color as the cap but paler. **Odor** very disgusting of acetylene and of sulfur dioxide. **Flavor** mild. **Gills** sparse, broad, thick, eroded near the stem; yellow. **Spores** white. In autumn, in woods, especially latifoliate woods. **Not edible**. Similar to it is *Tricholoma equestre* (page 100), **edible**, which however has not a disgusting but a pleasant odor, although slight.

TRICHOLOMA SULPHUREUM var. BUFONIUM (2)

Color brown or reddish brown, especially at the center; **not edible**, just as the typical form. *Tricholoma inamoenum*, **not edible**, has a disgusting smell, similar to that of *T. sulphureum*, cap 5–7 cm, whitish or tending to hazel; stem tall, thin, whitish; gills broad, sparse, whitish or yellowish; growing under conifers, in the mountains. A similar species is *Tricholoma sulphurescens*, **not edible**, cap 4–6 cm, whitish tinged with yellow, or with ochraceous spots; stem tall, with yellow down; flesh yellow; odor rancid or of turnip; flavor pungent or bitter.

TRICHOLOMA COLOSSUS

This is an extraordinarily big, thick, fleshy mushroom, with short and thick stem; of reddish brown color, flesh white becoming slowly red when exposed to air. **Cap** pinkish hazel or reddish brown; convex with involute margin; then plane-convex, 5–25 cm, rather gibbous, uneven and with the margin still turned downward; cuticle smooth or slightly squamose, sometimes somewhat cracked, especially at the center; slightly viscid in humid weather. **Stem** short, thick, even thicker in the middle; sometimes with bulbous base, sometimes with fusiform base; pruinose in the upper part; with a ring in the middle but only when unripe; slightly squamose; faded fuliginous brown; reddish or brownish at the base. **Flesh** thick, firm, white, then pinkish, finally hazel pink. **Odor** agreeable. **Flavor** bitterish. **Gills** very close, rather thick; adhering to the stem; sometimes rounded or eroded near the stem; white, then with reddish spots. **Spores** white. It grows solitary in coniferous woods. **Edible**: when fresh it is a little indigestible; better when preserved in oil; it can also be dried or used as a powder. It is likely to be confused with the following **edible** species: *Tricholoma robustum*, smaller and with thinner stem; *Tricholoma caligatum* (page 93), brown tending to violaceous, with taller stem; *Biannularia imperialis* (page 109), which has two rings and decurrent gills.

LYOPHYLLUM (Tricholoma) GEORGII (1)

Cap white or pale cream or pale ocher or hazel gray, but also yellow or reddish; sometimes spotted; smooth, dry; sometimes also slightly cracked, hemispheric, then more or less expanded, 5–15 cm; at a late stage plane and uneven; margin thick, rolled toward the gills; strewn with soft, evanescent powder; faded; then rather explanate and often undulate. **Stem** stout, often squat; slightly fibrillar; whitish; ochraceous at the base; stuffed. **Flesh** thick also near the cap's margin; white. **Odor** of flour. **Flavor** tasty. **Gills** very close, narrow, often bifid near the stem; rounded or eroded near it; free or almost free; cream colored. **Spores** white. It is found in wood clearings, under bushes, or in meadows, in groups, also in rings; in spring, rarely in summer, more rarely in autumn. **Edible**, of excellent quality, also in the following varieties: *gambosum* (2), cap spotted with reddish, gills quite broad in the middle; *graveolens* (3), cap cinereous, gills grayish; *palumbinum* (4), cap white or cream, but amethystine at the center; *albellum* (5) entirely white. Related to the previous ones is *Tricholoma goniospermum*, **edible**, with amethystine gills; found in large groups in hilly and mountain meadows and woods, not only in spring, but also in summer and autumn.

MELANOLEUCA VULGARIS (1)

Cap fuliginous, slightly paler at the margin; convex, cuspidate, then plane, 4–8 cm, with more or less prominent umbo at the center; moist and darker in humid weather. **Stem** slender, elastic; whitish; streaked, for its entire length, with brownish, well-visible fibrils; darker at the base, which is often bulbous and covered with white down; slightly flocculose in the upper part; then becoming darker, but always lighter than the cap. **Flesh** soft, whitish; slightly cinereous in humid weather; yellowish the flesh of the stem; becoming brownish and rather tough with age. **Odor** soft. **Flavor** mild. **Gills** close, eroded near the stem; whitish. **Spores** white. It grows in clearings and in pastures. **Edible**.

MELANOLEUCA COGNATA (2)

Cap 5–9 cm, golden ocher, as the stem which is rugose, rather curved, and slightly bulbous; from April to July, in grassy spots under conifers and poplars. **Edible**.

MELANOLEUCA EVENOSA var. STRICTIPES (3)

Cap 4–8 cm, white or slightly ochraceous; sometimes slightly bitterish; growing in groups, in autumn, in mountain pastures. **Edible**.

MELANOLEUCA CNISTA (Fries) (4)

Cap 5–9 cm, whitish; anise odor, acrid flavor; growing in spring and in summer, in the plains, in dry woods of latifoliate trees. **Edible**. Several authors make no distinction between *cnista* and *evenosa*.

LYOPHYLLUM (Tricholoma) AGGREGATUM (1)

Cap convex or campanulate, with involute margin; then plane, 4–12 cm, generally umbonate; gray brown, now more brown, now more gray; streaked with radial fibrils; bright and sericeous in dry weather; fading with age. **Stem** rather stout, often curved, and also slightly eccentric; thickened at the base; white, then whitish; fibrillar; the base is bunched together with the bases of other specimens on the same tuft; but sometimes the base is confluent with the bases of other specimens. **Flesh** elastic, thin, whitish. **Odor** agreeable. **Flavor** mild. **Gills** close, white, annexed-rounded; then slightly decurrent and whitish. **Spores** white. It grows in tufts, around stumps and on buried roots even outside the woods. **Edible**.

LYOPHYLLUM LORICATUM (2)

Cap 4–10 cm, gibbous; cuticle tough, corrugated; flesh also tough; growing more often singly; **edible**.

LYOPHYLLUM (Clitocybe) CONGLOBATUM (3)

Similar to *L. aggregatum*: cap 3–10 cm, cinereous or grayish or faded olivaceous; odor of wheat flour, bitterish flavor; found in autumn, in tufts, in clearings and meadows, along the edges of woods; **edible**, it is necessary to parboil it. Similar to *L. conglobatum* is *Lyophyllum connatum*, **edible**, of good quality; growing in humid places, on decayed wood, in dense tufts with the bases bunched together tight but not confluent.

1

3

2

107

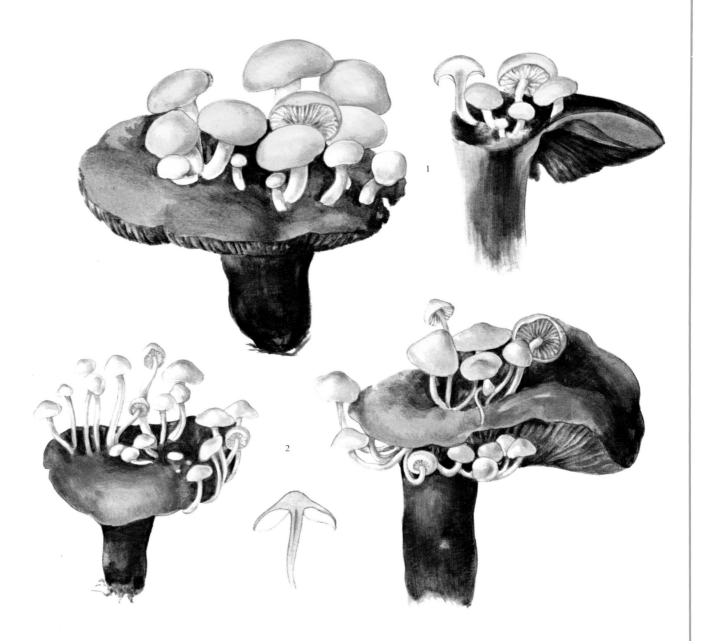

NYCTALIS ASTEROPHORA (1)

Cap globular or hemispheric, white, flocculose; then becoming convex 1–3 cm, and hazel colored; finally dissolving, for few millimeters, into a brownish powder containing spores, called chlamidospores. **Stem** often curved, white, sericeous and fibrillar; then fuliginous. **Flesh** thick, fishy smell, white; as we have said, in the end a good part of the cap's flesh becomes powder. **Gills** whitish, rather sparse, narrow; sometimes reduced to simple branched folds; sometimes completely lacking. **Spores**: the ones growing on the gills (basidiospores) are few and developed; the ones growing on the cap are brownish. It grows on decaying black russulas or on those that become black or blackish with age, and on decaying *Lactarius vellereus* (page 129). **Of no interest** from the alimentary point of view.

NYCTALIS PARASITICA (2)

Cap convex, 0.5–1.5 cm, generally cuspidate, whitish, then grayish; sericeous, filamentous, furfuraceous, with the margin often striate in the direction of the gills. **Stem** thin, curved, filamentous; grayish. **Flesh** thin, gray, dissolving into ochraceous powder. **Gills** rather sparse, thick, narrow; whitish; finally reduced to brownish powder. **Spores** whitish if growing on the gills (basidiospores); ochraceous when growing on the cap (chlamidospores). It grows on *Russula delica* (page 144) and on white *lactarii* in the decaying stage. **Not interesting** from an alimentary standpoint.

MELANOLEUCA GRAMMOPODIA

Cap grayish brown, slightly darker and moist in humid weather; convex, with large central umbo and involute margin; then plane, 6–26 cm, finally depressed, but still with large central umbo and with thin and deflexed margin; cuticle smooth, glossy. **Stem** slender, stout, hardy, cylindric, slightly bulbous at the base, which is covered with white down; whitish, but streaked for its entire length with dark, fuliginous, well-visible fibrils, which sometimes are slightly twisted. **Flesh** thick at the center, thin at the margin; rather watery; whitish, slightly smoky in humid weather. **Odor** strong and nauseating. **Flavor** mild. **Gills** very close, thin, adhering to the stem and then decurrent; whitish or cream, then slightly fuliginous. **Spores** white. It grows in the mountains, in pastures, in meadows, in gardens; in large groups, often in arcs, hidden by the grass where this is taller and greener; it can also be found in the plains, although rarely, with special characteristics. **Edible**; necessary to parboil it in water; otherwise it can be disgusting because of the smell. Of the same color as *grammopodia*, or even darker, is *Melanoleuca brevipes*, **edible**, entirely fuliginous gray; cap 3–6 cm, short stem, growing in woods. Also small and growing in meadows is *Melanoleuca exscissa*, **edible**, cinereous, with thin and sometimes eccentric stem.

BIANNULARIA IMPERIALIS

Cap globose, then convex, finally plane 5–20 cm, often somewhat undulate; margin tightly rolled, like an Ionic volute, toward the gills, then somewhat explanate and here and there fissured; cuticle dry, strewn for some time with few floccose remains of the general veil; slightly fibrous; cracking, starting from the center, while the mushroom is aging and drying up; more or less intense chestnut color or olivaceous brown. **Stem** squat, pointed at the base; hard stuffed; whitish, then yellowish; striate in the upper part. **Rings**: one around the stem, just below the gills, remnant of the partial veil; the other ascending from the base, remnant of the general veil; both membranous, whitish, slightly smoky. **Flesh** tough, white. Mixed **odor** of flour, cucumber, and bedbugs. **Flavor** agreeable, then sour. **Gills** close, narrow decurrent along the stem; whitish, then cream, finally cinereous, with blackish edges. **Spores** white. It grows in autumn, in coniferous woods, in groups, partly buried in the ground. **Edible**, but cooked fresh, it is rather indigestible, whereas preserved in oil, after boiling in diluted and aromatic vinegar, it is very tasty and much more digestible. A similar species is *Armillaria Zelleri*, **not edible** because it is bitter; with a single, frayed ring.

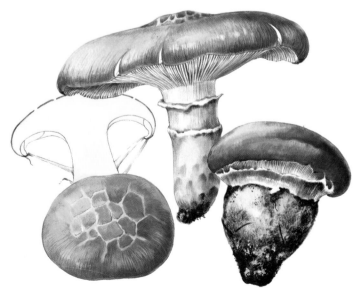

ARMILLARIELLA (Clitocybe) MELLEA

Cap 3–6 cm, umbonate; margin thin, involute, then explan-ate, undulate, striate, finally fissured; cuticle viscid in humid weather; with squamules more crowded at the center; but lacking squamules in older specimens; honey or cinnamon color, or brownish or reddish brown or olive, depending on the plants on which the mushroom develops; occasionally, when growing on acacia, it can be entirely white. **Stem** slen-der, fibrous, elastic, pithy; pinkish and striate in the upper part; brownish and gradually darker from the ring toward the base; base fuliginous, thickened but compressed by the bases of other specimens of the same tuft. **Ring** or armilla, quite thick, white and striate above, yellowish and flocculose underneath. **Flesh**: the cap's firm, the stem's fibrous. **Odor** not too agreeable. **Flavor** between acidulous and bitterish. **Gills** not too close, narrow, decurrent on the stem and then descending upon it with a tooth; whitish with yellow or pinkish hues; then faded and with reddish spots. **Spores** white. It grows in autumn, in tufts, on live trees that it dam-ages, but also on stumps or dead roots; sometimes it grows on rotting wood hidden in the grass, now singly, now in tufts; if solitary it can have large cap, 6–16 cm, and swollen base. **Edible**, only if well cooked and if the liquid secreted while cooking, which is toxic, is discarded; it can also be dried.

CLITOCYBE DEALBATA (1, 2)

Cap 2–6 cm, often depressed; margin involute, then explanate and undulate; cuticle covered with white bloom, not removable; then the bloom is reduced to irregular spots on a cream ocher background. **Stem** tall, slightly curved, white with ochraceous spots or with one side completely ochraceous; rather tough, fibrous; soon hollow. **Flesh** fibrous and tenacious, or tender and fragile; white, but, soaked with rain, it appears darker than the gills. **Odor** slight of flour. **Flavor** mild. **Gills** close, decurrent; whitish, then cream. **Spores** white. It grows in groups, in the grass, outside the woods. **Poisonous**.

CLITOCYBE RIVULOSA (3)

Distinguishable from *dealbata* because the bloom on the cap is resolved into concentric bands on a pale golden pink background; stem white, then rosy; flesh white, but golden pink under the cuticle. **Poisonous**. *Clitocybe fragrans*, edible but **better avoided** because it is easily confused with the poisonous species of *Clitocybe*; with anise smell, pale ocher, growing in woods.

CLITOCYBE CERUSSATA (4)

Cap 5–10 cm, now umbonate, now depressed; white as if whitewashed; then spotted with yellow and sometimes tinged with pink; margin odd, fissured; spores cream rosy; grows in woods, on plant debris; but the variety *difformis* is found on manured soil. **Poisonous**.

CLITOCYBE INFUNDIBULIFORMIS

Cap soon depressed, funnel shaped, 3–10 cm, often with small umbo in the center of the depression; cuticle sericeous, hazelnut colored; paler in the variety *catina*; in the variety *costata* (center) the cuticle is brownish and the margin is undulate or even lobate, with radiating grooves. **Stem** cylindric, thin, slender; rarely shrunken; of the same color as the cap; fibrous; streaked with brown fibers in the variety *costata*; tenacious, elastic, internally spongy; base rather swollen, covered with white down. **Odor** of bitter almonds, agreeable. **Flavor** somewhat tart. **Gills** close, not too broad; decurrent on the stem; whitish. **Spores** white. It grows especially in rainy summers and autumns, in rows of several specimens, just everywhere, also in woods, but especially at the edge of coniferous woods, in grassy and sandy grounds. **Edible**, it is good when well cooked; it can also be dried.

Similar to *C. infundibuliformis* are *Clitocybe* or *Lepista vermicularis*, **edible**, rather squat, with rootlike cords at the base, found in spring, in coniferous woods; *Clitocybe squamulosa*, **edible**, cap 3–5 cm, brown without umbo, with darker squamules; *Clitocybe incilis* (Gillet), **edibility unknown**, cap 3–10 cm, argillaceous brown with grooves along the uneven and festooned margin, with straw-colored gills, squat stem slightly paler than the cap, growing under conifers.

CLITOCYBE GIGANTEA

Cap white, then cream tinged with pink; later yellow ocher and finally reddish hazel; becoming slowly reddish brown where bruised; convex, with velvety and involute margin; then plane, 10–40 cm, and also more or less deeply depressed; margin glabrous, with light grooves in the direction of the gills, lobate, undulate, here and there fissured in the direction of the gills; cuticle thin, smooth, then cracked starting from the center, and finally torn, especially along the margin, into large pieces in concentric bands, turned upward, with the sericeous, paler subcuticle visible between the bands. **Stem** squat, strong, sometimes with thickened base; of the same color as the cap or slightly paler; fibrous, sometimes slightly rugose longitudinally, and here and there creviced. **Flesh** thick, elastic, fibrous; soft in mature specimens; white. **Odor** soft. **Flavor** agreeable. **Gills** very close, thin, here and there bifid; somewhat decurrent along the stem; easily detachable from the cap; slightly paler than the cap. **Spores** white. It grows in the mountains, in wood clearings, in pastures; often in rings. **Edible**. The *Clitocybe candida* (Bresadola), white, is probably only a *gigantea* still unripe.

CLITOCYBE GEOTROPA

Cap first campanulate, with the margin rolled toward the gills and slightly velvety; then depressed, funnel shaped, 10–20 cm, with explanate margin and with persistent umbo in the lower part of the funnel; of ochraceous yellow color, now paler, now tending to orange; glabrous, smooth. **Stem** thick, stout, thickened at the base; fibrous, elastic; slightly paler than the cap, sericeous; base enwrapped in white down; stuffed then spongy. **Flesh** white, then cream. **Odor** aromatic, of lavender or of bitter almonds. **Flavor** delicate and agreeable. **Gills** close, decurrent on the stem; here and there bifid; white, then rosy cream with distinctly pinkish hues; elastic; not fragile. **Spores** white. It grows in autumn, especially in rainy seasons; in large groups, often in circles, in the grass, or also under blackberry bushes, in wood clearings. **Edible** of good quality, but better use only the caps of the older specimes, and discard the stringy stems.

Clitocybe maxima, **edible**, of poor quality, has odor similar to that of *C. geotropa*: cap 20–60 cm, funnel shaped, broad brimmed, without central umbo; stem short, squat; grows in meadows, also in the mountains. *Clitocybe inornata,* **edible**, of poor quality, has floury taste, and pleasant turnip odor although it is soon rancid; small and rather rare, cap 5–10 cm, whitish or cinereous tinged with ocher, with woolly base; grows in groups, in coniferous woods.

geotropa Clit.

CLITOCYBE NEBULARIS

Cap convex, then plane 6–26 cm, often with large umbo at the center; finally depressed and somewhat uneven; cinereous or also slightly fuliginous; darker toward the center; discolored at the margin; faded in dry weather; initially finely furfuraceous, especially along the margin; then glabrous and lucid; margin involute, then explanate and undulate; cuticle thin, easily and almost entirely removable. **Stem** thick, slightly thickened at the base; elastic; stuffed, fibrous-spongy; then rather hollow; paler than the cap, furfuraceous, fibrillar, sometimes somewhat rugose; base covered with white down. **Flesh** firm but soon soft; slightly fibrous; white **Odor** strong, rather disgusting. **Flavor** acidulous. **Gills** easily detachable from the cap; whitish, then cream; close, unequal, narrow, decurrent on the stem; whereas the gills of *Entoloma lividum* (page 82), **poisonous**, are not decurrent but eroded near the stem and rusty pink. **Spores** white tending to cream. It grows in late summer and in autumn, especially after thunderstorms, in woods, in large groups, often in large circles. **Suspect:** probably toxic when raw; **edible** when cooked or dried; it must be boiled for few minutes in water, well drained, and only then can it be properly cooked; otherwise it can remain uneatable because of the disgusting odor, persistent even after cooking. Similar to *nebularis* is *Clitocybe gilva* (page 118), **edible**, but with shorter stem, and with aromatic, agreeable odor.

CLITOCYBE CLAVIPES (1)

Cap brownish gray, sometimes tending to olivaceous; with paler margin tending to yellow; with darker, fuliginous center. Sometimes, however, the color is almost identical to that of the cap of *Clitocybe nebularis*. Convex with central umbo; soon expanded, 4–8 cm, and then depressed more or less deeply; smooth; slightly viscid in humid weather; fibrillar, sericeous, almost velvety in dry weather. **Stem** more conical than cylindric; swollen base covered with white down; fibrillar; paler than the cap; soft, spongy inside. **Flesh** tender, soon flaccid; in humid weather so watery that liquid can be squeezed from it; whitish. **Odor** soft. **Flavor** mild. **Gills** not too close; rather thick and narrow, decurrent on the stem; cream, becoming gradually yellow as they ripen. **Spores** white. It grows in autumn, in woods, especially larch. **Edible**.

CLITOCYBE DICOLOR (2)

Cap 2–6 cm, almost immediately plane, then slightly depressed or umbilicate, or, on the contrary, slightly umbonate; brownish gray, darker at the center; more intensely colored in humid weather; in dry weather or with age, it fades until it becomes cinereous, remaining however, darker in the center. **Stem** rather slender, whitish in the upper part, at first fuliginous gray only at the base, but then gradually darkening upward. **Flesh** with aromatic odor. It grows in autumn in the woods, plains, or mountains. **Edible**.

CLITOCYBE ODORA (1)

Cap convex, moist, glabrous; then plane, 3–9 cm, with slight umbo in the center; finally depressed, with undulate margin, and completely dry; initially pale green or also somewhat bright green, tinged with blue green or blue; later paler and tinged with cinereous, yellowish, or pale ochraceous shades. **Stem** cylindric, stout, rather short; base thickened and covered with white down; fibrillar, whitish then slightly paler than the cap; elastic, fibrous; stuffed, then hollow. **Flesh** white tinged with green. **Odor** of anise. **Flavor** bitterish. **Gills** not too close, narrow, thin, slightly decurrent on the stem; greenish with blue green or bluish shades. **Spores** white tinged with pink. It grows in groups in woods, among dead leaves. **Edible**, but very aromatic even after cooking; it is better to use few specimens mixed with other species of mushrooms.

CLITOCYBE ODORA form ALBA (2)

Completely white with greenish shades. **Edible** as the typical form.

CLITOCYBE ODORA form VIRIDIS (3)

Gills white, then ochraceous yellow. **Edible** as the typical form. Also with anise odor are *Clitocybe suaveolens*, brownish, growing under firs, and *Clitocybe obsoleta*, reddish brown, but whitish in dry weather, growing under pines; both without any interest from an alimentary standpoint.

CLITOCYBE TABESCENS

Cap orange ocher or reddish brown with darker squamules in the center; convex, then expanded, 3–10 cm, sometimes with large hemispheric umbo in the center, sometimes plane or only slightly umbonate, sometimes even depressed; fibrillar. **Stem** very tall, tapering upward, thickening at the base, which is compressed by the bases of other specimens of the same tuft; fibrillar, smooth, without ring, slightly paler than the cap, except at the base which is brownish and fuliginous; stuffed, rarely hollow. **Flesh** thin; the cap cinereous white; the stem brownish and fibrous. **Odor** agreeable. **Flavor** slightly acrid. **Gills** close, somewhat broad, decurrent on the stem; cream with pinkish shades; then slightly paler than the cap. **Spores** white. It grows in dense tufts, near the stumps and the roots of latifoliate trees; it appears terricolous when the wood on which it feeds is buried. **Edible**, provided it is well cooked. The inexperienced amateur might mistake *Clitocybe tabescens* for other species of lignicolous, cespitose mushrooms which, if not always toxic, are sometimes at least not edible: *Clitocybe olearia* (page 117), **poisonous**, which is, however, all reddish brown; *Hypholoma fasciculare* (page 55), **not edible**, very bitter and with non-decurrent gills; *Pholiota mutabilis* (page 60), **edible**, with non-decurrent gills and a ring around the stem; *Armillariella mellea* (page 110), **edible**, which in the reddish form is the exact copy of *Clitocybe tabescens*, with the only difference being a ring around the stem.

CLITOCYBE (Pleurotus) ILLUDENS (1)

Cap convex, then plane, 6–12 cm; then depressed; often with small, persistent umbo at the center; margin thin, involute toward the gills, then somewhat explanate and irregularly lobate; cuticle dry, lucid, rather rugose, fibrillar; of a more or less faded orange color. Stem now tall, now short; curved, sometimes eccentric; sometimes with thinner base; of the same color as the cap, or also paler but with brown or blackish spots; striate or even rugose; firm, stuffed, fibrous. **Flesh** tenacious, fibrous; orange but often not uniform; some places deep orange, some others faded; the flesh of the stem darker. **Odor** unspecifiable or nauseating. **Flavor** delicate. **Gills** close, thin, narrow, several of them bifid; decurrent on the stem; orange, then fading; becoming phosphorescent at night, when the spores are ripe. **Spores** yellowish white. It grows in tufts in regions with cool temperate climate, on latifoliate trees, especially on oaks. **Poisonous**, it causes violent diarrhea.

CLITOCYBE OLEARIA (2)

Similar to *C. illudens* and equally **poisonous**; growing also in winter on olive trees and on the remains of the pressing of olives, in warm temperate regions: cap 6–18 cm, reddish brown. Many authors consider *Clitocybe olearia* identical to *Clitocybe illudens*.

illudens Clit.

HYGROPHOROPSIS (Clitocybe) AURANTIACA (3)

Cap bright orange yellow or ochraceous yellow; but whitish in the specimens growing in swampy grounds; convex with involute margin; then plane, 4–8 cm, or also depressed; sometimes regular, sometimes very irregular, with undulate and lobate margin; dry, velvety, sericeous. **Stem** cylindric, rather thin, often curved, sometimes eccentric; of the same color as the cap; elastic, stuffed, fibrous, then with hollow base. **Flesh** soft, rather spongy, slightly paler than the cap. **Odor** soft. **Flavor** mild or slightly acrid or even slightly disgusting. **Gills** rather close, thin, narrow, bifid or furcate; decurrent along the stem; sometimes with uneven edges; of the same color as the cap. **Spores** white. It grows in autumn, especially in coniferous woods. **Edible**, of poor quality; tasty when fried. Not to be confused with *Clitocybe olearia* and *Clitocybe illudens* (page 117), **poisonous**, which grow on latifoliate trees and not on conifers, with closer gills not bifid nor furcate.

HYGROPHOROPSIS AURANTIACA var. PALLIDA (1)

Gills white, then cream; **edible**.

HYGROPHOROPSIS AURANTIACA var. NIGRIPES (2)

Base fuliginous; it can be found on decaying stumps, probable feeding on hidden mold; **edible**.

CLITOCYBE CYATHIFORMIS (1)

Cap with involute margin and umbilicate center; but soon funnel shaped, 3–10 cm; later with striate margin; grayish brown or fuliginous brown, darker in humid weather. **Stem** slender, tapering upward; almost of the same color as the cap; but sometimes much paler than the cap, as in the specimens illustrated above; streaked with darker striae, sometimes reticulate; base covered with whitish down; elastic, stuffed, but soon hollow. **Flesh** thin, soft, watery, fuliginous. **Odor** and **flavor** mild. **Gills** somewhat sparse, annexed to the stem, then decurrent on it; whitish, then cinereous or yellowish cinereous. **Spores** white. It grows until the first frosts, in the ground or on wood debris, in the humid recesses of woods, meadows, and fields. **Edible**.

It is also **edible** in the following varieties: *suaveolens*, with anise odor; *expallens* (2), smaller and paler than the typical form, growing in meadows; *vibecina* (3), light as the *expallens*, with the margin of the cap striate and the base of the stem also striate, growing in woods; *brumalis* (4), grayish, flaccid, with an oily appearance in humid weather, growing in woods, under conifers, rarely under latifoliate trees; *pruinosa* (5), small, with brown cap, whitish stem, growing in woods, under firs.

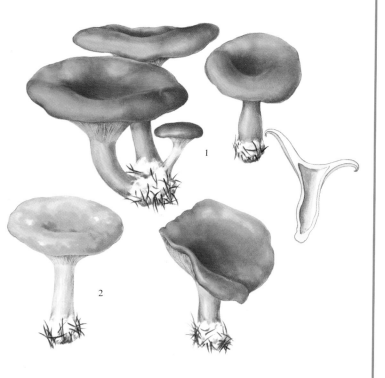

LEPISTA (Clitocybe) INVERSA (1)

Cap orange brown or orange ocher, often darker at the center; convex, then funnel shaped, 3–10 cm; glabrous, smooth, moist; but finally squamose in some varieties; margin involute and sometimes undulate. **Stem** short, firm, generally flared toward the cap and thickened at the base, enwrapped by whitish down; sometimes eccentric; whitish, then of the same color as the cap; smooth, fibrillar; stuffed, then spongy, finally hollow all the way up to the cap's cuticle. **Flesh** tough, thin, whitish or brownish. Slight anise **odor**. **Flavor** none or acidulous. **Gills** close, thin, narrow, decurrent on the stem; well shaped, sharp at both extremities, not bifid; easily removable in lumps; whitish, then tending to orange, with darker edges. **Spores** white. It grows in autumn, in groups, in latifoliate, but especially coniferous woods. **Edible**, of poor quality. It is likely to be confused, without danger, with *Lepista vermicularis* (page 111), **edible**, also found in coniferous woods, but in spring, with root-shaped cords at the base. *Lepista flaccida*, **edible**, smaller and paler than *inversa*, is considered by several authors simply as a form, with flaccid flesh, of *Lepista inversa*.

LEPISTA (Clitocybe) GILVA (Konrad) (2)

Cap 4–10 cm, yellowish or slightly smoky, more or less faded, with small, darker spots; gills bifid, aromatic odor, growing under latifoliate trees but especially under firs, in the mountains; **edible**.

LACCARIA LACCATA (1)

Cap convex, then expanded 3–6 cm, with a little depression in the center, more rarely with small umbo; undulate margin; cuticle rather rough, almost squamose; pinkish or yellowish or orange brown or brown; darker in humid weather. **Stem** cylindric, thin, slightly undulate; of the same color as the cap; fibrous, tough; first stuffed, then soon hollow. **Flesh** thin; of the same color as the cap, fading upon drying. **Odor** and **flavor** mild. **Gills** sparse, broad, thick, unequal, slightly decurrent; rosy, then covered with white powder: the **spores**. Terricolous, growing in humid woods, in grass or in moss, especially under poplars. **Edible**.

LACCARIA AMETHYSTINA (2)

Entirely violet, but soon faded; **edible**, better than *laccata*.

LACCARIA LACCATA var. PROXIMA (3)

Cap 6–12 cm, orange brown, squamose; gills rosy amethystine; **edible**.

LACCARIA LACCATA var. SANDICINA (4)

Cap lilac amethystine, then grayish; stem and gills lilac; **edible**.

LACCARIA TORTILIS (5)

Cap 1.5–2 cm, undulate, pale reddish; stem short, twisted and hidden by the cap; gills pinkish; growing in humid and muddy recesses; **of no alimentary interest**. Growing in the sands of the Great Lakes is *Laccaria trullissata*, **not edible**, because of the sand that covers the cap; 3–6 cm, reddish brown paler at the center; gills sparse, red amethystine.

RHODOPAXILLUS (Tricholoma) NUDUS

Cap 3–15 cm, with involute margin which then becomes explanate and even turned upward, undulate, sometimes with deep spoutlike folds; moist, smooth; violet tending to gray, brownish at the center; becoming faded in dry weather or with age. **Stem** stout, fibrous, stuffed; violaceous or cinereous amethystine; with thickened, downy base. **Flesh** of the cap fragile, of the stem fibrous; violaceous. **Odor** aromatic. **Flavor** agreeable. **Gills** close, thin, rounded toward the stem and annexed, then decurrent; violaceous, then ochraceous. **Spores** pinkish amethystine. It grows in woods, in autumn, sometimes also in other seasons, except during periods of frost. The variety *lilaceus*, smaller and of brighter color, grows under conifers; it is slightly **poisonous** when raw, **edible**, of excellent quality, when cooked; parboiling is recommended.

Similar to *R. nudus*: *Rhodopaxillus glaucocanus*, **not advisable**, cinereous-amethystine, then whitish, odor and flavor disgusting, growing in the shade, especially under beech trees; *Rhodopaxillus sadicus*, **edible**, less fleshy, rather gracilent, growing in manured ground; *Rhodopaxillus sordidus* (Singer), **edible**, smaller and paler than *nudus*, growing in late autumn, in tufts or groups, in the grass of meadows, parks, and gardens.

RHODOPAXILLUS (Tricholoma) SAEVUS

Cap convex, also rather cuspidate; then almost flat, 5–15 cm, sometimes rather gibbous; margin involute toward the gills and pruinose, then somewhat undulate; pale gray, pale pinkish gray, or pale fuliginous; rarely with amethystine shades; fading with age; cuticle smooth, moist, shining, easily detachable from the cap. **Stem** short, cylindric, often thickened at the base, stuffed, pale violet; covered with very fine, white or rosy fibrils or squamules. **Flesh** thick, tender; pale, slightly violet under the cuticle of the cap. **Odor** agreeable. **Flavor** mild. **Gills** rather close, broad, undulate; rounded near the stem; then sometimes decurrent on the stem; whitish, then with fuliginous shades. **Spores** rosy cinereous. It grows in late autumn, after the first cold weather until the first frost, in large rings in the grass of humid meadows and pastures; but wait for dry weather before collecting it. **Edible**, of good quality.

A similar species is *Rhodopaxillus truncatus*: **cap** 4–12 cm, rosy pale ocher; convex, but soon plane and depressed, uneven, with undulate and oddly lobate margin; slightly velvety in the center; cuticle almost not separable; margin discolored, thin, smooth. **Stem** short, squat, cylindric, sometimes like an upside-down cone; slightly paler than the cap; fibrous. **Flesh** thick, cream white. **Odor** agreeable. **Flavor** mild or bitterish. **Gills** thin, rather close, adherent to the stem and also slightly decurrent, cream colored, then ochraceous. **Spores** rosy. It grows in coniferous woods, especially under firs. **Edible**.

RHODOPAXILLUS (Tricholoma) IRINUS

Cap 5–12 cm, slightly umbonate, smooth, with slightly undulate margin; pale ocher to flesh pink, deeper in humid weather. **Stem** thick, fibrous, tenacious, than rather fragile; silvery, fibrillar, pruinose the upper part, with ochraceous shades toward the base. **Flesh** thick, white, marbled with rosy ocher. **Odor** of violet or of orange blossom. **Flavor** sapid. **Gills** close, narrow, rounded near the stem and adhering to it; ochraceous pink. **Spores** rosy. It grows in autumn, in groups, in clearings of mixed woods, especially of beeches and pines. **Edible**: laxative for some individuals.

The species with pink spores was taken off the genus *Tricholoma* and classified under the genus *Rhodopaxillus*. This explains the double denomination of *Tricholoma irinus* and *Rhodopaxillus irinus*. From the same genus *Tricholoma* was taken off the species with smaller, more slender carpophore, sensitive to humidity, which was classified in the genus *Melanoleuca*: thus we have the new denomination *Melanoleuca grammopodia* side by side with the old one *Tricholoma grammopodium*. The lignicolous species of the genus *Tricholoma* was reclassified in the genus *Tricholomopsis*: thus other double denominations came about: *Tricholoma rutilans* and *Tricholomopsis rutilans*. Similar transpositions were made for several species, which kept the species name but took a new genus name. Therefore, for practical purposes, the species denomination, more stable than the genus denomination, is much more important than the latter.

CLITOPILUS PRUNULUS

Cap cinereous white, slightly darker at the center, for some time entirely strewn with white, evanescent pruina, more persistent at the margin; convex, sometimes also uneven; then expanded, 5–12 cm, now plane, now depressed, sometimes uneven, gibbous; margin at first thick, very pruinose, rolled toward the gills, then more or less explanate, thinner, lobate, undulate, fissured in the direction of the gills; slightly viscid in humid weather; in dry weather it looks like suede; white, rather viscous, with very uneven margin in the variety *orcella*. **Stem** squat, often curved; sometimes eccentric: now unevenly swollen, now thickened at the base, which is covered with white cottony down; of the same color as the cap; pruinose in the upper part. **Flesh** rather thick, except at the margin; soft, fragile, white. **Odor** of bread dough. **Flavor** agreeable, but sometimes also bitter. **Gills** close, thin, narrow, decurrent along the stem; easily separable in lumps from the cap; white, then pinkish, finally rosy hazel. **Spores** yellow rosy. It grows in wood clearings, especially of oak woods, often near to *Boletus edulis* (page 177). **Edible**, excellent; it cooks very fast; can be dried. To avoid the bitter specimens, it is advisable to taste without swallowing some specimens now and then as you pick them. *Clitopilus orcella*, **edible**, white, more viscous than *C. prunulus*, with very uneven margin, is not considered a different species but only a different form of *prunulus*.

Do not confuse *Clitopilus prunulus* with *Clitocybe rivulosa, dealbata*, and *cerussa* (page 111), which are poisonous; it is necessary to remember that the ripe gills of these clitocybes are whitish, whereas those of *C. prunulus* are rosy.

RHODOPAXILLUS (Tricholoma) PANAEOLUS (2)

Cap cinereous-hazel colored, often with little, darker, round spots; paler at the margin; first convex, pruinose, with the margin rolled toward the gills and farinaceous; then becoming plane, 4–12 cm, or depressed, dry, glabrous, with margin undulate and sometimes lobate. **Stem** squat, cylindric, sometimes thickened at the base; even shorter in the variety *brevipes*; dry, striate, slightly paler than the cap; stuffed, fibrous, spongy; then hollow. **Flesh** tender, elastic, spongy, cinereous. **Odor** of flour. **Flavor** agreeable. **Gills** thin, annexed to the stem and then slightly decurrent, easily detachable from the cap; of the same color as the stem, then light hazel and finally rosy hazel. **Spores** rosy cinereous. It grows in autumn, in groups, in meadows, especially in hills and mountains. **Edible**, of good quality; it becomes a bit piquant with cooking.

RHODOPAXILLUS CAESPITOSUS (1)

Similar to *R. panaeolus*, but with whitish or white cap; growing in tufts, amid the grass of mountain pastures; **edible**.

Let us mention here the principal **edible** *Rhodopaxillus*: *nudus* (page 120), violet, aromatic, growing under conifers, autumn-winter; *saevus*, gray amethystine, stem fibrillar, growing in meadows, autumn-winter; *glaucocanus*, cinereous amethystine, slight mint flavor, found under conifers and beeches; *truncatus*, oddly depressed, rosy ocher, bitterish, growing under conifers; *irinus* (page 121), rosy ocher, white fibrillar stem, odor of roses and violets, found under conifers.

PLEUROTUS CORNUCOPIAE

Cap convex, then depressed or also funnel shaped, 5–12 cm, often uneven, sometimes with small umbo in the center of the depression; first covered with down, but soon glabrous and lucid; first whitish, generally tinged with red, then yellow ocher or also brownish. **Stem** sometimes eccentric, generally curved, covered with down, white, or yellowish gray, and finally slightly brownish, generally branched; covered for a long stretch by a reticulation formed by prolongations of the gills. **Flesh** thick, slightly fibrous, and yet tender and fragile; white, yellowish only if rubbed. **Odor** of flour or slightly nauseating. **Flavor** agreeable. **Gills** close near the margin of the cap because of numerous intermediate gills; less crowded near the stem along which they are decurrent for a long distance through fine threads connected as in a net; narrow, white, generally tinged with pink; then cream. **Spores** white with rosy amethystine shades. It grows from spring to summer, on oak, elm, poplar, and beech trunks, in dense tufts. **Edible**, of good quality; it is advisable to boil it in water and drain it well, before properly cooking it. Unfortunately it is very soon infested by larvae; it is necessary to examine very carefully every specimen and to use only those which are intact. *Pleurotus pulmonaris*, **edible**, is very similar to the paler forms of *Pleurotus ostreatus* (page 114) and of *Pleurotis cornucopiae*, but it has an odor different from that of *P. ostreatus* and less intense than that of *P. cornucopiae*, and the stem is not reticulate; it grows in autumn.

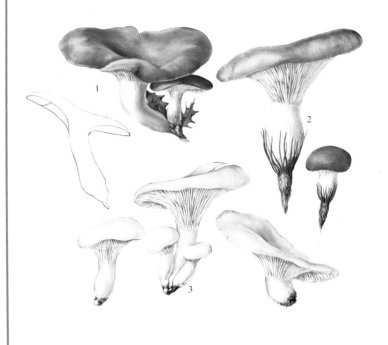

PLEUROTUS ERYNGII (1)

Cap brownish gray; fading with age; rarely pallid, whitish since the beginning; convex, then expanded, 4–15 cm, uneven, depressed; margin almost always turned downward; cuticle slightly velvety, but soon glabrous. **Stem** generally rather eccentric in relation to the cap; thick; fusiform at the base; smooth, glabrous, whitish, stuffed. **Flesh** firm, white. **Odor** soft. **Flavor** agreeable. **Gills** not too close, broad, decurrent on the stem, and here and there connected together along the stem; whitish, then with cinereous-ochraceous shades. **Spores** white. It grows between spring and summer, and again in autumn, in uncultivated, sandy grounds, at the edge of footpaths; on the decaying remains of some *umbellifers*, similar to the thistles, such as *Eryngium campestre*. **Edible**, excellent; it can be dried.

PLEUROTUS ERYNGII var. FERULAE (2)

Cap brownish gray or fuliginous, reaching larger size than in the typical form, 5–18 cm; stem bulging, with radiciform base; on the remains of an umbellifer called *Ferula Lanzi*, in warm temperate regions; **edible**, excellent; it can be exsiccated.

PLEUROTUS ERYNGII var. NEBRODENSIS (3)

Whitish or white, 4–15 cm; growing in the mountains and, on the Alps, at up to 2,200 meters of altitude, always on the remains, from the previous year, of some shrubs; **edible**, excellent, both fresh and exsiccated.

ostreatus Pleur.

PLEUROTUS OSTREATUS

Caps shell shaped, joint and superimposed like the tiles on a roof; blackish violaceous, brownish, or grayish ochraceous; fading to yellowish with age; margin rolled toward the gills; then explanate and undulate; cuticle smooth, but with glittering granules in the variety *glandulosus*; lucid, but slightly velvety near the stem; diameter of a single cap 5–15 cm, diameter of the tuft 15–35 cm. **Stems** lateral, slanted, sometimes rudimental; but very long in the variety *stipitatus*; with pubescent bases confluent in a single mass; stuffed, firm, white, smooth. **Flesh** thick, tender, then tough; white. **Odor** agreeable. **Flavor** sapid. **Gills** more or less close; broad; decurrent on the stem through a thread; not crossing one another; white or cream; also with shiny granules in the variety *glandulosus*. **Spores** white, tinged with amethystine. It grows in tufts, in autumn, until the first winter rigors, but also in winter when this is mild, on trunks and stumps of latifoliate trees, rarely on conifers. **Edible**, of good quality and very much in demand. On the other hand, the variety *columbinus* is **edible only with caution**, since it can cause diarrhea and other intestinal trouble, particularly in delicate individuals; cap reddish ocher, reddish at the center, blue violaceous at the margin; then green or blue green; sometimes entirely blue; growing on latifoliate trees but more often on conifers.

PLEUROTUS DRYINUS (1)

Cap 4–10 cm, irregular, often gibbous; with involute margin; cuticle white, grayish, or ochraceous, covered with felt that then breaks up into silvery or ochraceous, evanescent scales; in the variety *tephrotrichus* a coarse, grayish covering of the cap lasts for a long time. **Stem** firm, cylindric, eccentric, often horizontal; hard, fibrous, whitish; becoming yellow when bruised or with age. **Cortina** whitish, flocculose, fugacious. **Flesh** thick, white; soon hard, and somewhat tough; the flesh of the stem fibrous. **Odor** mild and agreeable. **Flavor** agreeable. **Gills** and intermediate gills close, broad, with uneven edges; decurrent through a thread; white, then yellow. **Spores** white. It grows on latifoliate trees, rarely on conifers. **Edible**, good as long as unripe.

PLEUROTUS (Tricholomopsis or Lyophyllum) ULMARIUS (2)

Cap 6–24 cm, yellowish, often with darker spots; gills close, annexed to the stem or eroded near it; odor rancid; flavor bitter; growing on elms, but not exclusively. **Edible** as long as completely unripe.

PLEUROTUS SEROTINUS (3)

Cap 4–10 cm, olive green or brownish green; margin yellow, rolled toward the gills; cuticle velvety, then glabrous and viscid; gills close, narrow, yellowish, then brownish; stem lateral, squat, yellowish, covered with olivaceous or brownish scales, denser in the upper part; flesh tenacious, mucilaginous; growing in autumn, on latifoliate trunks. **Not edible**.

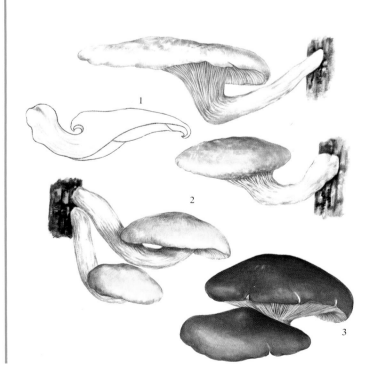

TRICHOLOMOPSIS EDODES

Cap convex, now round, now kidney shaped; ochraceous, brown, violaceous brown; sometimes adorned with white or ochraceous, evanescent warts, especially in the center and in a circular belt near the margin; then plane, 5–10 cm, and also depressed, uneven, often with zigzag crevices and covered with darker scales; with thin, explanate, undulate, festooned, light color margin. **Stem** squat, often eccentric in relation to the cap, sometimes curved, sometimes slanted or even horizontal; the upper part is white, smooth or with slight vertical striae; the rest is white or ochraceous, striate, fibrous, rough. **Ring** white, thin, formed by the filamentous remains of the cortina; evanescent. **Flesh**: the flesh of the cap white and firm; the stem whitish, fibrous and tough. **Odor** agreeable; aromatic when the mushroom is dried. **Flavor** agreeable. **Gills** close, rather narrow, bifid, eroded near the stem; white, then here and there ochraceous. **Spores** whitish. It grows in spring and in autumn in the mountains on old latifoliate trees, especially chestnut, ilex, oak, in groups or tufts. **Edible**, in great demand and intensely cultivated in the Far East: the Shiitake, cultivated in Japan on small logs of hodoghi (*Quercus pasania*). This species is often ascribed to the genus *Armillaria*, although it does not have decurrent gills; to the genus *Cortinellus* and *Tricholoma*, although not terricolous; to the genus *Lentinus*, although without denticulate edged gills. It seems to belong to the genus *Tricholomopsis*.

LENTINUS TIGRINUS

Cap: soon depressed funnel-like, 3–12 cm, whereas the cuticle, brown and velvety, resolves into squamules, denser in the center, among which is visible the white, sericeous, lucid background; margin thin, involute, fissured. **Stem** thin, flared toward the cap, curved, with filamentous remains of the cortina, forming a fugacious pseudo-ring; whitish; speckled with granular, evanescent squamules from the pseudo-ring to the base; stuffed, fibrous, tenacious; in the form *ramosipes* (bottom left) the stem divides into several branches, each supporting a cap. **Flesh** elastic, tenacious, thin, white; soon tough; it dries without rotting. **Odor** of cream. **Flavor** slightly acrid. **Gills** close, narrow, decurrent, soon with serrate edges; whitish, then cream with orange hues. **Spores** white or cream. It grows in groups or in tufts, from late spring to the beginning of autumn; on trunks or stumps of latifoliate trees, especially willow, poplar, beech, in humid ground. **Edible**, as long as completely unripe, as is *Lentinus degener*, 5–20 cm, red brown, squamose; stem thick, bulging; flavor agreeable. Related species, **not edible**: *Lentinus adhaerens*, 3–6 cm, whitish, then ochraceous; on firs and pines: from the gills it exudes resinous droplets; *Lentinus vulpinus*, 4–11 cm, rust colored, rugose and striate; cespitose; piquant as pepper; *Lentinus omphalodes*, small, 2–4 cm, color as of dried dates; stem thin, grooved; bitter or acrid; grows on buried wood debris.

ACANTHOCYSTIS GEOGENIUS (1)

Cap brown tending to cinereous, olivaceous, or fuliginous; dark orange brown in the variety *Queletii* (2); fan or funnel shaped, 6–10 cm, open along one side; uneven margin; covered with a gelatinous coat, removable and shining, and with a whitish or grayish pubescence, denser near the stem, lacking at the margin. **Stem** atrophic, lateral, white, hairy. **Flesh** tenacious, thick, white, here and there brownish. **Odor** of flour. **Flavor** of flour. **Gills** close, thin, narrow, decurrent, white, then cream. **Spores** white or pallid. It grows at the foot of trees. **Edible**. Similar to it is *Acanthocystis petaloides*, **edible**, less fleshy and paler.

CREPIDOTUS MOLLIS (3)

Cap whitish or yellowish, semicircular, 3–8 cm; covered with a gelatinous, removable coat; in the form *calolepis* covered also with brownish hair, which, in dry weather, after the gelatinous coat has dried out, appears as clar-cut, triangular tufts. **Stem** none or atrophic, cottony. **Flesh** flaccid, thin, watery, whitish. **Odor** and **flavor** mild. **Gills** close, narrow, whitish, then brownish. **Spores** brownish. It grows on latifoliate trees, in groups. Uninteresting from an alimentary standpoint, same as *Crepidotus applanatus*, which grows on conifers, and *Crepidotus fragilis*, which grows in the ground along humid footpaths. Both *applanatus* and *fragilis* lack, however, the gelatinous coat.

LENTINUS LEPIDEUS

Cap hemispheric, white, bristling with dark, coarse scales; soft cortina from the margin to the stem; becoming yellow when bruised; then convex, 5–12 cm, uneven, yellow, fibrous, creviced, almost without scales. **Stem** squat, fibrous, white, full of brown scales that simulate a ring; blackish at the base that is fixed into the support by a radiciform, flattened appendix. **Flesh** tough, white, then whitish, coriaceous spongy; it dries without rotting. **Odor** of anise. **Flavor** mild. **Gills** rather sparse, decurrent; with uneven edges; white, then yellowish. **Spores** white. It grows in tufts, during rainy seasons, on coniferous wood, especially old larches. **Not edible**.

Let us mention a few other mushrooms, of the genus *Panellus*, lignicolous, which dry without rotting, with fan-shaped cap and atrophic and lateral stem, or no stem at all, **not edible**: *Panellus stipticus*, 1–4 cm, ochraceous; peduncle like an upside-down cone, gills cinnamon, flesh soft but tenacious, bitter sour, growing all year round, on dead latifoliate trees; *Panellus mitis*, 1–2 cm, white or rosy cream, with gelatinous veil, mild flavor, on dead conifers; *Panellus nidulans*, 2–5 cm, orange ocher, gills close and saffron colored, without stem, with flesh mucilaginous, but tough. Similar to *Panellus* is *Schizophyllum commune*, **not edible**, 2–4 cm, gray, rugose, hairy; gills violaceous, halving along the edges, which are flocculose; growing also in winter on the crust of decaying tree branches.

PANUS CONCHATUS (1 fresh, 2 dried)

Cap fan shaped or irregularly funnel shaped, 5–10 cm; margin with more or less curled lobes and fissured in the direction of the gills; cuticle sometimes desquamating in concentric zones; brownish, with violaceous velvet in the unripe specimens. **Stem** unequal, lateral, short; brown and initially covered with a violet felt; base thickened and downy. **Flesh** thin, tough, elastic, white. **Odor** aromatic. **Flavor** almost of turnip. **Gills** very close, narrow, decurrent, not denticulate; cream amethystine, then hazel; becoming rusty when bruised. **Spores** white. It grows from spring to autumn, on latifoliate trees, more rarely on conifers; dries without rotting. **Not edible**.

LENTINELLUS (Lentinus) COCHLEATUS (3)

Cap funnel shaped, 3–10 cm, rather odd, open along one side, more or less extensively; reddish brown, fading upon drying; glabrous; margin curled, fissured in the direction of the gills. **Stem** entirely wrinkled and grooved longitudinally; twisted; of the same color as the cap; generally darker at the base; hard, fibrous, hollow. **Flesh** thin, cartilaginous, tenacious, elastic; whitish tending to reddish. **Odor** of anise; but odorless in the variety *inolens*. **Flavor** almost none. **Gills** close, narrow, decurrent, serrate; whitish, then pinkish cream. **Spores** white. It grows on old stumps especially of beeches; dries without rotting. **Edible** when unripe, but indigestible.

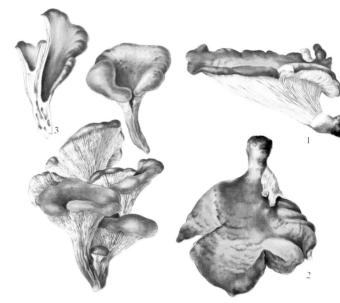

LACTARIUS VELLEREUS

Cap plane-convex, with margin rolled toward the gills; then plane, 8–15 cm, depressed in the center, finally funnel shaped with explanate and irregularly undulate margin; entirely covered with stiff down, more evident in dry weather; white, then whitish or yellowish, with brownish spots. **Stem** short and thick, hard, often misshapen; pointed at the base; white, then with brownish spots; velvety, like the cap. **Flesh** thick, hard, brittle; white, then yellowish, with greenish stains. **Odor** agreeable. **Flavor** acrid. **Latex** scarce, white, bitter; acrid in the variety_ *Bertillonii*. **Gills** somewhat apart, connected by fine veins; slightly decurrent along the stem; white, with blue green or yellowish hues; then pale ocher. **Spores** white. It grows in the humid recesses of latifoliate woods, in groups. **Not advisable**: it is not poisonous, but even well cooked and seasoned it is of a very poor quality.

Similar to *L. vellereus* are *Lactarius velutinus*, **not advisable**, with mildly flavored latex, but acrid-tasting flesh; and *Lactarius deceptivus*, **not advisable**, entirely white, including the latex that remains white even when exposed to air; as this mushroom ripens the cap gradually expands and the soft border along the margin detaches from it, ringlike, but remaining hanging down from the margin at various points; at the same time the cuticle in the center of the cap becomes brownish and breaks into numerous squamules.

LACTARIUS PIPERATUS

Cap convex, then depressed and also funnel shaped, 6–20 cm; smooth, regular; sometimes slightly cracked in dry air; margin rolled toward the gills, then explanate and undulate; white, then whitish, with hazel stains; always white along the margin. **Stem** squat, sometimes shaped as an inverted cone; white with reddish or greenish shades. **Flesh** hard, cream colored, becoming slowly greenish when exposed to air. **Odor** soft. **Flavor** slightly acrid. **Latex** abundant, syrupy, white then slowly greenish; very acrid flavor. **Gills** very close, thin, narrow; the bifid ones numerous; decurrent along the stem; white with ochraceous hues; then pale cream, stained green by the latex; spotted with brown where bruised. **Spores** white. It grows in shady and humid recesses in the woods; in large groups, in rows or in circles. **Not advisable**: in some regions it is eaten cooked on the grill; in others after it has been exsiccated; still in other regions, dried and reduced to powder, as seasoning; in others in small doses, fresh, in place of hot pepper; even cooked after parboiling it is left with a questionable taste of laundry soap and is difficult to digest. More common than the above and similar to it is *Lactarius pergamenus*, **not edible**: gills very close and narrow, stem long, cap not too fleshy, white, then yellowish and rugose, flesh that tends to become yellowish, and latex white not changing even in contact with air. All the *lactarii* that are neither acrid nor bitter are **edible**, since they are not poisonous; but they are not always tasty.

LACTARIUS CHRYSORRHEUS (1)

Cap soon depressed and then funnel shaped, 4–10 cm; dry; rosy tending to vermilion, with darker spots, rosy ochraceous, often arranged in concentric zones. **Stem** squat, stuffed, soon hollow; whitish, with reddish shades, with cream or ocher spots. **Flesh** white tinged with orange at the periphery; becoming quickly yellow when exposed to air. **Odorless**. **Flavor** acrid. **Latex** white, quickly changing to lemon yellow when exposed to air; with very acrid taste. **Gills** close, thin, decurrent along the stem; creamy white color. **Spores** creamy white. It grows in woods, especially under chestnuts. **Not edible**.

LACTARIUS TABIDUS (2)

Cap 4–7 cm, umbonate, ochraceous or bright orange; rugose in persistent dry weather. **Stem** long, slender, slightly paler than the cap. **Flesh** and **latex** white, both becoming yellow when exposed to air. **Flavor** of the flesh mild; of the latex slightly acrid. **Gills** rosy. Under latifoliate trees, especially birches, and under conifers, particularly pines. **Edible** when dried, but of poor quality; cooked soon after collection it remains slightly acrid. Also *Lactarius theiogalus* (non-Fries), **to be avoided**, has flesh and latex that become yellow in contact with air; it is however sturdier than *L. tabidus*, ocher rosy color as sometimes is *L. chrysorrheus*, and generally without umbo. It is to be noted that different authors have used the denomination *theiogalus* for different species.

LACTARIUS CONTROVERSUS

Cap plane with depressed center and margin rolled toward the gills; then funnel shaped, 6–30 cm, with rather explanate margin; viscid in humid weather; white, with concentric pinkish zones; at first completely velvety, then only at the margin; often encumbered with vegetable debris or with soil. **Stem** squat, smooth, whitish. **Flesh** thick, hard, fragile, granular; white, slightly pinkish under the colored parts of the cap. **Odor** of wine, acidulous, or disgusting. **Flavor** acrid. **Latex** white, acrid. **Gills** close, narrow, decurrent, white, but soon rosy. **Spores** white. Grows in large rings of many specimens, in the grass of thin woods, especially under poplars. **Edible with caution**: cooking for a long time can eliminate the acrid taste, but does not make the mushroom tasty; it is somewhat improved by preserving in oil after boiling first in diluted and aromatic vinegar. *Lactarius populinus* also grows under poplars, in the grass; it is **not edible**, with a darker cap than *L. controversus*, creamy pink, but with gray, concentric bands; misshapen, funnel shaped, 6–24 cm, viscid; flesh elastic, greenish white; acrid, very hot; gills close, rosy amethystine. Darker than *L. populinus* is *Lactarius insulsus*, **not edible**: cap often misshapen, 5–15 cm, ochraceous or chamois color, with darker zones; stem generally squat and eccentric; gills flesh colored and slightly wrinkled; flesh white, becoming slowly pinkish and then cinereous when exposed to air; odor of fruit, flavor of the latex acrid; growing under latifoliate trees, in the plains.

scrobiculatus Lact.

LACTARIUS SCROBICULATUS (1)

Cap 6–24 cm, margin involute with matted cilia; depressed center; viscid, plushy; rarely with zones and even then not clearly defined; yellowish. **Stem** cylindric, strong, hard, soon hollow; whitish, tending to yellow; speckled with ochraceous erosions. **Flesh** thick, hard, fragile; white, but yellowish at the base of the stem. **Odor** of fruit. **Flavor** acrid. **Latex** abundant; white, but turning quickly to sulfur yellow when in contact with air; acrid. **Gills** close, decurrent; cream, with yellow edges. **Spores** cream colored. It grows under conifers, in the mountains, is rare in certain areas, abundant and in groups in others. **Not edible**.

Similar to *L. scrobiculatus* and also **not edible**: *Lactarius cilicioides*, different from the one mentioned in the description of *Lactarius torminosus*: cap ochraceous, with darker zones and with matted cilia at the margin; stem with erosions; latex very acrid, white, becoming immediately yellow when exposed to air; growing especially under latifoliate trees; similar to it is *Lactarius resinus*, which grows under conifers and birches and is without zones on the cap and without matted cilia at the margin. *Lactarius repraesentaneus* (2) with latex that becomes violet: it is not acrid but bitter; grows in the mountains, under conifers.

Lactarius zonarioides (Kuhner-Romagnesi) (3) also grows in the mountains, under conifers; it is quite different from *L. scrobiculatus*: less sturdy; orange or orange brown; very acrid; latex white, not changing; the corresponding species in the plains is *Lactarius zonarius*, equally **not edible**.

LACTARIUS TORMINOSUS

Cap convex, then plane, 5–12 cm, depressed at the center, and finally funnel shaped; pale creamy orange or light pinkish hazel or light flesh pink; these colors are more or less intense in alternate concentric zones; covered with long, dense hairs that gradually join in matted tufts; these tufts then stick to the cuticle of the cap and become almost indistinguishable; cuticle dry, rough; margin rolled downward, like an Ionic capital, then breaking into numerous, long, whitish, matted hairs. **Stem** slightly paler than the cap, with a darker annular zone near the gills; sometimes externally sparsely stippled with some small, superficial erosions; soon entirely eroded and hollow. **Flesh** thick; faded cream color. **Odor** of fruit. **Flavor** slightly acrid. **Latex** abundant, white; not changing in contact with air; very acrid. **Gills** very close, thin, narrow, decurrent on the stem; resistant to breakage; pale creamy rosy. **Spores** white, tinged with pink or cream. It grows in latifoliate woods, especially near birches. **Poisonous**: causes intestinal disturbance; some authors have reported cases of deadly poisoning, presumably due to ingestion of this mushroom. Similar to *L. torminosus* and equally **poisonous**, but smaller, paler, without concentric zones on the cap: *Lactarius pubescens*, sometimes almost white, and *Lactarius cilicioides*, pale ocher color, different from the *cilicioides* dealt with in the previous description.

LACTARIUS DELICIOSUS

Cap 5–15 cm, funnel shaped and with more or less explanate margin; smooth, viscid in humid weather; orange, with darker concentric zones; upon ripening becomes entirely green, starting from the darker bands; also becomes green when bruised. **Stem** cylindric, soon eroded and hollow; of the same color as the cap, covered with rosy or ochraceous scurf. **Flesh** hard, brittle, granular; white; greenish under the dark zones of the cap; pale orange at the periphery; exposed to air it becomes quickly green, but this coloring then disappears. **Latex** orange; becoming green in contact with air. **Odor** acidulous. **Flavor**: the flesh more or less acrid, the latex mild. **Gills** slightly paler than the cap; unequal; decurrent. **Spores** white or cream. It grows in coniferous woods, especially under pines and near junipers. In the variety *salmonicolor*, of pine and fir woods, it does not become green and has a mild flavor. **Edible**, of good quality: it should be cooked quickly at high flame, not stewed. Similar to *L. deliciosus*, and also **edible**: *Lactarius semisanguifluus*: cap faded cinereous ocher, speckled with greenish spots arranged radially; gills soon blue green; flesh white, becoming speckled with blood red spots when exposed to air; latex orange, then violet brown; in autumn, in pine woods. *Lactarius indigo*, rare North American species, entirely indigo colored. *Lactarius hemicyaneus*: flesh of the cap and latex blue; flavor mild.

LACTARIUS SANGUIFLUUS (2)

Cap convex, then plane, 5–12 cm, with central depression; then depressed, funnel shaped; orange vermilion; sometimes with darker concentric zones, but not distinctly outlined; becomes green upon ripening. **Stem** rather squat, firm, cylindrical or tapering toward the base; hard, fragile; stuffed with pith, but soon hollow; whitish in unripe specimens; then gradually changing to the color of the cap; often speckled with small erosions more intensely colored at the bottom. **Flesh** thick, hard, brittle, granular; white; exposed to air it becomes quickly speckled at the periphery with dense, blood red dots; in *L. semisanguifluus* this process happens slowly; then becoming vermilion and finally greenish. **Odor** of fruit. **Flavor** rather acrid. **Latex** venous blood red; exposed to air, becomes slowly purple brown. **Gills** close, decurrent on the stem; ochraceous, then rosy orange, finally violaceous; slowly changing to greenish when bruised. **Spores** pale ocher. It grows in woods, generally under conifers, but sometimes also at more than one hundred meters from them. **Edible**, of good quality; it should be cooked at high flame.

LACTARIUS HATSUDAKE (1)

It has some of the characteristics of *L. sanguifluus* and of *L. deliciosus*, but it is much bigger than either of them; grows in Japan, where it is considered of **no alimentary interest**.

LACTARIUS DELICIOSUS var. JAPONICUS (3)

Pale orange, without green spots; **edible**.

LACTARIUS VOLEMUS

Cap convex, with margin tightly rolled toward the gills, then plane, 5–15 cm, uneven, depressed, funnel shaped, with explanate and undulate margin; yellowish or orange, golden orange, reddish orange, or brownish orange; generally darker at the center; cuticle dry, not translucent; cracking with age; in the variety *oedematopus* it is smaller and browner than the typical form. **Stem** sometimes slightly swollen in the middle; hard, fragile, stuffed; slightly paler than the cap. Base whitish, then gradually darker and darker brown. **Flesh** abundant, firm, brittle, whitish; becoming brownish when exposed to air. **Odor** agreeable; that of herrings in older specimens. **Flavor** mild. **Latex** very abundant, fluid, with mild flavor and herring odor; white; exposed to air, it finally coagulates into a viscous, hazelnut colored mass. **Gills** close, thin, narrow, rather decurrent; cream, then hazel; when broken they immediately ooze a white, abundant latex; becoming brown when rubbed. **Spores** white. It grows singly, in woods. **Edible with caution**: parboiling is advisable; it should then be cooked at high flame, on the grill, not stewed; however, even when properly cooked, it sometimes retains a disagreeable laundry-soap flavor, so that some people cannot eat it.

Similar to *Lactarius volemus* are: *Lactarius corrugis*, **edible**, with the cuticle of the cap corrugated along the margin, with gills cinnamon yellow, and *Lactarius rugatus*, **edible**, of very good quality, smaller than *L. volemus* and with rugose cap.

LACTARIUS UVIDUS (1)

Cap 5–8 cm, cinereous amethystine or ocher amethystine; sometimes discolored, whitish; without real zones; viscid or glutinous; margin thin; glabrous. **Stem** cylindric, soon hollow; viscid; paler than the cap; becoming spotted with violet. **Flesh** tender; fragile; white tinged with yellowish; becoming rapidly violaceous when bruised or when exposed to air. **Odor** mild. **Flavor** acrid. **Latex** white; becoming immediately violet in contact with air; flavor mild, but soon bitter, then acrid, persistently burning. **Gills** close, thin, decurrent, pinkish white, then yellowish. **Spores** white or cream. It grows in shady, humid, or even swampy woods, especially under birches. **Not edible**.

LACTARIUS VIOLASCENS (3)

Similar to *L. uvidus* in that the flesh becomes violaceous; different from *L. uvidus* in that the cap becomes darker, not viscid, with zones near the margin; flavor only slightly acrid; growing under conifers. **Edible**: parboiling necessary.

LACTARIUS ASPIDEUS (Konrad-Maublanc) (2)

This is another of the mushrooms with flesh and latex becoming instantly violet or blue violet when exposed to air: cap 6–12 cm, yellowish, often zonate; moist; gills cream color, then yellowish; latex at first mild, then bitter-acrid-burning. **Not edible**.

LACTARIUS BLENNIUS (1)

Cap 4–10 cm, depressed at maturity; olivaceous or greenish; but pale green in the form *viridis*; rarely with concentric zones; viscous, but soon dry; margin involute, then explanate, pale, velvety, sometimes speckled with dark dots. **Stem** viscous; slightly paler than the cap; almost white at the base; spongy, then hollow. **Flesh** brittle; whitish, becoming slowly cinereous greenish when exposed to air. **Odor**less. **Flavor** mild, then acrid. **Latex** white; becoming greenish gray in contact with air; acrid. **Gills** close, thin, annexed, finally decurrent; whitish, becoming gray when bruised. **Spores** greenish white. It grows in groups under latifoliate trees, especially beeches and oaks, among dead leaves. **Not edible**.

LACTARIUS VIETUS (2)

Cap 3–8 cm, elastic, then brittle; sometimes with slight umbo; cinereous amethystine or ocher amethystine, rarely without well-outlined zones; soon dry, shining. **Stem** slender, soon hollow; paler than the cap; slightly spotted. **Flesh** thin. **Odor** mild. **Flavor** slightly acrid. **Latex** scarce; white; gray green when dry; very acrid. **Gills** close, cream, then rosy cream. **Spores** cream colored. Under birches and pines. **Not edible**: slightly toxic. Similar to it is *Lactarius impolitus* (Fries) **of no alimentary interest**, cinereous amethystine, umbonate, with tenuous zones; dry; odor of fig leaves; flavor slightly acrid; latex white, unchangeable; grows under birches.

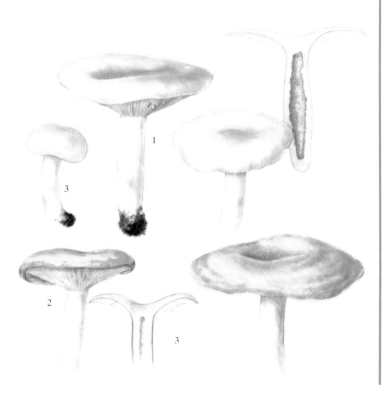

LACTARIUS PLUMBEUS

Cap convex and then plane-convex, 8–25 cm, rather depressed dark color, olive fuliginous, brownish olive, green, or brownish like the cap of *Paxillus involutus* (page 175); darker at the center, lighter at the margin, which is sometimes yellowish, always rolled toward the gills and, in unripe specimens, covered with thick, sulfur yellow velvet; the entire cap is a little velvety, viscid, or glutinous. If tested, ammonia stains it violet. **Stem** squat, hard, stuffed, then hollow; sometimes speckled with minute erosions; viscid in humid weather; slightly paler than the cap, blackish at the base. **Flesh** thick, firm; whitish, becoming slightly brownish, reddish gray, or violet gray when exposed to air. **Odor**less.

Flavor at first mild, then acrid. **Latex** white, becoming brownish in contact with air; flavor very acrid, burning. **Gills** close, decurrent on the stem; straw colored, becoming easily spotted with brownish gray; with brown edges. **Spores** cream. It grows in large groups, in late summer and in autumn, in the humid ravines of coniferous and latifoliate woods; but more frequently under birches, in peat-rich soil. **Not edible** because acrid; however, it is consumed in some regions, after special treatment, but only as an emergency food. It is easily distinguished from the green forms of *Lactarius blennius* (page 136), **not edible**, which is ordinarily smaller, with gills persistently white, and growing amid dead leaves, especially under beeches and oaks.

LACTARIUS PALLIDUS (1)

Cap plane-convex, 5–15 cm; sometimes with central umbo, sometimes slightly depressed from the beginning; then expanded and depressed, funnel-like or oddly shaped. Cream, rosy ocher, or light brown; viscid, glutinous; with slight ripples or even rugose; margin rolled toward the gills, only tardily rather explanate. **Stem** squat, cylindric, sometimes eccentric; stuffed, then hollow; moist or also viscid, especially at the base; slightly paler than the cap, **Flesh** thick, elastic; of pale cream color. **Odor** of fruit. **Flavor** slightly acrid. **Latex** rather abundant, whitish; at first of mild flavor, then slightly acrid. **Gills** close, unequal, largely annexed to the stem; whitish, with pink hues; then cream tinged with ocher. **Spores** cream. It grows in latifoliate woods, especially birch and beech. **Not advisable** although edible: even when properly cooked it is of a very poor quality.

LACTARIUS TRIVIALIS (2)

Cap 5–20 cm, violet amethystine, then later brownish or also pale ocher; viscid. Stem sometimes quite longer than that of the specimens illustrated here; violaceous white, with base yellow or yellowish and spotted with black; stuffed, but soon hollow. Latex, after few moments, very acrid; white, but, while coagulating in air, it becomes covered by a greenish pellicle. It is found amid moss in humid coniferous woods. **Not edible**.

LACTARIUS FULIGINOSUS (1)

Cap 3–11 cm, fuliginous brown to whitish; dry, furfuraceous, velvety, then glabrous; margin slightly grooved. **Stem** rugose, slightly paler than the cap, often spotted. **Flesh** whitish, in air rosy or saffron, especially at the periphery. **Latex** white, slowly changing to rosy. **Odor** of fruit. **Flavor** mild, then acrid. **Gills** annexed, then decurrent; whitish, then ochraceous pink. **Spores** fuliginous ocher. It grows under latifoliate trees, especially oaks, but under hornbeams in the variety *pterosporus*, with paler, rugose cap, and closer, more colored gills. **Not edible**.

Similar to *L. fuliginosus*, **not edible**: *Lactarius acris* (2), fuliginous, spotted with white, viscid; flesh white, then pinkish, finally brown; latex acrid, white, but, exposed to air, becoming quickly bright pink, then slowly brownish; under latifoliate trees. *Lactarius picinus* (3), from brown to blackish; the flesh, in contact with air, becomes speckled with pink and orange; latex white, acrid; grows in the mountains, under fir trees. Similar to *L. picinus* is *Lactarius lignyotus*, growing under the same conditions: even darker, rugose, umbonate, with sulcate margin; gills white or spotted with red; latex immediately brown red in contact with air; not acrid. *Lactarius pyrogalus* (4), olivaceous fuliginous to violet and faded ocher, with tenuous zones; gills sparse and thick; flesh and latex white, unchangeable; acrid; under hazelnut trees. Similar to this is *Lactarius circellatus*, violaceous brown, with distinct leaden zones; gills rather close and thin, orange; slightly acrid; growing under hornbeams.

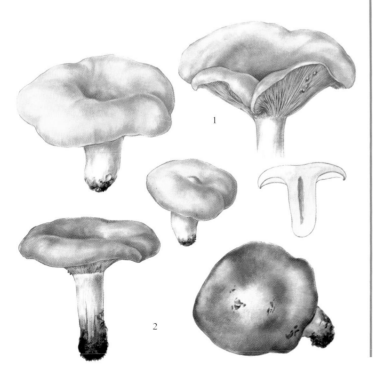

LACTARIUS RUFUS (1)

Cap campanulate, then plane, 3–10 cm, with prominent umbo at the center; reddish brown. Margin initially rolled toward the gills, pruinose and downy; then explanate and almost completely glabrous. **Stem** cylindric; reddish gray, pruinose; reddish after dissolution of the pruina; cottony at the base; firm; stuffed, but soon pithy. **Flesh** firm, brittle; reddish white, darker at the periphery and toward the base of the stem. **Odor** soft. **Flavor** very acrid. **Latex** white, unchangeable, acrid, burning. **Gills** close, narrow, decurrent; ivory color, then pale reddish ocher; covered, when ripe, with a whitish powder: the **spores** en masse. It grows under conifers. **Not edible**: in some regions it undergoes particular treatments, then is preserved in oil and consumed as a piquant seasoning.

LACTARIUS BADIOSANGUINEUS (2)

Smaller and less acrid than *L. rufus*; flesh reddish or liver red; growing in the mountains. **Not edible**. Its counterpart in the plains is *Lactarius hepaticus*, **not edible**, growing in spring and in autumn. *Lactarius acerrimus*, growing under latifoliate trees, and *Lactarius zonarioides*, growing under conifers (spruce) in the mountains, both **not edible**, are also of brown, reddish, or orange color, with unchangeable white latex, cap with concentric zones, and are very acrid.

LACTARIUS AERUMBONATUS (3)

Different from *L. rufus* only for its cap without umbo. **Not edible**.

LACTARIUS HELVUS

Cap 5–15 cm, umbonate, then depressed; ochraceous; velvety, dry; margin soon explanate and undulate. **Stem** cylindric, soon hollow; of the same color as the cap; sometimes woolly at the base. **Flesh** pallid. **Latex** watery, slightly cloudy; with odor of coconut or roasted chicory, and licorice flavor. **Gills** close, here and there bifid near the stem and decurrent on it; yellowish white, then of the same color as the cap. **Spores** white or pink. In humid recesses, under conifers. **Not edible fresh**: but dried it can be used in small amounts as seasoning. *Lactarius fuscus*, **not edible**, has aromatic odor of cinnamon: cap 3–10 cm, blackish gray, tinged with violet; latex white, unchangeable, finally acrid; grows in the mountains, under conifers.

Small and **not edible**: *Lactarius cyathula*, with watery latex as that of *L. helvus*, but slightly acrid: cap 1–3 cm, chestnut color, plane-depressed, with blackish green umbo; margin with well-outlined, long, radial striae; stem tall; grows in humid grounds, under alders. *Lactarius spinulosus*, with watery latex: cap 2–4 cm, umbonate and adorned with pyramidal flocci orderly arranged; entirely ocher amethystine, flavor at first mild, then acrid; grows on humid ground, especially under birches and elms. *Lactarius lilacinus*, very similar to *L. spinulosus* but bigger and with less prominent umbo.

helvus Lact.

LACTARIUS MITISSIMUS (Fries) or FULVISSIMUS (Romagnesi) (top)

Cap 3–6 cm, umbonate; viscid; brown, then bright orange; fading, drying out, and becoming slightly corrugated with age. **Stem** cylindric, soon hollow; of the same color as the cap. **Flesh** firm, soon soft; brittle; yellowish, becoming spotted with brown. **Odor** mild, of plant bugs. **Flavor** mild, then bitter. **Latex** scarce, white, unchangeable, with mild flavor. **Gills** close, decurrent, ochraceous cream. **Spores** cream. It grows under latifoliate or coniferous trees. **Edible**, of poor quality. Very similar to it is *Lactarius ichoratus* (Kuhner-Romagnesi), to be avoided because it is acrid; found under latifoliate trees.

LACTARIUS AURANTIACUS (Fries) or MITISSIMUS (Romagnesi) (bottom)

Similar to *Lactarius mitissimus* (Fries), grows in the mountains, under conifers; rarely in the plains and under latifoliate trees; cap orange tending to yellow; the flesh a bitterish acrid flavor; the latex bitter and throat-irritating; **edible**, of poor quality because slightly acrid even after cooking; tastier if used after exsiccation.

Similar to the two above is *Lactarius Poninsis*, **edible** only if parboiled and then further cooked: cap convex, then plane 3–8 cm, and then, sometimes, slightly depressed; margin rolled toward the gills; altogether of a shape almost geometrically regular; bright orange pink; lucid; gills close, white, then pale orange; stem cylindric, of the same color as the cap; latex white, unchangeable; growing in groups under larches.

LACTARIUS QUIETUS (1)

Cap 3–10 cm, rarely umbonate; slightly rough; brown or pale rosy brown with darker spots, arranged sometimes along the margin in tenuous, concentric zones. **Stem** rather long, firm, soon hollow; fibrillar and rugose; slightly paler than the cap, then slightly darker. **Flesh** firm, white, with rosy brown stains. **Odor** of plant bugs. **Flavor** mild. **Latex** scarce, cream colored, with mild flavor. **Gills** close, broad, bifid near the stem; decurrent; rosy cream, then brownish. **Spores** rosy white. Grows especially under oaks. **Edible**.

LACTARIUS SUBDULCIS (Fries) (2)

Cap 2–6 cm, thin; dry, smooth or pruinose, non-zonate; reddish brown. **Stem** equal, slightly paler than the cap, dark at the base. **Flesh** tender, fragile; reddish. **Odor** slightly of plant bugs. **Flavor** mild. **Latex** white, with mild flavor, then bitter or bitterish acrid. **Gills** fragile; cream, then reddish; decurrent. **Spores** white. Grows under beeches and hornbeams. **Edible**, but of little alimentary interest. It could be mistaken, without danger, for *Lactarius mitissimus* and *Lactarius aurantiacus*.

Similar to *L. subdulcis*, but more on the pink side, is *Lactarius decipiens*, with acrid latex, changing to deep yellow in few minutes, and with geranium odor; growing in dry latifoliate woods; it is **edible** only if cooked at high flame so as to dissolve the substance imparting the acrid flavor to the latex.

quietus Lact.

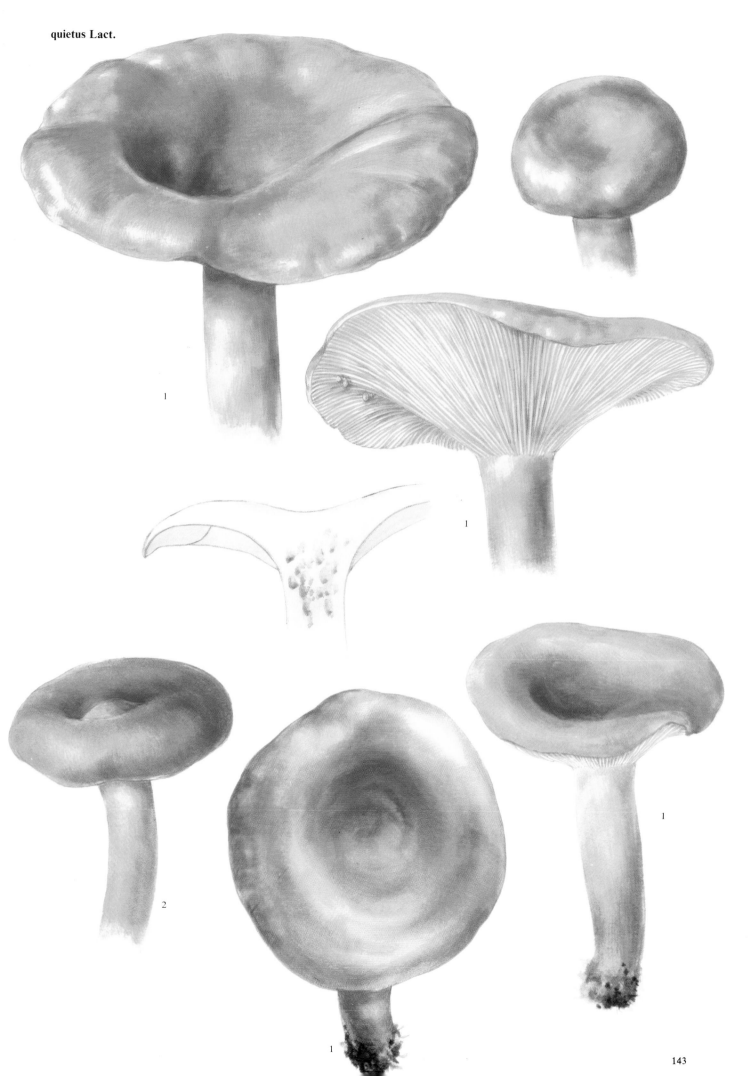

1

1

1

2

1

143

LACTARIUS CAMPHORATUS (2)

This mushroom is ordinarily small and slender; rarely somewhat big and stout (3). **Cap** deep red brown, darker at the center, lighter along the margin; becoming very discolored with age; convex, with umbo in the center; then expanded, 3–6 cm, occasionally 9 cm, and then depressed, but generally retaining the central umbo; margin rolled toward the gills, then explanate and with grooves in the direction of the gills; dry, not translucent. **Stem** stuffed, of the same color as the cap, or darker; pulverulent. **Flesh** thin, reddish; the stem darker. **Odor** of plant bugs, roasted chicory, or camphor, but light. **Flavor** mild, slightly bitterish. **Latex** somewhat abundant; faded white; sweetish flavor. **Gills** close, bifid near the stem, annexed then decurrent; slightly violaceous, then reddish, finally of the same color as the cap; covered with a cream colored powder: the **spores** en masse. It grows in groups or in tufts, even in dry seasons, from spring to late autumn, under conifers, especially pine, and under latifoliate trees, especially chestnuts and oaks. **Edible**: it is better to exsiccate it and use it as seasoning.

LACTARIUS SERIFLUUS (1)

It has the same odor as *Lactarius camphoratus*, but it looks generally sturdier: cap 4–9 cm, umbonate, sometimes paler than the dark form of *L. camphoratus*, but sepia brown in the center; stem of the same color as the cap, thick; latex scarce, watery; gills yellow; spores pinkish; growing under conifers and latifoliate trees. **Edible**, but of very poor quality.

RUSSULA DELICA (1)

Cap convex, but slightly depressed, then funnel shaped, 5–17 cm; white, then with pale ocher stains or completely pale ocher; margin rolled toward the gills, then explanate, undulate, fissured; cuticle soiled by various debris, sometimes of large size. **Stem** thick, short; white, sometimes with blue green hues on the top near the gills; then with ochraceous spots; smooth, then rugose. **Flesh** thick, firm, granular; white, becoming slowly brownish or vinous when exposed to air. **Odor** of ripe fruit or even slightly brackish. **Flavor** of the gills slightly acrid. **Gills** with numerous intermediate lamellae, somewhat thick, rather sparse; the less broad, the thicker the flesh of the cap; several bifid ones; slightly decurrent; white, then cream; sometimes with blue green hues; dewy as long as the mushroom is unripe. **Spores** white or with a cream shade. It grows in large groups, often partly buried, under conifers and latifoliate trees. **Edible**, of poor quality: it is, however, particularly sought after by woodsmen, who cook it in the woods on the grill on nonsmoking embers, seasoned with salt and a few drops of oil.

RUSSULA PSEUDODELICA (2)

Similar to *R. delica*, but with gills with rosy or yellowish hues, and odor of herrings. **Edible**.

RUSSULA CHLOROIDES (3)

Similar to *R. delica*, but with closer, narrow, thin, gills; **edible**. The absence of latex is sufficient to distinguish these russulas from the white Lactarii *piperatus* (page 130), *vellereus* (page 129) and *controversus* (page 131), all not advisable for eating.

RUSSULA NIGRICANS (1)

Cap convex, then plane, 7–20 cm, often also depressed and funnel shaped; white or whitish, then brownish gray or fuliginous gray, finally blackish; margin thick, turned toward the gills, smooth, remaining white longer than the rest of the cap; cuticle dry, slightly velvety in dry weather and often cracked. **Stem** short, thick; white, then gradually more and more gray and blackish; stuffed, then pithy. **Flesh** hard, very fragile; whitish; when bruised or broken or cut, it becomes blood red in few minutes, then blackish. Any part of the mushroom, when bruised or broken, changes color just as the flesh does. **Odor** soft, of fruit. **Flavor** mild; but the gills are slightly acrid. **Gills** distant from one another, unequal, very thick, with interspaced intermediate gills; fragile; adhering to the stem; whitish or faded yellow; then becoming brownish and finally black, starting from the edge and the exterior part. **Spores** white. It grows in woods. **Edible**, of poor quality.

RUSSULA DENSIFOLIA (2)

Similar to *R. nigricans*: cap 5–16 cm, fuliginous with blue green or olivaceous shades; gills very close, thin, narrow, slightly decurrent, white with blue green hues and gray or reddish spots; slightly acrid; every part of this mushroom becomes first reddish, then blackish; **edible**, of very poor quality. Very similar to *Russula densifolia*, and equally **edible**, of poor quality, is the mushroom classified by Heim as *Russula densifolia* variety *densissima*, with milky white cap, sometimes tinged with ochraceous shades.

RUSSULA LEPIDA (1)
Cap hemispheric, then plane 4–12 cm; red, sometimes vermilion, sometimes carmine; it can fade and become yellowish or even whitish, although retaining some red spots, especially near the margin; in the variety *lactea* (2) it is white; not translucent; it looks as if made of painted plaster; to the touch the cuticle feels as if of suede, dry; it is difficult to separate it from the cap; it cracks with age, but the margin is seldom fissured. **Stem** hard but brittle; sometimes white, often tinged, at least partly, with pink and reddish color. **Flesh** thick and very hard, as of unripe apples; but brittle, granular; white. **Odor** of pencil made of cedar wood; cooked it smells of lye. **Flavor** of the gills bitterish; flavor of the rest of the mushroom, first mild, then slightly resinous, acrid or bitterish; very bitter in the variety *amarissima*. **Gills** close, especially in unripe specimens; fragile, milky white, with cream or blue green hues, and sometimes with the edges pink near the margin of the cap. **Spores** creamy white. It grows in coniferous or latifoliate woods, especially oak and beech. **Edible**, of poor quality; parboiling necessary; it is, however, sought after and preserved in oil, after boiling in water and aromatic vinegar. Similar to this mushroom: *Russula aurora*, **edible**, better than *R. lepida*, rosy, with white and flocculose stem; and *Russula Linnaei*, **not advisable**, characterized by the reddish stem.

RUSSULA ALBONIGRA (2, with section at center left)
Cap convex, then plane 7–14 cm, finally concave or also funnel shaped; white, then gray, then blackish gray; paler along the margin; cuticle smooth, not lucid; margin involute toward the gills, smooth. **Stem** short, stout; white, then brownish gray and blackish. **Flesh** hard, brittle; white, exposed to air it becomes blackish in a few minutes and black as charcoal in half an hour. Any part of this mushroom, when bruised, changes its color the same way as the flesh does. **Odor** soft. **Flavor** slightly acrid. **Gills** close, unequal, now and then bifurcate; slightly decurrent; white or pale cream, then blackish gray. **Spores** white. It grows especially in beech woods. **Edible**, of poor quality.

RUSSULA ADUSTA (1, with section at bottom right)
Similar to *R. albonigra*, sometimes quite larger, 7–24 cm, fuliginous brown, slightly viscid; the flesh, exposed to air, does not become black but rosy, and then very slowly fuliginous brown; **edible**, of poor quality.

Note: *Russula albonigra*: cap white, then blackish; gills close; flesh white, rapidly blackish, after half an hour black. *Russula adusta*: cap fuliginous; gills close; flesh white; slowly pink, then fuliginous. *Russula nigricans* (page 145): cap white, then blackish; gills sparse; flesh white, rapidly red, then blackish. *Russula densifolia·* cap fuliginous; gills close; flesh white, then reddish, finally blackish. *Russula densissima*: cap milky white; gills close; flesh white, then reddish, finally blackish.

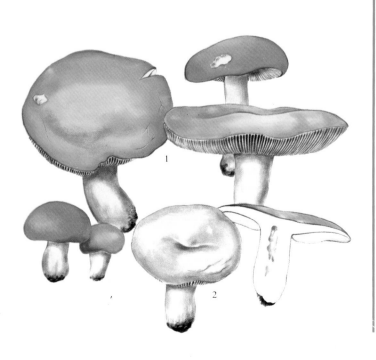

albonigra Russ.

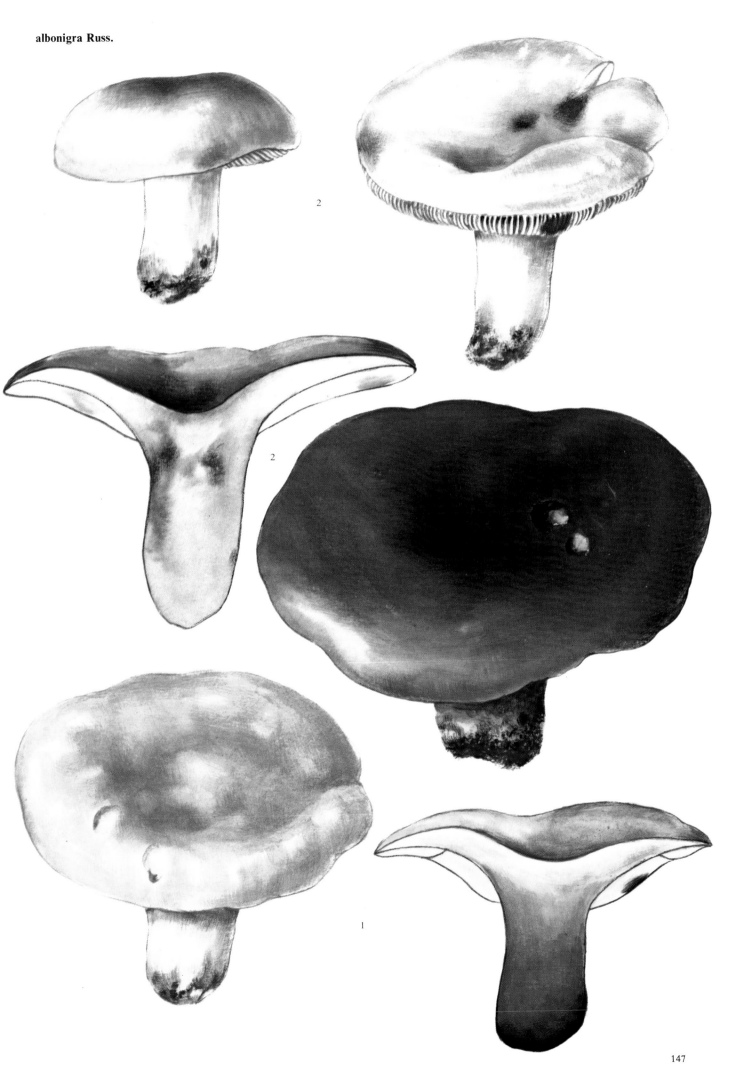

2

2

1

RUSSULA CYANOXANTHA

Cap 5–15 cm, often depressed; black violet, blue violet, gray violet, coeruleous gray, or slate gray, amaranth black or green black; in the variety *Peltereaui* (bottom left) is, from the beginning, olive green or yellowish green; with pigeon-neck hues; cuticle soon dry, with radiating fibrils, then with radiating wrinkles; margin tardily striate. **Stem** white, then tinged with gray or violet; often with brownish spots; rugose, somewhat elastic. **Flesh** rather elastic; white; pinkish or amethystine under the cuticle; slowly changing to cinereous when exposed to air. **Odor** soft. **Flavor** agreeable; but slightly acrid after mastication in the variety *variata*. **Gills** somewhat thick, rather close, broad; numerous bifid ones; connected by fine veins; annexed to the stem; lardaceous, elastic, not brittle; white with blue green or bluish hues. **Spores** snow white. It grows in woods. **Edible**, excellent. Similar to it and equally **edible**: *Russula grisea*, cap 5–10 cm, of the same color as *cyanoxantha*, more often amethystine gray, sometimes paler in the center; but with gills tinted with lemon yellow, brittle; grows under birches. *Russula grisea* variety *ionochlora*, cap 5–10 cm, violet gray, but olivaceous in the center; gills yellowish; slightly acrid when unripe; grows under latifoliate trees. *Russula brunneo-violacea*, cap 3–9 cm, dark violet brown color due to a dense, adhering bloom, sometimes with yellow spots; decorticable; stem with yellowish shades; gills white, then cream; grows especially under oaks and beeches.

RUSSULA HETEROPHYLLA

Cap convex, then depressed, 5–12 cm; cuticle smooth and shining or rugose and velvety, except at the center; gelatinous in humid weather; not easily separable from the cap; cracked in dry weather; margin smooth, striate only at a late stage; bright green, olive green, or yellow green; but gray green in the variety *livida*; greenish gray with white center in the variety *galochroa*; white and then hazel in the variety *virginea*; often with more deeply colored center. **Stem** cylindric, often tapering toward the base; striate or reticulate; white, then brownish starting from the base. **Flesh** firm, somewhat elastic, white. **Odor** soft. **Flavor** mild. **Gills** very close until almost fully ripe; thin, narrow, especially toward the stem, where they join together irregularly and on which they are decurrent through fine veins; snow white, sometimes with blue green shades; then with rusty or fuliginous spots; with yellow spots in the variety *livida*. It grows under conifers, but especially under latifoliate trees; the variety *galochroa*; under birches; the variety *virginea* grows under oaks and beeches. **Edible**, of good quality. *Russula heterophylla* differs from *Russula vesca*, **edible**, primarily for the color; from *Russula aeruginea* (page 152), **edible**, because in the latter the ripe gills are yellowish and the spores cream; and from *Russula virescens* (page 149), also **edible**, primarily because the latter's cuticle is dry and cracks in many characteristic polygonal squamules.

RUSSULA VIRESCENS

Cap spheroid, then more or less expanded, 5–12 cm, sometimes slightly depressed, sometimes somewhat knobby; margin undulate, smooth, seldom with tenuous radial grooves; cuticle separable only along the margin; white, with small, sandy farinaceous spots tending to hazel or greenish; then the cuticle, which has thickened, cracks into many polygonal spots, which gradually move away from each other, becoming green, yellowish green, olivaceous green, or gray green; in between these spots the background appears, yellowish, but gray green in the center; then everything tends to discolor, though not uniformly. **Stem** stout, furfuraceous, then slightly rugose; white, then with a slight hazel shade. **Flesh** firm; white, then with pink or reddish hues; greenish under the cuticle. **Odor** agreeable, then slightly disgusting, of cheese. **Flavor** pleasant. **Gills** somewhat close, brittle, white or pale cream, with rosy cream shades, often with brown or reddish spots. **Spores** white tending to pale cream. It grows in groups, from spring to autumn, especially in birch, oak, and chestnut woods, in the grass. **Edible**, of good quality, either cooked or raw, seasoned with lemon juice, olive oil, salt and pepper. Another species of *Russula* with a fragmented cuticle is *R. cutefracta*, which, besides being green and olivaceous, can be violaceous; paler lines, generally reddish as the flesh immediately under the cuticle, form a gratelike pattern on the fragmented cuticle. This *Russula* is **edible**.

vesca Russ.

RUSSULA VESCA

Cap first convex, then more or less depressed, 5–11 cm; cuticle slightly rugose, often retracted from the margin, so that the extreme end of the gills is uncovered; decorticable up to half radius; margin smooth or slightly striate in the direction of the gills; the typical color of the cap is ochraceous brown or amaranth brown, deeper in the center, sometimes with violaceous or greenish spots, but it can also be hazel or gray green colored, paler in the center and with rosy zones along the margin, or faded pink with yellowish spots; it is never pure red or pure violet; it discolors with age. **Stem** cylindric, often pointed at the base; white, then yellowish; brownish at the base; firm, stuffed, then spongy and infested by larvae. **Flesh** thick, firm, when healthy; white, then with yellowish shades; slightly colored under the cuticle of the cap; the flesh of the stem tends to become spotted with brownish. **Odor** irrelevant. **Flavor** characteristic, of hazelnuts. **Gills** close, here and there bifid, almost decurrent; white, often with rosy brown edges; then slightly cream, speckled with rusty dots due to dried droplets of lymph; not very elastic. **Spores** white. Grows under latifoliate trees, in the plains; seldom in the mountains, under conifers. **Edible**, of good quality. This *russula* is distinguishable from the **edible**: *heterophylla* (page 148), primarily in the color, and *cyanoxantha* (page 148), because the gills of the latter are lardy and elastic.

RUSSULA AMOENA (Quelet) (1)

Cap 2–8 cm, often depressed; from amethystine to violet or to olive green or with olive green zones; soon dry, farinaceous, with dark granules; smooth margin. **Stem** slightly paler than the cap, furfuraceous. In the variety *citrina* (2, the smaller specimen, upside down) the cap is yellow and the stem is white; in the variety *violeipes* (3) the cap is either yellow or green and the stem is violaceous. **Flesh** white. **Odor** of cooked shrimps. **Flavor** mild. **Gills** thin, white, then cream, with violaceous edges; then ochraceous cream. **Spores** cream. It grows especially under conifers. **Edible**.
The following edible species are similar to *Russula amoena*: *Russula azurea* (Bresadola): cap violaceous, cloudy violet, violet brown, violet gray, blue violet, light blue with spots sometimes darker, sometimes lighter; margin only tardily striate; cuticle soon dry, rough, thin, separable; stem white; gills broad, unchangingly milky white like the spores. *Russula lilacea* (Quelet): cap rosy violet or dark brown red; stem reddish or white with reddish flocci; spores yellowish; grows especially under oaks, beeches, and hazelnuts; to be distinguished from *Russula firmula*, **not edible**, very acrid, cap purple violet, gills and spores egg-yolk yellow; growing in latifoliate and coniferous woods.

RUSSULA XERAMPELINA

Cap and **stem**: when the mushroom grows under conifers, especially pines and spruces, the cap is blood red, with darker center, almost black; and the stem is pink or reddish rosy (variety *erythropus*, 1). When it grows under latifoliate trees, the cap is olivaceous or olivaceous yellow, darker in the center; the stem is white but veiled by a color the same as the cap's (variety *olivascens*, 2); or the cap can be brown or violaceous brown, darker in the center, with the stem white, but veiled by a color the same as the cap's (variety *fusca*, 3). **Cap** hemispheric, sometimes somewhat knobby; then expanded, 8–15 cm, and sometimes also slightly depressed in the center; margin ordinarily even; seldom slightly striate in the direction of the gills; cuticle not easily separable from the cap. **Stem** sometimes thickened at the base, sometimes rather curved; marked by fine veins or fine reticule. **Flesh** firm, whitish or slightly yellowish; becoming brownish when bruised or with age, especially that of the stem. **Odor** of cooked shrimps, stronger after picking. **Flavor** of hazelnuts. **Gills** not too close, broad, rather unequal, often bifid; fragile; first whitish, then cream or pale yellow; hazel color only in older specimens. **Spores** pale ocher. **Edible**. Similar to *R. xerampelina* is *Russula Barlae*, **edible**, rusty orange or green. *Russula xerampelina* grows together with *Russula sardonia* (page 158), **not edible**, characterized by a very acrid flavor.

RUSSULA AERUGINEA

Cap hemispheric, but soon plane 5–10 cm, depressed in the center; pale green, grass green, or olive green, more intense in the center; faded in the margin; sometimes speckled with rusty spots; margin smooth, then slightly sulcate in the direction of the gills; cuticle smooth, slightly viscid, separable almost up to the center. **Stem** sometimes somewhat thick and unequal; white, then spotted with brown, starting from the base. **Flesh** white, tending to become cinereous. **Odor** slight or none. **Flavor**: the gills slightly acrid, especially in unripe specimens, then becoming mild. **Gills** first close, then somewhat apart; bifid, rounded toward the stem and sometimes slightly decurrent; elastic; pallid, then cream yellowish, with few brownish spots. **Spores** cream. It grows under birches, pines, and spruces. **Edible**, of poor quality. Similar to *R. aeruginea*, but paler and smaller is *Russula smaragdina*, **edible**, of poor quality: cap 2–5 cm, very fragile, with striate margin, lemon yellow tending to green or olivaceous; flesh of the stem cinereous; flavor mild; some authors consider it a dwarf form of *R. aeruginea*. Also similar to *R. aeruginea* is *Russula parazurea*, **edible**: cap 4–7 cm, dark blue green, dark olivaceous green, or blue gray, sometimes reddish in the center; decorticable; stem white; gills white; odor mild of cheese; flavor mild; growing especially under latifoliate trees.

RUSSULA OLIVACEA (Fries)

Cap hemispheric or also almost spherical, then expanded, 7–20 cm, and depressed; purple red, olivaceous brown, olivaceous or yellowish; cuticle viscid in humid weather; not separable from the cap; pulveraceous in dry weather and then concentrically corrugate and cracked; margin not striate. **Stem** white, sometimes with some red spots; not rugose. **Flesh** white. **Odor** imperceptible. **Flavor** of hazelnuts. **Gills** not too close, thick, broad, brittle; for long time yellowish with lemon yellow edges; then darker. **Spores** ocher. It grows in latifoliate and coniferous woods. **Edible**, of good quality. It is similar to the following russulas, also **edible**: *Russula alutacea* (page 155), which, however, has the cuticle separable from the cap up to almost half the radius, the margin of the cap striate, gradually better and better outlined until wrinkled in knobby grooves, with gills brownish ocher, that is, darker than those of *olivacea*; *Russula xerampelina* (page 152), which however is different for the cap, red, when growing under conifers, and olivaceous green when growing under latifoliate trees, and with even margin, with characteristic odor of cooked shrimps and spores of lighter color than those of *olivacea*; *Russula Romellii* (page 154) with gills broader than those of *olivacea*, and very fragile.

RUSSULA CAERULEA (1)

Cap conical, then plane 3–10 cm, also depressed, always umbonate; violet or violaceous, with indigo colored spots; margin thin, even, then with short grooves; cuticle separable, viscid in humid weather; glossy in dry weather. **Stem** slender; white, then here and there grayish or brownish. **Flesh** firm, white. **Odor** mild. **Flavor** mild, if peeled; the cuticle of the cap is bitterish. **Gills** close, narrow toward the stem, broad toward the margin; thin; faded yellow, then yellowish. **Spores** faded yellow. It grows in grassy places of pine woods. **Not edible**: bitter, acrid, and tough even if well cooked.

RUSSULA TURCI (2)

Similar to *R. caerulea* but paler; becoming yellowish with age, at first in spots, then entirely; cuticle velvety in dry weather, viscid in humid weather, especially in the central depression; flesh thin, white; base of the stem with walnut-husk odor; flavor pleasant; gills close, but soon apart, thick, cream color, then ochraceous yellow; spores light ocher; growing under firs and pines; **edible**. *Russula amethystina*, **edible**, differs from *R. Turci* for the yellow spots that speckle its cap. *Russulae* similar to those above: *Russula nauseosa* variety *laricina*, **edible**, violaceous, gibbous, fragile, mild flavor, found under larches; *Russula firmula*, **not edible** because very acrid, with violet cap and egg-yolk yellow spores; growing especially under firs.

RUSSULA INTEGRA (2)

Cap 5–15 cm, smooth; soon concave, with sulcate and undulate margin; cuticle separable, viscid in humid weather, sericeous in dry weather; color basically brown but tending to green, amaranth, violet, chestnut brown, or purple; never red or orange. **Stem** long, thick, white, smooth; then slightly rugose and with brownish shades. **Flesh** firm, then soft; white, then yellowish. **Odor** soft of honey in ripe mushrooms. **Flavor** of hazelnuts. **Gills** close, then somewhat apart; broad, thick, here and there bifurcate; not always adhering to the stem; white, then yellowish, with the edges appearing white when seen at an angle. **Spores** yellow. It grows in the mountains, under conifers; is rare in the plains. **Edible**, of good quality. Quite different from *R. integra* is *R. pseudointegra*, **edible**: cap 7–14 cm, bright red or rosy, which becomes discolored and speckled with flocci; gills ochraceous; odor of laudanum, flavor bitterish of wild mint; growing especially under oaks.

RUSSULA ROMELLI (1)

The picture used here is that of a specimen of modest size; but this mushroom can reach a quite large size: cap 7–20 cm, red, tending to violet along the margin, and to green toward the center; margin striate and then sulcate; cuticle smooth and lucid, viscid in humid weather, separable; gills broad, brittle; growing under latifoliate trees; **edible**.

RUSSULA ALUTACEA (Fries)

Cap hemispheric, then expanded 7–20 cm, and also depressed; purple red with olivaceous or yellowish spots, or olivaceous yellow, green, brown, or leather brown; tends to fade until it becomes almost white; the cuticle is viscid and separable from the cap almost up to half the radius; margin marked radially by striae and then by knobby grooves. **Stem** more or less extensively rosy or reddish, on a white background; seldom without any trace of red; somewhat rugose. **Flesh** white. **Odor** imperceptible. **Flavor** mild. **Gills** not too close, rather thick and broad; yellow ocher almost from the beginning and then leather color; sometimes with the edges reddish near the margin of the cap. **Spores** ocher. It grows in latifoliate and coniferous woods. **Edible**, of good quality. The striae, the grooves of the cap's margin and the separable cuticle are sufficient to distinguish it from *R. olivacea* (page 153). *Russula integra,* **edible** of good quality, has also a striate cap's margin and a cuticle easily separable and viscid but soon dry and sericeous; moreover it is smaller, 5–12 cm, than *alutacea*; the color is more often cocoa brown, the stem white, then ochraceous; and it grows almost exclusively in the mountains. *Russula Velenovskyi,* **edible**, is much smaller than *R. alutacea*: cap 3–8 cm, brick brown or violaceous brown, but yellow ocher in the center, velvety and granular; grows under beeches and birches.

RUSSULA AURATA

Cap convex, then plane 4–9 cm, and sometimes slightly concave; bright red, orange red, or leather red; often with golden yellow or lemon yellow zones; rarely entirely lemon yellow or golden yellow; margin even; slightly sulcate in the direction of the gills only in the very old specimens; cuticle separable only along the cap's margin. **Stem** often somewhat unequal; white; yellowish at the base and sometimes sparsely spotted. **Flesh** rather firm, but fragile; white; yellowish under the cap's cuticle. **Odor** soft. **Flavor** mild. **Gills** sometimes more, sometimes less close, often connected together by fine veins; creamy white color; with lemon yellow or golden yellow edges; this color is more easily noticeable along the cap's margin. **Spores** light yellow. It grows toward the end of spring and in the summer, in humid places of latifoliate woods. **Edible**, of good quality, cooked fresh: to be cooked at high heat, not stewed.

Bigger than *R. aurata* is *Russula melliolens,* **edible**, of good quality, characterized by an unmistakable honey smell, either when fresh or dried: cap 6–15 cm, bright red or purple red or also deep pink; ripe gills yellow; stem white with rosy spots; flesh white with brownish spots; under latifoliate trees. *Russula obscura,* **edible**, cap 6–12 cm, dark red or violaceous red or vinous red; flesh and gills' edges become blackish; growing on humid grounds, under conifers.

RUSSULA LUTEA (1)

Cap thin and fragile; convex, then plane 2–6 cm, and also depressed; cuticle totally separable even with a single pull; viscid in humid weather, lucid in dry weather; margin even, then slightly striate radially; narcissus yellow or ochraceous yellow, sometimes deeper in the center. **Stem** thin and slender, slightly rugose; fragile, white. **Flesh** thin, brittle, white. **Odor** imperceptible. **Flavor** acidulous. **Gills** more or less close, thin, equal, connected by minute veins; fragile; cream colored, then the same color as the cap's. **Spores** yellow slightly ochraceous. It grows in woods. **Edible**, delicate; cooks very fast.

RUSSULA CHAMAELEONTINA (2, 3)

Small and fragile as the previous species, but of more varied colors; yellow, ochraceous yellow, orange, pink, or cherry red; often yellowish in the center and pink along the margin; soon with radially silcate margin. Gills somewhat apart, yellow. Flesh odorless when fresh, then with odor of roses; with vinegar odor in the variety *vitellina*; always odorless in the variety *ochracea*. It grows especially in coniferous woods; **edible**. Similar to *R. chamaeleontina* is *Russula nauseosa*, also called *Russula venosa* subspecies *nauseosa*, **edible**: cap violaceous, greenish, yellowish, with brown center, almost totally decorticable; stem white; gills yellow; flavor of the gills slightly piquant; grows in the mountains, under conifers, from spring to autumn.

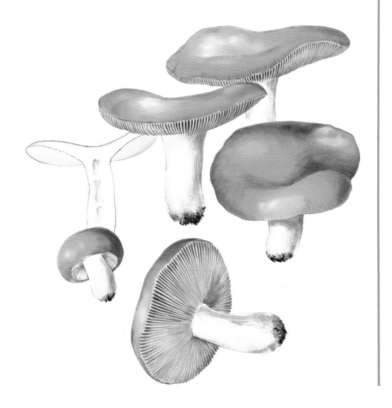

RUSSULA ATROPURPUREA

Cap convex, then plane, 5–15 cm, or depressed; dark purple, but almost black in the center; sometimes strawberry red or brick brown; faded, almost amethystine in the variety *depallens*, found in humid places; with lighter spots, vinous or brownish; margin paler and not striate; cuticle viscid in humid weather, shining in dry weather, only partly separable. **Stem** thick, squat, cracked, squamose; white, then grayish, but brownish at the base; stuffed, then hollow. **Flesh** firm, fragile, white. **Odor** mild. **Flavor** of the unripe specimens slightly acrid, otherwise mild. **Gills** broad, sometimes bifid, white with cream hues. **Spores** snow white. It grows under conifers, but especially under oaks. **Not edible.** Similar to *R. atropurpurea* and also **not edible**: *Russula atro-*

rubens, cap 4–8 cm, dark red or blood red, almost black at the center; cuticle separable, stem white, but reddish or rosy at the base or along one side; gills narrow; flesh fragile, red under the cuticle, acrid; grows in sandy woods. *Russula aquosa*: cap 4–9 cm, violaceous pink, with darker violaceous center; cuticle separable; flesh brittle with odor of radish and with acrid flavor; under conifers. *Russula maculata*, cap 4–10 cm, deep red and here and there yellow, speckled with more deeply colored dots; then turning to yellowish while the dots become rusty; viscid and lucid in humid weather, opaque in dry weather; margin even; stem short, hard, white; gills ochraceous; odor of apples, roses, or cedarwood; flavor mild, then very acrid; grows under beeches.

RUSSULA SANGUINEA

Cap convex, then plane 4–10 cm, or also slightly depressed in the center; margin even, only tardily radially striate; cuticle not separable from the cap, dry; viscid and glossy only in humid weather; blood red, tomato red, pinkish red, or rosy; fading with age until it becomes totally or at least partly white. In the variety *exalbicans* (center) the cap is violet red or rosy with yellowish center, but becomes rapidly and totally discolored to cinereous and then whitish except at the margin; also the flesh becomes cinereous. **Stem** thick, tall, slightly rugose, elastic, soon hollow; rosy red or rosy, rarely white; becoming yellowish and then hazel with age. **Flesh** white, firm, fragile. **Odor** mild of fruit. **Flavor** now distinctly acrid, now only slightly pungent or bitterish. **Gills** narrow, soon apart; almost always somewhat decurrent on the stem; white, but soon cream, then ochraceous; in the variety *pseudorosacea* the gills do not adhere to the stem and, when bruised, become yellow as does the flesh. **Spores** pale ochraceous. It grows in late summer and in autumn, under conifers, especially pines. **Not edible**: becomes bitter by cooking. It is similar to the following, **not edible** species: *Russula atropurpurea* (page 157), which has, however, a thicker white stem; *Russula emetica* (page 160), viscid, shining, decorticable, with white gills and stem; *Russula badia* (page 160), which has, however, the odor of cedarwood.

RUSSULA SARDONIA (1)

Cap umbonate or campanulate, then expanded, 5–10 cm, and also depressed; violet, purple violet, purple red, brown red, or violaceous brown; sometimes totally or partly green or yellowish; with age it becomes a faded olivaceous color; cuticle separable only along the margin; margin involute, then explanate, smooth, tardily with radial striae. **Stem** often slightly swollen in the middle; the color of the cap but a little subdued by the grayish particles that cover it; seldom totally or partly white. **Flesh** firm, then soft; white, slightly colored under the cap's cuticle. **Odor** slightly of fruit. **Flavor** acrid. **Gills** close, then more sparse; narrow, cream color or yellow from the beginning. **Spores** pallid ochraceous. It grows in pine woods, in the plains. **Not edible**: it loses the acrid flavor but becomes bitter in cooking.

RUSSULA QUELETII (2)

Very similar to *Russula sardonia* but smaller and more tender; grows rarely in the plains, frequently in the mountains, under spruces: cuticle moist, then dry and opaque; margin of the cap soon marked with radial grooves; stem more or less deeply violaceous; gills free or almost free from the stem, white, then cream, without yellow iridescence; odor of geranium or fruit, and acrid flavor; spores cream; **not edible**. Very similar to *R. Queletii* is *Russula torulosa*, which, as the *sardonia*, grows in pine woods, in the plains; **edible** only when of mild flavor; often, in fact, is acrid.

sardonia Russ.

159

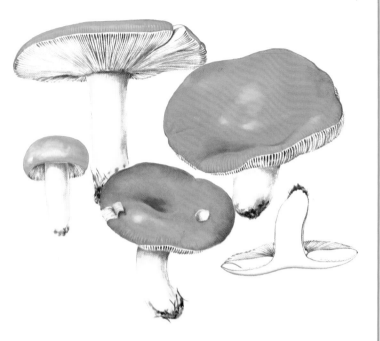

RUSSULA EMETICA

Cap 3–11 cm, carmine red, seldom pinkish, yellowish, or whitish; it discolors easily; margin paler, smooth, but with radial grooves in the older specimens; cuticle smooth, slightly viscid, separable. **Stem** thick, hard, smooth, white; stuffed, then somewhat hollow. **Flesh** rather brittle in the typical form; more resistant in the other forms; often watery, whitish, slightly reddish under the cuticle. **Odor** varied, depending on the different varieties. **Flavor** first mild but soon acrid and persistently hot. **Gills** rather sparse in the typical form, closer in the other forms; free or almost free from the stem; white, often with greenish or yellowish shades. **Spores** snow white. It grows on sandy and humid grounds, in woods, in the moss, but also in swampy ground or soil deposited on rotting stumps. **Not edible**; however, it is possible to use it, mixed in small quantities with other mushrooms, as a hot seasoning. Generally smaller than *R. emetica* is *Russula Mairei*, **not edible**: cuticle velvety, dry, not too separarable; flesh less brittle, rosy just under the cuticle. In the variety *silvestris*, **not edible**, *Russula emetica* reaches a more modest size, 3–5 cm; and in the variety *betularum*, **not edible**, growing under birches, is of a more varied but generally deeper and darker color. *Russula venosa*, **edible**, can be distinguished from the latter because it has ochraceous, not white gills, and mild, not acrid, flavor.

RUSSULA BADIA

Cap 5–12 cm, thin, now depressed, now umbonate; cherry red, brownish, amaranth; lighter at the margin; almost black at the center; often with lighter spots; cuticle first viscid, then dry; separable; margin tardily with radial grooves. **Stem** rugose; white, often with pinkish or amethystine stains. **Flesh** white. **Odor** of the gills: of cedarwood. **Flavor** mild, then unbearably hot. **Gills** somewhat close, fragile; yellowish, then slightly ochraceous, sometimes with paler edges, and with reddish iridescence toward the cap's margin. **Spores** light ocher. It grows in coniferous woods, especially pine and fir woods, in sandy grounds; more frequent in the mountains. **Not edible**.

Also growing under conifers, mostly red, but only slightly acrid: *Russula paludosa*, **edible**, of good quality; cap hemispheric, then convex or also depressed, 4–14 cm; bright red or strawberry red or orange; for long time viscid and with even margin; decorticable almost up to the center; stem cylindric or fusiform, long, white with pink spots, stuffed, then spongy; flesh white, odorless, slightly acrid; gills yellowish; spores deep cream; grows in swampy grounds. *Russula viscida*, **edible**, of poor quality: cap 5–13 cm, dark brown red, wine red, or amaranth, with lentiform ochraceous spots, viscid; stem thick, rugose, yellowish, hard then flaccid; gills narrow, close, ivory white; flesh white, finally brownish; flavor slightly acrid; grows in the mountains, in fir woods.

RUSSULA FRAGILIS (1)

Cap 3–7 cm, now depressed, now with slight umbo; now red, wine red, dark red, or violet; now carmine or pinkish with almost black center; now brown or olivaceous; sometimes with lighter or coeruleous spots; sometimes white; however colored, it soon fades; margin radially sulcate; cuticle moist, separable. **Stem** white, it tends to grow yellow; without any trace of red. **Flesh** tender, fragile, white, also under the cuticle. **Odor** of apples. **Flavor** acrid, then mild. **Gills** close, then sparse; thin, fragile; white, then cream. **Spores** white. It grows in woods, especially humid and shady ones, on the ground, in the moss, or on decayed stumps. **Not edible**.

RUSSULA VIOLACEA (2)

Similar to the previous one, but with violet cap, becoming discolored, with whitish spots; margin radially striate from the beginning; stem hollow, white, but yellow at the base; spores cream; grows in the clearings of pine woods, in autumn. **Not edible**, because even after proper cooking it is still very acrid.

RUSSULA PUELLARIS (3)

Similar to the previous one in shape, but with the cap viscid, ochraceous, purple brown, scarlet red, or violaceous red, darker at the center; margin turned downward, soon discolored and with knobby grooves; stem with yellow spots; flesh firm, white, soon soft and yellow; becomes yellow also when bruised; odor and flavor mild; gills yellowish with golden shades; spores yellowish; grows in groups in the moss, especially under pines, birches, and alders. **Edible**.

RUSSULA FELLEA

Cap globular, then convex, finally plane 4–9 cm, or also depressed; margin thin, almost always with radial striae and then with knotty grooves; cuticle viscid, not easily separable from the cap; uniformly ocher, more or less intense. **Stem** generally thick; pallid, then yellowish; then, starting from the base, it becomes ochraceous. **Flesh** cream, then ocher. **Odor** sweetish. **Flavor** very acrid and bitter. **Gills** close also in the ripe mushroom; thin; pointed toward the stem, rounded toward the cap's margin; with some dewy droplets hanging from the edges; white, then acquiring slowly the color of the cap. **Spores** white or tending to cream. It grows in woods, especially under beeches and also under solitary beech trees. **Not edible.** The beautiful *Russula solaris* also grows under beeches; **not edible**, smaller than *R. fellea*, cap 3–5 cm, chrome yellow, with yellowish margin; scented, piquant like mustard. Also very acrid and **not edible**: *Russula foetens* (page 164), cap 5–10 cm, ochraceous, margin with bumpy grooves; not only acrid but also bitter and fetid. *Russula farinipes*, cap 4–7 cm, ochraceous; stem farinaceous; odor of fruit, but flavor very pungent and bitter. *Russula ochroleuca* (page 163), cap 4–10 cm, yellow or slightly ochraceous, viscid; even margin. *Russula consobrina*, cap 3–9 cm, fuliginous; even margin; odor of fruit, flavor very pungent; grows under conifers. The *Russula consobrina*, *farinipes*, and *foetens* belong, as does *R. laurocerasi* (page 164), to the group of "fetid" russulas, to which either *fellea* or *ochroleuca* does not belong.

RUSSULA OCHROLEUCA (1)

Cap 4–10 cm, slightly depressed, ocher tending to yellow, red, or olivaceous, often brown in the center; moist; sometimes strewn with brown granules; margin somewhat undulate, always slightly involute, smooth, then channeled. **Stem** white, often spotted. **Flesh** white. **Odor** mild. **Flavor** mild or acrid. **Gills** broad, cream colored. **Spores** white or whitish. It grows especially under pines. **Not edible**, at least when it is acrid. In the variety *citrina* (3) the cap is clearly yellow and the flesh immediately under the cuticle is yellowish.

RUSSULA DECOLORANS (2)

Cap 5–15 cm, soon dry; decorticable; margin even, then sulcate; orange tending to yellow or to red; then grayish, finally blackish. **Stem** sometimes thick; rugose; white, then grayish. **Flesh** tender, white, then gray, finally blackish. **Odor** and **flavor** mild. **Gills** rather close, bifurcate near the stem, to which they adhere little or not at all; white, finally grayish. **Spores** ochraceous white. It grows in autumn, in the mountains, especially in fir woods. The cap discolors and the flesh becomes cinereous also in the following **edible** russulas: *paludosa*, cap dark red, with ochraceous spots, viscid, decorticable; growing in autumn, in humid ground, under conifers; *claroflava*, cap chrome yellow, stem white, flavor mild, growing under birches; *punctata* (Krombholz), cap violaceous red, but initially with small, white spots at the margin; growing under conifers.

ochroleuca Russ.

RUSSULA FOETENS

Cap globose, then expanded 6–24 cm; finally more or less depressed; color ocher yellow, sometimes tending slightly to gray; darker in the center; fading with age; margin thin, from the beginning sulcate in the direction of the gills; then becoming undulate and fissured in the direction of the gills, while the grooves become gradually more prominent and knobby; cuticle viscid, separable from the cap only along the margin. **Stem** stout; white, then spotted with brownish, starting from the base; stuffed, then hollow and fragile; the stem's cavity is filled with brownish pith. **Flesh** white, then brownish; brittle. **Odor** fetid. **Flavor** of the gills acrid and nauseating; the flavor of the stem sometimes mild. **Gills** somewhat apart, narrow and thick, unequal; here and there bifid; connected together by minute veins; whitish, then cream or yellowish, with brown or reddish brown spots; dewy in humid weather in the unripe specimens. **Spores** pale cream. It grows in summer and early autumn, in the woods, on humid grounds, in groups. **Not edible.**

Similar to *R. foetens* for the general characteristics, but with odor of bitter almonds; *Russula laurocerasi*, quite smaller than *foetens*, cap 4–7 cm; *Russula illota*, cap 5–16 cm, covered with a violaceous veil as long as it remains moist, and with the gills' edges speckled with blackish dots. These mushrooms are not poisonous, but they are **not edible** because of their not too attractive appearance and their odor and flavor.

RUSSULA PECTINATA (1)

Cap 4–7 cm, exceptionally 10 cm; ochraceous brown, dark brown, or yellowish; often rather grayish in the center; seldom totally brown gray or olivaceous gray; margin undulate and with knobby radial grooves; cuticle moist, not easily separable from the cap. **Stem** first stuffed with pith, then eroded and partly hollow; fragile; white, then grayish, finally brownish. **Flesh** white, with zones of the same color of the cuticle. **Odor** nauseating. **Flavor** not too acrid, but nauseating, then bitter. **Gills** somewhat sparse, narrow, connected together by veins; white, then cream. **Spores** deep cream. It grows in wood clearings, in the grass. **Not edible.** A very similar species is *R. pectinatoides*, **not advisable**, although slightly or not at all acrid or bitter, with ochraceous spots on the stem, and rust colored at the base.

RUSSULA SORORIA (2)

Very similar to *Russula pectinata*, slightly bigger, fuliginous brown, sometimes blackish in the center of the cap; less fetid than *pectinata*, with acrid flavor; growing in the clearings of latifoliate woods, in the grass; **not edible.** Similar to *R. sororia* is *Russula consobrina*, **not edible**: cap 3–9 cm, fuliginous brown, viscid, with even margin; odor mild of fruit; flavor very acrid; found under conifers. On the other hand, *Russula mustelina*, **edible**, can sometimes have a brown cap, similar to that of the previous species, but the rest of the mushroom is different: cap 6–15 cm, partly buried, convex, thick, with even margin; stem white, pyriform; odor light, flavor of walnuts; grows in the mountains under pines and firs.

HYGROPHORUS (Limacium) CHRYSODON (1)

Cap hemispheric, then expanded, now somewhat uneven, now with umbo in the center, now depressed; margin almost always undulate; cuticle very viscid; at first entirely covered with a golden yellow, lemon yellow, or sulfur yellow veil; then the veil folds into flocci, loosely spread on the white cuticle, but especially along the margin; it becomes spotted with yellowish when bruised; becomes completely yellowish with age. **Stem** slender, sometimes curved, soon hollow; viscid, tender, white, adorned on top with yellowish flocci; when bruised it becomes spotted with yellow. **Flesh** tender, juicy, white. **Odor** soft. **Flavor** sometimes imperceptible, sometimes tasty. **Gills** sparse, not too thick; first annexed to the stem, then decurrent on it; white, with floccose or yellowish edges; then cream colored. **Spores** white. It grows in the grass, in mountainous woods. **Edible.**

Similar to the previous species and equally **edible**: *Hygrophorus leucophaeus* (2): the center of the cap and the base of the stem are rusty brown; the margin of the cap is not golden like that of the previous species, but sometimes the entire mushroom is slightly ochraceous pink, growing under latifoliate trees. *Hygrophorus discoideus*: the entire cap is rusty brown, darker in the center, growing especially in the mountains, under conifers, but also in the plains under latifoliate trees. *Hygrophorus Karstenii*, **probably edible**: entirely white, but with yellow gills, growing in the moss, under firs, in the northern mountainous regions.

HYGROPHORUS (Limacium) RUSSULA (1)

Cap 4–18 cm, viscid; violaceous rosy, with darker squamules, denser in the center; sometimes, on the contrary, it is whitish, with few purplish squamules; margin involute, velvety, discolored; then somewhat explanate, undulate, lobate, fissured. **Stem** thick, stuffed, white; spotted with purple pink; flocculose in the upper part. **Flesh** thick, firm, juicy; white or tinged with pink; reddish when exposed to air. **Odor** soft. **Flavor** mild or bitterish. **Gills** somewhat close, thick, eroded near the stem, and briefly decurrent on it; white, tending to pink; becoming spotted with violaceous rosy or blackish red. **Spores** white. It grows in groups, in the plains, under latifoliate trees, especially under beeches. Only the non-bitter specimens are **edible**; it is necessary therefore to taste each collected specimen and to keep only those with mild flavor. Similar to *H. russula*, growing in the mountains, under conifers, **edible**: *Hygrophorus capreolarius*, entirely violaceous, inside and outside; granular-squamose in the center of the cap; with brownish or purple gills. *Hygrophorus purpurascens*, reddish, with pallid gills with red edges, and with remains of the cortina on the stem. *Hygrophorus erubescens* (2): more slender and less viscid than *H. russula*; white, spotted with violaceous red; gills sparse, decurrent, pale; stem without cortina, with violaceous red dots; becoming spotted with yellow where bruised; flesh bitter, therefore **not edible**.

HYGROPHORUS (Limacium) EBURNEUS (1)

Cap 4–8 cm, glutinous, often umbonate; white, then yellowish, especially in the center. **Stem** slender, viscid, white, then slightly yellowish; granular in the upper part. **Flesh** white, somewhat firm, brittle. **Odor** slightly unpleasant. **Flavor** mild. **Gills** sparse, decurrent, white. **Spores** white with ochraceous or pinkish shades. It grows in groups, especially under beeches. **Edible**, of poor quality because of its viscosity and odor.

Similar, although not identical to *eburneus*, but quite ill smelling, is *Hygrophorus cossus*, **not advisable**. Smaller and less viscous than *Hygrophorus eburneus* is *Hygrophorus piceae*, found in the mountains, under conifers; it is **edible**, but of little alimentary interest.

Also edible are the following two varieties of *Hygrophorus*

eburneus: *chrysaspis* (3), characterized by an antlike odor and by the color, pale orange, of the gills; *carneipes* (2), with the upper part of the stem covered with white flocci, but tinged with pink or red also internally.

HYGROPHORUS (Camarophyllus) NIVEUS (4)

Cap 1–5 cm, not viscous; white; but cinereous and with the center brown in the variety *fuscescens*; grows in the meadows, in autumn, until early winter; **edible**, delicate.

HYGROPHORUS (Camarophyllus) VIRGINEUS (5)

Bigger and fleshier than *niveus*, of which it is considered only a variety: cap sometimes spotted with red; **edible**, rather tasty.

HYGROPHORUS (Limacium) PUDORINUS

Cap delicate rosy orange, darker at the center; globose, with velvety, white, involute margin; then convex, and also depressed, 5–18 cm; margin lobate and undulate; viscid, soon dry. **Stem** cylindric, stout; viscid, soon dry; glabrous, white with rosy orange shades; white for a long time near the cap, and sprinkled with dewy droplets, then covered with farinaceous flocci; becoming, with age, entirely ochraceous and squamose, starting from the base; stuffed. **Flesh** thick, hard, white; ochraceous under the cuticle of the cap, rosy at the periphery. **Odor** of resin. **Flavor** of resin. **Gills** sparse, broad, thick, annexed to the stem, then decurrent on it; white, soon tending to pink, starting from the edges. **Spores** white. It grows in groups, under firs and red pines, in the mountains; rare in the plains. **Edible**: to free it from the resinous taste, which becomes stronger with cooking, it has to be left immersed in salted water or in water and vinegar for some time; it can also be preserved in oil. It differs from *H. poëtarum* because the latter is paler, and grows under latifoliate trees.

Much smaller and much more brightly colored is *Hygrophorus aureus*, **edible**: cap 3–6 cm, first umbonate, then depressed, with undulate margin; viscid, rosy orange or orange vermilion with golden margin; stem long, viscid; flesh white, yellow under the cuticle; gills sparse, adhering to the stem, yellowish; growing in mixed woods of coniferous and latifoliate trees.

HYGROPHORUS (Limacium) POETARUM

Cap rosy cream; rarely white and only with few rosy cream zones; convex or cuspidate, then plane and uneven, 5–20 cm; slightly viscid; sericeous, shining. **Stem** rather long, stout, flared upward near the cap, often tapering and curved toward the base; fibrillar, sericeous, shining, strewn on top with limpid, dewy droplets; then finely velvety; white with rosy cream shades. **Flesh** thick, brittle; white or rosy white, at least under the cap's cuticle. **Odor** mild; sometimes more intense, of Peruvian balsam. **Flavor** of hazelnuts. **Gills** sparse, decurrent along the stem; ivory white, with light rosy yellow hues. **Spores** white. It grows in latifoliate woods, especially beech, in the mountains; seldom in the plains. **Edible**, of very good quality. It is distinguishable from *H. pudorinus* almost only because the latter is more intensely colored and grows under conifers. Also *Hygrophorus melizeus*, **edible**, of poor quality, initially white, takes, with age, a rosy cream coloring; but it is much smaller than *H. poëtarum*, more slender and pretty: cap 3–6 cm, covered with gluten in humid weather; stem long, thin, often undulate; odor strong, disgusting; gills sparse, slightly decurrent, white, then yellowish; grows under latifoliate trees. As small as *melizeus*, and of ochraceous color, darker in the center, is *Hygrophorus arbustivus*, **edible**: cap 2–7 cm, umbonate; stem long; gills cream colored, then slightly decurrent; growing under oaks and hazelnut trees.

HYGROPHORUS (Limacium) AGATHOSMUS (1)

Cap 3–8 cm, viscid, smooth, glabrous; cinereous tending to brown or violet; more rarely discolored or whitish; darker at the center, where it is covered with glutinous papillae; lighter, almost white, at the margin, which is first involute, then somewhat explanate. **Stem** rather tall, cylindric; white tending to brown, speckled in the upper part, with white, and then brownish, flocci. **Flesh** tender, juicy, white; gray under the cuticle. **Odor** of bitter almonds or anise. **Flavor** mild. **Gills** sparse, broad, thick, decurrent, connected together by minute veins; white, then whitish. **Spores** white. It grows under conifers, especially firs, in the mountains; it is rare in the plains. **Edible**. *Hygrophorus hyacinthinus*, **edible**, differs from *H. agathosmus* practically only in its odor of sweet-smelling violets or hyacinths, in the radiciform base of the stem, and in being slightly bigger.

HYGROPHORUS (Camarophyllus) CAMARO-PHYLLUS (2)

Cap 6–12 cm, brown, fuliginous, or blackish, with blue hues; with olivaceous brown spots in persistent dry weather; umbonate, then depressed, with uneven margin; moist, but not viscid; dry in dry weather; decorticable only along the margin. **Stem** thick, fibrous, dry, smooth in the upper part, almost velvety in the lower part, cinereous. **Flesh** tender, white, cinereous under the cuticle. **Odor** soft. **Flavor** mild. **Gills** white, then cinereous; sparse, crescent shaped, connected by nervations, decurrent. It grows in pine woods, in the mountains. **Edible**, of good quality.

HYGROPHORUS (Limacium) HYPOTHEIUS (1)

Cap olivaceous brown, more or less intense; fibrillar; initially covered with a glutinous, olivaceous brown coat; after this coat has dried out, the cap appears olivaceous green, orange, or yellow, darker in the center; convex, with the margin rolled toward the gills; then plane and also depressed, 3–7 cm, but with slight central umbo, with margin explanate and often fissured in the direction of the gills. **Stem** cylindric, whitish, with yellowish or olivaceous zones; glutinous from the ring down; stuffed. **Ring** glutinous, soon disappearing. **Flesh** tender, white; yellowish under the cuticle of the cap and toward the periphery of the stem; becoming slightly reddish when exposed to air. **Odor** mild. **Flavor** agreeable. **Gills** sparse, broad, decurrent, whitish, then golden yellow. **Spores** white. It grows in autumn with the coming of the first cold nights, in the woods, especially under pines and firs. **Edible**.

HYGROPHORUS (Limacium) EXPALLENS (2)

Similar to *H. hypotheius*, but smaller and paler; by some authors considered as the winter form of the latter; **edible**.

HYGROPHORUS (Limacium) OLIVACEOALBUS (3)

Similar to *H. hypotheius*, but thicker, with prominent umbo at the center of the cap, and with white gills; found in woods, especially under pines; **edible**, of good quality. Similar to *H. olivaceoalbus* is *Hygrophorus limacinus*, **edible** of good quality; it has, however, cinereous greenish gills, and grows especially under hornbeams and beeches.

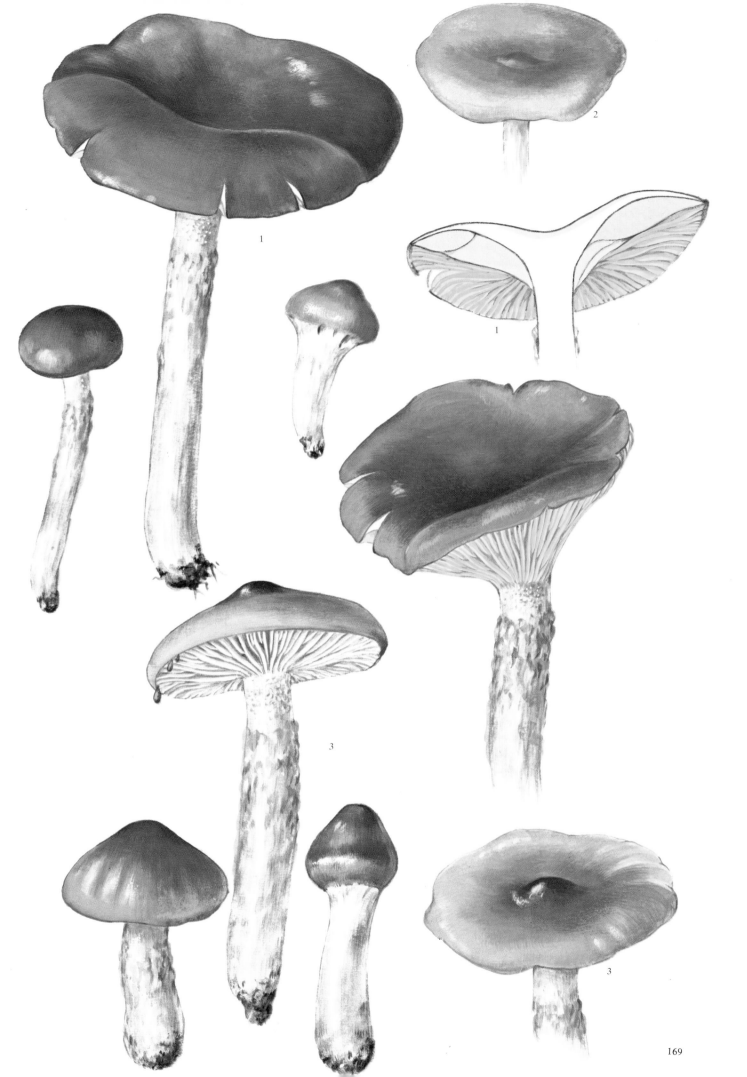

HYGROPHORUS (Camarophyllus) NEMOREUS (1)

Cap orangy ocher or rosy hazel, slightly deeper at the center; covered with pubescence, often gathered in tufts slightly darker than the surface; dry, not viscous, hemispheric or campanulate, with involute margin; then plane 4–10 cm, with large umbo in the center, and with the margin explanate or even slightly upturned. **Stem** cylindric, rather slender, tapered at the base, and sometimes also slightly curved; slightly paler than the cap; fibrillar; strewn with a fine scurf on the upper part; stuffed or medullar. **Flesh** tender, white. **Odor** soft, of flour. **Flavor** pleasant. **Gills** sparse, very broad, thick, decurrent; rosy cream color, then slightly paler than the cap. **Spores** white. It grows in autumn, in woods. **Edible**, of poor quality.

HYGROPHORUS (Camarophyllus) PRATENSIS (2)

Cap 4–8 cm, slightly paler than the cap of *H. nemoreus*, without pubescence, without scurf; margin thin. **Stem** stouter than that of *H. nemoreus*, and without scurf on the upper part. **Flesh** whitish, then ochraceous; firm, brittle; fibrillar. **Odor** pleasant. **Flavor** mild. **Gills** sparse, broad, decurrent, connected by minute veins; cream, then pale orange. **Spores** white. It grows in meadows, not in the woods. **Edible**, of good quality. Of more lively color is *Hygrophorus (Camarophyllus) leporinus*, **edible**: cap 2–7 cm, cuspidate, rosy, flocculose or squamose; stem pale pink; gills sparse, pinkish; grows in grassy and mossy places, under conifers, in the plains and in the mountains, where, however, it is of smaller size.

HYGROCYBE (Hygrophorus) PUNICEA

Cap campanulate, then expanded more or less evenly, 5–12 cm, often umbonate; not too fleshy, so that looking through it against the light one can see the outline of gills in transparency; viscid and shining; first scarlet red, then gradually losing color; discolored in dry weather; margin thin, undulate, then fissured. **Stem** thick, orange yellow, covered by reddish fibrils; with a white cotton at the base; soon hollow. **Flesh** white, tending to the coloring of the cap; orange under the cuticle, yellow in the stem. **Odor** and **flavor** agreeable. **Gills** sparse, broad, thick, adhering, then detached from the stem; yellow or cream; then reddish, but with yellow edges. **Spores** white. It grows in summer, in grassy meadows, in the mountains, in groups; it is rare in the plains. **Edible**, very good. Similar to *H. punicea* and **edible**: *Hygrocybe intermedia*, cap 3–6 cm, orange, fibrillar and squamose at the margin; stem orange; gills sparse and fragile, whitish, then yellowish and finally orange. *Hygrocybe Bresadolae*, small as *intermedia* but taller; cap yellow with orange center, stem yellow, floccose and viscous; grows in autumn, in meadows. *Hygrocybe lucorum*, entirely yellow except at the margin of the cap, which is white and flocculose; stem smooth; grows in autumn, under larches.

HYGROPHORUS (Camarophyllus) MARZUOLUS

Cap soon plane or depressed 3–10 cm, uneven, gibbous; cinereous, sometimes faded, more rarely with ochraceous shades; then becoming plumbeous, blackish, spotted; cuticle soon dry and not translucent. **Stem** squat, white and furfuraceous in the upper part; always grayer toward the base. **Flesh** abundant, tender, although slightly fibrous; white with grayish shades under the cuticle and toward the margin of the cap. **Odor** soft. **Flavor** mild. **Gills** first close, narrow, thick; then thinner and quite apart; curved and decurrent on the stem; connected together by small veins; here and there bifurcate; white, then gray or blackish with lighter edges. **Spores** white. It grows in groups, in the mountains, under conifers and oaks, chestnuts, and beeches, appearing sometimes with the first autumnal chills, but usually toward the end of winter, after the melting of the snow and then until May; often hidden under dead leaves, the debris of wood, under moss; after finding one, remove the dead leaves around and usually you will find several more. **Edible**, excellent.

Hygrophorus (Limacium) pustulatus, **edible**, is autumnal, and somewhat similar to *H. agathosmus* (page 168) but smaller and more slender; cap 2–6 cm, brownish gray, but entirely gray in the form *tenebratus*, viscid, with woolly squamules in concentric zones; stem thin, long, cylindrical, white, but covered on the upper part with brownish pimples; gills waxy, white, decurrent; grows under pines and firs.

conica Hygr.

HYGROCYBE CONICA (1)

It contains a latex that becomes black when exposed to air, making the whole mushroom black. **Cap** yellow or red or orange, often asymmetric, 3–6 cm, umbonate; margin lobate, soon fissured; fibrillar, rather moist. **Stem** tall, yellow; soon hollow. **Flesh** thin, brittle; white; yellow under the cuticle. **Odor** soft. **Flavor** mild. **Gills** thin, broad, annexed, but soon free from the stem; white, with yellow edges, then greenish. **Spores** white. It grows in the grass.

Hygrocybe nigrescens (4): cap bright red, fibrillar, base white; latex amethystine in contact with air. *Hygrocybe coccinea* (2): cap bright red, soon faded; *Hygrocybe miniata*, velvety, often umbilicate cap, and *Hygrocybe turunda*, umbilicate and squamose, seem almost miniature versions of *H. coccinea*; equally small is *Hygrocybe citrina*, entirely lemon yellow. *Hygrocybe psittacina* (3): first green because of the viscous coat covering it, then brownish yellow tending to reddish; gills green with yellow edges; similar to it is *Hygrocybe laeta*, color ranging from tawny to flesh color. *Hygrocybe chlorophana* (5): yellow, it does not become black; margin of the cap involute; similar to it is *Hygrocybe ceracea*, with yellowish and waxy cap and striate margin. All are **edible**.

GOMPHIDIUS GLUTINOSUS

Cap 5–12 cm, violaceous gray or violaceous brown; then with some blackish spots; covered with a glutinous, removable coat, which, on drying, turns into a waxy, shining crust; cuticle completely removable. **Stem** whitish in the upper part, yellow or yellowish downward and at the base; then with violaceous or blackish stains; stuffed. **Cortina** glutinous, cinereous or amethystine; with age it coagulates on the stem. **Flesh** of the cap white and soft, cinereous under the cuticle; the stem yellowish and tougher; the flesh of the base deep yellow. **Odor** mild. **Flavor** none or acidulous. **Gills** sparse, thick, with rather undulate edges; furcate outward; decurrent; easily detachable; whitish, then fuliginous. **Spores** blackish. It grows in groups, under conifers, often near a decaying *Boletus viscidus* (page 191). **Edible**, good: the glutinous coat must be discarded; it becomes blackish with cooking; it can also be dried. Similar to it is *Gomphidius nigricans*, **edible**, which becomes completely black in dry weather. Smaller is *Gomphidius maculatus*, **edible**: cap 3–5 cm, rather viscid, ochraceous; paler and tending to pinkish in the variety *gracilis*; with small blackish spots; stem long, white, speckled with small red spots; flesh rosy under the cuticle, yellow at the base of the stem; found in the mountains, under larches.

BOLETUS (Gyroporus) CYANESCENS (1)

Cap 5–15 cm, rather uneven; whitish or with yellow or brown or gray or olivaceous shades; white in the form *lacteus* (2); cuticle dry, soft, velvety, with squamules, hairs and flocci slightly darker than the surface. **Stem** stout; of the same color as the cap and pubescent, but white and smooth in the upper part; hard, fragile; stuffed, soon partly hollow. **Flesh** thick, firm, white; exposed to air it becomes blue or indigo, it changes more intensely and rapidly the more the air is humid. **Odor** mild. **Flavor** pleasant. **Pores** small, round; whitish, then yellowish; becoming quickly blue when bruised. **Tubules** adhering to the stem little or not at all; whitish. **Spores** yellowish. It grows especially in pine, chestnut, and oak woods, on loose and rocky grounds. **Edible**, excellent.

PHYLLOPORUS RHODOXANTHUS (3)

Cap brown or orange brown or olivaceous brown; hemispheric, then plane 2–10 cm, and also depressed, funnel shaped; velvety, sometimes cracked. **Stem** sometimes thin, sometimes stout; fibrillar; first whitish, but reddish brown and striate in the upper part, then brownish; greenish yellow at the base. **Flesh** with reddish shades, becoming livelier in contact with air. **Odor** soft. **Flavor** mild. **Gills** sparse, thick, broad, unequal, decurrent, connected by septa, narrower than the gills themselves; with uneven edges; yellow; becoming blue green when bruised. **Spores** olivaceous brown. It grows in autumn, in the woods. **Edible**.

GOMPHIDIUS VISCIDUS (1)

Cap 3–10 cm, umbonate; viscid, but soon dry; fibrillar; copper colored or slightly vinous; more rarely brownish or yellowish. **Stem** tall, fibrillar, yellow, then of the same color as the cap, but yellowish at the base; initially viscid, with annular, violaceous ocher, squamose zones; then with coagulated, ochraceous remains of the cortina, a little under the gills. **Cortina** glutinous in humid weather, filamentous in dry weather; amethystine, evanescent. **Flesh** firm; ocher yellow tinged with violaceous shades; darker in the stem, more yellow at the base. **Odor** soft. **Flavor** pleasant. **Gills** sparse, thick, rather broad, bifid, decurrent; easily detachable; cinereous yellow, then grayish violet, finally fuliginous, with yellow and flocculose edges. **Spores** fuliginous brown. It grows in coniferous woods, especially under pines, in the moss. **Edible**, of poor quality. Similar to it is *Gomphidius helveticus*, **edible**, cap not viscous but dry, somewhat rough, hairy, fibrillar, terra-cotta colored as are the gills; found in the mountains, under spruces and pines.

GOMPHIDIUS ROSEUS (2)

Cap pinkish red; stem short, white, with rosy zones, and yellow base; growing under conifers, often together with *Boletus bovinus* (see page 194); **edible**. In North America, under pines, the following **edible** species grow: *Gomphidius vinicolor*, pale violaceous red, and *Gomphidius rutilus*, cap olivaceous brown or gray, then ochraceous; stem at first ochraceous, then pale violaceous red.

PAXILLUS INVOLUTUS

Cap 6–12 cm, often depressed; brown tending to olivaceous, fuliginous, or grayish; sometimes spotted; discoloring with age; viscid in humid weather; cuticle feltlike, especially along the margin; margin rolled toward the gills, like Ionic volutes. **Stem** short, flared upward, often pointed at the base; of the same color as the cap, lighter upward; firm, stuffed. **Flesh** soft, then flaccid; yellowish; becoming saffron colored or rosy brown when in contact with air. **Odor** agreeable. **Flavor** acidulous. **Gills** close, here and there connected together, especially near the stem on which they are decurrent; easily detachable in lumps; cream, then ochraceous. Like the gills, all the other parts of the mushroom become brown at the slightest touch. **Spores** ochraceous. It grows in humid recesses, under latifoliate trees. **Poisonous** when raw. **Edible**, of good quality when cooked, provided it is still unripe; it becomes blackish by cooking. Smaller than the above is *Paxillus leptopus*, **edible** with the same precautions as for the previous species; cap yellowish and smooth, then squamose except at the margin and at the center; margin not involute, then with radial knobby grooves; stem thin, sometimes eccentric, slanted; flesh yellowish; found from late spring to autumn in all kinds of woods, coniferous, latifoliate or mixed, but especially in alder woods. It is considered by some authors only as a variety of *Paxillus involutus*.

PAXILLUS ATROTOMENTOSUS

Cap convex, then plane 10–30 cm, and also depressed, but with the margin always somewhat rolled toward the gills; surface and margin rather uneven in the ripe specimens; brown, more or less deep, and fuliginous; during long periods of dry weather it can become much lighter, grayish ocher or cinereous yellow; cuticle dry, velvety, then glabrous. **Stem** squat, often eccentric or even lateral, with the base extending rootlike into the stump on which it grows; covered with a more or less blackish felt, hirsute in the form *hirsutus.* **Flesh** thick, soft, often watery; whitish. **Odor** pleasant. **Flavor** bitterish. **Gills** close, confluent, especially near the stem; decurrent; easily separable from the cap; pale olivaceous yellow, then ocher yellow. **Spores** pale ocher. It grows in autumn, on stumps, especially pine and spruce, in groups or in tufts of three or four specimens. **Not advisable**.

Paxillus panuoides grows also on crumbling pine stumps: cap 2–14 cm, bowl or funnel shaped, supported by a short peduncle; narcissus yellow, pubescent; gills thin, rather uneven, decurrent to the peduncle, confluent, saffron yellow, fragile; flesh soft, thin, cream; **edible**, when unripe, otherwise it is too tough. The small *Paxillus corrugatus* grows on decaying shrubs; without stem, with sinuous gills with uneven edges; **not advisable**, because of its very disagreeable odor.

BOLETUS (Cyroporus) CASTANEUS

Cap globose, then convex, finally plane 3–10 cm, and sometimes also depressed; margin thin, slightly undulate in the older specimens; cuticle velvety, almost plushy; then more or less glabrous and shining; not easily detachable from the cap; chestnut color, sometimes tending to cinnamon, sometimes to orange brown. **Stem** rather unequal, covered by a hard bark; somewhat rugose, velvety, of the same color as the cap or slightly lighter, but with darker spots and nodules; stuffed, but soon spongy; then with small cavities, and finally hollow. **Flesh** of the cap hard and brittle; flesh of the stem soft and spongy; white; rosy or hazel under the cuticle; in contact with air it acquires sometimes a light rosy shade; when bruised it becomes spotted with yellow. **Odor** soft. **Flavor** slightly of hazelnuts. **Pores** small, round, white, then yellowish. **Tubules** short, rounded toward the cap's margin, and toward the stem; white, then yellowish. **Spores** greenish yellow. It is found singly or in small groups, in the gravelly clearings of coniferous, but especially latifoliate woods, more frequently under beeches, oaks, and chestnuts. **Edible**, of good quality: the stem of the ripe specimens should be discarded. *Boletus fellus* (page 179), **not edible**, has also chestnut color and grows in gravelly woods; but the stem is stuffed, covered by a prominent reticulation, the pores are rosy amethystine, and it is very bitter.

BOLETUS (Tubiporus) EDULIS (Edible Boletus)
Together with *Amanita Caesarea* (page 17) this well-known boletus is rightly considered the king of mushrooms.
Cap hemispheric, then convex more or less regularly, 5–25 cm; seldom somewhat depressed; ochraceous or tawny brown or grayish brown; sometimes, however, also faded, whitish; with the margin generally paler; cuticle smooth or somewhat rugose; not velvety; dry and shining in dry weather; slightly viscid in humid weather. **Stem** first ovoid, then rather cylindrical, often with thickened base; always thick; stuffed; whitish or hazel or tawny hazel; covered by a fine reticule, white upward, then gradually darker toward the base that, however, it does not reach. **Flesh** rather firm and compact; soon becoming soft; under the cuticle it has the same color as the cuticle; white in the rest, even near the tubules. **Odor** and **flavor** agreeable. **Pores** small, round, regular; white, then yellowish, finally olivaceous. **Tubules** long and relatively thin; almost detached from the stem; whitish, then yellowish, finally olivaceous. **Spores** olivaceous brown. It grows in the plains, in sunny spots in woods of latifoliate trees such as oak, linden, beech, hornbeam, but it is more frequent in the mountains, in sunny spots in fir woods, especially in warm summers following rainy springs. **Edible**, excellent when cooked; raw, in salads, must be eaten in small quantities, otherwise it can be harmful. Some authors have also described a *Boletus albus*, white, and a *Boletus citrinus*, yellow; but they are actually specimens of *Boletus edulis* grown in very shady places.

BOLETUS RETICULATUS

Cap 5–18 cm, somewhat irregular and sometimes depressed; hazel color or gray brown more or less intense; more rarely yellowish or even whitish; the margin of the same color as the cap; the cuticle, finely velvety, dries out easily, cracking into many irregular small pieces; these pieces form an irregular net through which the lighter color of the background, and that of the flesh becomes visible. Hence the denomination *reticulatus*. **Stem** same color as the cap; covered from the top to the base with a rather regular reticule, with medium-size meshes, lighter than the color of the surface and rather in relief with respect to it. **Flesh** compact, firm, but soon soft; milky white, even immediately below the cuticle of the cap; yellowish near the tubules. **Odor** and **flavor** pleasant. **Pores** small, white, then yellowish; finally olivaceous; near the margin of the cap they are frequently somewhat pinkish. **Tubules** white, then yellowish, and finally olivaceous; sometimes very long; almost always abruptly shortened near the stem. **Spores** olivaceous brown. It grows from April to October, but especially from May to September, near oaks and beeches. **Edible**, excellent.

Similar to *Boletus reticulatus*, of which it could be a variety, is *Boletus rubiginosus*, **edible**; cap first reddish brown and velvety; then becoming gradually glabrous and of a faded brown color where the reddish pubescence has disappeared, while the margin becomes somewhat corrugated.

BOLETUS (Tylopilus) FELLEUS

Cap ochraceous, then gradually darker brown; hemispheric, then convex and finally plane, 5–12 cm, and also somewhat depressed; margin involute, then explanate or also turned upward, and undulate. **Stem** thick, cylindric or slightly thickened at the base; slightly paler than the cap; velvety; covered by a brownish reticule with large, oblong meshes, in relief. **Flesh** thick, soft, tender; white, becoming pink in contact with air; brown under the cuticle of the cap. **Odor** mild. **Flavor** very bitter, as bile. **Pores** small, but soon somewhat large, angular; whitish, then pinkish and finally blackish violet. **Tubules** rather long, shortened near the stem, to which they adhere only by a tooth or not at all. **Spores** pink tinged with brown. It grows in woods, especially in sandy grounds. **Not edible**: easily mistaken, if one does not taste it, with some specimens of *Boletus edulis* (page 177) or of *Boletus aereus* (page 180), and cooked together with them it will make everything bitter and not eatable; to avoid such mistake, better remember that *B. felleus* has pinkish pores and reticule in high relief, whereas *B. edulis* and *B. aereus* have olivaceous yellow pores and a fine reticule, only slightly marking the stem. According to Fries, *Boletus felleus* exists also in the variety *alutarius*, with the pores white and slightly pinkish only when fully ripe; flavor not bitter, and therefore **edible**. This opinion is, however, not shared by others and the specimens described by Fries could have been hybrids.

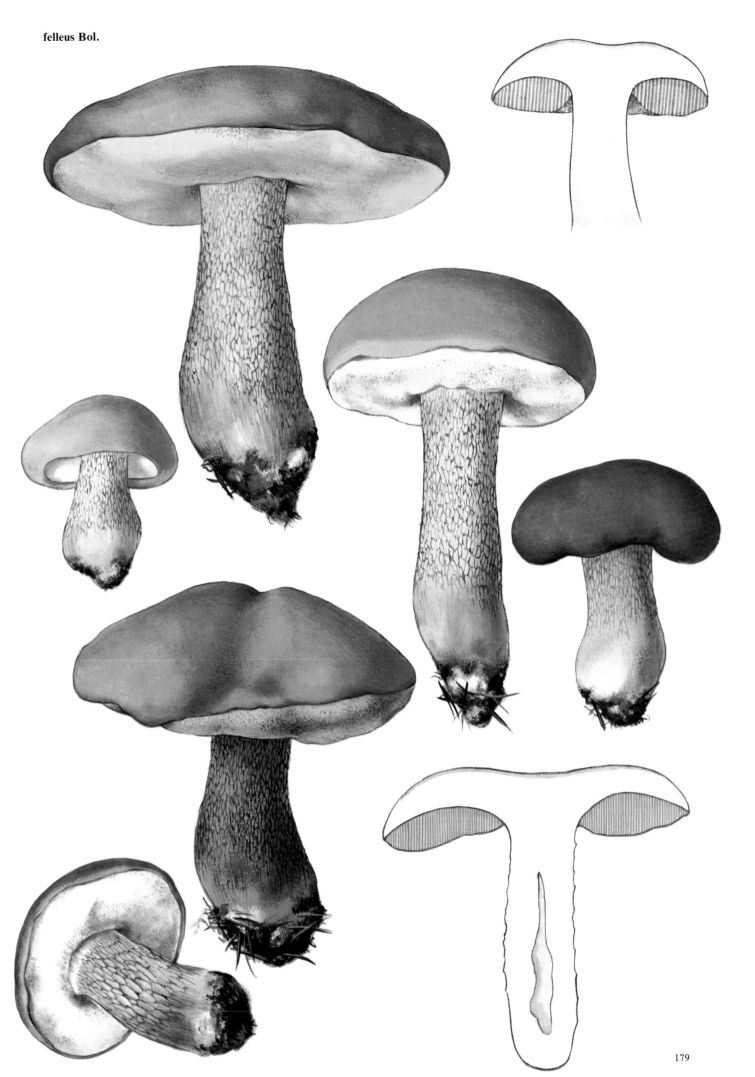

felleus Bol.

BOLETUS (Tubiporus) AEREUS

Cap hemispheric, then convex 10–20 cm; velvety and dry; first black brown, then it discolors slightly, maintaining darker bronze brown areas that give it a somewhat marbled appearance; never with reddish or garnet red shades, but sometimes with a very faded ochraceous coloring. **Stem** thick, cinnamon or saffron color; becoming discolored with age; almost always covered with a fine reticule, white upward, brick brown at the base. **Flesh** firm and compact; white also under the cap's cuticle. **Odor** and **flavor** agreeable. **Pores** small, rounded, white or whitish, and pruinose; then slightly larger, yellowish, finally olivaceous. **Tubules** whitish and close; then olivaceous; shortened near the stem and almost free from it. **Spores** olivaceous brown. It grows in bushy clearings and on hilly ridges of mixed woods, but especially in oak and chestnut woods, in warm summers and autumns of the Mediterranean regions. **Edible**, excellent. *Boletus edulis* variety *fuscoruber*, **edible**, cap 5–15 cm, deep pure brown, that is, of a color intermediate between that of *Boletus aereus* and of *Boletus edulis* (page 177) in the typical form, and very similar to the color of *Boletus pinicola* (page 181): with pyriform stem, with a diameter sometimes equal, sometimes even larger than the diameter of the cap; white without reticule or only slightly striate; found in mixed woods, especially beech and spruce.

BOLETUS (Tubiporus) PINICOLA
Cap hemispheric, then pulvinate 18–30 cm, exceptionally 40 cm; often somewhat uneven; rugose; reddish brown or garnet brown; cuticle slightly wrinkled, but not velvety; initially furfuraceous, lasting longer along the margin; margin initially knobby, then undulate, lobate, and easily stained with whitish, yellowish, or greenish colorings. **Stem** very hard; first oval, then pyriform or with bulbous base; white, then ochraceous, covered by a reticule, first white, then faded violaceous, but brownish toward the base, which is also brownish and covered with darker reticule. **Flesh** very thick; white; with garnet brown shades under the cuticle. **Odor** agreeable, somewhat aromatic. **Flavor** mild and agreeable. **Pores** small, round, regular; creamy white, then yellowish, speckled with rusty dots; finally olivaceous. **Tubules** rather long and thin; shorter near the stem, from which they are almost detached; first creamy white, then yellowish, finally distinctly olivaceous green. **Spores** olivaceous brown. It grows in the mountains, especially in the summer, in dry woods, particularly pine, fir, chestnut, and beech woods. **Edible**, delicate: the water in which it is cooked becomes greenish.

Similar to it is *Boletus mirabilis*, **edible**, excellent, which grows in North America: cap rough, stem rather long, reddish, with or without reticule.

BOLETUS (Tubiporus) APPENDICULATUS
Cap 8–20 cm, sometimes somewhat uneven; slightly velvety, dry; reddish brown, brown, or ochraceous. **Stem** thick, often barrel shaped; yellow, covered with a fine reticule. Base bulbous, but with radiciform appendix; brownish. **Flesh** compact, but soon tender; yellowish; in contact with air it acquires a soft light blue or even pinkish coloring; violaceous pink at the base. **Odor**, when cut, of fresh bread. **Flavor** agreeable. **Pores** close; yellow with pink hues from the beginning; becoming spotted with blue when touched. **Tubules** short and thin, yellow or yellowish, generally annexed to the stem. **Spores** olivaceous. It grows in latifoliate woods, especially under birches and linden trees. **Edible**, of excellent quality. Similar to *B. appendiculatus*: *Boletus impolitus*, **edible**: cap 8–20 cm, less fleshy, and paler than the cap of *B. appendiculatus*; stem not reticulate; base with radiciform appendix, often buried in the ground, especially if this is soft; flesh white, unchangeable; odor slight of vinegar; in latifoliate woods, especially oak woods. *Boletus fragrans*, **edible**: cap 4–18 cm, often uneven; cinereous ocher, then brown; stem not reticulate, brownish marbled with dark red; yellow upward; fusiform with radiciform base buried deep in the ground; odor of vinegar or fruit but light; flavor acidulous, then bitterish; growing in the mountains and hills, in sunny woods, and in clearings or latifoliate woods.

BOLETUS (Tubiporus) CALOPUS (1)
Cap 5–20 cm, gibbous; ochraceous or olivaceous ocher; but white in the variety *albus* (3); cuticle dry; almost plushy, then smooth, not easily detachable. **Stem** thick; yellow with white reticule; then carmine, with pale carmine reticule. **Flesh** thick; yellowish, brownish or reddish at the base; becoming bluish in contact with air. **Odor** slightly acidulous. **Flavor** mild, then bitter. **Pores** small, round; yellow, then olivaceous yellow; becoming bluish blue if bruised. **Tubules** thin; rounded toward the stem and adhering to it; yellow, then olivaceous or blue green. **Spores** olivaceous ocher. It grows in groups, in sunny spots in woods, especially coniferous ones, in the mountains. **Not edible.**

BOLETUS (Ixocomus) PLACIDUS (2)
Cap 3–12 cm, white, then yellow, but amethystine in the center, then brownish; cuticle viscid, easily removable. **Stem** slender; white, with yellow spots, and with red brown granules or variegations. **Flesh** white; yellowish toward the periphery. **Odor** and **flavor** mild. **Pores** white, then golden, secreting dewy droplets; finally olivaceous brown. **Tubules** short, annexed to the stem; whitish, then olivaceous. **Spores** ochraceous. It grows in tufts, under pines. **Edible.** Similar to it is *Boletus plorans*, **edible**, which grows in the mountains, under conifers: slightly darker than *B. placidus*, stem with only some brown dots or lines; in the form *cembrae*, however, it has velvety dark brown or almost black cap.

BOLETUS (Tubiporus) ALBIDUS (1)
Cap convex, then plane, 6–24 cm; white, then whitish, with hazel shades and with spots tending to greenish; finely pruinose, dry and almost plushy; margin involute toward the tubules, then thinner, explanate and sometimes fissured. **Stem** pyriform, then somewhat cylindric, with the base prolonged into a radiciform appendix; white and finely reticulate in the upper part; whitish, with cinereous or yellowish shades in the middle; spotted with gray and green, without traces of red, at the base. **Flesh** thick, whitish, with yellow iridescence; the stem more intensely colored; yellow and then blue green where the tubules are attached, becoming blue when exposed to air, especially in unripe specimens. **Odor** slight. **Flavor** at first mild, then slightly or distinctly bitter. **Pores** small, round; white, then pale lemon yellow; stained green when bruised. **Tubules** thin, almost free from the stem; greenish yellow, then olivaceous. **Spores** yellowish. It grows in the clearings of latifoliate woods, especially under oaks and beeches. **Not edible**, primarily because of its bitterness.

BOLETUS ALBIDUS variety EUPACHYPUS (2)
Cap pale ochraceous, that is, of a slightly darker color than in the typical form; stem more bulging, often somewhat bulbous at the base even when the mushroom is ripe, with carmine red zones, spots, or reticule, at least in the part nearer to the cap; flesh with distinctly bitter flavor, although less bitter than the flesh of *B. felleus*, but enough to make this mushroom disgusting and therefore **not edible.**

BOLETUS (Tubiporus) REGIUS (1)

Cap 8–20 cm, often uneven; carmine red, strawberry red, brownish-purple-red, or brownish-violaceous-red; here and there olive green; cuticle finely velvety or fibrillar or plushy; dry; in fully ripe specimens often cracked, especially at the center. **Stem** often bulging at the middle; yellow or yellowish; with fine reticule whose meshes are sometimes lighter than the background color in the upper part of the stem, and darker toward the base; the stem becomes blue at the touch. Base often rather bulbous; terminating with a short radiciform appendix; spotted with brown or with reddish. **Flesh** compact, yellowish; the flesh of the base rosy amethystine; exposed to slightly humid air it becomes blue. **Odor** mild.

Flavor agreeable. **Pores** small, golden with a pinkish iridescence; becoming blue or blue green at the touch. **Tubules** yellow, then olivaceous yellow; shorter near the stem and free or almost free from it. **Spores** olivaceous brown. It grows from spring to autumn, in the sandy and humid ravines of latifoliate woods, such as oak, linden, and birch. **Edible**, of excellent quality: to be used preferably together with other species of mushrooms; alone it is slightly indigestible.

BOLETUS (Tubiporus) PALLESCENS (2)

Often considered only a variety of *B. regius*, it has slightly ochraceous or whitish cap; **edible**, just as tasty as *Boletus regius*.

BOLETUS (Tubiporus) LURIDUS

Cap 5–20 cm, brown tending to olivaceous, reddish, orange, or cinereous ocher; velvety, then furfuraceous; viscid in humid weather. **Stem** now squat and very big, now thin, curved; hard, stuffed; yellow above, yellowish and reddish in the middle, brownish at the base; with a fine, dark reticule. **Flesh** whitish in the cap; tending to orange in the stem; dirty and verminous at the base; exposed to air the flesh becomes instantly blue, then greenish, finally grayish; the same happens to every other part of this mushroom when bruised; the surface of attachment of the tubules is orange, rosy orange, or red. **Odor** soft. **Flavor** sapid. **Pores** small, round; first orange, then red; those nearer to the cap's margin tending to yellow. **Tubules** thin, long, but short near the stem; yellowish, then olivaceous. **Spores** olivaceous brown. It grows in the woods. **Poisonous** when raw. **Edible**, agreeable, when cooked: it becomes yellow with cooking.

Equally becoming blue at the touch and equally **edible** when well cooked: *Boletus junquilleus*, 4–18 cm, entirely yellow, then orange or brownish, except the pores, which become olivaceous; grows under beeches. *Boletus Frostii*, amaranth color, then brick red, shiny; pores yellow, then rusty as the stem, which is covered with a high-relief reticule with large, yellow meshes; grows in North America, under young oaks.

BOLETUS (Tubiporus) ERYTHROPUS

Cap 5–20 cm, brown, olivaceous brown, fuliginous brown, or purple brown; occasionally rather pallid or with yellowish spots; slightly moist initially and in humid weather; but soon dry and somewhat velvety. **Stem** thick, swollen; yellow or orange yellow; speckled with red flocci, denser in the middle part; brownish or olivaceous brown at the base; not reticulate. **Flesh** yellow also on the surface of attachment of the tubules; exposed to air it becomes instantly blue, then red; seldom infested with larvae. **Odor** and **flavor** agreeable. **Pores** small, round; red or orange; bruised, they become blue, then greenish. **Tubules** free from the stem; yellow, then greenish. **Spores** olivaceous brown. It grows from spring to autumn, in wood clearings. **Poisonous** when raw; **edible** when well cooked; it remains yellow when cooked. Similar to *B. erythropus*, in bulk, in the yellow coloring of the stem, and in the instantaneous blue coloring of the flesh when exposed to air is *Boletus torosus*, cap yellow, then yellowish with red spots; stem spheric, then pyriform, yellow, reddish at the base; with a yellow reticule; flesh yellow, changing immediately to deep blue in contact with air, then slowly to green yellow; tubules yellow; pores yellow, then purple red; spores olivaceous brown; found in woods of latifoliate trees, especially beeches; **poisonous** when raw; given as **edible** when cooked, by some authors.

erythropus Bol.

BOLETUS (Tubiporus) QUELETII

Cap 5–12 cm, often uneven; velvety; dry; olivaceous yellow, olivaceous brown, orange brown, or carmine red, but garnet red in the variety *lateritius* (top left); bruised, it becomes deep blue, but orange yellow where nibbled by small animals. **Stem** stout; yellow above, purple brown toward the base; then gradually becoming entirely purple brown; covered with fine, brownish flocci. **Flesh** of the cap thick, firm, but soon soft; the stem fibrous; the base hard; the cap yellow, becoming immediately deep blue in contact with air; red brown in the base, changing to blackish violet when exposed to air. **Odor** mild. **Flavor** acidulous, then bitterish. **Pores** small, first reddish, but yellow along the cap's margin; then olivaceous yellow with rosy hues; becoming deep blue at the touch. **Tubules** greenish yellow, then olivaceous; changing to blue green when bruised; free or almost free from the stem. **Spores** olivaceous brown. It grows in latifoliate woods. **Edible**. A species, when ripe, that can be confused with *B. Queletii* variety *lateritus* is *Boletus Dupainii*: cap viscid, scarlet red; then dry and yellowish with red or yellow spots; stem yellowish, covered with red granules; flesh yellowish, reddish under the cap's cuticle, yellowish under the tubules; exposed to air, it becomes slightly blue, but greenish at the base of the stem; grows in summer, under latifoliate trees. Some authors consider it edible, like *Boletus luridus* and *Boletus erythropus*, whereas others list it as suspect; therefore it is **better avoided**.

BOLETUS (Tubiporus) PURPUREUS (3)

Cap 5–20 cm, sometimes rather uneven; at least initially whitish, but yellowish cream in the variety *rhodoxanthus* (1); covered with a fine, whitish pubescence, but grayish brown in the variety *rubro-sanguineus* (2); it is however difficult to find it in this stage because at the slightest breeze or at the slightest contact the pubescence becomes instantly blue and then more slowly pink or carmine; then, with age, it becomes stained violet and blackish. **Stem** oval or pyriform; then more or less cylindrical; yellow, with deep yellow reticule; but soon purple brown with reticule either red or darker than the surface that it covers; slightly velvety; becoming blue at the slightest touch. **Flesh** firm, soon tender, spongy; yellow, becoming instantly blue, and then slowly dark red, when exposed to air. **Odor** of must. **Flavor** sapid. **Pores** small, first yellow, soon vermilion, then almost orange; changing to deep blue at the touch. **Tubules** not too long, shorter near the stem and almost free or free from it. **Spores** olivaceous brown. Singly or in small groups, in summer, in the clearings of latifoliate woods, especially under oaks and beeches. **Poisonous** when raw; but also when well cooked it can cause intestinal discomfort and vomiting in particularly sensitive individuals; nevertheless, some authors dare to consider it as **edible** after long cooking; however, it is not advisable to try it, because even prolonged cooking does nothing to improve the flavor.

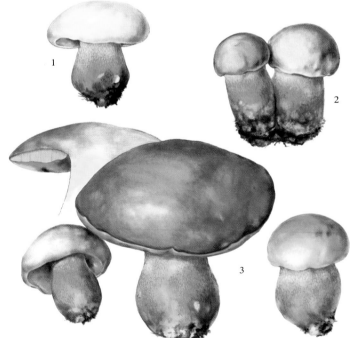

BOLETUS (Tubiporus) SATANAS

Cap globose, then convex 6–30 cm; velvety, but soon glabrous; whitish or with olivaceous shades, then with yellow, red, brownish, olivaceous, and fuliginous spots. **Stem** thick, squat, firm, stuffed; it appears red, but ochraceous at the base, because of the reticule which covers it and which is prevailingly red, but also rosy brown and olivaceous, on a paler background, mostly yellow; sometimes instead of the reticule there are stains of the above colors. **Flesh** thick, soon spongy; whitish, with yellowish spots; exposed to air, it becomes slowly bluish, then again whitish. **Odor** and **flavor** agreeable in the unripe specimens; later disgusting. **Pores** small, round, yellow, soon red, then faded; when bruised, they become blue, then blue green. **Tubules** little or not connected to the stem; yellow, then olivaceous. **Spores** olivaceous brown. It grows in spring and in summer, in the sunny clearings of dry woods of latifoliate trees. **Poisonous**. Similar to it: *Boletus lupinus* (Romagnesi), **suspect**, which, however, in general, does not have a real reticule on the stem, but minute, hairy, brownish lines. *Boletus lupinus* (Bresadolae), **suspect**, whose cap assumes also a greenish coloring; also the stem is less red than that of *B. Satanas* and is covered with a blood red reticule, except in the upper part, where it is bright yellow. *Boletus eastwoodiae*, **poisonous**: cap olivaceous ocher, pores scarlet, stem red and yellow, with scattered, very fine and reddish ocher reticulations; becoming dark blue when bruised; found in North America.

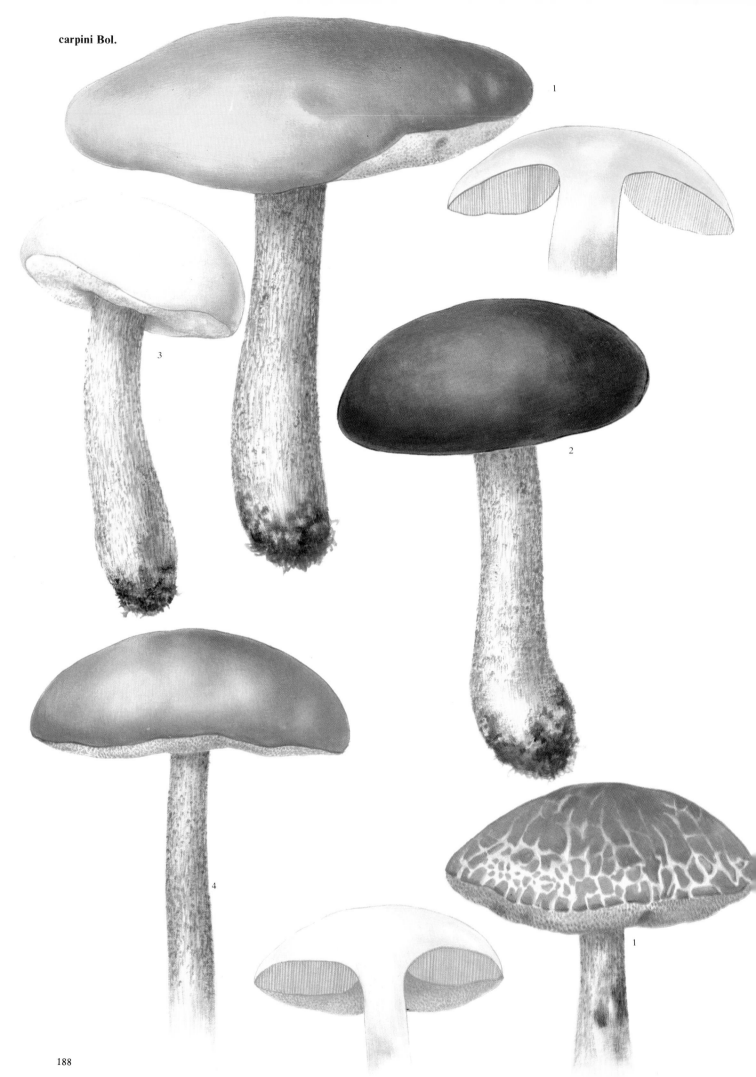

carpini Bol.

1

3

2

4

1

BOLETUS (Trachypus) CARPINI (1, with section)
Cap 4–16 cm; ochraceous, brown, olivaceous brown, or fuliginous brown; but white in the variety *niveus* (3), which grows under birches; almost black and velvety in the variety *oxydabilis* (2), which also grows under birches; glabrous; cuticle slightly viscid in humid weather, becoming corrugated and cracked in dry weather; not decorticable. **Stem** long, thick, thickened downward; fibrous; whitish, covered with rough, cinereous filaments, soon blackish. **Flesh** soon flaccid; whitish; becoming quickly rosy, then gray, when exposed to air; but the flesh of the base greenish, then blackish. **Odor** mild. **Flavor** agreeable. **Pores** small, round; white, then yellowish, finally grayish yellow. **Tubules** thin, long, little or not at all connected to the stem; grayish. **Spores** light brown. It grows in groups, under hornbeams, oaks, and hazelnut trees, but not under poplars and birches. **Edible**: it becomes black with cooking.

BOLETUS LEUCOPHAEUS (4, with section)
Cap 6–18 cm, brownish; cuticle slightly velvety, never cracked into tilelike pieces; stem somewhat thin, long; the flesh white, changes to cinereous pink, but greenish at the base, but so slowly and faintly that this change can go unnoticed; pores white, then cinereous pinkish, not yellow, and finally grayish; tubules long, of the same color as the pores; spores light brown; grows in groups, since spring, under birches; **edible**.

BOLETUS (Trachypus) AURANTIACUS (3)
Cap 4–20 cm, orange tending to brown or to red or to yellow; cuticle velvety, protruding beyond the cap's margin; it cracks in dry weather. **Stem** soon long, thick; whitish, covered with very fine, snow white filaments gathered in parallel cords; at the slightest touch they become reddish, then shrink into rusty roughnesses; the base, when bruised, becomes greenish or deep blue. **Flesh**: the cap soon soft; the stem slightly tough; exposed to air it becomes cinereous rosy, then blackish. **Odor** mild. **Flavor** agreeable. **Pores** small, round, cinereous. **Tubules** thin, long, not adhering to the stem; whitish. **Spores** light brown. It grows under hornbeams, birches, and poplars; seldom under other plants. **Edible**: it becomes black with cooking.

BOLETUS RUFESCENS (2)
Similar to *B. aurantiacus*, but with lighter cap, darker pores, cinereous yellow, then olivaceous and finally fuliginous, and with firmer and tastier flesh; stem covered with flocci blackish from the beginning, and spores light brown; found under birches; **edible**.

BOLETUS DURIUSCULUS (1)
Cap gray or fuliginous; velvety; stem streaked with grooves or prominent ridges; base spotted with green; flesh remaining for some time cinereous pink before changing to blackish, when exposed to air; spores fuliginous; found under poplars; **edible**.

BOLETUS (Trachypus) CROCIPODIUS

Cap hemispheric, then expanded, 3–12 cm; yellow, lemon yellow, olivaceous yellow; then brownish, olivaceous brown, ochraceous brown; cuticle not easily detachable from the cap, velvety, then glabrous and fragmented in many small irregular pieces, against which the paler background shows. **Stem** ovoid, then rather tall, tapered at the base; pale lemon yellow; adorned with granules of the same color; then the granules become brown, while the stem becomes yellowish. **Flesh** thick; firm, but soon soft and watery; the flesh of the stem remains hard and is fibrous; yellowish, changing to reddish or amethystine, and then black, in contact with air. **Odor** and **flavor** agreeable. **Pores** whitish and rounded; then brighter and brighter lemon yellow, but finally olivaceous brown, and angular. **Tubules** rather long; little or not adhering to the stem; lemon yellow, then olivaceous yellow. **Spores** brownish yellow. It grows in groups, in woods of latifoliate trees, especially oaks and beeches. **Edible**, of poor quality: it becomes mushy with cooking. Of small size as *B. crocipodius* and of bright colors as *B. aurantiacus* (page 189) is *Boletus volpinus*, **edible**, growing on sandy grounds, under pines and spruces, among bilberries. Similar to the previous ones is *Boletus lepidus*, characterized by the fact that it grows toward the end of November, along the French Atlantic coast, and perhaps only there.

BOLETUS (Ixocomus) ELEGANS

Cap 4–15 cm, often umbonate; yellow or orange, with brown spots in the center; somewhat viscid in humid weather. **Stem** stuffed, fibrous; with brown reticule above, but with brown striae and dots from the ring downward, and olivaceous brown or blackish at the base. **Ring** white, viscid; then dry, shrunken on the stem, brownish. **Flesh** firm, but soon flaccid; watery after rain; yellow, becoming rosy or violaceous brown if exposed to air. **Odor** tenuous. **Flavor** acidulous. **Pores** yellow, then yellowish, finally olivaceous yellow. **Tubules** yellow; when compressed they become rosy gray; with age they become olivaceous brown; somewhat decurrent on the stem. **Spores** light olive yellow. It grows in groups, not far from larches, in grassy and sunny spots. **Edible**: the cuticle, easily detachable, and the ring, viscid and indigestible, must be discarded; it can be preserved dried, or in oil, after boiling in diluted and aromatic vinegar. Slightly smaller than *B. elegans* is *Boletus flavus*, **edible**, but slightly indigestible: grows near larches, but the pores are larger than in *B. elegans*, and the ripe tubules are gray, not olivaceous brown. Even smaller is *Boletus flavidus*, **edible**, growing near pines, not larches, and with umbonate cap. Similar to the above-mentioned species is *Boletus sibiricus* variety *helveticus*, **edible**, with red brown spots on the cap, cottony, not viscid, ring, persistent around the stem, and sometimes with some pendulous remains at the cap's margin.

BOLETUS (Ixocomus) VISCIDUS (1)

Cap 4–12 cm, cinereous or tending to brown or greenish; in the variety *Bresadolae* (3) it is amethystine yellow or violaceous brown, with yellowish and rather rugose margin; cuticle viscid in humid weather; easily separable, slightly desquamated in dry weather. **Stem** of the same color as the cap, then brownish; finely reticulate above, then with brownish powder; stuffed. **Ring** thin, white; then shrunken on the stem, brownish. **Flesh** soon flaccid, watery; cinereous white, becoming cinereous when exposed to air, with zones of various colors; more brownish at the base. **Odor** and **flavor** agreeable. **Pores** large, angular; whitish, then of the color of the cap. **Tubules** long, but very short near the stem; decurrent; grayish tending to olivaceous. **Spores** brownish. It grows from spring to autumn, near larches. **Edible**: the cuticle, viscid, must be discarded.

BOLETUS TRIDENTINUS (2)

Cap 5–15 cm, viscid, yellow, then reddish orange or rusty brown; made somewhat rugose by squamules that tend to move apart while the mushroom is ripening; stem the color of the cap, or slightly lighter; marked by a soft reticule on top, next to the tubules; flesh soft, yellow, pink at contact with air, acidulous; pores rosy ocher, then more and more brownish; tubules a little decurrent; spores greenish yellow; growing near larches; **edible**.

BOLETUS (Ixocomus) LUTEUS

Cap hemispheric or conical, then somewhat expanded, 4–14 cm, often umbonate; with fine, radial striae; brown, ochraceous, or reddish brown; sometimes with violaceous shades due to the glutinous coat that covers it; this coat is very thick and persistent in *subluteus*, **edible**, which grows in North America; drying or with age, it discolors; cuticle easily detachable; margin often adorned with the remains of the membrane that was protecting the tubules; this membrane, whitish at first, becomes then olivaceous, lacerated, and hangs down like a ring around the stem. **Stem** solid; from the ring to the cap it is faded yellow and strewn with ocher granules more or less deep colored; toward the base it is brownish. **Ring** large, with dilacerated margin; first glutinous and whitish, then it dries around the stem, becoming brownish violet. **Flesh** soft; becoming watery with age; lemon color or whitish, sometimes pink under the cuticle of the cap; exposed to air it does not change color considerably. **Odor** and **flavor** insignificant. **Pores** yellow, round, small; but soon angular, yellowish, then olivaceous. **Tubules** rather long, adhering to the stem; yellow, then with olivaceous or ochraceous shades. **Spores** brownish ocher. It grows in late summer and autumn, in the grass, in pine woods. **Edible**, pleasant tasting when unripe and free from all glutinous parts; of poor quality when very ripe, and then the tubules and the stem should also be discarded.

BOLETUS (Ixocomus) GRANULATUS

Cap 4–14 cm, but 6–24 cm in Palestine; sometimes uneven; brown tending to ocher, yellow, or red; it discolors with age; viscid or dry depending on the weather; cuticle separable. **Stem** thick; the upper part, when still unripe, exudes, as the pores, dewy droplets; yellow, with yellowish then brown granules. **Flesh** soft; yellow; the stem brownish. **Odor** and **flavor** mild. **Pores** yellowish, slightly angular. **Tubules** short, adhering to the stem; yellowish, then olivaceous. **Spores** ochraceous. Grows under pines; it forms fruiting bodies several times a year. **Laxative** when old. **Edible**, sapid as long as unripe and freed from the viscid cuticle: while removing the cuticle it is advisable to protect the hands with gloves in order to avoid persistent spots on them. However, the decorticated mushroom is less tasty; to free it from the viscid substance, indigestible and not very pleasant to the eye, leave the mushroom for a few minutes in boiling water, then drain it thoroughly and cook it with the proper seasoning.

Similar to the above and **edible**: *Boletus albidipes*, paler and with festooned margin; *Boletus brevipes*, more viscid and without granules on the stem; *Boletus collinitus*: stem slender, all dotted by granular spots, base wrapped in yellow rosy filaments; it does not secrete droplets from the pores; found in the mountains; *Boletus leptopus*, similar to *B. collinitus*, from which it can be distinguished for the lighter cap and the squatter stem; furthermore it grows along the coast, under pines, not in the mountains.

granulatus Bol.

193

BOLETUS VARIEGATUS

Cap hemispheric, then convex, 5–15 cm, or also plane, somewhat uneven, with thin margin; first covered with an unbroken, ochraceous, moist, rough cuticle; then this cuticle becomes smooth and fragments into furfuraceous, brownish squamules, regularly spread on the cap; the ochraceous yellow subcuticle can be seen between the squamules. **Stem** cylindric, thick, stout, sometimes in the shape of a truncated cone; base often thickened and curved, generally covered with white down; smooth; more or less faded ochraceous yellow. **Flesh** thick, soft; yellowish or saffron or faded orange; but the flesh of the base of the stem reddish; becoming bluish when exposed to air. **Odor** slight of vinegar, radish, or chlorine. **Flavor** sweetish. **Pores** small, then larger; olivaceous yellow, then fuliginous; becoming bluish when bruised. **Tubules** short, annexed to the stem; not easily detachable from the cap; olivaceous. **Spores** olivaceous brown. It grows in groups of many specimens, spread here and there near pines. **Edible**. There are those who consider it as the driest of the *Ixocomus* and those who consider it as the moistest of the *Xerocomus*. Also *Boletus sulphureus*, **edible**, has the cap, 5–10 cm, squamose, the flesh that becomes, for a short time, bluish when exposed to air, and grows near pine trees; it is however completely sulfur yellow; when growing very large and in tufts, on pine sawdust, it takes the name *sphaerocephalus*.

BOLETUS (Ixocomus) BOVINUS

Cap convex, then expanded, 4–12 cm, often somewhat cuspidate, with the margin thin, lobate and undulate; ocher yellow, orange, or faded brown; cuticle viscid in humid weather, cartilaginous in dry weather and soon cracked; separable from the cap with difficulty. **Stem** thin, often curved, often short; sometimes flared toward the cap and with tapered base; of the same color as the cap, more yellow near the cap, paler, seldom brownish, at the base. **Flesh** of the cap yellowish, soft, having a particular spongelike elasticity; soon mucilaginous and verminous; flesh of the stem more brightly colored and slightly fibrous; exposed to air it becomes sometimes pinkish; less often slightly cerulean. **Odor** mild. **Flavor** agreeable. **Pores** soon very large, angular, separated by thin septa; grayish, then yellowish, finally olivaceous brown. **Tubules** short, decurrent, not easily separable; olivaceous yellow, becoming olivaceous brown with age or when bruised. **Spores** olivaceous brown. It grows in the grass, in mountainous pine woods, often together with *Gomphidius roseus* (page 174); in rings or in tufts of several specimens, sometimes with the caps welded to one another. **Edible**, of poor quality. Similar to *B. bovinus* is *Boletus mitis*, **edible**, with the cap's margin tending to pinkish or to amethystine. *Boletus americanus*, **edible**, which grows in the pine woods of North America, resembles *bovinus* in its color, viscosity, tubules, and pores, but the margin of the cap is covered with downy remains of the partial veil, and the stem is slender, thin.

BOLETUS (Ixocomus) PIPERATUS (1)

Cap 2–6 cm, ochraceous brown; glabrous, smooth; viscid in humid weather. **Stem** thin, fragile; slightly paler than the cap; yellow and downy at the base. **Flesh** tender; ochraceous yellow; the flesh of the stem yellow; it does not change color in contact with air. **Odor** soft. **Flavor** like that of pepper. **Pores** large, denticulate, reddish brown. **Tubules** reddish brown, slightly decurrent. **Spores** olivaceous brown with reddish shades. It grows in small groups, under conifers and latifoliate trees, more frequently under birches. A little paler and bigger than *B. piperatus* is *Boletus (Ixocomus) lignicola*, **edible**, with mild flavor, growing in coniferous wood: with pores yellow, then greenish, and the flesh yellow, but becoming bluish for a short time when exposed to air.

BOLETUS AMARELLUS (2)

Cap 2–6 cm, ochraceous, reddish at the margin; slightly viscid in humid weather. **Stem** squat, yellow; with red granules in the upper part. **Flesh** white, rosy near the tubules; yellow at the base of the stem; acidulous, then bitter. **Pores** yellow, then red. **Spores** brownish. Under conifers. **Not edible**. Also *Boletus rubinus*, **not edible**, is bitter; but it grows in the summer, under latifoliate trees, and its stem, pores, and tubules are red.

BOLETUS CRAMESINUS (3)

Cap 2–6 cm, red, soon discolored; viscid. *Stem* yellow with reddish or brownish shades or spots. **Flesh** whitish, slightly rosy under the cuticle, fibrous in the stem; of mild flavor. **Tubules** and **pores** yellow. **Spores** brownish. It grows in the grass, under latifoliate trees. **Edible**. *Boletus cramesinus* is considered a *Xerocomus*, that is, with dry cap, even though in humid weather it is just as viscid as the *Ixocomus*.

BOLETUS (Xerocomus) SUBTOMENTOSUS (2)

Cap 3–15 cm, olivaceous yellow or olivaceous brown; velvety; drying and with age it fades and cracks. **Stem** yellowish, sometimes with reddish or brownish spots; finely velvety or flocculose; with ridges, connected in a reticule, more or less in relief and of orange brown color; but sometimes smooth with few brownish dots; firm, stuffed, fibrous. **Flesh** thick, firm, then soft; the cap yellowish white, brownish under the cuticle; the flesh of the stem of a more intense color, and that of the base even deeper. **Odor** soft. **Flavor** acidulous, then mild. **Pores** large, uneven, denticulate, bright golden yellow; they do not become bluish when bruised. **Tubules** rather long, annexed to the stem; yellowish, then olivaceous. **Spores** yellow with olivaceous shades. It grows from spring to autumn, in grassy places in the woods. **Edible**, of poor quality: it becomes mucilaginous with cooking.

BOLETUS SPADICEUS (1)

Similar to *B. subtomentosus,* but with the cap purple brown, sometimes with pinkish shades, covered by a soft, yellowish velvet; the stem is yellow and covered with flocculose, reddish brown granulations, arranged to form a reticule, or at least ridges, more evident in the upper part of the stem; the flesh of the cap is yellowish, more deeply colored in the stem and even more in the base; grows under conifers. **Edible**, not in great demand, but, nevertheless, of good quality.

BOLETUS (Xerocomus) CHYRSENTERON (1, five specimens)

Cap 3–12 cm, ocher brown or olivaceous brown; reddish at the margin; velvety, dry, soon cracked; the surface showing between the cracks, and the bottom of the erosions are red. In autumn it appears darker, brown or sepia brown, and without cracks, so that it could be denominated *scotioarrhagadosus*. **Stem** firm; yellow, with red striae in the upper part, with red dots or spots or striae in the lower part; when bruised, it becomes blue; stuffed. **Flesh** soft; yellow; red under the cuticle; brownish at the base; when exposed to air, the flesh near the tubules becomes bluish, while that of the stem becomes reddish. **Odor** of fruit. **Flavor** agreeable. **Pores** large, angular, yellowish, then greenish; becoming blue when bruised. **Tubules** annexed to the stem; olivaceous yellow. **Spores** olivaceous brown. It grows in the woods, in the grass and moss. **Edible**, but becoming mushy when cooked.

Similar to *B. chrysenteron* and **edible**: *Boletus Russelii*: cap olivaceous brown, then reddish and cracked; stem long, with reticule and fibers lacerated and protruding; grows in North America. *Boletus versicolor* (2), pinkish, red, or purple, soon faded and spotted; stem not striate, yellow above, reddish in the middle, brownish at the base; a layer, one millimeter thick, of flesh under the cuticle, is of the same color as the cuticle; it avoids grassy places. *Boletus armeniacus* (3): small, cap 2–5 cm, apricot color; stem golden ocher, yellow above, carmine in the middle; grows under latifoliate trees.

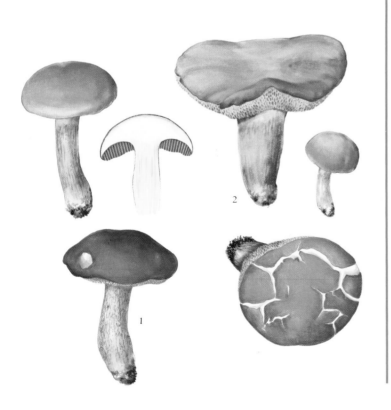

chyrsenteron Bol.

BOLETUS (Xerocomus) BADIUS
Cap first hemispheric, then convex or plane, 4–14 cm, sometimes rather uneven; brown, at times very dark, almost black, other times discolored, ochraceous; cuticle dry, velvety; slightly viscid in humid weather; not easily removable from the cap. **Stem** sometimes thick, sometimes thin; stuffed; fibrillar; much paler than the cap, except at the base where it is of the same color as the cap. **Flesh** firm, then soft, finally flaccid; fibrous in the stem; whitish, but here and there yellowish; brown just under the cuticle of the cap; becoming bluish when exposed to air, especially near the tubules and here and there along the stem. **Odor** tenuous, of fruit. **Flavor** mild. **Pores** very small and white, then large, angular, and olivaceous yellow; becoming deep blue when bruised. **Tubules** adherent to the stem; yellowish, then olivaceous yellow. It grows in large groups, also in woods of latifoliate trees, oaks, beeches, chestnuts, but more frequently in coniferous trees, oaks, beeches, chestnuts, but more frequently in coniferous woods. **Edible**, of good quality. Similar to *Boletus badius*, but also to *Boletus pinicola* (page 181), is *Boletus badio-rufus*. **Edibility unknown**, since only few specimens have been found until now, exclusively in France: cap pulvinate, with the margin involute toward the tubules; purple brown; stem with radiciform base, olivaceous, with a reticule of hexagonal meshes in the upper part; flesh white, unchangeable in air; strong odor and sapid flavor; tubules decurrent, of olivaceous color when fully ripened.

BOLETUS (Xerocomus) PULVERULENTUS
Cap brown, olivaceous brown, vinous brown; lighter, tending to yellow in the unripe specimens; becoming blue, then olivaceous where bruised; hemispheric, with the margin involute toward the tubules; then expanded, 3–14 cm, gibbous, with undulate margin; velvety, then glabrous; viscid in humid weather. **Stem** rather thin but firm; cylindric but flared upward; often curved, with a pointed base, from which a radiciform appendix runs horizontally on the ground; velvety; golden yellow above, brown speckled with purple red in the middle, fuliginous brown or olivaceous brown at the base; stuffed. **Flesh** soft, yellowish, which becomes immediately deep blue, then green gray when exposed to air. **Odor** tenuous. **Flavor** pleasant in the unripe specimens, bitter in the old ones. **Pores** somewhat large and uneven, golden yellow and lemon yellow; becoming blue, then greenish at the slightest touch. **Tubules** long, annexed to the stem and sometimes also decurrent; chrome yellow, then eventually olivaceous. **Spores** olivaceous. It grows in the humid and mossy recesses of fir, chestnut and beech woods. **Edible**, of good quality. At first sight it appears similar to *Boletus subtomentosus* (page 196) or to *Boletus badius*, but it is unmistakably characterized by the color, bright yellow, of the upper part of the stem, and by the deep blue coloring acquired by the flesh when wounded or bruised, due to oxidation in air.

BOLETUS (Boletinus) CAVIPES

Cap similar to a small onion with acute umbo; then it expands, 5–14 cm, becoming uneven, gibbous, with the margin often lobate and festooned; cuticle dry, like suede, covered with a coarse down, denser at the center, darker than the background, and which, depending on its color, makes the cap brown, in the form *ferrugineus,* or yellow, in the form *flavidus,* or other intermediate colors. **Stem** slightly lighter than the cap, but yellow from the ring upward; generally barrel shaped; fragile and hollow even in the unripe specimens; in the stem's cavity very often there is a small amount of water. **Ring** white and glutinous, then cottony and yellowish. **Flesh** soft and yellowish in the cap; fibrous and with rosy shades in the stem, or at least near the base. **Odor** soft.

Flavor agreeable. **Pores** large, angular, arranged in radial or curved-radial rows; larger near the stem; yellowish, then olivaceous yellow. **Tubules** short, decurrent; not easily detachable from the cap; yellowish, then olivaceous yellow. **Spores** olivaceous yellow. It grows in groups, in the mountains, near larches, in sunny spots, especially those facing north. **Edible**, of poor quality: it can be dried making it a better food.

BOLETUS (Boletinus) PICTUS (2, 3)

Similar to *Boletinus cavipes,* but quite smaller and of a nice vinous red color; grows in the Far East, especially in Japan, and in North America; **edible**.

BOLETUS (Strobilomyces) STROBILACEUS

This mushroom is initially entirely whitish, then it becomes rosy cinereous and finally fuliginous and black in all its parts. **Cap** grayish, hemispheric, then convex, more or less expanded, 3–15 cm, covered with large, woolly scales, darker than the background, triangular, arranged like roof tiles and protruding, roof-gutter-like, from the margin, from which sometimes hang long, blackish, filamentous tails. **Stem** long, thick, flared toward the cap; but sometimes, vice versa, tapered toward the cap and distinctly bulbous at the base; cinereous, covered with darker, flocculose scales; but with a light reticule, on reddish white background, above the ring; then it becomes blackish there too. **Ring** filamentous, blackish, evanescent. **Flesh** firm, somewhat tough; whitish, becoming reddish and then smoky violaceous in air; but blackish in the variety *floccopus*; with age, it dries out, instead of rotting. **Odor** and **flavor** mild. **Pores** large, polygonal, quite regular; bigger near the stem; smaller near the margin of the cap; whitish; becoming reddish when bruised; then black. **Tubules** long, annexed to the stem and sometimes slightly decurrent; but other times, rounded toward the stem and detached from it. **Spores** sepia brown or purple black. It grows singly or in small groups, in the hills and mountains, in latifoliate and mixed woods, especially on soft soil, like that loosened by moles. **Edible**, while unripe, but mediocre, tough.

BOLETUS (Porphyrellus) PORPHYROSPORUS

Cap 5–15 cm, grayish or brownish gray or fuliginous; becoming black when bruised; velvety, dry, not shining; cracked in lasting dry weather; margin thin, and initially involute toward the tubules. **Stem** thick, first oval, then cylindric, often curved, sometimes slender; of the same color as the cap, a little discolored at the base; fibrillar, covered with very fine, darker granules, but not rugose. **Flesh** thick, but thin at the margin of the cap; first firm, then soft; the stem fibrous; white, then whitish; when exposed to air it becomes slate pink, especially at the top of the stem, but blue green near the tubules; then it becomes entirely blackish gray. It stains the paper green, and the water fuliginous brown. **Odor** mild. **Flavor** acidulous. **Pores** rather large, now round, now angular, uneven; first cinereous cream, then gradually ochraceous, olivaceous gray, purple brown, fuliginous brown; becoming greenish blue, then fuliginous at the touch. **Tubules** long, shorter near the stem and only partly annexed to it; cinereous cream, then olivaceous gray; at contact with air they become purple pink, then cinereous pinkish. **Spores** cocoa colored. It grows singly or in groups, in the mountains, in coniferous woods, especially under firs; rarer in the plains and in mixed woods. The variety *fuligineus*, smaller and darker, grows only under conifers; the color of the tubules and of the flesh near them does not change when in contact with air. **Edible**, of poor quality.

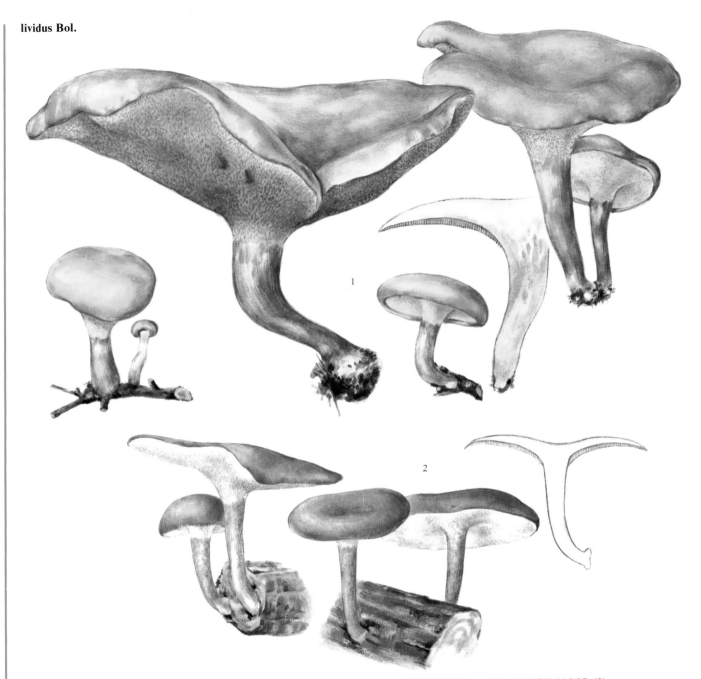

BOLETUS (Gyrodon) LIVIDUS (1)

Cap 4–20 cm, sometimes unevenly depressed; margin undulate; yellowish ocher or rusty ocher; glabrous, viscid, covered by fuliginous fibrils. **Stem** gracilent, also eccentric, flared upward, thickened at the base; often undulate; pruinose; slightly darker than the cap; stuffed, fibrous, then spongy. **Flesh** tender; yellowish; becoming blue, at least near the tubules, when exposed to air. **Odor** soft. **Flavor** acidulous. **Pores** small, denticulate; yellow, then greenish, finally blackish. **Tubules** short, decurrent, olivaceous yellow. **Spores** olivaceous brown. It grows in humid woods, especially under alder, birch, and hazelnut trees. **Edible**, of good quality, and therefore unjustly neglected by the collectors.

POLYPORUS (Polyporellus) BRUMALIS (2)

Cap 2–12 cm, faded ocher, ochraceous, or fuliginous; margin involute and, at least initially, protected by cilia; velvety, squamose, but soon glabrous. **Stem** slender, strong, paler than the cap; squamose and granulous; then glabrous. **Flesh** elastic, tenacious, thin, white. **Odor** and flavor agreeable. **Pores** small, round, white or cream, then cinereous. **Tubules** short, decurrent, white, then cinereous. **Spores** white. It grows in spring, on wood of latifoliate trees. **Edible**, while unripe. Similar to it, but not edible: *Polyporus arcularius,* with the pores so large as to resemble small alveoli of a honeycomb, and *Polyporus ciliatus,* with very large pores and with the margin of the cap with a characteristic fringe.

POLYPORUS (Melanopus) SQUAMOSUS

Cap semicircular or circular, 10–60 cm, flat, slightly depressed near the stem; cream or light ocher, covered with darker scales, arranged in concentric curves, less dense along the margin. **Stem** squat, often eccentric and obliquely outstretched; whitish, but soon blackish brown, starting from the base. **Flesh** white, tender; but soon elastic and tough, and finally corky; often inhabited by small coleopters, which contribute to the propagation of the mushroom. **Odor** sometimes of honey, sometimes of rancid flour. **Flavor** sometimes agreeable, sometimes sweetish. **Pores** small and whitish; then gradually bigger, denticulate, and yellowish. **Tubules** short, sometimes almost unperceivable, decurrent netlike along the stem; whitish, then yellowish. **Spores** white. Grows in tufts of several specimens with confluent bases, in the summer, on live or dead latifoliate trees, such as poplars, willows, elms; seldom on firs; sometimes it sprouts for the first time at the beginning of spring and a second time in late summer; it can sprout for several years at the same place. **Edible**, while unripe. The base of the stem is black also in *Polyporus varius*, **not edible** because coriaceous: cap 3–12 cm, ochraceous, thin, without scales, smooth. On the contrary, the stem is never black in *Polyporus Forquignoni*, **edible** while unripe, which looks like a miniature *P. squamosus*: cap 1–6 cm, squamose, with fringes along the margin, brittle, fleshy, not coriaceous.

POLYPORUS (Polystictus) PERENNIS (1)

Cap funnel shaped, 3–9 cm, yellowish, rusty, or brown; with radial striae and darker concentric circles; velvety, then glabrous; margin thin, sericeous, with cilia and fringes. **Stem** thin, yellow, velvety, then rusty and glabrous; fibrous, stuffed. **Flesh** thin, tough, rust colored. **Odor** and **flavor** soft. **Pores** small, round, then angular, uneven; first pruinose and whitish, then grayish brown. **Tubules** short, decurrent, grayish brown. **Spores** yellowish. It grows in groups of several specimens, sometimes with the caps joined together; it can live for several years. **Not edible**.

POLYPORUS (Melanopus) PICIPES (3)

Cap bowl shaped, 5–15 cm; brown; slightly viscid, fibrillar, glabrous, sericeous, shining, even if slightly rugose and uneven; margin thin, elastic. **Stem** blackish brown toward the base, lighter upward; velvety, then glabrous; sometimes eccentric or lateral, sometimes atrophic or completely lacking. **Flesh** elastic, thin, coriaceous, white. **Odor** strong. **Pores** small, white or cream. **Tubules** short. **Spores** white. It grows in tufts, on latifoliate trees; rare on conifers; it can live for several years. **Not edible**, not only when several years old, but also when still young.

POLYPORUS ELEGANS (2)

Similar to *P. picipes,* but with the stem blackish brown from the base to halfway up, and then abruptly white to the top; it is **not edible**; nor is *Polyporus melanus*, smaller, with pruinose and floccculose cap, and with short, twisted and blackish stem.

3

1

2

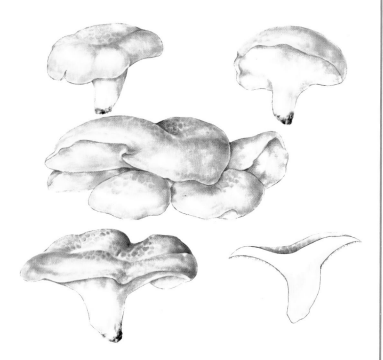

POLYPORUS (Caloporus) PES CAPRAE

Cap brownish, even though with greensih cuticle, since the latter is covered with brownish or fuliginous filaments, gathered in tufts, sometimes rather ruffled; first convex with the margin rolled toward the tubules; then plane-convex, 6–12 cm, with the margin rather explanate and slightly undulate; often divided in two sections by a deep groove, which continues down to the base and makes the mushroom resemble a cloven hoof. **Stem** short, thick, somewhat uneven, often divided, as already said, and also slightly curved; smooth, whitish with ochraceous or yellowish shades; stuffed. **Flesh** white, tinged with greenish. **Odor** mild. **Flavor** agreeable, of hazelnuts. **Pores** large, whitish. **Tubules** short, decurrent along the stem. **Spores** whitish. In wood clearings, especially beech and fir woods. **Edible**, of good quality when still unripe, even raw in salads; it is convenient to discard the cuticle and part of the stem. Equally under firs, or better on the stumps and on the roots of the firs, more rarely on other conifers or latifoliate trees, one can find another mushroom with brownish cap, *Phaeolus Schweinitzii,* **not edible**: turbinate, 10–30 cm, with the upper surface knobby and felted; laterally covered, down to the base, with large, uneven, yellowish or olivaceous, then brown, pores; flesh saffron colored, soft and spongy, but finally tough and cork-like; sometimes shaped like a horse hoof, without stem, planted sideways on the wood on which it feeds.

POLYPORUS (Caloporus) OVINUS

Cap convex with the margin lobate and involute; whitish, smooth, glabrous; then plane, 6–12 cm, or also depressed, uneven, with undulate margin; yellowish, then olivaceous yellow, and finally olivaceous brown, with yellow spots, cracked in tilelike pieces, starting from the center. **Stem** squat, often tapered at the base; sometimes curved, sometimes eccentric in relation to the cap; of the same color as the cap; with some darker spots, furfuraceous. **Flesh** thick, firm, brittle, whitish, then yellowish. **Odor** agreeable. **Flavor** of almonds. **Pores** very small, white, then yellowish. **Tubules** very short, decurrent unevenly along the stem; whitish, then yellowish. **Spores** white. It grows in groups of several specimen or also in tufts of two or three individuals, sometimes with the caps welded together, in coniferous woods, especially under pines, in the mountains; rare in the plains. **Edible**, of good quality, when unripe; parboiling advisable; it becomes yellow with cooking; it can be preserved in oil. *Polyporus cristatus,* **not edible**, can reach the size of *P. ovinus*; the color of the cap, olivaceous brown, is the same as that of the fully ripe *P. ovinus*; but the cuticle is velvety, then finely squamose and cracked; the stem, yellowish or olivaceous, is covered with pores down to the base; the flesh, soon tough and brittle, is greenish, acidulous or bitterish; growing on humus and on rotted wood, in the woods, especially under oaks.

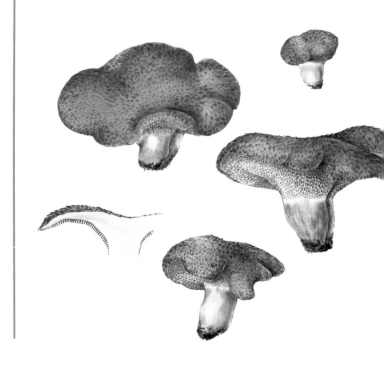

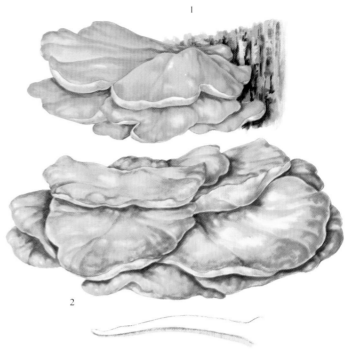

POLYPORUS (Caloporus) CONFLUENS

Caps of various shapes, with uneven surfaces and lobate margins; numerous, close together, lying upon one another forming a tuft of 15–35 centimetres in diameter; cuticle not separable from the cap, smooth and rosy yellow; then sometimes somewhat lacerated and ochraceous pink or ochraceous. **Stems** short, unequal; flared upward and bending with the caps; confluent in a single, fleshy mass at the base; smooth, furfuraceous, whitish, with a pinkish shade toward the base; firm, fragile, stuffed. **Flesh** firm and compact; brittle; becoming corky with age; white, sometimes becoming shaded with pink at contact with air. **Odor** soft. **Flavor** acidulous-bitterish; but the flesh of the older specimens is distinctly bitter, especially near the cuticle. **Pores** first white or rosy white, very small; then becoming larger and of the color of the cap, but lighter. **Tubules** decurrent almost to the base of the stem; short, not separable from the flesh of the cap and of the stem; whitish, later yellowish. **Spores** white. It grows in coniferous woods. **Edible** when still unripe, but mediocre and bitterish if cooked without parboiling; tubules and cuticle must always be discarded; this is easily done with a sharp potato peeler; with cooking, the mushroom becomes yellow; if eaten in great quantities it has a laxative effect; it can be dried; it improves if preserved in oil.

POLYPORUS (Polypilus) SULPHUREUS (2)

Caps numerous, with irregular, bizarre shapes, gibbous, horizontally protruding, lying one upon the other, shelflike, 20–40 centimeters in all; with the margins undulate and divided into lobes by deep grooves; confluent at the base in a single mass, sometimes in a single, short trunk, whitish and then yellowish. The upper part is yellow, rosy yellow, or lemon yellow; but of a beautiful rosy color in the variety *miniatus* (1), which grows in the·Far East; fading with age, but becoming stained with brownish yellow. The lower part is covered with small **pores**, first round, then angular, sulfur yellow, excluding dewy, yellowish droplets. When the **spores** are ripe, they cover with a thick powder, first yellow, then white, the caps on which they fall. **Flesh** thick, soft, juicy, yellowish; with agreeable **odor** and acidulous **flavor**; then it becomes light, hard, brittle, and exhales a sweet smell. It grows from spring to autumn on the trunks of latifoliate trees, also on fruit trees, which it erodes and causes to fall; found less frequently on the trunks of conifers or on felled trunks. **Edible** when still unripe.

Only the margin is yellow in *Trametes odorata* or *Osmoporus odoratus,* **not edible**, which can be found all year round on larches and firs, in the mountains, but which grows only in humid weather: cap of irregular shape, 6–14 cm, sometimes multiple, rusty, rugose, hairy, with yellow margin sometimes very showy; pores angular, cinnamon colored; tubules long, furfuraceous; flesh hard, rusty, with persistent odor of anise, therefore the denomination *odorata*; spores white, then brown.

POLYPORUS (Polypilus) UMBELLATUS

From a large trunk, whitish with pinkish and ochraceous shades, several cylindrical ramifications branch out, which divide further in numerous shorter and smaller branches, each bearing a cap at the tip: fifty, a hundred, two hundred, each with a diameter of 2–4 centimeters. These **caps** are at first convex, with central umbo; then they expand, and finally become depressed at the center; hazel color, tending sometimes to gray, sometimes to brown; covered with darker squamules; often somewhat cracked; with the margins thin, undulate, and sometimes radially fissured. On the lower side they are white, covered with short, whitish **tubules** terminating into round, then angular, **pores**, decurrent along the stem. The **flesh** is white, tender; the flesh of the branches is, however, rather fibrous; it has slight **odor** of flour and agreeable **flavor**. **Spores** white. It grows in the summer, but sometimes also in autumn, in woods of latifoliate trees, especially beeches and oaks, not only on the stumps but also on buried roots, and then it mistakenly appears terriculous; each tuft can reach 30 centimeters in diameter and in height, but sometimes it can grow to half a meter; **edible**, worth considering also because of its size, but it spoils very quickly and then is no longer edible, especially because of the very bad smell; therefore, once cooked, it should be consumed as soon as possible.

POLYPORUS (Boletopsis) LEUCOMELAS

Cap from gray to blackish with violet shades; becoming reddish brown when bruised; smooth, fibrillar, sericeous; then rather rugose and cracked; hemispheric, with the margin divided into lobes adhering to the stem; then expanded, 6–15 cm, and gibbous or depressed, with the margin undulate and sometimes also oddly curled. **Stem** unequal, generally squat, firm, slightly eccentric with respect to the cap; of the same color as the cap, with whitish or yellowish spots; initially velvety and squamose, then glabrous; stuffed, then with few cavities. **Flesh** very thick, tender, fibrous, white; becoming pinkish and then blackish when exposed to air. **Odor** unperceivable. **Flavor** of the cap agreeable, of the stem bitterish. **Pores** somewhat large, oblong or angular, sometimes denticulate; white, then cinereous. **Tubules** short, decurrent on the stem, cinereous. **Spores** white. It grows in the mountains, in the woods, especially of conifer trees; seldom in the plains. **Edible**, but of poor quality: should be boiled in water for a few minutes, drained, and then cooked with the proper seasoning.

Let us mention here another mushroom, although of different genus, with the pores large, angular, almost like the alveoli of a honeycomb: the small *Favolus europaeus*, **not edible**, cap cream colored, squamose, not more than 6 centimeters in diameter, stem, black at the base, not more than 3 centimeters long; found on ash and fruit trees.

leucomelas Pol.

POLYPORUS (Polypilus) FRONDOSUS (1)

From a thick, whitish, and pruinose stem or trunk branch out obliquely numerous branches each bearing a horizontal spatulate or flabellate cap with undulate margin; the upper surface of the cap is brown, grayish brown, or grayish, somewhat rugose, velvety, covered lengthwise by darker fibrils; in the lower side they are covered with **pores**, the openings of the very short **tubules**; the **pores** are small, rounded, but gradually more oblong toward the stem, so that the last ones are decurrent on the stem like minute gills. Diameter of the tuft: 15–40 centimeters. **Flesh** brittle, rather fibrous, white. **Odor** aromatic, rather strong. **Flavor** agreeable. **Spores** white. It grows in summer and autumn, on the trunk or stump of various latifoliate trees, especially oaks. **Edible** when still unripe.

POLYPORUS FRONDOSUS variety INTYBACEUS (2)

Caps gray, then fuliginous; turned obliquely outward or also upward, with lobate margins, so that as a whole the fruiting body looks like the head of an endive; peduncles very close together, undulate, whitish or cinereous, spotted with yellow confluent in a trunk or stem, reddish brown; pores large, whitish, then cinereous; odor of flour; **edible** when still unripe.

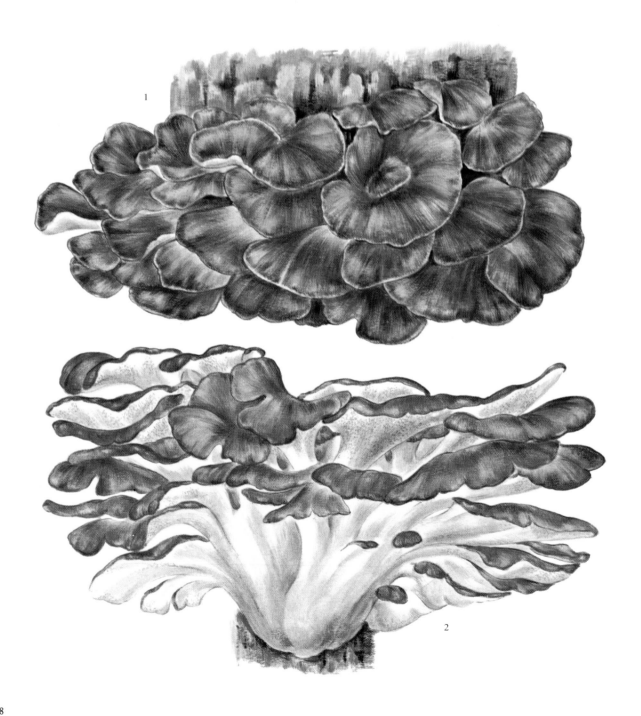

POLYPORUS (Polypilus) GIGANTEUS

Caps flabelliform, lying upon one another, shelflike; brown, rusty, or fuliginous brown; with blackish spots; with coarse, radial wrinkles; with concentric depressions more deeply colored; with the margins light, granulous, lobate, often fissured; the whole mushroom, when aging or drying, becomes blackish; on the whole, it can be over 50 centimeters in diameter. **Stems** hardly singled out, conglobated in an irregular mass; whitish. **Flesh** soon fibrous and tough, whitish; becoming reddish, then blackish, when exposed to air or bruised. **Odor** strong, agreeable. **Flavor** acidulous. For some time the lower surface of the caps appears smooth and whitish; then short **tubules** begin to form on it, terminating in small, white and then cinereous, **pores**; both tubules and pores become blackish when bruised. **Spores** white or whitish. It grows on the stumps of latifoliate trees, especially of beeches and oaks, in huge masses, sometimes covering the entire stump. **Edible** only as long as unripe and therefore still tender. *Polyporus (Polypilus) montanus* grows in the mountains, on the trunks of still vegetating conifers; it is **edible**: several caps, similar to cornucopiae, stuffed and ochraceous, sprout here and there along a stem similar to the trunk of a latifoliate tree; the tubules are decurrent on the lateral surface of the cap as far as the stem; flesh whitish and unchangeable in air; it can reach the same size as *P. giganteus*. The unripe specimens are of remarkable dimensions and are **edible**.

CORIOLUS VERSICOLOR (2)

It is formed by several caps, with a total diameter of 6–12 centimeters, thin, coriaceous, flabelliform, with undulate margin, attached together laterally, spread out in various directions, horizontally, lying one upon another. The upper surface is marked by concentric zones of various colors, velvety, with a silken sheen. The lower surface is covered with small pores, dug in the very tissue of the cap, white, round, then uneven and yellowish. Spores whitish or ochraceous. It grows throughout the year, on decaying wood of latifoliate trees, rarely on coniferous wood. Similar to it is *Coriolus zonatus*, less thin, gibbous, brownish, with the zones lacking the silken sheen, the pores white, then gray and green gray.

LENZITES SAEPIARIA (1)

Similar to *Coriolus versicolor*, when seen from above, but with less conspicuous colors, among which brown predominates; velvety, but hispid. The lower surface has close, thin, furcate gills, connected toward the center like pores; rigid, yellowish, then brownish, pulverulent. Flesh rather thick, corklike, rusty. Spores white. It grows throughout the year on the wood of conifers, even on lumber. *Lenzites abietina* also grows on processed wood: brown, with orange ocher margin, and sparse gills.

Equally lignicolous, thin, zonate, woolly, hispid, coriaceous, but with a smooth lower surface: *Stereum purpureum*, cinereous above, brownish underneath, and *Stereum hirsutum*, yellowish above, brownish underneath.

None of the above mushrooms is edible.

DAEDALEA QUERCINA (2)

Semicircular 6–30 cm, more or less bulky; with surface of a corklike color, rugose, with concentric zones more or less noticeable near the margin. Lower surface covered with pores, dug into the very tissue of the cap; first rounded, then unevenly dilatate, with the separations among them eventually resembling gills, intersecting one another labyrinthlike. Flesh odorless, with color and consistency of cork; stratified, but with not too distinct layers. Spores white. It grows on latifoliate trees, especially on oak and chestnuts, either live or felled, or even on lumber; rarely on conifers; it can live for several years. Similar to it, but with hexagonal, regular pores, is *Trametes hexagonoides*, found more frequently on lumber.

TRAMETES GIBBOSA (1)

Seen from above, it looks like *Daedalea quercina,* but it is paler and slightly velvety; the part nearer to the host is greenish, a color due to algae; the margin is rosy cinereous. The lower surface is covered with pores, dug into the tissue of the cap, sometimes rounded, sometimes fused together here and there, so that the septa among the pores look like gills; white, then yellowish. Flesh corky, tenacious, white. Spores white. It grows throughout the year, on latifoliate trees, or on lumber.

Similar to the preceeding one is *Trametes hispida,* which, however, is smaller and of a darker color both on the upper surface and internally. **None of the above mushrooms is edible**.

UNGULINA MARGINATA (1)

Hoof shaped: 10–30 cm by 8–16 cm. In the first years: crust of a tissue distinct from that of the rest, rugose, resinous, with white, yellow, and brown zones; margin swollen, discolored; flesh corky, whitish. In the following years: fissured, blackish brown; margin even, dark vermilion; flesh brown. Pores small, round, whitish or yellowish. Tubules stratified. Grows on latifoliate trees and on conifers.

UNGULINA FOMENTARIA (2)

Hoof shaped: 10–40 cm by 10–20 cm. In the first year: crust with concentric grooves, pruinose, cinereous; margin rounded, paler; flesh corky, spongy. Afterward: crust hard, bulky, ocher or brownish; margin rusty; crust always whitish in the variety *Inzengae* (3), and black from the start in the variety *nigricans*; flesh corky, tough; reddish brown. Pores small, round, cinereous, then ochraceous. Tubules long, rusty, multilayered. Spores whitish. It grows on live or dead latifoliate trees, on which it grows during the favorable seasons, for several years.

Another pluriannual species, which can grow to even bigger sizes than the above, is *Ungulina officinalis*: white, cinereous, yellowish, often polychrome; flesh soon tough, corky, white; odor of fresh flour, flavor bitter; grows on larches; much in demand in earlier times for the preparation of drugs and bitter liqueurs.

None of the above mushrooms is edible.

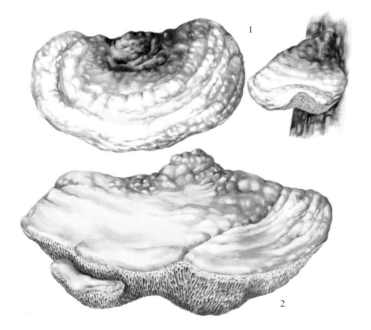

marginata Ung.

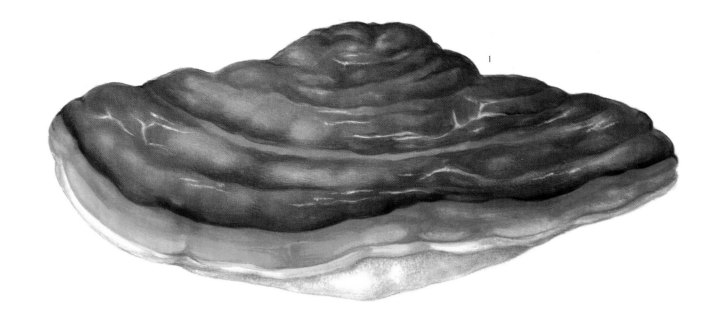

POLYPORUS (Piptoporous) BETULINUS (1)

Cap hoof shaped, 8–16 cm, planted by the hock into the trunk of the host; then expanded, flattened and semicircular; gray or brown, becoming discolored and fissured with age; cuticle thin, papery, and for a while easily separable from the cap; margin permanently involute toward the tubules. **Stem** reduced to a peduncle rising from the rear part of the cap and infixed under the bark of the birch. **Flesh** first tender, juicy, almost gelatinous; then corky; white, then whitish or slightly yellowish. **Odor** and **flavor** acidulous. **Pores** very small, round, white, then whitish. **Tubules** short, whitish; sometimes, in the end, detached from the cap. **Spores** white. It grows in summer, on birches, which eventually it causes to die. **Not edible**.

TRAMETES RUBESCENS (2)

Semicircular, 6–12 cm, smooth, gibbous; sometimes white, becoming spotted with red if bruised; more often yellowish, reddish, or brownish; sometimes, starting from the part adhering to the support, it becomes purple black, more or less deep. **Flesh** either thick or thin; corky, white, then pinkish, eventually brownish. **Pores** and **gills**: the lower surface is sometimes perforated by pores, first round and white, then oblong and pinkish; sometimes it has gills, connected together by fine veins, white, then rosy cream and finally brownish. **Spores** cream. It grows throughout the year, on latifoliate trees, rarer on conifers; more frequent in the plains, in warm regions; harmful for the host plant. **Not edible**. *Lenzites tricolor*, **not edible**, is a form of *Trametes rubescens*, thin, pliable, of brighter colors and with the hymenium formed by gills.

INONOTUS (Xanthochrous) HISPIDUS (1)

Hoof shaped: 15–40 cm by 10–20 cm, yellowish, orange, or rusty, then blackish; covered with hispid fur; flesh spongy, watery, yellowish, then dry, brittle, rusty; pores small, round, yellowish, then brown; tubules long, clearly distinct from the flesh, exuding a dewy juice; spores rusty; in the summer, on latifoliate or also fruit trees, to which it is harmful; annual, but growing again on the same trunk year after year; **edible**, when still unripe.

PHELLINUS ROBUSTUS (2)

Similar to *Ungulina fomentaria* (page 210): 10–30 by 10–30 cm, pluriannual, brown; but for a long time with a crust not clearly differentiated from the rest of the tissue of the mushroom; flesh and tubules reddish ocher; spores yellowish white; grows on oak trees.
Similar to it are: *Phellinus Hartigii,* growing on firs; *Phellinus igniarius,* growing on willow trees and with a browner flesh; *Phellinus pomaceus,* small, 3–6 cm, uneven; found on the branches of apple, cherry, and plum trees.

PHELLINUS NIGRICANS (3)

Shaped as a horse hoof: 5–20 by 5–20 cm, protected by a hard, black crust, but of a tissue not clearly differentiated from that of the rest of the mushroom; this distinguishes it from *Ungulina fomentaria* variety *nigricans*; shiny, marked by prominent grooves, gradually more and more numerous; with whitish or ochraceous margin; found on latifoliate trees. **None of the above mushrooms is edible**, with a partial exception for *Inonotus hispidus.*

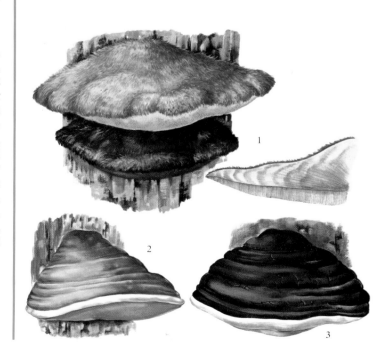

GANODERMA LUCIDUM (2, 3)

Cap circular or flabellate, 5–12 cm; generally horizontal but sometimes also slanted; supported laterally by a vertical or slanted stem; surface of the cap divided into concentric steps, centered on the top of the stem; margin sometimes undulate; these undulations often have corresponding depressions oriented toward the top of the stem; covered with a shiny, violaceous brown, reddish brown, reddish fuliginous, or yellow crust. **Stem** of the color of the cap; at times slightly black; unequal, now 15–30 cm high, sometimes contracted, sometimes not present at all. **Flesh** elastic, then coriaceous, rusty. **Pores** small, white, then brownish. **Tubules** short, then rather long; white, then yellowish. **Spores** brownish. It grows rapidly on stumps, especially of oaks and chestnut trees, and therefore is, undoubtedly, lignicolous; although it may often seem terricolous, when growing on buried wood.

GANODERMA TSUGAE (4)

Larger than *G. lucidum,* vermilion, with yellow margin, found in Japan.

GANODERMA APPLANATUM (1)

It can reach even 60 cm in diameter; without stem or with only a short peduncule; knobby or corrugated, sometimes on concentric zones; not shiny, but opaque; basically brown with a lighter margin.

None of the above mushrooms is edible, but since they are oddly shaped, shining and unputrescible, they can be used as bizarre, ornamental trinkets.

FISTULINA HEPATICA

Shaped as an ox tongue, 10–20 cm, extended horizontally and infixed into the trunk of the host plant through a peduncule that is sometimes well differentiated and other times atrophic and unnoticeable. Margin generally thin, sometimes even, sometimes lobate. It is of a liver red color, subdued by the yellow color of the papillae that cover it as long as the mushroom is unripe; then it becomes dark and velvety, and eventually gelatinous. The lower surface is covered with very small **tubules**, distinctly separated from one another like the bristles of a brush; first yellowish, then pinkish; becoming brownish when bruised. **Flesh** red, juicy, fibrous, with paler streaks. **Odor** mild. **Flavor** between acidulous and bitterish. **Spores** rosy or cinereous rosy. It grows on old trunks of chestnut and oak trees. **Edible**: one must discard the upper cuticle and the tubules and leave the rest for a few hours in the seasoning, in order to wash away the acidulous-bitterish juice; then it should be well drained, and moderately seasoned again before serving; it can also be cooked like a cutlet or preserved in oil. Sometimes, some simple specimens of *Polyporus sulphureus* variety *miniatus* (page 205) can be confused with *Fistulina hepatica*; however, the former has true tubules, yellow and exuding yellowish droplets from the pores; distinctly different from the minute tubules of *Fistulina hepatica*, which are arranged like the bristles of a brush.

HYDNUM (Sarcodon) REPANDUM (1)

Cap 5–15 cm, uneven, with lobate and undulate margin; ocher tending to red or reddish; orange with white stem in the variety *rufescens* (3); white in the variety *albidus* (on the left of *rufescens*); velvety, pruinose. **Stem** thick, sometimes unequal and eccentric; of the same color as the cap. **Flesh** hard, brittle; slightly fibrous; white, becoming yellowish in contact with air. **Odor** mild. **Flavor** acidulous, but bitter in the older specimens. **Teeth** close, uneven, decurrent on the stem; whitish, then the color of the cap; fragile. **Spores** creamy white. It grows in groups, in rows, in rings; in autumn, in the woods. **Edible**, good, when still unripe; then bitter and disgusting; free it from the bitterish teeth, using a stiff brush; parboiling recommended.

HYDNUM LEVIGATUM (2)

Cap smooth, not squamose, brownish gray; teeth of the same color, long, with white points; flesh amethystine white, then cinereous white, bitter; grows under conifers; **not edible**. Similar to the previous species: *Hydnum umbilicatum*, **edible**, depressed in the center, thin, brown or orange, often zonate, with long teeth; *Hydnum fuligineo-album*, **not edible**, white with fuliginous or brownish margin, squamose stem, flesh white, rosy in contact with air, coriaceous.

HERICIUM (Dryodon) CORALLOIDES (1)

Densely branched, with branches intersecting one another from a short, whitish, horizontal, corrugated trunk. Teeth in tufts, up to two centimeters long, sharp, thin, white, then cream, with rosy iridescence, hanging from the lower surface of the branches. On the whole, this mushroom can reach a diameter of 30 centimeters. Flesh white, brittle; odor mild and agreeable, flavor slightly bitter. Spores whitish. It grows in autumn and in winter, until the first frost, on felled trunks or on old trees, especially beeches, elms, ash trees, oaks, and pines. **Edible**, but it must be boiled a few minutes in water and well drained before cooking it with proper seasoning.

HERICIUM ERINACEUS (3)

Smaller and more compact than the previous one; teeth neatly crowding one another, fleshier, pruinose, elastic. **Edible**, parboiling necessary. Similar to *H. erinaceus* is *Hericium caput Medusae*, which, however, has the main branches well separated from one another; teeth oddly outstretched in all directions. **Edible** when still rather unripe and after a short parboiling in water.

HERICIUM CAPUT URSI (2)

Branched like *H. coralloides*, but with the teeth similar to those of *H. erinaceus* and hanging in tufts from the tips of the branches. **Edible** when still unripe and after parboiling in water.

coralloides Her.

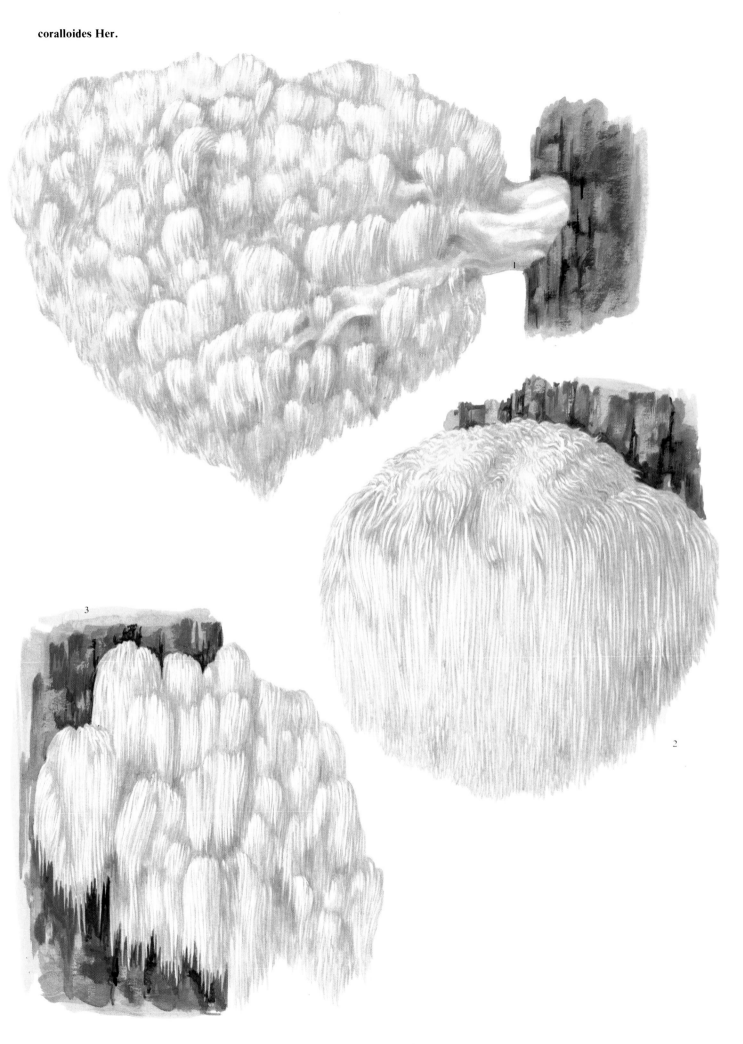

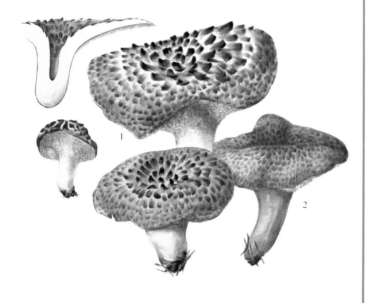

SPARASSIS CRISPA
It resembles a sponge or a head of lettuce. **Stem** short, thick, fleshy, fibrous, whitish. Branches numerous, flat, ribbonlike, undulate, stretching upward or outward, here and there confluent, ruffled, with serrate margin; whitish, tending to yellowish, then faded brownish. **Flesh** white, elastic, fibrous. **Odor** soft, resinous. **Flavor** of hazelnuts. **Spores** whitish. It grows in autumn, near old pines; but not exclusively: a specimen of this *Sparassis* was once found, in autumn, at the foot of a mulberry tree, in the form *candida*. **Edible**, excellent, when still unripe and quickly cooked.

Similar to *S. crispa* and equally **edible**: *Sparassis radicata*, with small, flattened, very crispate branches, branching out from a thick, cylindric stem or trunk that is not too visible at ground level because buried for the most part under the wood debris that feeds the mushroom's mycelium; found in North America, under conifers. *Sparassis laminosa,* with few branches that are ribbonlike, long, regular, slightly or not at all crispate, and sometimes spread only vertically; grows especially under oaks, but not exclusively: a specimen of this *Sparassis,* formed by four white, large, upright, and only slightly intertwined branches, was once found, in autumn, in the dried bed of a ditch, between a hedge of blackberry bushes and a paved road.

HYDNUM (Sarcodon) IMBRICATUM (1)
Cap funnel shaped, 5–25 cm, with lobate or undulate margin; fuliginous brown; covered with squames and scales that are larger near the center of the cap. **Stem** squat, ochraceous gray. **Flesh** firm, tenacious; whitish, then soft and fuliginous. **Odor** mild, disgusting in the older specimens. **Flavor** sour and bitterish. **Teeth** close, thin, long, decurrent; cinereous, then brownish; fragile. **Spores** ochraceous. It grows in groups under conifers. **Edible**, unripe, after discarding the cuticle and the teeth, and parboiling; it improves when preserved in oil, dried, or even pulverized.

HYDNUM SCABROSUM (2)
Cap 5–15 cm, brownish, squamose; teeth whitish; acrid; under pines; **not edible**. Similar to it is *Hydnum squamosum,* **edible**, of poor quality: cap 4–8 cm, with fibrillar, reddish scales; stem short, white; teeth thin, reddish; flesh white; flavor mild.

Other **non-edible** species of *Hydnum*: *Hydnum amarescens,* smooth, reddish ocher; with short teeth, bitterish. *Hydnum fennicum,* base of the stem blue, even inside. *Hydnum fuligineo-violaceum,* smoky violet, choking flavor. *Hydnum acre*, bitter and peppery: cap 5–10 cm, rough, yellow, then olivaceous; autumnal, growing under latifoliate trees on sandy grounds. *Hydnum abietum*, white, greenish at the center, viscid; teeth very long; grows under conifers in North America.

CALODON SUAVEOLENS (1)

Cap turbinate, 4–9 cm, whitish, then bluish ocher; knotty, floccose; margin undulate, discolored. **Stem** short, velvety; blue, then fuliginous. **Flesh** fibrous, corky; indigo color at the base of the stem and then lighter and lighter, in concentric zones, up to the margin of the cap, where it is white. **Odor** of anise. **Teeth** thin, short, decurrent, bluish, then brownish. **Spores** grayish ocher. It grows in the mountains, under firs. **Not edible**.

Calodon coeruleum (2), bluish, then brownish; flesh whitish with blue zones; found in the mountains, under firs. *Calodon aurantiacum* (3), orange yellow, white at the margin; stem orange yellow; teeth white, then yellow, finally rusty; grows in the mountains, under conifers. *Calodon ferrugineum* (center left), white, velvety, exuding red droplets, then rusty; found under latifoliate trees. *Calodon nigrum* (6), blue black, margin white and ciliate, odor of licorice. *Calodon gravelens* (5), cap thin, rosy ocher, stem thin, blackish, teeth white; odor strong of licorice or coffee substitutes. **None of the above is edible**.

AURISCALPIUM (Leptodon) VULGARE (4)

Cap heart shaped, 1–2 cm, thin, coriaceous, hispid, brown, then blackish. Stem lateral, slender, pubescent, the color of the cap. Teeth tenacious, grayish. Throughout the year, on decaying pinecones. **Not edible**.

CLAVARIA (Ramaria) BOTRYTIS (1)

At first sight this mushroom looks like the head of a ripe cauliflower, 6–16 cm by 8–20 cm, with tips that are very small, short, bifid, rosy or amethystine, confluent in bigger and bigger branches and finally in a single trunk, thick, short, fleshy, rounded at the base, whitish, then ochraceous. **Flesh** white, firm, brittle. **Odor** tenuous. **Flavor** acidulous or bitterish. **Spores** pale ocher. It grows in autumn, in thin woods, especially of beech trees; seldom in coniferous woods. **Edible** with caution: in particularly sensitive individuals it produces laxative effects, although not violent ones; moderate use is recommended, and then only the stem, not the branches; it should be boiled for a few minutes in water, then carefully drained and finally cooked properly.

CLAVARIA BOTRYTIS variety PARVULA (2)

Of smaller size than *C. Botrytis*; tips of the branches pink or purple pink; **edible** with caution. *Clavaria botrytis* variety *rufescens*, **edible** with caution; it can attain larger sizes than *C. Botrytris*: branches yellowish, then ochraceous; tips rosy red or amaranth red; acidulous; grows in coniferous and latifoliate woods, on the ground, on which, at first sight, it appears orange on top and white below.

CLAVARIA (Ramaria) FORMOSA (1)

Total height 10–20 cm. Trunk yellow pink, branches light orange pink, long, cylindric, elastic; tips bidentate, lemon yellow; flesh fragile, whitish, tending to reddish at contact with air; acidulous or bitterish; spores pale ocher; grows under latifoliate trees. **Drastic laxative.** Very similar to it is *Clavaria elegantissima*, **not edible**, entirely orange pink.

CLAVARIA FLAVA (2)

Total height 8–16 cm. Trunk whitish or yellowish, with vinous spots; branches cylindric, smooth, yellow, with short tips; flesh brittle, white; odor and flavor mild; spores pale ocher; found in the mountains, especially under firs and beeches. **Edible**, but in certain individuals it produces laxative effects.

CLAVARIA AUREA (3)

Total height 10–14 cm. Trunk pale cream; branches golden yellow, short, stiff, tips bidentate, golden yellow; flesh firm, white: odor and flavor agreeable; spores pale ocher; found in the woods, especially under conifers. **Edible**, but with laxative effects in certain individuals.

Similar to the preceding species is *Clavaria gelatinosa*, which grows in the forests of latifoliate trees and of conifers of North America: yellow flesh that appears gelatinous, when cut, and marbled like polished agate. **Not edible** because it can cause intestinal discomfort in particularly sensitive individuals.

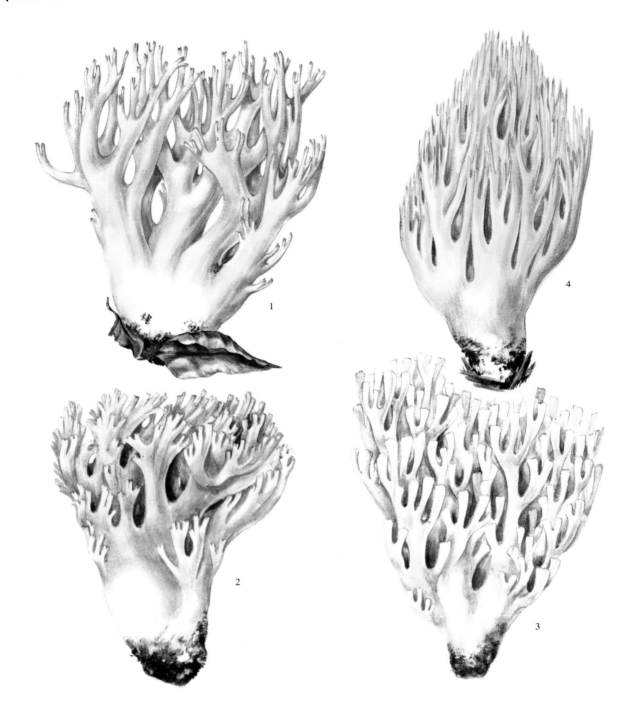

CLAVARIA (Ramaria) PALLIDA (1)

Total height 6–12 cm. Base pallid, stem cinereous ocher, branches rosy cream, tips slightly amethystine; flesh tough, white; odor mild; flavor agreeable; spores pale ocher; grows in late summer and in autumn, under latifoliate trees; **drastic laxative**.

CLAVARIA CINEREA (2)

Total height 5–10 cm. Trunk whitish, cinereous, grayish; branches uneven, rugose, smoky, with blue hues; tips dentate, obtuse or sharp like awl's points; flesh fragile, white; odor mild; flavor pleasant; spores white, with blue green shades; grows in autumn, in the woods; **edible**, but a laxative to some individuals.

CLAVARIA PYXIDATA (3)

Total height 7–14 cm. Trunk thin, whitish, spotted with brown; branches like inverted cones; tips like inverted cones, crowned with white or yellowish teeth; flesh piquant; grows on decaying wood; **edible**, but a laxative to some individuals.

CLAVARIA STRICTA (4)

Total height 5–10 cm. Base floccose; trunk thin, brownish or violaceous brown; branches vertical, stiff, parallel, reddish yellow; tips yellow, pointed; then the entire body becomes thinner, with longer, farther apart, olivaceous branches; flesh soon tenacious; odor of spices; flavor bitter, piquant, metallic; found in autumn, on wood debris; **not edible**.

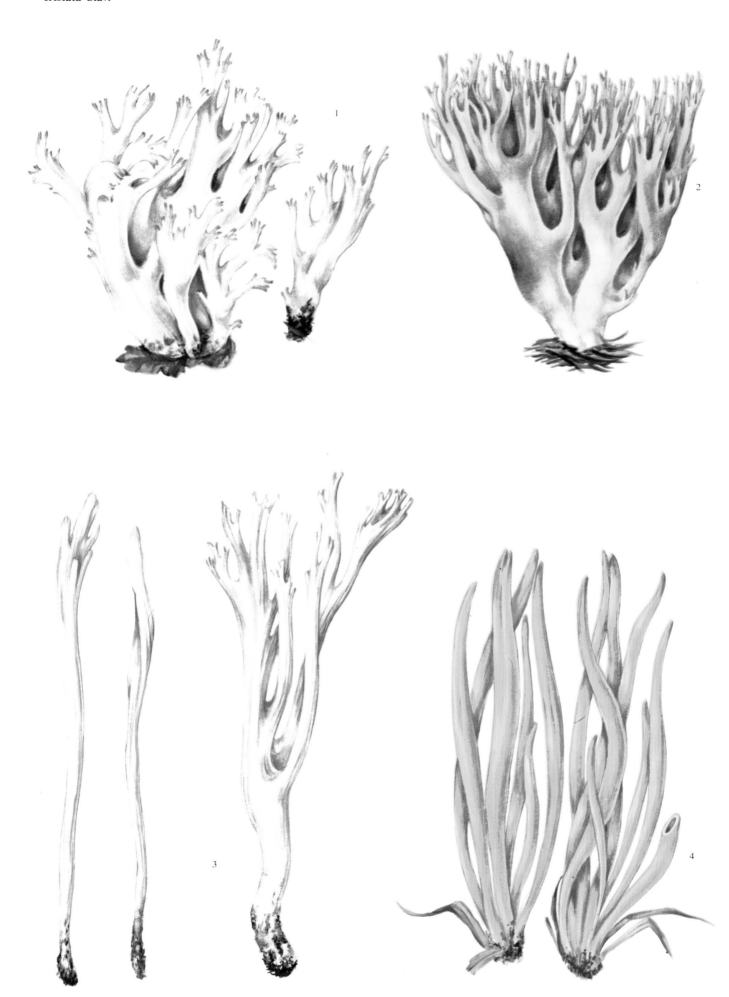

CLAVARIA (Ramaria) CRISTATA (1)

Total height 2–6 cm. Trunk whitish, smooth, pruinose, velvety at the base; branches flat, uneven, sometimes few, sometimes numerous and close; whitish; tips yellow or gray, subdivided into pointed crests; flesh tenacious, white; spores white; growing in the ground, in woods, at the edges of footpaths. **Edible**, but of little alimentary interest.

CLAVARIA ABIETINA (2)

Total height 2–6 cm. Trunk thin, cream or slightly ochraceous; branches close, rugose; tips crowded, sharp, bidentate or tridentate; yellow, then orange, finally ochraceous and olivaceous; flesh flaccid; odor soft; every part of this *Clavaria* becomes green when bruised; spores rusty ocher; under conifers. **Edible**, but of little alimentary interest. Similar to it is *Clavaria flaccida,* **not edible** because it is tough and elastic, not becoming green when bruised.

CLAVARIA RUGOSA (3)

Total height 5–12 cm. Of varied shape; now simple, now branched; whitish, yellowish, or cinereous; marked lengthwise by distinct ridges or grooves; flesh fragile, white; odor and flavor very soft; spores white; grows along forest paths. **Edible**.

CLAVARIA FUSIFORMIS (4)

Simple, spindle shaped, 5–12 cm high, hollow, yellow; in tufts of many specimens, tightly bunched together at the base; found in autumn, in grass, along trails. **Edible**.

CLAVARIA (Clavariadelphus) PISTILLARIS (1)

Club shaped, 8–24 cm high, yellowish or ochraceous, sometimes tending to orange; first smooth, then slightly rugose; furfuraceous; flesh soft, whitish, bitterish; spores yellowish white; **edible**, of poor quality.

CLAVARIA (Clavariadelphus) TRUNCATA (2)

Similar to the latter, but with the top truncated and flattened; sulcate and rugose; 6–16 cm high; flesh sweetish; found under conifers; **edible**, of poor quality.

NEVROPHYLLUM (Gomphus or Cantharellus) CLAVATUM (3)

Club shaped or turbinate, 3–6 cm high, fleshy, truncate, depressed or slightly funnel shaped, often more or less open on a side, lengthwise; with the margin oddly lobate and crispate; ochraceous above, violaceous or rosy on the sides, and finally brownish; marked, from the top down, by viens, larger and larger as the mushroom ripens, purple violet, then ochraceous. **Flesh** white, aromatic, sometimes bitterish; often infested by larvae, starting from the base. **Spores** ochraceous. It grows in woods, especially fir woods, in large groups, in rings, in rows. **Edible**: some consider it excellent, some mediocre; always slightly bitter, even after prolonged cooking; in that case the specimens are probably too old.

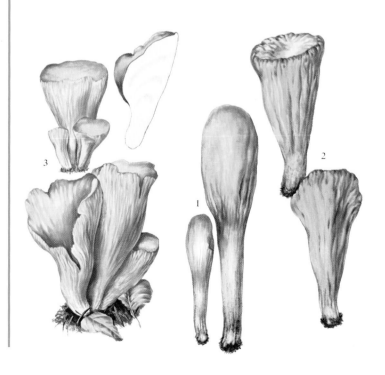

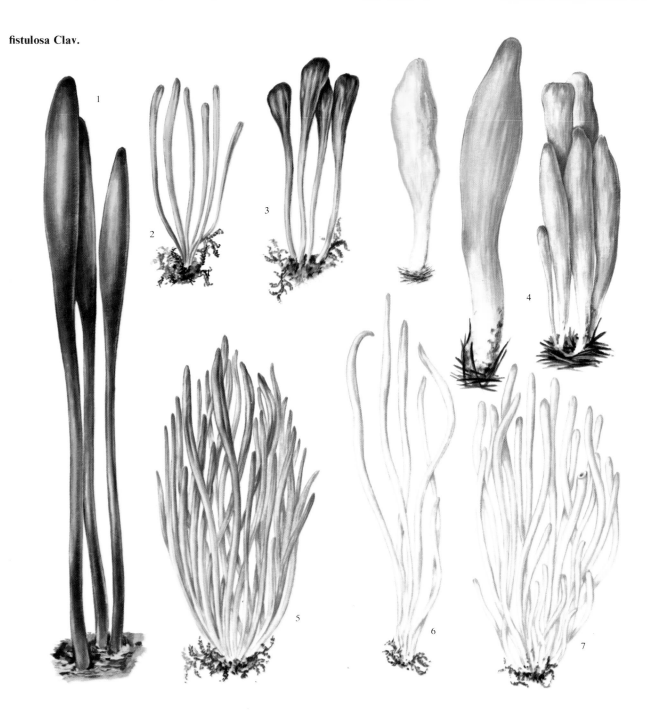

CLAVARIA FISTULOSA (1)
Club shaped, slender, 10–20 cm high, brownish; hollow; the upper part fragile, the lower tough; grows under latifoliate trees, on wood debris; **edible**.

CLAVARIA HELVOLA (2)
Club shaped, slightly compressed on top; yellow; 3–6 cm high; flesh whitish, elastic, odorless, tasteless; grows in the moss, in tufts; **edibility unknown**.

CLAVARIA ARGILLACEA (3)
Club shaped, 3–8 cm high, flattened, with longitudinal grooves; sometimes dilated or bilobate upward; the lower part yellow, the upper part grayish, greenish, or yellowish; with floccose base; growing in sandy or peaty grounds, in autumn, in the moss, in tufts; **edible**.

CLAVARIA (Clavariadelphus) LIGULA (4)
Club shaped, 4–12 cm high, rounded on top, or truncate or pointed; cinereous amethystine or amethystine ocher; flesh white; grows at the foot of conifers, in thousands of specimens; **edible**.

CLAVARIA FUMOSA (5)
Shaped like several long spindles, 6–10 cm high, connected at the base, sometimes flattened and with longitudinal grooves; amethystine yellow, then fuliginous; fragile; growing in tufts, in woods, in the moss; **edible**.

CLAVARIA VERMICULARIS (6)
Worm shaped, 6–15 cm high, yellowish on top, fragile; grows in the moss, in dense tufts; in the variety *fragilis* (7) it is hollow; **of no alimentary interest**.

CRATERELLUS (Cantharellus) CORNUCOPIOIDES (1)

It has the appearance of an empty cornucopia, 5–12 cm high, with lobed margin; with crispate margin in the form *crispus*. The internal surface is fuliginous or brownish gray, with darker squamules; the lateral surface is smooth or slightly rugose, cinereous, grayish, or amethystine gray, and pruinose, In humid weather the whole mushroom appears blackish. **Flesh** thin, membranous, elastic. **Odor** and **flavor** mild. **Spores** white. It grows in tufts, sometimes huge, in the humid and muddy recesses of the woods. **Edible**, much sought after; it can be preserved dried or also reduced to powder.

CANTHARELLUS CINEREUS (2)

Similar to *Craterellus cornucopioides*, generally smaller, of grayish color; however, the lateral surface is covered with nervations, similar to coarse lamellae with obtuse edges; connected together here and there either directly or through crossveins; plumbeous cinereous with or without bluish shades. **Flesh** elastic. **Odor** of plums. **Flavor** pleasant. **Spores** white. It grows in humid woods, especially beech woods. **Edible**. Similar to it is *Cantharellus carbonarius*, **edible**, gray, with white ribbings, stem whitish and stuffed; found on grounds scorched by fire.

CRATERELLUS (Cantharellus) LUTESCENS (1)

Cap infundibuliform 2–5 cm, with its cavity soon communicating with that of the stem. Margin undulate and crispate. The upper part initially gray and flocculose, then glabrous, striate, brown or fuliginous. The lower part initially rosy yellow, smooth; then orange yellow and covered with low ridges, sparsely connected, veinlike. **Stem** long, tapered at the base; yellow or orange yellow, rugose; stuffed, but soon hollow. Total height 7–12 cm. **Flesh** thin, fibrous, tenacious, yellowish. **Odor** of fruit. **Flavor** agreeable. **Spores** white. It grows in the mountains, in humid coniferous woods, in groups or tufts, often hidden in the heather. **Edible**, of good quality, although slightly tough.

CANTHARELLUS TUBAEFORMIS (Fries) (2)

Similar to the preceding form, 5–15 cm high, with funnel-shaped cap, pubescent, brown, then yellowish; but with prominent veins, similar to lamellae, often bifurcate and connected together by transversal veins; yellow, then gray. It grows in latifoliate woods but especially in coniferous woods, particularly under pines. **Edible**, of good quality.

CANTHARELLUS TUBAEFORMIS variety LUTESCENS (Fries) (3)

Cap yellow with olivaceous shades. **Edible**. Let us mention also the small *Cantharellus muscigenus*, **edible**, which grows on wood fragments, in the moss, in large groups; dried and reduced to powder it makes a very good, aromatic seasoning.

ANTHURUS ASEROIFORMIS (1)

It appears at first egg shaped, whitish tending to rosy. Then the membranous wrapping breaks, and from five to seven tentacles emerge, some of them, at least initially, united two by two at the tips; white pinkish color outward, scarlet red inward. Then the tentacles curve outward so that the mushroom acquires the appearance of a flower, supported by a short peduncle, sometimes rising above the margin of the volva. Total height 7–14 cm. The scarlet red tissue decays early, becoming rugose, eroded, blackish, malodorous. Grows in cool, humid places. **Not edible**.

PSEUDOCOLUS SCHELLENBERGIAE (2)

Looking like an octopus with few tentacles, united at the tips, and with the head buried in the volva; it appears therefore like a small spindle, 4–7 cm high, rosy, split lengthwise; grows in autumn, in the woods of Japan, North America, and Cuba. **Not edible**.

CLATHRUS RUBER form KUSANOI (3)

Smaller than *Anthurus aseroiformis*, 4–7 cm high, paler, and with fewer tentacles; grows in the woods, in Japan. **Not edible**.

CANTHARELLUS CIBARIUS (1)

It has the shape of a filled -up funnel, 3–10 cm; the upper part velvety, moist, but soon glabrous and dry; with undulate and crispate margin; from slightly above the base, to the margin, it is covered with coarse lamellae; entirely golden yellow; but the variety *neglectus* (2) is paler, thinner, and with violaceous down on the lamellae; the variety *albus* (6) is white; the variety *amethysteus* (5) is yellow, but with squamules or with a violet disk on the cap; the variety *ianthinoxanthus* has amethystine gills. **Flesh** slightly fibrous and tenacious; white or yellow, depending on the different varieties. **Odor** agreeable. **Flavor** slightly acrid. **Spores** white or yellowish. It grows from spring to autumn, in woods, in the moss, in groups. **Edible**. Similar to it and also **edible**: *Cantharellus Friesii*, orange color, *Cantharellus olidus,* rosy, with odor of candy; grows in autumn, near spruces. *Cantharellus sinuosus*, brown or fuliginous, with ridges atrophic and faded yellow; found under latifoliate trees.

CANTHARELLUS FLOCCOSUS (3)

Hollow, 12–24 cm high, yellow, tending here and there to pink and to red; squamose internally; grows in the Far East and in North America; **edible**.

CANTHARELLUS PALLIDUS (4)

Whitish, with amethystine cinereous shades; grows in Japan; considered as **not edible**. However, the small *Cantharellus cinnabarinus* is **edible**; it is entirely red; found in North America.

cibarius Canth.

1   2   3

DICTYOPHORA DUPLICATA (3)

Cap thimble shaped, hollow, open at the top; the exterior surface alveolate, covered with a greenish yellow, then olivaceous yellow gluten; eventually the gluten dissolves into a blackish, dense liquid, and the white surface underneath becomes visible. **Stem** cylindric, hollow, with spongy walls, white. Total height 12–24 cm. **Net**: hangs curtainlike from the cap's margin, generally halfway down the stem; with large meshes; fragile; evanescent. **Volva**: enwraps the entire unripe mushroom, giving it an egglike appearance; white, pinkish, or yellowish; then it opens, remaining adherent to the base of the stem, and assuming an ochraceous color. **Flesh** porose, fragile, white, fetid. **Spores** greenish yellow. Grows singly, in warm and rainy seasons, in Northern Europe and in North America.

DICTYOPHORA INDUSIATA (1)

The meshes of the net are more substantial than in *D. duplicata*; grows in Japan.

PHALLUS IMPUDICUS (2)

Similar to *Dictyophora,* but without the characteristic net; grows in fields, meadows, parks, under hedges. *Mutinus caninus* is smaller than the preceding species, 6–12 cm high, without net, thin, very fragile, fetid, ending in a point or like the head of a match; initially green, glutinous, then red.

All these mushrooms, ripe, are fetid and absolutely **not edible**; there are, however, people who will eat sometimes one, sometimes another, when still unripe, at the egg-shape stage.

SCLERODERMA AURANTIUM (1)
Globose, 3–12 cm, clinging to the ground through radiciform filaments. Involucre bulky, elastic, coriaceous; yellowish or orange, then ochraceous; rugose, verrucose; with the top open craterlike, when ripe. Flesh white, then pinkish, then blackish violet, turning eventually into an olivaceous brown powder: the spores. Odor of ink. It grows in the arid, warm ravines of the woods, in the ground or on old stumps. **Not edible**: it can cause gastric trouble; it is used to adulterate dried truffles.

SCLERODERMA VERRUCOSUM (3)
Smaller than *S. aurantium*, 3–7 cm, and with a less bulky involucre, covered with almost granular, crowded warts, darker than the brownish surface. Supported by a squat and rugose peduncle. Grows in the dry, warm, sandy ravines of the woods, on the ground or on old stumps. **Not edible**.

BOLETUS (Xerocomus) PARASITICUS (2)
Cap 3–8 cm, olivaceous yellow, velvety, often cracked by the dry air. **Stem** fibrillar, curved, with pointed base. **Flesh** firm, thick, yellow. **Odor** and **flavor** mild. **Pores** large, round, yellow, then reddish yellow. **Tubules** short, annexed to the stem. **Spores** olivaceous yellow. Grows on *Scleroderma aurantium*, more rarely on *Scleroderma verrucosum*, making them sterile. **Edible**. Similar to *B. parasiticus* is *Boletus astraeicola*, **probably edible**, which grows in Japan, on unripe *Astraeus hygrometricus* (page 232): cap and stem smoky gray.

CYATHUS CRUCIBULUM (1)
Similar to a nest, 0.5–1 cm, closed by a soon broken veil; brown outside, ocher inside; with 8–10 small peridioles, flat, white, attached to the wall by a minute peduncle. Lignicolous, grows from spring to autumn.

CYATHUS STRIATUS (2)
Similar to a nest, 0.5–1 cm, outside velvety and fuliginous, inside cinerous and with vertical ridges; with 10–12 peridioles, cinereous. Terricolous and lignicolous.

CYATHUS OLLA (3)
Similar to an inverted campanule, 0.5 cm by 1.5 cm; outside fuliginous and pruinose; inside cinerous; with 6–8 peridiolès, cinereous and serceous. Lignicolous.

SPHAEROBULUS STELLATUS (4)
Globose, 0.2–0.3 cm, yellow; then it opens, starlike, showing a small, protruding, cinereous, shining sphere that is afterward flung away. Lignicolous.

TYLOSTOMA BRUMALE (5)
Globose, 0.5–2.5 cm, brownish, then cinereous; protected by a double involucre; lying on the ground; then a long, squamose, hard, stiff stalk develops underneath; finally a round opening is formed on the top of the sphere and a brownish powder of ripe spores comes out through it. It grows in autumn and winter, in the sun, on sand, on rubble, in the moss.

TYLOSTOMA GRANULOSUM (6)
Similar to *T. brumale*: opening denticulate; base of the sphere encrusted with sand; stem with granular squamules. It grows in autumn, on barren soil, which is rich in nitrogen compounds. **These mushrooms are not edible**.

LYCOPERDON (Calvatia) MAXIMUM

Globose, sometimes somewhat depressed and slightly corrugated toward the base; with diameter ranging from 5 to 50 centimeters. It clings to the ground through a short peduncle, sometimes atrophic and almost unnoticeable. It is wrapped by a double involucre: the outer one, very thick, is first white and velvety; then it becomes rather smooth, with yellowish or brownish coloring; finally it breaks, dividing into many tilelike pieces, which gradually fall. The inner involucre is thin and white; then it becomes grayish, fuliginous, and more and more fragile, until it lacerates irregularly, starting from the top. **Flesh** initially compact and white; then yellowish and soft; afterward olivaceous, flaccid, and mushy; finally it becomes clotted-pulverulent, dark brown, and comes out from the involucre, like smoke, at every breath of air or when the involucre is squeezed between the fingers. **Odor** and **flavor** of the flesh, when still white and unripe, mild and agreeable; when it has become pulverulent, disgusting. **Spores** tobacco colored. It grows on all sorts of ground, but especially on truck farms and in gardens; sometimes also in the mountains, in the pastures, along the trails, in the sunny clearings of woods. **Edible**, excellent, when still unripe, both raw in salads, and fried in butter; it cooks in few minutes; the outer involucre should be discarded.

CLATHRUS CANCELLATUS

Initially egg shaped, 2–3 cm, wrapped in a thick, white volva; attached to the ground through a short, radiciform appendix, mousetail-like; often corrugate from the base to middle height. Then a pinkish sphere emerges from the dilacerated volva, 6–12 cm, perforated, netlike. This net has polygonal meshes, either quadrangular, or slightly rounded, and the tissue is spongy and fragile. As the net enlarges the meshes grow thinner, acquiring a lenticular section, and becoming blood red or brick red; outside transversally striped, inside eroded, alveolate, stained by a granular, green and brown mucilage, containing the ripe spores. At this stage it exhales an unbearable cadaveric stench. It grows from spring to autumn, in humid recesses, in the shade of latifoliate trees, but sometimes also in the middle of a meadow. **Not edible**.

Sometimes *Clathrus cancellatus* is found in a form for which the denomination *discancellatus* is more appropriate, since the spheroidal net of the typical form is reduced to 5–6 red tentacles, stretching upward from the volva, and united at the tips; this form could be identified as the form *Kusanoi* of *Clathrus ruber* (page 224), were it not for the different color, pinkish rather than vermilion.

cancellatus Cla.

LYCOPERDON (Calvatia) COELATUM

This mushroom has the shape of an inverted pear, even very large, 6–16 cm. As long as it is unripe, it is white, entirely covered with small, pointed warts; later these warts fall and the mushroom becomes cinereous and covered by small, polygonal, cuspidate areas, diminishing toward the stem where these are no cuspidate areas. Under the thick, outer involucre covering the mushroom, stalk included, there is another, thinner involucre, which enwraps a mass of white pulp, and does not reach to the spongy mass of the stem. As the mushroom ripens, the pulp changes from white to yellowish, then to olivaceous, finally to mushy and brownish. At the same time the outer involucre, by now brownish, has started to disintegrate, beginning from the top; and the inner involucre, now cartilaginous and brownish, breaks on top, unevenly, craterlike. Through this opening, little by little, the wind blows away the internal, grumous pulverulent, tobacco-colored substance: the spores. Year after year it is possible to find in the meadows the remains of this or of other *Lycoperdon* of large size, like brown or fuliginous bowls, empty, looking as if made of thick paper in the upper part and of pith at the base. The flesh, when still white, has a mild and agreeable odor and flavor. It grows in summer, in the grass, in the mountains, in groups or in rows of several specimens. **Edible**, of very good quality, also raw, in salads, or sliced and fried, like a breaded veal cutlet; the stalk and the two involucres must be discarded; as soon as the pulp becomes slightly yellowish this mushroom **becomes not edible**.

LYCOPERDON GEMMATUM (1)

Peridium globose, white, with rosy, cinereous, or yellowish shades, often with slight umbo in the center, where, when fully ripe, it will open craterlike; covered with pointed warts, which however easily fall, leaving on the mushrooms' surface a reticule with polygonal meshes. **Stem** short, cylindric, tapered at the base and flared upward, or shaped like an inverted truncated cone; whitish; smooth or slightly furfuraceous: total height 3–8 cm. **Flesh of the peridium** white and firm, with delicate odor and flavor; then it becomes greenish yellow and doughy, finally grumose, pulverulent, and fuliginous brown: the **spores** en masse. **Flesh of the stem** white and spongy, then yellowish and tough; no septum separates it from the flesh of the peridium. It grows in woods, singly, in groups, and even in tufts. **Edible**, of very good quality, even raw; one must use only the flesh of the peridium, when still unripe, white and firm. Similar to it is *Lycoperdon furfuraceum*, with smaller peridium, 2–4 cm, tinged with pink, smaller pointed warts and more easily caducous; **of no alimentary interest**.

LYCOPERDON (Calvatia) SACCATUM (2)

It can become much bigger than *L. gemmatum*, particularly because of the stem, generally long, often rugose lengthwise. When still unripe, the peridium is covered with evanescent, minute granules and thorns; when ripe, a spheric bowl of the external involucre detaches itself from the top of the peridium, while the internal involucre opens up, craterlike, to let out the spores in an olivaceous brown mass. **Edible**, like *L. gemmatum*.

LYCOPERDON ECHINATUM (1)
Similar to an upside-down pear, 3–6 cm high, brownish, with hairs clustered in pyramids, which, falling off, leave a polygonal mark; flesh whitish, then similar to soot; **not edible**.

LYCOPERDON PIRIFORME (2)
Similar to an upside-down pear, 3–7 cm high, whitish, then yellowish, furfuraceous, rugose at the base; flesh white, then similar to soot; lignicolous; **edible** when unripe.

LYCOPERDON UMBRINUM (3)
Similar to an upside-down pear, 3–5 cm high, often umbonate, yellowish, then brownish; with hairs clustered in tufts; flesh whitish, then sootlike; **not edible**. *Lycoperdon pratense*, of the meadows, **edible** when unripe, is whitish like *L. piriforme*, but with thorns like *L. echinatum*. Similar to *L. echinatum*, but smaller, are *Lycoperdon pulcherrimum* and *Lycoperdon pusillum*, which, however, once the pubescence is lost, appear smooth, without marks,

BOVISTA NIGRESCENS (4)
It differs from *B. plumbea* because the inner involucre, initially plumbeous, changes to brown and finally to black; found in mountain pastures; **edible** when still unripe.

BOVISTA PLUMBEA (5)
Globose, 2–5 cm, nearly without peduncle, white, glabrous, then rugose; under the outer involucre, which dissolves, there is an inner one, plumbeous, cartilaginous, which will open on top; flesh white, without sterile base, then sootlike; found in mountain pastures; **edible** when unripe.

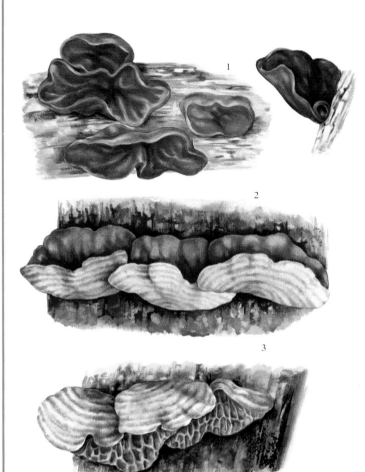

AURICULARIA (Hirneola) AURICULA JUDAE (1)
Shaped like a cup or an ear, 3–10 cm, without base or with very short, lateral peduncle; with thin, elastic, translucent walls. The external surface is crossed by veins, sparsely connected; velvety and olivaceous gray. The internal surface, initially smooth, becomes later noticeably rugose; gray, violet gray, brown, or purple brown, and finally blackish. As the mushroom ripens, it enlarges and flattens. **Flesh** gelatinous, tough. **Spores** white. It grows throughout the year, but especially in winter and in spring, on old trunks, especially elder, walnut, beech, robinia, and willow. **Edible**, even raw, much appreciated in the Far East.

AURICULARIA MESENTERICA (2)
Leaf shaped, 5–12 cm, thick, with uneven lobes, with the lower half attached to the tree, and the upper half stretching out in the form of an oddly shaped roof gutter. The surface partly adhering to the trunk is velvety, marked by concentric zones, and is cinereous, gray, or brownish. The other surface is crossed by venous wrinkles, connected netlike, and is purple gray, later becoming very dark, violaceous brown. **Flesh** gelatinous in humid weather, but dries up, toughens, and can become coriaceous in dry weather. **Spores** white. It is found throughout the year, but especially from autumn to spring, on stumps and dead trunks of latifoliate trees. **Not edible**.

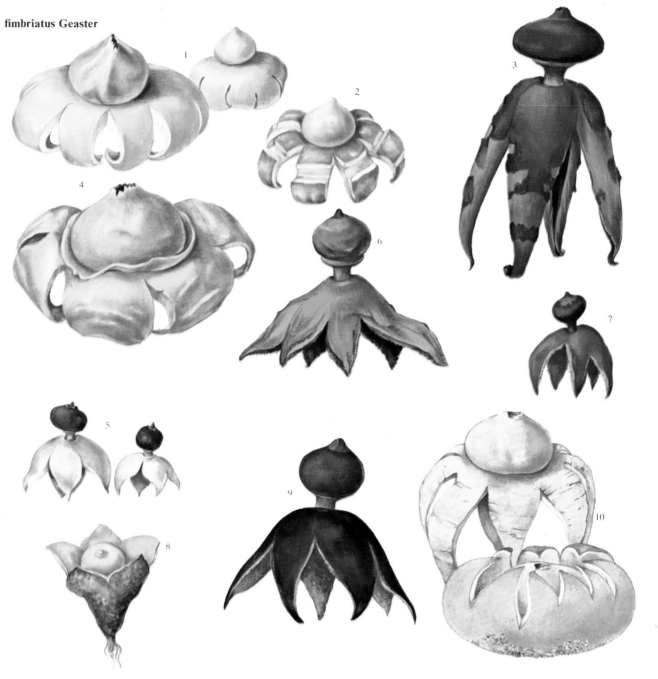

GEASTER

The mushrooms of the genus *Geaster* are globose, protected by a thick involucre. This splits, star shaped, then it opens up, as a flower's petal (rays) would, showing a smaller umbonate globe; then the rays recurve under the globe. The spores, similar to soot, come out from the lacerated umbo. **Of no alimentary interest**. The numbers indicate the diameter of the star from point to point.

(1) GEASTER FIMBRIATUS: 4–8 cm, with fringed operculum; autumnal.

(2) GEASTER RUFESCENS: 4–8 cm, the flesh becomes reddish when cut and exposed to air.

(3) GEASTER FORNICATUS: 5–10 cm, total height 7–15 cm; with four rays. Similar to it is *Geaster melanocephalus*, with the central sphere appearing black when the spores, which cover it, are ripe.

(4) GEASTER TRIPLEX: 6–10 cm, with a third pseudo-involucre, under the central sphere; grows under latifoliate trees.

(5) GEASTER QUADRIFIDUS: 2–3 cm, with four rays, small globe supported by a peduncle.

(6) GEASTER STRIATUS: 3–7 cm, globe supported by a little column and capital.

(7) GEASTER NANUS: 1.5–2.5 cm, in sandy grounds, on sea dunes.

(8) GEASTER MIRABILIS: 1.5–2 cm, with five rays, not completely involute; on dead leaves, in warm regions, also in Japan.

(9) GEASTER PECTINATUS: 3–7 cm, purple brown, pruinose, with 6–12 rays.

(10) ASTRAEUS HYGROMETRICUS: 4–10 cm, without umbo, with 6–10 rays, dark underneath and lighter and reticulate above, which open up in humid weather without curling under the central sphere, and fold again over it in dry weather; in sandy woods.

TREMELLODON (Pseudohydnum) GELATINOSUM (1)

Cap 4–8 cm, of very varied shapes; it can look like an oyster shell, but it can also assume very irregular shapes. Ranging in color from cinereous white to fuliginous brown or bluish brown. Margin thin, lobate, also very unevenly undulate. Lower surface of the cap covered with gelatinous teeth. **Stem** sometimes rather well developed, sometimes straight, more often rather curved; sometimes reduced to a short peduncle. **Flesh** gelatinous, tremulous, elastic; white with blue green iridescence. **Odor** and **flavor** resinous. **Spores** coeruleous white. It grows in summer and in autumn, but also in winter, on stumps of conifers, especially of pines. **Edible**, even raw in salads, but with rather resinous flavor.

CALOCERA VISCOSA (2)

Its shape, as a young tree densely branched, 3–6 cm high, makes it look like a *Clavaria*; but the texture of the **flesh**, tenacious and elastic, although slightly gelatinous, makes it clearly distinguishable from the latter. Yellow tending to orange; on drying it becomes hard as bone, and orange. Each branch ends with two or three points, like a molar tooth. The **base** is always dry and hairy. A long white cord extends from the base into the host. **Spores** ocher yellow. It grows throughout the year, on the stumps of rotting conifers, especially of pines. **Of no alimentary interest**.

GYROCEPHALUS RUFUS (Guepinia Helvelloides)

Shaped like a cornucopia, 3–12 cm high, with thin walls, open from top to bottom along a side; rosy or red; internal surface smooth; external surface either smooth or slightly rugose lengthwise, furfuraceous when the spores are ripe; attached to the ground through a short, stuffed, faded peduncle. **Flesh** gelatinous, diaphanous, shining, elastic, viscid, tenacious, pinkish. **Odor** of moss. **Flavor** agreeable. **Spores** whitish or rosy cream. It grows in the mountains, in the humid recesses of coniferous woods, in the grass or in the moss, in groups or in tufts. **Edible**, even raw in salads, when unripe; otherwise it can be consumed only after proper cooking.

Let us mention here two more mushrooms, also found in coniferous woods, but very different from the preceding species: *Pisolithus tinctorius*, globose 5–15 cm, with a thin, yellowish involucre, later fuliginous and unevenly breaking in the upper part; flesh yellow, aromatic, divided in many small cells; then dissolved into a brownish mass; grows under conifers, in sandy grounds; edible, when unripe, with good, aromatic flavor, used as seasoning. *Rhizopogon luteolus*, globose, uneven, 2–6 cm, with a thin, whitish, woolly involucre; then ochraceous and covered with sparse, brown red filaments; whitish, then ochraceous inside; grows buried or semiburied in pine woods; edible, when still unripe, but of poor quality.

GYROMITRA ESCULENTA

Cap similar to knobby brain, brown, internally hollow and whitish. **Stem** often compressed, rugose, whitish or pinkish; soon hollow; the cavity of the stem is connected to that of the cap. Total height 8–16 cm. **Flesh** thin, with the appearance and consistency of wax; whitish or pinkish. **Odor** mild. **Flavor** soft and agreeable. **Spores** light yellow. It grows in groups, in spring, very rare in autumn, in the cool, humid, and sandy recesses of coniferous woods; in untilled soil, in meadows, and also along road edges. **Edible with great caution**: it can be **deadly** if eaten raw; for particularly allergic people it can be harmful even cooked, especially if only briefly cooked and consumed in excessive quantity, or twice in the same day; and if consumed with the water in which it cooked. Those who try it for the first time should eat only a very small amount. It is advisable to boil it for a few minutes in water, to drain it, and then cook it with the proper seasoning. Completely harmless when exsiccated. Only the perfectly healthy and unripe specimens should be dried. It is, however, sold in various markets, in Europe, where it has been used for a very long time, so much so that is been deemed worthy of the name of *esculenta,* that is, edible. In the mountains one can find the *Gyromitra gigas,* **edible**, larger and paler than *esculenta;* only the unripe specimens should be used, after parboiling.

HELVELLA (Physomitra) INFULA (1)
Height 8–16 cm. Cap mitriform, deeply sulcate; brown, with the other surface, half-hidden, white and velvety. Stem whitish, pruinose, rugose, soon partly hollow. Flesh thin, fragile, whitish. It grows in autumn, but sometimes also in spring. **Edible**.

HELVELLA CRISPA (2)
Height 6–14 cm. Cap whitish, with the other surface cinereous. Stem squat, corrugated and alveolate; whitish; autumnal. **Edible**.

HELVELLA MONACHELLA (3)
Height 5–10 cm. Cap mitriform, fuliginous, with the other surface whitish. Stem white, smooth or slightly rugose. It grows in spring. **Edible**.

HELVELLA LACUNOSA (4)
Height 6–12 cm. Cap blackish, with the other surface lighter. Stem whitish, corrugated. It grows in the clearings of latifoliate woods. **Edible**.

HELVELLA CALIFORNICA (5)
Height 6–12 cm. Similar to *H. lacunosa,* but squatter, with the ribs of the stem simpler. **Not edible**. It grows in the woods of North America, as does the *Helvella caroliniana,* with cap with brainlike convolutions, **edible**, but likely to be confused with the poisonous *Helvella underwoodii,* which has, however, squatter stem, is compressed and without ribs.

HELVELLA ELASTICA (6)
Height 4–8 cm. Cap mitriform, cinereous white or rosy white. Stem whitish, slender, smooth or with few, slight, vertical grooves. **Edible**, but somewhat tough.

PEZIZA ACETABULUM (Acetabula vulgaris) (1)

Goblet shaped, 4–11 cm high. Walls thin, fragile, like wax. Margin rolled inward, undulate, often lobate. External surface, sterile, grayish brown, first lighter, then gradually darker; furfuraceous. Internal surface, fertile, darker than the external one; smooth. **Stem** thick, whitish; with grooves that make it look like a miniature trunk of an old oak tree; with branching ribs enwrapping the base of the goblet. **Spores** of faded color. It grows in the spring, especially on sandy soils, in large groups. **Poisonous**, if eaten raw; **edible**, if well cooked.

PEZIZA (Disciotis) VENOSA (2)

Goblet shaped, 3–15 cm large. Inside brown, with corrugate bottom. Outside whitish and furfuraceous. Also whitish is the short and atrophic peduncle that supports the goblet. The walls of the goblet are thin and fragile like wax. In the variety *reticulata,* the bottom of the goblet is formed by a reticule of fine, well-distinct veins. **Poisonous**, if eaten raw; **edible**, if well cooked. Similar to it is *Peziza costifera,* gray both inside and out; margin lobate and undulate, stem lighter, with ribs branching and enwrapping the goblet for about one-half its height. **Poisonous**, if eaten raw; **edible**, if well cooked.

PEZIZA (Otidea) ONOTICA (1)

Shaped like a donkey's ear, 3–8 cm high, elastic, waxy-fleshy; yellow and smooth outside; rosy yellow and hairy inside; on a hairy peduncle; grows under latifoliate trees; **edible**. Similar to it is *Otidea auricula,* which, however, is brown.

PEZIZA (Otidea) LEPORINA (2)

Shaped like a rabbit's ear, 2–4 cm high, brownish inside, lighter outside; on conifer needles; **edible**. Similar to it is *Otidea alutacea,* outside yellowish and variegated.

PEZIZA (Scutellinia) SCUTELLATA (3)

Shaped like a watchglass, 0.5–1.5 cm, inside scarlet, outside reddish and pubescent; grows on soils rich in organic substances and on wood debris; **of no alimentary interest**.

PEZIZA (Aleuria) CATINUS (4)

Goblet shaped, 1–4 cm, all ochraceous; outside pruinose; with festooned margin; on a peduncle; **of no alimentary interest**.

PEZIZA (Sarcoscypha) COCCINEA (5)

Bowl shaped, 2–6 cm, scarlet inside, outside amethystine cinereous and velvety; on a peduncle; found in winter, on wood debris; **edible**.

BULGARIA INQUINANS (6)

Globose, 2–4 cm, rusty, pubescent, full of gelatin, tenacious, smoky; then it opens up a little, while the inside becomes black; spores black, staining, spread all around; grows in winter, on the bark of felled oaks and beeches, in groups; **not edible**.

PEZIZA RUTILANS (7)

Similar to an upside-down campanule, 1–2 cm; orange red inside; orange and pruinose outside; pubescent margin; found in mossy places; **of no alimentary interest**.

rotunda Mor.

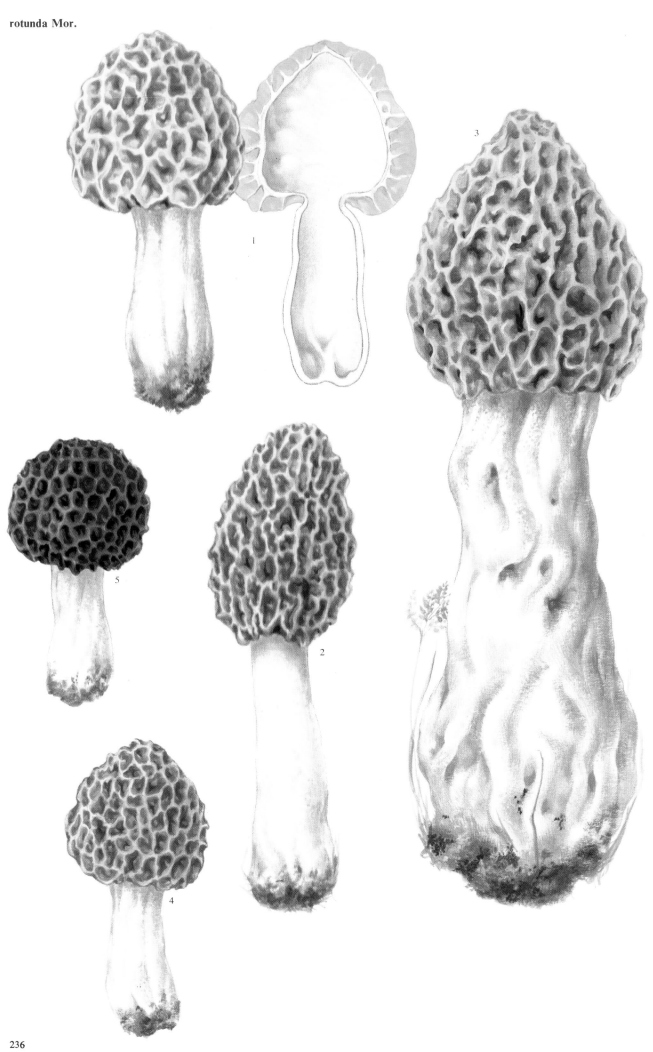

MORCHELLA

The *Morchellae* are hollow, with flesh of a waxy texture and appearance; they are found in the spring; **edible**, and some of them are very delicious if unripe, healthy, cleaned from the sand and the snails that often infest them, and if well cooked. The cap, globose, conical or uneven, either adheres to the upper part of the stem, in the true *morchellas*, or descends around the stem, roof-gutter-like, in the *Mitrophorae*. The cap soon becomes alveolate. The stem, basically white is sometimes cylindric, sometimes bulging; rugose, pruinose. The spores are ochraceous. The numbers indicate the height in centimeters (cm).

MORCHELLA ROTUNDA (1)
12–24 cm, cap globose, reddish ocher; large alveoli; found in meadows, near latifoliate trees.

MORCHELLA VULGARIS (2)
8–16 cm, cap ovoid, fuliginous, then ochraceous; but sometimes also grayish or even whitish.

MORCHELLA CRASSIPES
15–30 cm, cap conical or uneven; stem bulging, long, furfuraceous.

MORCHELLA SPONGIOLA (4)
6–12 cm, cap globose, ochraceous; alveoli small, deep, uneven; stem firm; on sandy soils, even along the seashore.

MORCHELLA UMBRINA (5)
6–10 cm, cap globose, very dark; alveoli somewhat regular, large, rounded.

MORCHELLA HORTENSIS (1)
10–15 cm, cap ovoid, fuliginous, with the base separated from the stem by a horizontal collar; alveoli remarkably uneven.

MORCHELLA COSTATA (2)
10–25 cm, cap with vertical ridges and with the base separated from the stem by a horizontal collar. Similar to it, but thinner, is *Morchella angusticeps*, growing under conifers, in North America.

MORCHELLA CONICA (3)
5–15 cm, cap olivaceous brown, distinctly conical, with distinct ridges from the apex to the base; base separated from the stem by a horizontal collar.

MORCHELLA ELATA (4)
7–14 cm, cap tall, generally conical, olivaceous brown, with the base separated from the top of the stem by a horizontal collar; stem ochraceous; found under conifers.

MORCHELLA (Mitrophora) HYBRIDA (5)
9–16 cm, cap ochraceous brown, small, conical, with vertical ridges; about one-half of it descending around the stem.

MORCHELLA (Mitrophora) RIMOSIPES (6)
12–24 cm, cap small, conical, olivaceous brown, descending about one-third around the stem; stem long, thick, rugose, furfuraceous. *Verpa bohemica* differs from the *Mitrophorae*, for having alveolate caps entirely descending around the stem; similar to it is *Verpa digitaliformis*, cap not alveolate, but only rugose; both are **edible**.

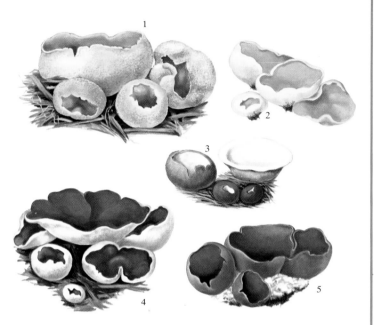

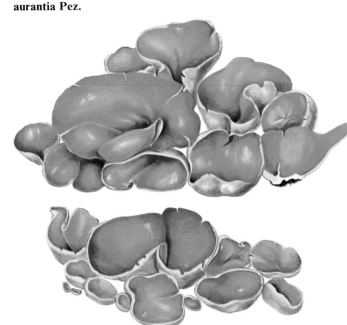

PEZIZA (Aleuria) VESICULOSA (1)

At first globose, hollow, with a slanted cleft; then opened, cuplike, 3–9 cm; margin denticulate; inside ochraceous; outside slightly lighter, pruinose, flocculose; on a peduncle; flesh without latex; grows from spring to autumn, in manured soils; **poisonous**, if eaten raw; **edible** if well cooked.

PEZIZA (Galactinia) SUCCOSA (2)

Similar to *P. vesiculosa,* but juicy; the latex becomes yellowish in air; found in woods, on the ground; **poisonous**, if eaten raw; **edible**, if well cooked.

PEZIZA (Lachnea) HEMISPHAERICA (3)

First globose, then basin shaped, 2–4 cm; inside whitish and lucid; outside brownish and hairy; **of no alimentary interest**.

PEZIZA (Aleuria) UMBRINA (4)

Cup shaped, 3–8 cm; inside fuliginous and undulate; outside whitish and pruinose; found on the ground, especially on scorched soil; **poisonous**, if eaten raw; **edible**, if well cooked.

PEZIZA (Aleuria) BADIA (5)

Cup shaped, 2–7 cm; margin uneven; lying on cottony down; inside brown; outside ochraceous, granular and furfuraceous; flesh juicy; **poisonous**, if eaten raw; **edible**, if well cooked. The following species are **of little alimentary interest,** even after cooking: *Peziza nigritella,* blackish inside, brown outside, without stem; *Peziza saniosa,* blackish inside, brown outside, on a peduncle; *Peziza repanda,* brown inside, whitish outside, without peduncle; *Peziza perlata,* fuliginous inside, whitish and rugose outside, without peduncle; *Peziza macropus,* entirely gray, with the cup on a long, cylindrical stem.

PEZIZA AURANTIA

It is the best representative of those species which, according to the most recent classifications, have been left in the genus *Peziza.* At first this mushroom looks like a small sphere, hollow, pale pink, furfuraceous; then the small sphere increases in size, breaks, and opens up like a cup, 5–15 cm in diameter, somewhat asymmetric, with a slanted margin gradually more and more uneven; but it never unrolls completely; outside it is rosy or faded orange, but later, with age or upon drying, it becomes whitish; inside it is bright orange, more seldom orange yellow. **Flesh** rather thick, but fragile, pink or pale orange. **Odor** agreeable. **Flavor** pleasant. It grows in late summer and in autumn, in sandy soils, in glades, sometimes in large groups or in tufts. **Edible,** even raw, in salads. It differs from *Sarcoscypha coccinea* (page 235), **of no alimentary interest,** because the latter is lignicolous, grows in winter and is of a different color; and from *Gyrocephalus rufus* (page 233), **edible,** because the latter is gelatinous, shaped like a cornucopia open sidewise, and is of a different color. We add here a note concerning another mushroom, red and oddly shaped, easy to find in the mountains, on the branches of **Rhododendrum ferrugineum:** the **Exobasidium rhododendri,** shaped like a berry, 1–4 cm, red with white, yellow and green spots; internally hollow, felted, white; sometimes used to adorn flower bouquets.

flavida Spath.

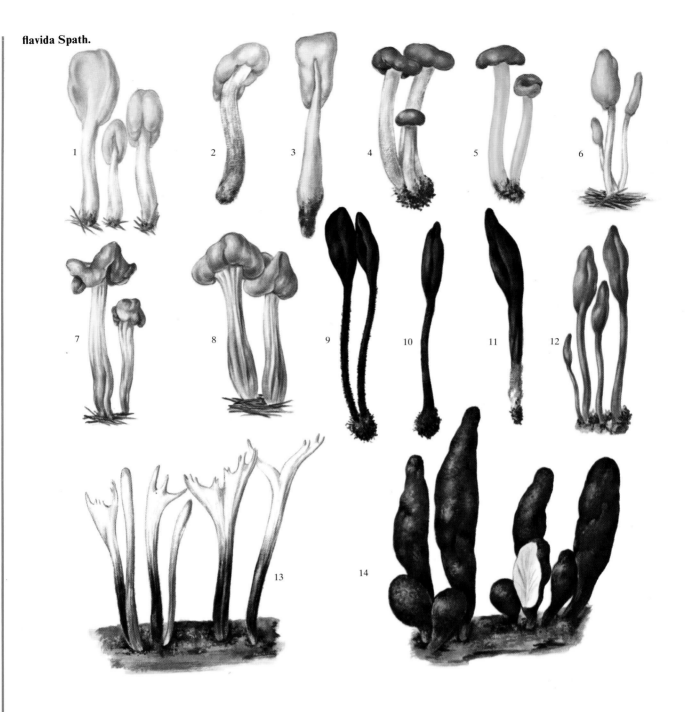

SPATHULARIA FLAVIDA (1)
Spathulate, 3–5 cm high, rugose, yellow; on a cylindric, yellowish stem; autumnal, grows on conifers' needles. Similar to it is *Spathularia neesi*, of ocher color. Other known *Spathulariae*: *S. velutipes* (2), with velvety stem, and *S. clavata* (3) with stem thickened at the base.

LEOTIA LUBRICA (4)
Nail shaped, 1–4 cm high; cap olivaceous brown, gelatinous; stem olivaceous yellow, pruinose, viscid. *Leotia lubrica* variety *aurantipes* (5) has a green cap and a yellow stem.

MITRULA PALUDOSA (6)
Height 1–4 cm; cap mitriform, odd, hollow, yellow; stem long and whitish; grows in spring, on leaves fallen in water.

CUDONIA CIRCINANS (7)
Nail shaped, 1–3 cm high; cap yellowish, oily; stem lightly colored, rugose; grows on conifer needles. Also *Cudonia confusa* (8) with swollen cap and swollen stem base.

GEOGLOSSUM (Trichoglossum) HIRSUTUM (9)
Shaped like the tongue of a bell, 2–5 cm high, on a thin and hairy stem; all fuliginous; grows in the summer, in grassy places. Other known *Geoglossum*: *Geoglossum fallax* (10), with nonpubescent stem; *Geoglossum cookei* (11), with cottony stem; *Geoglossum viride* (12), green.

XYLARIA HYPOXYLON (13)
Shaped like deer antlers, 4–8 cm high, blackish, often pruinose, corky; found in winter, on wood of latifoliate trees. Also known is *Xylaria polymorpha* (14), with numerous club-shaped hymenia, black and rugose, 4–8 cm high, joined together at the base; flesh white, corky; on wood of latifoliate trees.

All the above mushrooms are **worthless** from an alimentary point of view; however, strictly speaking, those of the genus *Spathularia* are **edible**.

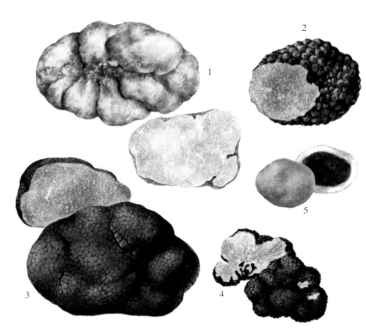

PEZIZA (Sarcosphaera) EXIMIA
Initially shaped as a sphere, 3–8 cm, compressed at the poles, often uneven; hidden into the ground, covered by a soil crust; then it comes to the surface, breaking the soil crust, even when hard and pressed and dry; as it grows it splits, star shaped, and it opens like a flower spreading out the petals (rays) more or less extensively; generally the diametral distance between two extreme points of such a star is 6–12 cm; but sometimes it can reach quite larger diameters, especially in humid weather, when it spreads out completely and becomes almost flat. Initially the external surface is whitish, then it becomes amethystine here and there, and eventually brownish; smooth or very slightly velvety. The internal surface is velvety and amethystine; then, gradually, it becomes violet, more and more intense, particularly at the bottom of the cup; but sometimes it remains pale or with few amethystine spots even on the inside. **Flesh** one to four millimeters thick, cartilaginous, tough, brittle; amethystine, cinereous, or ochraceous white; with mild odor and pleasant flavor. **Spores** discolored. It grows in large groups, in hills and mountains, in spring and at the beginning of the summer; not far from pines and spruces. **Poisonous** when raw: it can cause rather serious intestinal trouble. **Edible** only if unripe, parboiled and well cooked; however, even after cooking, it retains a rather elastic texture.

TUBER MAGNATUM or White Truffle (1)
Similar to a tuber, 3–15 cm, ochraceous, rugose with darker furfur and granules; cuticle not separable, thin; flesh soapy, rosy white, then silver amethystine, marbled; odor of garlic and cheese; grows in autumn and winter, buried, near oaks and other latifoliate trees, in northern Italy. **Edible**, very much in demand, delicious.

TUBER AESTIVUM or Summer Truffle (2)
Globose, 3–7 cm, blackish brown, with pyramidal warts, not contiguous; flesh white, then brownish marbled; aromatic; grows in the summer, in temperate regions, buried near latifoliate trees; **edible**, very much in demand.

TUBER MELANOSPORUM or Black Truffle (3)
Globose, 3–15 cm, blackish brown, with polygonal appressed warts; flesh white, then brownish violaceous; piquant odor; autumnal, grows in temperate regions, buried near oaks and other latifoliate trees; **edible**, very much in demand.

TUBER BRUMALE or Winter Truffle (4)
Globose, 2–8 cm, blackish brown, with polygonal, evanescent warts; flesh whitish, then blackish, marbled; odor strong; found in winter, in temperate regions, buried near oaks and other latifoliate trees; **edible**, very much in demand.

ELAPHOMYCES GRANULATUS or Deer Truffle (5)
Globose, 2–5 cm, brownish or faded, with warts and granules; involucre thick, fragile, reddish; flesh reddish, then fuliginous; found in·winter, even with the ground, in the moss, under latifoliate trees; **not edible**. Also **not edible** are *Elaphomyces muricatus*, smaller, brownish, with pointed warts, growing under conifers, and *Elaphomyces variegatus*, even smaller, growing more frequently under beeches.

Part Two
Fungi: An Outline of Some of Their Characteristics

How to Preserve Mushrooms

At certain favorable times of the year mushrooms grow in large numbers: a short trip to the right places is often sufficient to bring back home an overflowing basket; this happy event can happen for several days in a row. It might not be possible to use all the collected mushrooms at once. What can you do? Give them to your friends? What if they do not trust your experience? Often, out of kindness, they will accept your gift, but, as soon as you leave, the mushrooms go into the garbage can. Then it might be more convenient to use one of the various treatments that would ensure preserving the mushrooms you collect, so that during the winter, you will be able to enjoy the rewards of your collecting much more. Around the table on a gray, cool winter day, you will remember the happy days of your trips to the countryside, and you will think of future trips with much more pleasure.

Sometimes, instead of preserving the mushrooms, it might be more convenient to preserve, in the form of an extract, only their delicate taste and aroma. The steps in preparing a mushroom extract are as follows: Clean the mushrooms and discard their bruised parts. Then cook them at low, constant heat, without water and without adding any ingredients. In cooking, the mushroom will lose its juice. From time to time, collect this juice, pour it into a suitable container, and pour warm water—as much or slightly more than the volume of the juice—over the mushrooms. Repeat this operation several times, and stop when the juice appears discolored, or loses its fragrance and taste. Discard the mushrooms, which are now exhausted. Put the juice on the fire and let it boil slowly until it appears as a concentrated, thick extract. Practically all the mushrooms that taste good and have a good aroma can be used for the preparation of mushroom extracts. Mushroom extracts are used in a way similar to that of meat extracts.

Some mushrooms can be preserved in oil. One should use unripe or medium-ripe mushrooms; one should not use those which are too ripe. After careful cleaning, the mushrooms should be cut into pieces not larger than the size of half a walnut, and boiled for two to three minutes in water. On the side, you should boil for about ten minutes an equal volume of water and vinegar containing some whole small onions, laurel and rosemary leaves, pepper in grains, and salt. Pour mushrooms and the water used to boil them into the aromatized vinegar and continue to boil for about fifteen minutes. Then let them drain in a sheltered place to avoid contamination from molds; afterward place them in glass jars that can be tightly sealed; fill the jar with oil of good quality and close the jar tight.

Preservation of mushrooms is most often obtained by exsiccating them. This operation, when done well, is long and time consuming, but the results are sure. Discard the unhealthy mushrooms, clean the chosen ones and cut them into long, medium-thick slices; scald the slices in boiling water for two to three minutes to sterilize them. This operation will be easier if you have a large-size colander. Put the sliced mushrooms into the colander and immerse it in boiling water for four to five minutes (this longer time is necessary to allow the heat to reach the mushrooms in the center of the mass), then take the colander out and let the mushrooms drain and cool off a little. Place the mushrooms on a small wooden board and expose them to dry air in the shade. It is convenient to have a raised edge around the wooden board to prevent the mushrooms from flying away with the wind. It is often said that mushrooms exposed to the sun lose all their good qualities. Surely, if one does not pay attention they become horny and can no longer be regenerated; but, if you keep an eye on them, if you turn them around frequently, they will dry well even in the sun, more quickly than in air, and they will retain their fragrance and taste. If you dry mushrooms in the sun, sometimes there is no need to scald them with boiling water; the rapid drying and the sun will sterilize them. But if you do not scald them in boiling water make sure to use only fresh and very healthy mushrooms. In the evening, when the air becomes humid, you should put the mushrooms in a place where dew will not form; during the night they should be stored in a place where they will not re-absorb part of the water lost during the day. In the morning, after the air is dry, the mushrooms are exposed again to the sun or to the air. Two or three days are sometimes sufficient to ensure a perfect drying. The mushrooms are completely dry when they have lost about nine-tenths of their fresh weight. They should look dry, light, somewhat horny and no longer pliable. They should be kept inside hermetically sealed glass containers. If you prefer plastic bags instead, make sure there are no holes in them; the air could let in humidity and spores and the mushrooms could become moldy.

To regenerate dry mushrooms place them in lukewarm water a few hours before cooking. If the water looks very dirty it should be discarded, if it does not look too dirty, it can be filtered and used as seasoning either for the mushrooms or for other food.

Almost all mushrooms can be dried, except those that are somewhat fibrous, such as the *Cantharellus cibarius* (page 225), those that are easily putrescible, such as the *Coprinus comatus* (page 51), those that would dissolve into a powder, such as the *Lycoperdon*; and those that would acquire a woody texture, such as the species of the genus *Lactarius*, with the exception of the *Lactarius piperatus* (page 130), which, after drying, should be pulverized, using a strong grinder. The pulverized *Lactarius piperatus* should be used with moderation since it is very peppery.

All the mushrooms that can be preserved by drying can be pulverized. The powder takes up less space than the whole mushrooms. Mushroom powder should be stored in plastic bags or in hermetically sealed containers. It is used to season foods according to one's preferences. Naturally the better the mushrooms used to prepare it, the better the powder is. While is is possible to mix together the powder of mushrooms of different species, it is advisable to keep separated that of the *Lactarius piperatus* because of its very strong, peppery taste.

Many foods can be preserved for a long time either refrigerated or frozen, but fresh mushrooms deteriorate under such conditions. However, it is possible to keep fresh mushrooms without spoiling, in a refrigerator for a few days, provided the temperature is a few degrees above zero (centigrade scale). Once taken out of the refrigerator they should be used immediately; they would deteriorate if put back into the refrigerator. Cooked mushrooms take longer to spoil, so it is safe to eat them after warming them up, provided they have been kept in non-oxidizable containers, such as earthenware, glassware, or enamel.

Mushrooms which can be preserved under oil and vinegar

Armillaria mellea	110
Biannularia imperialis	109
Boletus (*several species*)	174 seq
Cantharellus (*several species*)	225 seq
Clavaria botrytis	218
Clitocybe Alexandri	114
Clitocybe geotropa	113
Clitocybe infundibuliformis	111
Clitocybe nebularis	114
Coprinus comatus	51
Cortinarius praestans	69
Cortinarius violaceus	76
Entoloma aprilis	83
Entoloma clypeatum	83
Entoloma Saundersi	83
Entoloma sepium	83
Fistulina hepatica	213
Gyrocephalus rufus	233
Hydnum (*several species*)	214 seq
Lepista gilva	119
Lepista inversa	119
Lyophyllum aggregatum	107
Lyophyllum Georgii	105
Lyophyllum loricatum	107
Pleurotus eryngii	123
Pleurotus eryngii variety *ferulae*	123
Pleurotus nebrodensis	123
Pleurotus ostreatus	124
Polyporus confluens	205

Polyporus frondosus	208
Polyporus giganteus	209
Polyporus intybaceus	208
Polyporus leucomelas	207
Polyporus ovinus	204
Polyporus pes caprae	204
Psalliota (*several species*)	42 seq
Rhodopaxillus irinus	121
Rhodopaxillus nudus	120
Rhodopaxillus panaeolus	122
Rozites caperata	62
Russula cyanoxantha	148
Russula virescens	149
Tricholoma albobrunneum	94
Tricholoma caligatum	93
Tricholoma colossus	104
Tricholoma columbetta	102
Tricholoma populinum	97
Tricholoma terreum	99

Lepiota procera

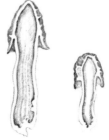

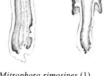

Morchella rotunda

Amanita caesarea

Mitrophora rimosipes (1) and *hybrida* (2)

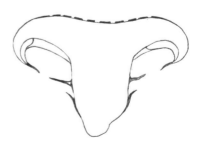

Biannularia imperialis

Nutrient Properties of Mushrooms

The human organism needs food. Foods contain in various proportions those alimentary principles that the organism utilizes to grow, to renew itself, to operate. The various principles have different functions: plastic, energetic, plastic-energetic, excipient, stimulant.

Plastic principle. The living organism grows and, either while growing or after reaching its full development, needs to renew itself continuously. The plastic material necessary for growth, development, and renewal is furnished by a group of organic substances known as proteins and by some minerals.

One hundred grams of fresh mushrooms provide, on the average, five grams of proteins assimilable by our body; more than our daily requirement of phosphorus and potassium; zinc, about our daily requirement; iron, about one-third of our daily requirement; plus other necessary minerals, but in smaller quantities.

Energetic principle. A living organism also needs substances that can provide it with the energy necessary to maintain its vital activities. These substances are used in the organism through a process of biochemical oxidation. Body heat is one of the results of these biochemical processes. The most important energetic aliments are the carbohydrates or sugars. Bread is the king among the energetic aliments. Meat generally contains only traces of carbohydrates; one hundred grams of fresh mushrooms contain about ten grams of carbohydrates, more than that contained in the same quantity of milk, string beans, or sugar beets.

Plastic and energetic principles. This group is represented by the substances known as fats or lipids. The adipose (fat) tissue of a healthy organism has protective, insulating, and lubricating functions. The organism, in emergencies, can use up the fat as a source of energy; the energy released by the oxidation of the lipids is higher than that produced by an equal quantity of carbohydrates. Lipids are important components of cell membrane systems. Therefore one can attribute to them both a plastic and an energetic function. Lipids do not abound in mushrooms: one hundred grams of fresh mushrooms contain slightly less than one gram of lipids, just about as much as in fat-free broth or in white bread, more than in sweet bread or in fresh codfish, and much more than in potatoes.

Excipients. They are represented by water and cellulose, a carbohydrate indigestible by our digestive apparatus, but, at the same time, quite necessary. *Corpora non agunt nisi soluta*: substances cannot act unless solubilized. Water is the medium necessary for all vital activities, present in every cell, circulating throughout all the systems. The higher the amount of water of an organism, the younger and stronger an organism is. With the exception of sugar and lard all aliments contain water.

To be digested and assimilated by the organism, the alimentary principles must not only be dissolved in water but also dispersed in some inert excipient substance, which can be softened. Ordinarily this excipient function is provided by the cellulose. Without cellulose there are scarce gastric secretions, weak intestinal peristaltic movements, constipation, pathological putrefactions, absorption of toxic substances, and, as a consequence, a long list of illnesses.

On the average, one hundred grams of fresh mushrooms contain eighty-five grams of water and a few grams of cellulose. Some of the water is lost during cooking.

Seasoning. Many aliments, to be tolerated by the organism, have to be taken with some seasoning which, by lending them aroma and taste, stimulates the activity of the digestive apparatus. The various condiments do not constitute a definite group of alimentary principles, but belong to one or another of the groups mentioned above: oil is a lipid, sugar is a carbohydrate, salt is a mineral.

Most of the edible mushrooms have a good aroma and good flavor, and can impart these qualities to other foods, making them more appetizing and therefore more easily digestible. Just think of the flavor imparted to a dish of spaghetti or risotto by a few slices of dried *Boletus edulis* (page 177).

Vitamins. The ingestion of foods containing all the alimentary principles indicated above, and well seasoned, is not yet sufficient for good digestion and is of no use for our organism if there is a deficiency of those substances known as vitamins. Vitamins have no plastic or energetic function, nor are they used as seasoning; the function of vitamins is that of catalyzers of biochemical processes; without vitamins, the food is not food, but poison. The main source of vitamins is provided by fresh fruits and vegetables, but even aliments of animal origin contain vitamins, derived from the plants eaten by the animals. *Cantharellus cibarius* (page 222) and *Amanita caesarea* (page 17) contain large quantities of vitamin A, which is absent in Boletus edulis (page 177). Fresh mushrooms generally contain high levels of vitamin PP and other vitamins of the B group, including choline, a vitamin with a protective action on the liver, in cases of mushroom poisoning. Mushrooms, like meat, are deficient in vitamin C; however, one hundred grams of *Fistulina hepatica* (page 213) can contain up to 150 milligrams of vitamin C, about fivefold our daily requirement. Vitamin D_2 is also abundant in fresh mushrooms, only slightly less than in butter and egg yolk: 100 grams of fresh mushrooms contain from 100 to 500 I.U., a level higher than our daily requirement. Although precise data are not available, it is believed that vitamin K is also abundant in fresh mushrooms. Fresh mushrooms also contain various organic acids that can stimulate respiration.

As a conclusion it can be said that mushrooms should not be considered just as a condiment to give more flavor to our food, but also as a proper food, more similar to eggs and meat than to vegetables. The abundance of alimentary principles, and their digestibility, depends on the state of ripeness of the mushrooms: they are at their best slightly before reaching full ripeness.

Mushrooms Are Fruiting Bodies

The professional collectors go searching for mushrooms with assurance gained through practice and, since they know the good places, they come back in a few hours with large harvests. The amateur could do the same for many species of mushrooms neglected by the professionals, but which, however, are not only comestible but also very tasty and of excellent quality. It is only necessary to know the life cycle of the mushrooms and when and where they gorw.

In some places people think that purple mushrooms are poisonous; but the *Rhodopaxillus nudus* (page 120) is purple, and yet it is perfectly edible once cooked well. Actually this mushroom is slightly toxic if eaten raw, but not because of its color. The most favorable season is late autumn. Mushrooms grow in groups, in circles (fairy rings), or in arcs in grassy grounds in the woods of either coniferous or latifoliate trees. If you do not collect all the samples in a group, and leave a mature sample in place, you can go back next year and find more mushrooms of the same species in the same place. The lamellae (gills) of the mature mushroom produces a powderlike substance, made up of microscope spores; these spores are so small that you need several million of them to make one gram. At first sight, even under a microscope, the spores of mushrooms of the same species seem to be equal. But sometimes, some of them have male characteristics and others female ones. The spores that fall on the soil germinate, under suitable conditions, forming threadlike structures, the hyphae, made of several cells, known as primary mycelium. The fusion of a male primary mycelium with a female primary mycelium produces a secondary mycelium, which, in turn, will produce the fruiting bodies (basidiocarps), sometimes improperly called carpophores (fruit-bearing), sometimes called hymeniophore, that is, hymenium-bearing (the hymenium is the structure producing the spores); they are also called receptacles. The mushroom that we collect is nothing else but the fruiting body of the fungus; the main body of the fungus goes unnoticed in the soil or in decomposing materials, or stumps or logs from which the fungus obtains the nutrient substances.

The fungi do not reproduce only through the formation of spores; they can form conidia, asexual spores formed on the mycelium, not in the fruiting bodies; the conidia germinate producing a secondary mycelium; or they can reproduce from pieces of mycelium separated from the parent fungus. After a period of growth and having reached the proper stage of development, the secondary mycelium produces new fruiting bodies, the reproductive structures that will ensure the perpetuation of the species through a new dissemination of spores. This life cycle has repeated itself without change for several million years. The scientists tell us that even the oldest mushrooms known to us are the same as those growing today.

In our example we have mentioned the gills (lamellae) because in the vast majority of the species of mushrooms of interest to us, the spore-bearing structures are in the form of lamellae. Actually this structure can assume different shapes. Sometimes, as in the genus *Boletus*, it is formed by tubules; sometimes, as in the genus *Hydnum*, by spines or toothlike projection; and, in other genera, can assume other shapes that will be described later.

Sometimes the spores are produced on the outside of specialized structures called basidia (singular = basidium); sometimes they are produced inside saclike structures called asci (singular = ascus). Basidium means base, support, and ascus means sac. The fungi with basidia form the class *Basidiomycetes*, and the fungi with asci form the class *Ascomycetes*. These two classes are further divided into subclasses, orders, families, genera. The genera are divided into species. Various characteristics are of importance in the classification and identification of the species. The color of the spore powder (that is, of the spores en masse) is one such characteristic, and it has been indicated for each species in the Atlas, except where it is of little diagnostic importance. Sometimes the proper identification of species cannot be based solely on macroscopic characteristics, those that one can see with the naked eye, but it is necessary to study microscopic characteristics, first of all, the structure of the spores. Under the microscope the color of the single spores is generally much paler than that of the spores *en masse* and one can recognize specific differences in shapes, dimensions and surface structures.

Fungi are a group of plants not containing chlorophyll, the pigment responsible for the green color of the leaves; without chlorophyll there is no photosynthesis; it is through photosynthesis, a light-dependent biochemical process, that green plants can transform the carbon dioxide in the air into sugars and starch. The fungi, without chlorophyll, depend, for their nutrition, on the organic materials that they can find in the environment. It is for this reason that fungi are often found associated with living green plants. The type of association in which there are mutual advantages for the plant and the fungus is called symbiosis. The mycorrhizae are an example of symbiosis between fungi and higher plants; they are formed by an association between fungal hyphae and roots of higher plants.

The great majority of the higher fungi, the mushrooms in which we are interested here, are either symbiont or mycorrhizical. It would be perfectly useless to look for *Boletinus cavipes* (page 199) in places without larch trees, of which this mushroom is a symbiont, and without which it can not grow. Once you have found a place where it grows, keep it in mind. *Boletinus cavipes*, which is found only on the mountains, is another of those species overlooked by professional people, but it is a fairly edible mushroom as long as it is unripe; it can also be preserved by drying.

Other mushrooms are parasites of living higher plants. One such example is the *Polyporus sulphureus* (page 205), which establishes itself on the wounds of living trees; it grows into tufts of large dimension, with a sulfur yellow color, and, in a few years, it succeeds in hollowing out the trunk of the infested trees. The trees can continue to look quite healthy for several years until the day they suddenly fall under the weight of the foliage that the rotten, empty trunk can no longer support.

The *Armillaria mellea* (page 110) is another parasitic mushroom. This mushroom has caused large destruction of mulberry trees. Once the infested trees are dead, this mushroom continues to grow on the decomposing stumps and roots. This type of life, on dead organic material, is called saprophytic life. The *Armillaria mellea* is initially a parasite and later a saprophytic mushroom.

Mushrooms do not grow every year with the same abundance: there are good years and bad years. The most important factors for the growth of mushrooms are temperature and humidity. Light, so important for the green plants, is not an important factor for the growth of mushrooms. But you must remember that there are some mushrooms of the genus *Tylostoma* that càn grow under the intense light and heat of the desert, whereas there are others, such as *Lactaria laccata* (page 119) that are found only in darker places, in woods.

A Few Words about the Microscopic Fungi

The structures that are commonly known as mushrooms are nothing else but the fruiting bodies of those organisms that the mycologists call higher fungi, or macromycetes (macromycetes = large fungi), even though the dimensions of the caps of some mushrooms might be only a few millimeters across. Several thousand species of macromycetes have been described so far; some authors list about seven thousand of them; but other authors think that many of the species described are not true species but unstable hybrids. Much more numerous, about one hundred thousand, are the species of microscopic fungi, that is those fungi that cannot be identified with the naked eye. Thus, for the mycologists, fungi are the *Oidium* (powdery mildew), the *Plasmopara viticola* (downy mildew of grapes), the rusts (*Puccinia*) and smuts (*Ustilago*) of grains and thousands of other parasites of wild and cultivated plants. The molds of various colors that so often develop on foodstuff, especially fruits, are also fungi. The blue and green molds so frequent on oranges, lemons, and tangerines, and responsible for the decay of large quantities of these fruits during transportation and storage, belong to *Penicillium*, a genus with many species.

The first antibiotics to be used against infectious diseases, the penicillins, were isolated from cultures of *Penicillium notatum*. Later on, several other antibiotics were isolated from numerous other molds. Molds of the genus *Penicillum* are responsible for the highly prized flavor of Gorgonzola, Roquefort (*Penicillium roqueforti*), Camembert (*Penicillium camemberti*), and various other cheeses.

Numerous species of molds are grown industrially on a large scale for the production of various organic substances, such as citric, lactic, gluconic, and fumaric acids and various enzymes; alone or together with yeasts they are used in the production of ethyl alcohol and alcoholic beverages from sugars and starches. The yeasts are also fungi and their practical importance is certainly higher than that of many mushrooms. It should be sufficient to remember that yeasts are responsible for the transformation of grape juice into wine, of malt into beer and for the leavening of bread dough; the yeasts themselves are nutritive products very rich in proteins, vitamins, and enzymes.

One should not forget that there are numerous microscopic fungi that are parasites of man and animals, mammalians, reptiles, fishes, birds, and insects.

Mushrooms in the Kitchen

In cooking, mushrooms like fish, should be used as soon as possible, because they spoil very quickly. Even mushrooms of excellent quality and healthy at the time they are picked can give trouble when they are not so fresh any longer or when one waits a long time before cooking them. In a few hours eggs deposited by insects start hatching; the maggots invade the mushrooms and help in putrefying them. The excellent *Coprinus comatus* (page 51) is one of the mushrooms that spoil very quickly, even when not infested by worms and maggots; it should be consumed no latter than twenty-four hours after it is picked.

As soon as a mushroom loses its natural odor and color, it should be thrown away without regrets. As we have already said, with few exceptions one should also throw away those mushrooms that have undergone freezing while still in their natural habitat.

We have already recommended cleaning the mushrooms immediately after picking them and before placing them in the basket. We have also recommended discarding immediately the tubules and the lamellae of ripe mushrooms, if tubules and lamellae are too flaccid. In this manner one contributes to the dissemination of the spores produced by the tubules and lamellae of the mature mushrooms; the spores falling on the soil in their natural habitat will germinate and produce more mushrooms. Only at home the mushrooms can be easily cleaned to perfection. One should eliminate all the insipid and indigestible parts: scales, warts, volva, ring, the stalk (part or all), if hard, fibrous, or infested by worms. The cap cuticle, if dry, should be kept, because it is the most aromatic and tasty part of the mushroom. Lamellae and tubules, if still healthy and not flaccid, should not be thrown away because they are generally the most nutrient parts of the mushrooms.

One should take care to preserve the natural taste and aroma of the mushrooms. Therefore in preparing the mushroom for eating one should not go to the extreme with the washing, parboiling, and adding sauces. Washing mushrooms, especially for too long, impoverishes them enormously. When absolutely necessary, the washing should be done with clean, cold water and—we repeat it again—quickly; then the mushrooms should be carefully dried. Sometimes a good washing is the only way to free completely from sand and small snails the *morchellas*, spongy alveolate mushrooms, which are internally empty and grow in sandy places. The addition of vinegar to the water used to wash mushrooms, advisable according to some mycologists, seems completely unnecessary, if not really damaging. Mushrooms, exceptions aside, are tastier, more aromatic, digestible, and nutrient the

less they are cooked; and when it is not possible to eat them raw, the cooking process should be quick and simple. We have said exceptions aside, because this general rule has numerous exceptions. The species of mushrooms that can be eaten raw are not numerous, although among them there are some of excellent quality that will be mentioned later in the text. Generally it is sufficient to season these mushrooms with lemon juice, oil, and salt; some pepper and aromatic herbs can also be added. Sometimes it might be necessary to leave them soaking in lemon juice and salt for a few hours to eliminate all those acrid, sour, bitter, too aromatic or somewhat toxic substances that are present in them.

As for the mushrooms that need cooking, one should remember species of the genus *Lactarius*, such as, for example, *Lactarius delicious* (page 134), that if cooked on a grill, or generally on an open fire, lose their acrid, intensely peppery taste, but if they are cooked as a stew, often become an inedible mush. Species of the genus *Russula* should also be cooked on an open fire because in the pot they become very hard and absolutely inedible.

Sometimes, before cooking certain mushrooms one should parboil them in water for a few minutes. Generally, exceptions aside, one should parboil all those mushrooms that are acrid, sour, bitter tasting, resinous, and have a coarse texture. The water used for this parboiling should be thrown away; don't use it, not even for livestock, because it could be harmful. One should not parboil the tender and delicate mushrooms because one would deprive them of most of their taste and aroma. Mushrooms with a viscid cap should be kept for a few minutes in a hot oven to dry up the viscid pellicle, which, after this treatment, will not form again, even if the mushrooms are cooked in a stew.

When cooking mushrooms, the pot should be left uncovered at the beginning to allow most of the water contained in the cells to evaporate. But then, if there are not other reasons to the contrary, it is advisable to cover the pot to preserve the aroma. As for the juice that collects in the pot, if one is cooking mushrooms of good quality, it is generally tasty and makes a very good sauce; but if one is using mushrooms of not good quality, often it is better not to use it. Taste it: if it is rather bitter or sweetish or in any way unpleasant, drain the mushrooms carefully and throw the juice away.

Too often people cook mushrooms with large additions of onions, garlic, aromatic herbs, tomatoes, green peppers, and assorted spices, and then wines of all sorts. The most exquisite mushrooms, when cooked this way, lose their characteristic taste and aroma, suppressed by those of the various additions. Therefore, be moderate in using spices and condiments. Some gourmets also advise to add salt and pepper only after cooking, just before serving.

The gourmets also advise cooking together mushrooms of different species, when they can be cooked using the same recipe. For instance, at the beginning of the season: *Psalliota campestris* (page 45), *Clitopilus prunulus* (page 122), *Lepiota procera* (page 35), *Pholiota mutabilis* (page 60), *Lyophyllum Georgii* (page 105), *Gomphidium viscidus* (page 174); later in the season: *Cantharellus cibarius* (page 225), *Armillaria mellea* (page 110), *Clitocybe infundibuliformis* (page 111), *Amanitopsis vaginata* (page 33), *Lepiota naucina* (page 39), *Russula virescens* (page 149), *Russula integra* (page 154), *Russula cyanoxantha* (page 148); in the fall: *Armillaria mellea, Rhodopaxillus nudus* (page 120), *Hygrophorus pratensis* (page 170), and some *Russula*; at the end of the season: *Armillaria mellea, Pleurotus ostreatus* (page 124), *Collybia velutipes* (page 90), *Agrocybe aegerita* (page 64). Once cooked, mushrooms will keep for several days; they can be eaten safely even warmed up.

Recipes for Mushrooms

It is to be understood that the mushrooms used in all recipes are to be cleaned.

Salads. To what we said before, we want only to add that to make a mushroom salad one should use only unripe mushrooms; they should be left to soak for some time in the seasoning; if you want to add some aromatic herb use a knife to chop it, not a machine.

On the spit. You could cook mushrooms using this method on your trips through the countryside. You should use fleshy mushrooms, not fibrous ones. Spit them on a green, thin, decorticated branch and cook them on nonsmoking embers. From time to time baste them with melted butter, sprinkle with salt and, at the end, with some pepper. The *Russula virescens* (page 149) prepared this way is quite delicious.

On the grill. This recipe is very good for *Lepiotas* of large size, some *Lactarius*, such as the *L. delicious* and *L. sanguifluus* (page 134) and for the *Russula virescens* (page 149). The stalks should be either discarded or cooked separately. Instead of a grill, you can use the hot plate of a charcoal stove or an iron frying pan on a gas range. The mushrooms should be dipped into hot, melted butter, until they are well soaked with it. Sprinkle them with salt and pepper. Place them on the grill, lamellae side up for a few minutes; then turn them on the other side, again for a few minutes. Sometimes instead of a few minutes, a few seconds will be sufficient. Serve them immediately.

In the frying pan (skillet). You can cook this way only the most tender species, such as *Coprinus comatus* (page 51), *Russula aurata* (page 156), *Psalliota campestris* (page 45), *Lyophyllum Georgii* (page 105), *Lycoperdon maximum* (page 228). Slice the mushroom, dip them in beaten eggs, then in a mixture of bread crumbs and finely grated cheese. Fry in hot oil for a few minutes.

Mushroom casserole. All mushrooms can be cooked using this recipe with the exception of all species of *Lactarius*, which would dissolve into a mush, and of *Russula*, which become very hard. Heat a mixture of oil and butter in equal parts and add some small onions. Then add the mushrooms. Cook on a high heat for about 5 minutes, uncovered; then for another 25 minutes, covered, at low heat. Shortly before taking them off the fire, sprinkle with minced parsley (chopped with a chopping knife, not with a machine). *Variation*: after the first five minutes, you can add some tomatoes or some diluted tomato sauce. *Variation*: if you do not add tomato and parsley, you can pour some white, dry wine on the mushrooms. *Variation*: if no tomato, parsley, or wine has been added, you can pour the mushrooms, after cooking, on eggs frying in butter; add some bread crumbs and grated cheese and cook for another five minutes in the oven. No matter how you cook them, do not forget the salt.

Mushroom stew. Cut the mushrooms in slices about one centimeter thick and cook them in a mixture of oil and butter, in equal parts, with some garlic cloves, not cut, but squashed. To keep them moist, add some broth as the water given out by the mushrooms evaporates. Or instead of broth you can use a meat sauce or a meat bouillon of good quality dissolved in warm water. Add salt as necessary and, if you like it, some pepper.

Stuffed mushrooms. One should use mushrooms with fleshy caps of large size, such as edible species of *Boletus, Psalliota, Amanita*. Cut off the stem and dig a hole in the cap. Fill the hole with stuffing prepared by mixing the minced stems with oil, bread crumbs, parsley, pepper and salt. Add some butter. Cook in an oven or, at least, covered. If the mushrooms are selected carefully, about half an hour of cooking should be sufficient.

Mushroom balls. Cut the mushrooms in small cubes. Cook them in a mixture of oil and butter in equal parts. Then mix with eggs, sausages, ground meat, bread crumbs, a little flour, and enough broth to keep the mixture workable. Prepare small balls. Dip them in beaten eggs and then in bread crumbs. Fry in oil. Besides salt, you can add a little pepper.

Mushrooms au gratin. Choose good potatoes. Boil them with skins on in salted water. Peel them and cut them into thick slices, but while peeling and cutting the potatoes, take care that they do not cool off too much, because this would make them hard. First place a layer of potato slices on the bottom of a casserole; cover this layer with finely minced mushrooms, bread crumbs, and butter curls; continue to make alternate layers of potato and mushrooms. Sprinkle the top layer with grated cheese. Place the casserole in a hot oven until you have a nice, golden crust. But don't forget the salt.

Mushrooms with Fontina. Only for mushrooms of very good quality. Cover the bottom of a casserole with oil and melted butter. Place a first layer of mushrooms. Cover the mushrooms with slices of Fontina or some other soft melting cheese. Make several layers alternating with mushrooms and Fontina. Cook at low heat to allow the cheese to melt; otherwise the cheese could harden. Halfway through cooking, add some milk or cream. This fondue of mushrooms with Fontina is to be served very hot, as soon as you have a light, bread-color crust on top. No other ingredients are required; as usual, salt is necessary, but in lesser quantity than for other recipes, since the cheese is already salted.

Pickled (Marinated) mushrooms. Use mushrooms of medium size. Sprinkle salt on them and let them stand salted for a day or two. Throw away the juice given out. Sprinkle with mustard seeds, clove, ginger, black pepper and as many spices as you like; bring to a boil. Let it stand for 15 days. Drain well. They are ready for use, as hot seasoning, for well-armored throats, such as those of sailors.

Mushroom sukiyaki. This is a Japanese recipe; it is used for the preparation of the Matsutake mushroom, which is similar, perhaps identical, to the *Tricholoma caligatum* (page 93). But one can use also the *Armillaria mellea* (page 110), the *Cantharellus cibarius* (page 225), the *Polyporus pes caprae* (page 204), or the *Pleurotus ostreatus* (page 124). Cut the mushrooms in thin slices; also slice some pork meat, veal, or chicken. Around the mushrooms and the meat, place celery, scallions, green pepper, leeks, in small separate groups. Add soy sauce and some sake, an alcholic Japanese beverage prepared from rice. Or instead of sake, use a strong, dry wine. Cook covered. You can eat this dish with boiled rice, dry. Do not forget the salt.

Mushrooms with cream and eggs. Clean and cut medium-thick slices of mushrooms of the genus *Psalliota*, that are medium ripe, healthy and firm; put some butter in saucepan and as soon as it starts frying briskly add the mushroom slices; sprinkle with salt, and let them cook until they are lightly—very, very lightly—browned. Then add, in spoonfuls, some Marsala or sherry, in such a quantity as to evaporate quickly. Then add some fresh, unsweetened whipped cream, stir gently, and let cook for another ten minutes, so that the total cooking time will be about half an hour. Pour the cream with the mushrooms on a plate; cover with slices of toasted bread and on each slice a poached egg, prepared ahead of time, and serve.

Mushroom Omelette. Fry some *psalliotas* as in the previous recipe, until they are well done. Pour over them some beaten eggs and increase the heat. While the mixture is still soft, add parsley, other aromatic herbs as you wish, and the necessary salt. Stir a little, continue to cook until done, and serve on a warm plate.

Mushrooms and veal shanks. Roll in flour as many veal shanks as there are people to serve; place them in a skillet in which you have melted butter (15 grams per person); add salt, pepper, and let them brown. Then sprinkle them with some dry, white wine, one spoonful for each veal shank. Now add some sliced Meadow mushroom (*Psalliota campestris*), 100 grams per person, some minced parsley, and continue to cook for about half an hour, adding some broth if necessary. Cook until done and serve with or without a sprinkle of lemon juice.

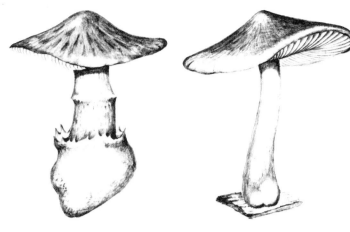

Squamanita Schreieri   *Pluteus astromarginatus*

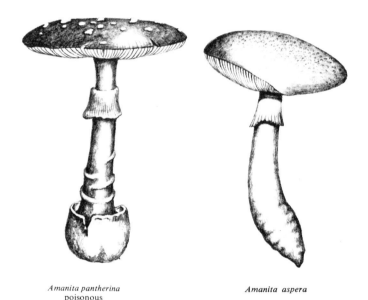

Amanita pantherina
poisonous

Amanita aspera

Russula paludosa   *Russula maculata*

Gastronomic Classification of Mushrooms

This classification has been prepared by Mr. Umberto Nonis, an expert mycologist and experienced collector. He has personally tested, using all the prescribed methods, the edibility of more than six hundred species of mushrooms. Therefore, this classification should be given careful consideration even in those rare instances in which it differs from the opinion of the mycological community as reported in the Atlas. In this classification the mushrooms are divided into four groups, from the best ones, first quality, to the not-so-good ones, fourth quality. Following this classification, there is a short list of mushrooms that can be eaten raw. In each group the mushrooms are listed in alphabetical order (the numbers indicate the pages where the various species are described).

Mushrooms of first quality

Agrocybe aegerita	64
Amanita caesarea	17
Boletus aereus	180
Boletus appendiculatus	181
Boletus cyanescens	174
Boletus edulis	177
Boletus pinicola	181
Clitopilus prunulus	122
Coprinus comatus	51
Hygrophorus marzuolus	171
Hygrophorus pratensis	170
Lepiota excoriata	37
Lepiota procera	35
Lyophyllum Georgii	105
Morchella conica	237
Morchella elata	237
Morchella rotunda	237
Morchella umbrina	237
Morchella vulgaris	237
Peziza aurantia	238
Pleurotus eryngii	123
Pleurotus eryngii variety ferulae	123
Pleurotus nebrodensis	123
Pleurotus ostreatus	124
Russula cyanoxantha	148
Russula lutea	156
Russula virescens	149
Tuber magnatum	240
Tuber melanosporum	240
Volvaria bombycina	41

Mushrooms of second quality

Amanita rubescens	21
Amanita solitaria	23
Amanitopsis vaginata	33
Armillariella mellea	110
Boletus badius	198
Boletus castaneus	177
Boletus duriusculus	189
Cantharellus cibarius	225
Cantharellus cinereus	223
Cantharellus tubaeformis	223
Clitocybe geotropa	113
Clitocybe infundibuliformis	111
Collybia velutipes	90
Coprinus atramentarius	50
Craterellus cornucopioides	223
Craterellus lutescens	223
Fistulina hepatica	213
Gomphidius glutinosus	173
Gyrocephalus rufus	233
Hydnum repandum	214
Hygrophorus poëtarum	167
Lactarius deliciosus	134
Lactarius sanguifluus	134
Lepiota rhacodes	36

Lepiota umbonata	34
Lycoperdon caelatum	230
Lycoperdon maximum	230
Polyporus ovinus	204
Polyporus umbellatus	206
Psalliota arvensis	46
Psalliota bispora	43
Psalliota campestris	45
Psalliota silvicola	48
Rhodopaxillus irinus	121
Rhodopaxillus nudus	120
Rhodopaxillus panaeolus	122
Rhodopaxillus saevus	120
Rozites caperata	62
Russula vesca	150
Sparassis crispa	216
Stropharia Ferrii	55
Tricholoma columbetta	102
Tricholoma equestre	100
Tricholoma matsutake (caligatum)	93
Tricholoma portentosum	101
Tricholoma terreum	99
Tricholomopsis edodes (shiitake)	126
Tuber aestivum	240

Mushrooms of third quality

Amanitopsis inaurata	31
Boletus aurantiacus	239
Boletus carpini	188
Boletus erythropus	185
Boletus granulatus	193
Boletus leucophaeus	188
Boletus luteus	192
Boletus luridus	184
Boletus rufus	189
Boletus scaber	189
Clitocybe gigantea	112
Clitocybe odora (small doses)	115
Gomphidius viscidus	174
Hericium erinaceus	215
Hygrophorus chrysodon	165
Hygrophorus olivaceo-albus	169
Hygrophorus virgineus	166

Laccaria laccata	119
Laccaria amethystina	119
Lacrymaria velutina	53
Peziza venosa	235
Peziza vulgaris	235
Pholiota mutabilis	60
Pleurotus dryinus	125
Polyporus frondosus	208
Russula aurata	156
Tuber brumale	240

Mushrooms of fourth quality

Auricularia auricula-Judae	231
Collybia fusipes	86
Helvella crispa	234
Helvella lacunosa	234
Hericium coralloides	215
Peziza onotica	235
Peziza vesiculosa	238
Volvaria gloiocephala	40

Mushrooms edible even raw

Amanita caesarea	17
Auricularia auricula-judae	231
Boletus aereus (small doses)	180
Boletus edulis (small doses)	177
Boletus pinicola (small doses)	181
Cantharellus cibarius	225
Fistulina hepatica	213
Gyrocephalus rufus	233
Lycoperdon caelatum	230
Lycoperdon maximum	228
Peziza aurantia	231
Psalliota arvensis	46
Psalliota bispora	43
Psalliota campestris	45
Psalliota nivescens	46
Psalliota silvatica	44
Psalliota silvicola	48
Rhodopaxillus panaeolus	122
Tremelloden gelatinosum	233
Tuber magnatum	240
Tuber melanosporum	240

Ignorance on Trial

The responsibility for so many "accidental" poisonings should not be blamed on mushrooms, but on prejudices as to their edibility. Most often it is perfectly useless to try to convince people of the falsity of most of these prejudices. People will listen to you, and smile at you, the way they smile at a poor idiot who doesn't know any better; they will even agree with you, but everything will remain as it was before. It might be worthwhile to examine some of these absurd prejudices, which, for so many people, have the value of incontestable truth and on which so many people rely faithfully, until they are poisoned by mushrooms that home-made tests had certified safe and edible.

It is said that all the spring mushrooms are edible. Actually during the spring you may find the *Amanita verna* (page 28), which is deadly and the *Hypholoma fasciculara* (see page 55), which is bitter like bile and rather toxic.

It is said that all mushrooms growing in late autumn are edible. Actually, even in the late fall, you may find the deadly *Amanita phalloides* (pages 26–27), as well as the *Amanita muscaria* (pages 18–19) and the *Entoloma lividum* (page 82), both of which are highly toxic, although not deadly.

It is said that all the lignicolous mushrooms growing on live trees are edible. But *Clytocibe olearia* (page 117), which grows on live olive trees, oaks, or on other fully live and healthy trees, is poisonous although not very dangerous.

It is said that all mushrooms growing on dead trees, rotting stumps, rotting wood debris, decaying straw, or manure are posionous. But *Coprinus comatus* (see page 51), which got got its name because it can grow on manure (*copros* in Greek), is an excellent edible species, of delicate flavor and easily digestible.

It is said that even the edible mushrooms can become poisonous through some strange influence exercised by vipers, toads, or poisonous plants growing nearby. All this is false. The presence of certain plants might inhibit the growth of mushrooms but it is not going to change a good mushroom into a poisonous one. An edible mushroom becomes toxic on spoiling; this is true, but even a beefsteak, if spoiled, is harmful; and this is not a reason to classify the beef as poisonous.

It is said that mushrooms eaten by snails or by other small animals are edible. Actually, snails are quite fond of the *Amanita muscaria* (page 18), which is poisonous, and of the *Amanita phalloides* (pages 26–27), which is deadly.

It is said that violet colored mushrooms are poisonous. Actually, *Laccavia amethystina* (see page 119), *Mycena pura* (page 46), and *Cortinarius violaceus* (page 76) are violet and edible. *Rhodopaxillus nudus* (page 120), of a violet color,

although rather toxic if eaten raw, is edible and quite good after cooking.

It is said that all viscid mushrooms are poisonous. Actually, *Boletus viscidus* (page 191), *Boletus luteus* (page 192), and sometimes *Boletus elegans* (page 191) are perfectly edible even though they are viscid; and *Gomphidius glutinosus* (page 173) is completely glutinous, but is edible and tasty.

It is said that all mushrooms whose flesh changes color after cutting are poisonous. In fact, the flesh of *Boletus cyanescens* (page 174) becomes ink blue immediately after cutting. However, this still is one of the most delicious mushrooms, whereas the flesh of the deadly amanitas does not change color after cutting, and they are deadly.

It is said that all the mushrooms that exude latex, either normally or after fracturing, are poisonous. Actually, among the mushrooms exuding latex, which are called *lactarii* because of it, there are numerous edible species, such as, for instance, *Lactarius deliciosus* and *Lactarius sanguifluus* (see page 134), which are edible and good.

It is said that the mushrooms with bitter, acrid, or pungent flavor are poisonous. It is true that there are some mushrooms so bitter, acrid, or pungent that nobody can eat them; but there are others, in fact quite a large number of them, that, upon cooking, will lose their disgusting flavor and acquire a tasty one. On the other hand, the deadly amanitas have a tasty flavor, both raw and cooked, and yet are deadly, both raw and cooked.

It is said that all mushrooms smelling like flour are edible. Not all. *Entoloma lividum* (page 82) has a distinct smell of flour and is dangerously poisonous.

It is said that all mushrooms lose their poison if boiled in water with or without salt or vinegar. Actually, the deadly amanitas remain deadly even after prolonged and repeated boiling.

It is said that all mushrooms lose their poison through exsiccation. This is true for *Gyromitra esculenta* (page 234), which, when fresh, can cause serious intoxication, especially in particularly sensitive people, but, after exsiccation, is completely harmless. However, this is not true for the deadly amanitas, which remain deadly even after exsiccation.

It is said that the mushrooms that are not poisonous to cats and dogs are also harmless to man. This is not true. The digestive system of a cat or dog is different from man's; dogs and cats can tolerate and sometimes are fond of aliments that are disgusting or completely uneatable by men. Concerning the deadly amanitas, one should keep in mind that in cats and dogs that eat them the symptoms of poisoning might not become evident until several hours after ingestion.

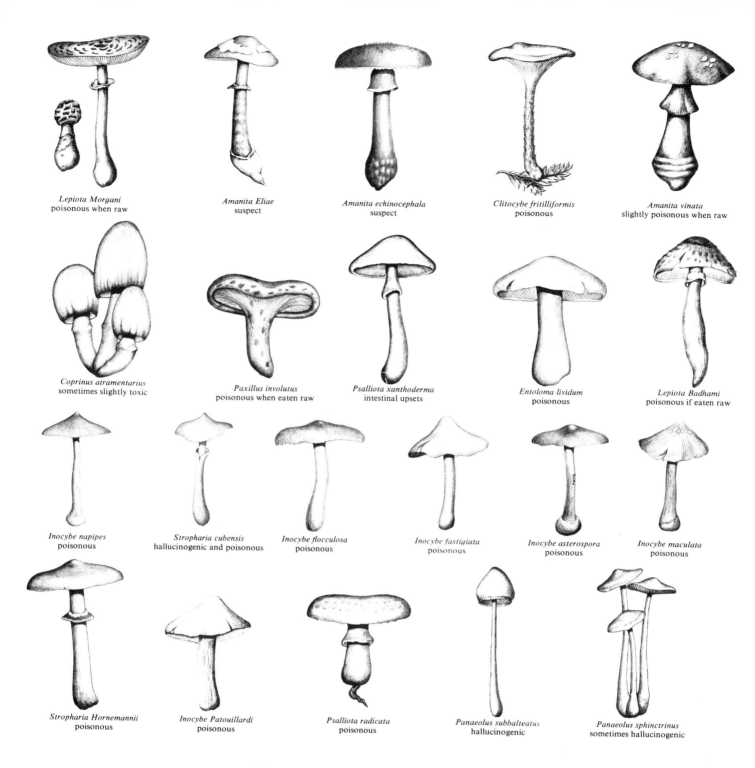

Lepiota Morgani
poisonous when raw

Amanita Eliae
suspect

Amanita echinocephala
suspect

Clitocybe fritilliformis
poisonous

Amanita vinata
slightly poisonous when raw

Coprinus atramentarius
sometimes slightly toxic

Paxillus involutus
poisonous when eaten raw

Psalliota xanthoderma
intestinal upsets

Entoloma lividum
poisonous

Lepiota Badhami
poisonous if eaten raw

Inocybe napipes
poisonous

Stropharia cubensis
hallucinogenic and poisonous

Inocybe flocculosa
poisonous

Inocybe fastigiata
poisonous

Inocybe asterospora
poisonous

Inocybe maculata
poisonous

Stropharia Hornemannii
poisonous

Inocybe Patouillardi
poisonous

Psalliota radicata
poisonous

Panaeolus subbalteatus
hallucinogenic

Panaeolus sphinctrinus
sometimes hallucinogenic

To be on the safe side, mushrooms tested on cats or dogs should not be eaten by humans for at least 48 hours after they are given to the animals. And, if these animals are fed only a small quantity of the suspect mushrooms, this homemade test would be even more useless. A much safer test would be that of feeding the suspect mushrooms to somebody willing to risk his life for us. Such a person would surely be somebody dear to us and we would certainly not like to let him do it for us.

It is said that the mushrooms that discolor, while cooking, a silver object put into the pot with them are poisonous, and, that all mushrooms that do not cause a color change are edible. Besides silver pieces, people also use pieces of gold, tin, iron, onion or garlic cloves, or bread crumbs to make the test. Actually the dead amanitas do not change the color of the above substances any more so than the *Amanita caesarea*

(page 17) or the *Boletus edulis* (page 177), both edible and excellent.

It is said that all poisonous mushrooms cause milk or egg white to coagulate; those that do not do so are edible. But even for this test we have to report that *Amanita caesarea* (page 17) and *Boletus edulis* (page 177) give a reaction similar to that of the deadly amanitas. Therefore this test is worthless. The list of these prejudices could be much longer; every country seems to have its own peculiar ones; it does not seem worthwhile to try to list all of them. At present we have not yet found a universal and safe test to distinguish the edible mushrooms from the poisonous ones. Let's discard all these deceiving homemade tests and let's instead learn to identify the edible mushrooms and the poisonous ones, so as to be able to avoid the latter and to enjoy the former in complete safety. This is an easy, pleasant, and useful task.

The Poisonous Mushrooms

As soon as mushrooms start appearing in the woods the newspapers begin to report stories about mushroom poisoning. In spite of the warning provided by these news items, year after year there are accidental poisonings caused by mushrooms. Yet there is no family that does not read at least one newspaper, and there is hardly anyone unaware of these reports. If these accidents continue to happen, with a frequency proportional to the (larger or smaller) number of mushrooms grown during a given season, it means that most people do not benefit from newspaper reports: they get a little frightened, but it's soon forgotten, and that is all. Most people do not pay attention to the shape and characteristics of the dangerous mushrooms and contine to rely blindly on their own intuition or on some arbitrary and misleading homemade tests.

Many a human life could be saved if, as an addition to the reports of poisoning accidents, the newspapers would publish the description of the mushrooms responsible for them and a list of first-aid procedures to help victims of such accidents. This would be a relatively easy task since, in comparison with several hundred species of edible mushrooms, there are only about a dozen really dangerous species. The newspaper willing to carry such a service for its readers would probably add to its prestige and sales.

Deadly mushrooms. The most dangerous, and the one responsible for most of the deaths resulting from mushroom poisoning, is the *Amanita phalloides* (pages 26–27), which is found very frequently in woods, in summer and autumn, especially in its forms or varieties *viridis* and *virescens*. The lethal dose for a man of medium size is twenty grams of fresh *Amanita phalloides*. Mushrooms as poisonous as *Amanita phalloides* are *Amanita bisporigera* (page 28), *Amanita verna* (page 28), *Amanita virosa* (page 28), *Lepiota helveola* (page 38) and *Cortinarius orellanus* (page 75); these species are less common than *A. phalloides* and completely absent in some regions.

Some deaths have also been attributed to *Gyromitra esculenta* (page 234), in spite of the fact that its name, esculenta, means edible. Once exsiccated, this mushroom is completely harmless; but when it is fresh it is not well tolerated by everybody, especially if it is only slightly cooked, consumed with the water in which it has been cooked, and eaten in a large quantity. For some people it is particularly harmful when eaten in successive meals. But over the years it has been sold in many markets and consumed without harm by many people. However, one should pay attention to how it is cooked. It should be parboiled in water first, then cooked well. The juice produced by the mushroom while cooking should not be used; it is also advisable to eat only small quantities of it and wait at least four days before eating more. The symptoms of poisoning from eating the deadly amanitas become evident only some time after eating, from 8 to 40 hours. It begins with vomiting, diarrhea, heavy perspiration, and consequent insatiable thirst; the feet and hands become cold, calf cramp develops; the eyes look deep-sunk, the face is drawn and pale, and sometimes yellow, as in jaundice. This is followed by a state of anxiety, deep prostration, and an imperceptible pulsebeat; and eventually rattling, paralysis, convulsive spasms, death. All this can last from 10 to 20 days. Sometimes, during the first 48 hours, there might be a slight improvement, but then the illness continues its inexorable course. Prompt and proper care can save adult and robust people; but it is much more difficult to save children. Poisoning symptoms from *Lepiota helveola* (page 38), from *Cortinarius orellanus* (page 75), and from *Gyromitra esculenta* (page 234) are fundamentally similar to those caused by the deadly amanitas; the cure is also essentially the same. The symptoms of intoxication due to *Cortinarius orellanus* become evident only very late, from 3 to 14 days, after eating this mushroom and, although very similar to those caused by *Amanita phalloides*, there are a few differences.

The cure, for which only a physician can assume full responsibility, aims to eliminate the poisonous substances from the organism through an evacuation of the digestive system and a stimulation of kidney activity; it aims to calm the pain and sustain the general condition, especially the heart. The cure should specifically fight against suffocation, nervous depression, and organism dehydration; it must protect kidneys and liver, which are directly threatened by the toxic substances of the mushrooms. Choline and thioctic acid are found very useful in protecting the liver in cases of mushroom poisoning.

Mushrooms harmful to the nervous system: *Amanita muscaria* (pages 18–19), *Amanita pantherina* (page 18), *Inocybe Patouillardi* (page 79), *Clytocibe dealbata* (page 111), and species related to them. In several areas of Italy, France, and Russia, *Amanita muscaria* is consumed regularly without harm, but one must consider that this might be due partly to the fact that often this mushroom is eaten after first being treated, which reduces its poison level, and partly to the fact that the amount of toxic principles contained in this mushroom varies depending on the area and the season. Still we believe it better to avoid this mushroom.

Luckily, the symptoms of intoxication caused by this group of mushrooms show up quickly: from half an hour to four hours after eating them. The principal symptoms are:

abundant secretion of saliva, of nasal mucus, and tears; slowing down of the pulse and a sensation of suffocation. In these instances the doctor should administer a good laxative, some diuretic beverages in large quantities, including tea and coffee but not alcholic beverages, and sometimes an injection of atropine if the subject is particularly weak.

Russula emetica (page 160) is another mushroom containing substances toxic to the nervous system; but since its ingestion causes immediate vomiting, the subject eliminates the toxic principles and there are no other consequences. At the same time it is so acrid to the taste that it is almost important to eat a large and dangerous amount of it.

Mushrooms harmful to the digestive system. A mushroom that is known to cause serious intoxication and also lethal, although rarely, is *Entoloma lividum* (page 82). Those that can cause a strong intoxication include: *Tricholoma pardinum* (page 98), *virgatum* (page 99), and *groanense* (page 99), *Clitocybe olearia* (page 117), *Boletus Satanas* (page 187), and *purpureus* (page 186), *Clavaria formosa* (page 218), and *pallida* (page 219). *Psalliota xanthoderma* (page 49) can cause a weak intoxication. The less these mushrooms are cooked, the more serious is the resulting intoxication. Within one hour from ingestion the subject experiences nausea, colic, vomiting, diarrhea, and fainting. The cure is essentially identical to that used for poisoning by *Amanita muscaria*.

Mushrooms harmful when eaten raw: almost all mushrooms belonging to the genera *Peziza, Morchella, Helvella*, those related to them, and a few other species, such as *Amanita rubescens* (page 21) and *Rhodopaxillus nudus* (page 120). The cure is essentially identical to that for poisoning by *Amanita muscaria*. Sometimes the symptoms of the poisoning are slight and disappear spontaneously in a short time. Several other mushrooms belonging to the genera *Russula* and *Lactarius* are also toxic when eaten raw; but their taste, acrid and bitter, is sufficient to prevent people from eating them. Once cooked, they often lose not only their disgusting taste but also their toxic properties. Sometimes fermentation is sufficient to destroy the toxic substances: this method is used in different parts of East Europe and the people in those places eat, after the mushrooms are fermented, not only

Lactarius torminosus (page 119), *Lactarius piperatus* (page 130), and *Lactarius plumbeus* (page 138), which are acrid when raw, but also *Lactarius rufus*, which, when eaten raw, has a taste that can only be described as a very hot fire. The collector of edible mushrooms could follow a simple rule when picking russulas and lactarii, and that is to discard, when in doubt, all the specimens with acrid or bitter flavor, and to conisder edible all the others, provided they are not too ripe or infested by larvae.

Coprinus atramentarius. This is an edible mushroom (page 50) which, however, can be quite harmful to some people, especially when one drinks alcoholic beverages, or, sometime, even coffee or tea, while or after eating it. The most characteristic symptom is a deep reddening of the face, together with an acceleration of the pulse, a loss of stength, and a cooling of hands and feet. These disturbances are not dangerous; they last only a short time and disappear without further consequence.

First aid while waiting for the doctor. The proper cure requires the knowledge of the species of mushroom ingested by the poisoned person. Often the poor victim does not know their name himself. Therefore, at times, to identify the suspect mushroom it is necessary to examine the parts discarded in the garbage can, the remains left after the meal, or even the vomit itself. As for vomiting, it is useful to remember that it is absolutely useless to induce it, if more than 8–10 hours have elapsed since the ingestion of the mushrooms, because the mushrooms are probably no longer in the stomach but in the intestine.

While waiting for the doctor, one could administer a laxative; but, if the poisoned person has strong visceral pains, use castor oil instead of a salt-type laxative, and use only a moderate dose: 30 grams for an adult, 15 grams for a child. You can administer beverages, even in large doses, such as milk, water with sugar, water with salt; or even tea or coffee, but in moderate doses. Keep the patient well covered, quiet, and in a warm place.

If the mushroom ingested is the *Amanita phalloides*, take the patient to the hospital immediately, but in the meantime even before he reaches the hospital give him, every half an hour, a teaspoon of salt dissolved in a glass of water.

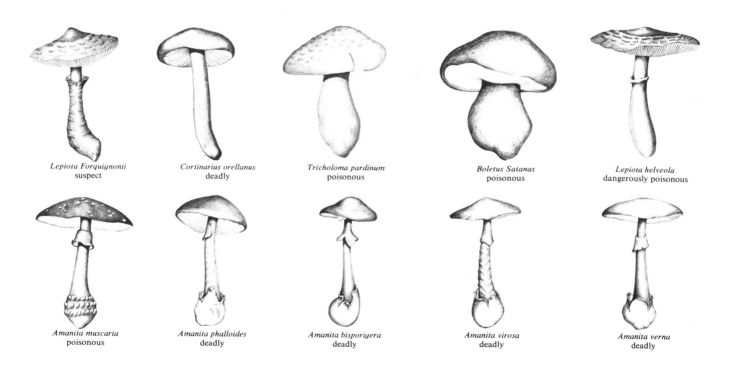

Lepiota Forquignonii
suspect

Cortinarius orellanus
deadly

Tricholoma pardinum
poisonous

Boletus Satanas
poisonous

Lepiota helveola
dangerously poisonous

Amanita muscaria
poisonous

Amanita phalloides
deadly

Amanita bisporigera
deadly

Amanita virosa
deadly

Amanita verna
deadly

The Cultivation of Mushrooms

Nicandros, a Greek doctor of the second century B.C., taught people to cultivate mushrooms on manure placed in holes dug around the roots of fig trees. The Greeks and Romans cultivated *Agrocybe aegerita* (page 64), which grows on poplars, according to a method that came to us through a description by Dioscorides, a Greek doctor of the first century B.C.: First they scattered pulverized bark of poplar on very rich soil. The dissemination of the spores of the mushroom on this cultured soil was probably left to the wind, since they prepared the soil almost certainly near to the poplars, and therefore to mature specimens of *Agrocybe aegerita*, whose spores were dispersed by the winds.

Andrea Cesalpino, an Italian doctor who lived between the sixteenth and seventeenth centuries, successfully used the same method in his experiments, and tried to spread it. Today we often use the following method: Poplar trunks are cut into disks, a few centimeters thick; one side of the disk is rubbed with the mature gills of *Agrocybe aegerita*; the disks are then placed, rubbed side up, on the ground, and covered with a thin layer of soil; they are watered regularly, but with moderation, since if they imbibe too much water, they would putrefy without forming the fruiting bodies. The first mushrooms appear in about ten months. The harvest is abundant and pays back generously for the small cost and little labor. In Italy, during the past century, various methods of mushroom cultivation, either newly developed or old ones brought back to use, were tried, apparently with successful results. Paolo Barbieri, of the Botanical Garden in Mantua, was successful in cultivating the *Volvaria bombycina* (page 41) in tanks, covered on the bottom with straw and small branches, horse and donkey manure, and eventually filled up with leaves of *Quercus aegilops* (Valonia oak), which had already been used for tanning hides. The tanks had double walls with a space between to circulate warm air. Antonio Perego, of the Botanical Garden of the Lyceum of Brescia, cultivated the *Pleurotus ostreatus* (page 124) on berries of laurel after the oil, in which they are rich, had been pressed out; the berries were compacted into holes dug in open grounds in shaded areas. A very similar method had probably been used for several centuries, and certainly in the eighteenth century in the area around Lake Garda. In Ligury, at Porto Maurizio, mushrooms were grown in large quantities on pressed olives (olive husks). In Naples, a *Clytocibe*, called *Agaricus neapolitanus*, was cultivated with success on coffee grounds, after some nuns found the mushroom growing on coffee grounds that were piled up in a shaded corner of their vegetable garden. In other places, also on coffee grounds, people succeeded in cultivating a species of *Volvaria*. In all these instances, with the exception of the first one, the dissemination of the spores was trusted, more or less unconsciously, to the action of the wind. The wind was also responsible for the cultivation of edible mushrooms in China, where they were grown on decaying debris covered with soil and placed in holes facing south, but in shaded places. The wood debris was further fertilized by the addition of potassium nitrate.

Today the mushrooms most intensively cultivated belong to the genus *Psalliota*. The cultivation of this mushroom on a large scale started about a century ago in France and from there rapidly spread to several other countries, from North America to Japan. The cultivation of this mushroom can be carried out both in an open and a close environment; it is usually preferable to do it in close environments, such as caves, old abandoned tunnels, and cellars, where it is easier to control ventilation, humidity, temperature, and light.

The mushrooms feed on the lignin provided by manure. Horse manure is preferred since it is very rich in chaff especially when the horse has been fed oats. The horse manure must be well fermented, of homogeneous texture, brownish and almost without smell; it takes a few weeks of work to bring it to the proper condition. The manure is used to prepare culture beds of parabolic sections, 40 centimeters wide at the base, slightly less than half a meter high, and as long as permitted by the space available. A little mycelium, easily available commercially, is placed in small holes, about 15 to 20 centimeters apart, along the sides of the culture beds. After about twenty days new mycelium starts appearing on the surface of the beds, which are then covered with a layer, two to three centimeters thick, of calcareous sand (ground limestone) well pressed but not forming a hard crust. The resistance provided by the sand stops the growth of the vegetative mycelium and compels it to produce the fruiting bodies, which appear a few weeks after the beds are covered and continue to be produced for three to four months. After the lignin in the culture beds has been used up, new beds have to be prepared with fresh manure. Besides cultivations with horizontal expansion, a new type of cultivation, with vertical expansion on shelf beds, is beginning to take hold. The ideal temperature for the cultivation of mushrooms is, at the beginning, about 19°C, and the relative humidity of the air should not exceed 85%, but, after about a month of production the temperature can gradually be lowered to about 13°C, while the relative humidity can be gradually increased to 90% and above.

To obtain continuous productivity, it is necessary to arrange the culture beds on a system of continuous rotation; so that the decrease of productivity in one section is balanced by the increase in another. In winter it is advisable to increase the thickness of the culture beds to compensate for the natural decrease of the temperature of the atmosphere, unless a thermostatic heating system is available. Circulation of air can be regulated through ventilation shafts or openings on opposite walls. There is no need to worry about light, because these mushrooms grow well even in darkness. However, it seems that when they are cultivated in open air and are exposed to daylight, they have more flavor. But the cultivation in open air is riskier than the one in a closed environment. To water the culture beds sprayers or nebulizers can be used, but it is important to use water with moderation: an excess could cause the putrefaction of the manure and ruin the harvest.

The mushrooms should be harvested when they reach a medium state of development, taking care not to pull out those still unripe, along with those of the right size. Only after long experience can one take care of the emergencies that arise in the process of cultivation—cultivation that can be as attractive and remunerative as it is exacting and binding. In several countries, and especially in the United States, there is an increase in the home cultivation of *Psalliota bispora* (pages 43–44). In this method of cultivation culture media are placed in drawers of specially designed cabinets, and the cabinets are kept in suitable places, even in open air. But the cultivation of the *Rhodopaxillus nudus* is somewhat aleatory (page 120); it involves mixing the mycelium of the mushroom with soil and watering this mixture with luke-warm water, sometimes with a little sugar. The mycelium necessary to start the culture is easy to find: you just dig around the ripe specimens of the mushroom in the places where you find them growing naturally. The mycelium is made of whitish filaments entangled in soil, twigs, and, sometimes, conifer needles.

Equally aleatory is the cultivation of the following species: *Volvaria bombycina* (page 41), *Coprinus comatus* (page 51), *Clitopilus prunulus* (page 122), *Clytocibe infundiboliformis* (page 111), several species of *Morchellae, Tuber magnatum* and *Tuber melanosporum* (page 240). In some regions, *Pleurotus cornucopiae* (page 123) is cultivated on disks of alder tree, with satisfactory results. Good results are also obtained in the cultivation of other lignicolous species, such as *Armillaria mellea* (page 110), *Craterellus cornucopioides* (page 223), *Collybia velutipes* (page 90), *Pholiota mutabilis* (page 60), and *Pleurotus ostreatus* (page 124).

The *Shiitake* (*Tricholomopsis edodes*, page 126) is cultivated on a large scale in Japan. These mushrooms are cultivated on small logs of *hodoghi*, chestnut, or holm oak. The mushroom farmers cut small disks of bark, attach small fragments of mycelium on the inner surface, and put them back in place on the logs. These logs are then placed, in an almost vertical position, in woody places pervious to sunlight, that are well ventilated, not excessively humid (remember that Japan is a rainy country), and with a temperature as close as possible to 17°C. As soon as the first mushrooms appear, watering must be increased. This procedure gives very good results.

There are botanical gardens and forest nurseries (parks), which with the cooperation of scientific institutions, and with a knowledge of the relationship between mushrooms and higher plants, that have attempted with success the cultivation, near to their symbiont trees, of several species of woodland mushrooms of the following genera: *Amanita, Tricholoma, Cortinarius, Lactarius, Gomphidius, Paxillus, Boletus,* and a few others. The purpose of these serious and cautious experiments, under controlled conditions, is to obtain a production of edible mushrooms worthy of consideration from an economical point of view.

At present, also being promoted is the cultivation of various mushrooms of the genera *Morchella, Boletus, Psalliota, Cantharellus, Lepiota*; it is done through dissemination of their spores, which are sold for a very low price. The spores are already mixed with pulverized and sterilized soil and can be disseminated on various types of grounds—vegetable gardens, gardens, parks, woods—after first being given a simple cleaning from weeds, branches, and undecayed leaves. There are no reliable data on the efficiency of this method. But we do know of one experience involving some shepherds living in the region of the orobian Prealps. It seems they threw some mushrooms of the genus *Gomphidius* onto a dunghill and were surprised later to find an unbelievably large number of mushrooms growing in the fields fertilized by the manure from that dunghill.

Let us conclude this short discussion with an odd fact. It is believed that ants started cultivating mushrooms long before man appeared on this earth. We know there are numerous species of ants in equatorial America that feed almost exclusively on fungi. To maintain a constant supply of food, these ants cultivate the fungi, depositing pieces of mycelium on carefully selected cultural grounds, fertilizing them with the proper fertilizer, and carefully following the growth of the crop. They transfer the mycelium from an old culture ground to a new one shortly before they lay their eggs. The ants take a piece of the old mycelium in their mouth, never putting it down along the way until they arrive to the new ground where they deposit it near the new anthill. They do not feed on this mycelium, not even in instances of extreme starvation; they would rather eat their own eggs. As soon as the larvae are transformed into worker ants, they begin their search for leaves or other material suitable for the growth of the mushrooms: they grind them, then place them near the hyphae of the growing mycelium. Then the ants start cutting the hyphae, at various points, so as to induce the formation of the mushrooms, which, after so much work and privation, are a well-deserved, safe, and abundant food for the entire colony.

Other ants, such as the leaf-cutting ants of Brazil, do not feed on the mature mushroom, but on the mycelial hyphae. These ants cultivate a mushroom similar to an *Amanita*, the *Rozites gongylophora*, whose hyphae form swellings full of plasma. The ants eat these swellings as they are formed. Thus the mushrooms can form and ripen only on abandoned anthills.

There are various species of mushrooms that grow abundantly in Palestine during winter, the rainy season, but strangely, the Bible, which is an estimable treasury even of natural history, seems to make no mention of any of them. We will only mention the *Boletus granulatus* (page 193) and the *Tricholoma terreum* (page 99), which are very frequent under the conifers of the high Judea region. The Hebrews must have known of the mushrooms growing in their woods and fields and, even though they might not have cultivated them, must surely have tried them as food especially in the not too infrequent times of serious famine. For these reasons, some people have put forward the hypothesis that the word *fungus* should be present in the Hebraic text of the Bible, but that it has been erroneously interpreted to indicate some other kind of plant.

A Brief Outline of the History of Mycology

The first records on the use of mushrooms as foods or drugs are relatively recent: they do not go beyond the fifth century B.C. Hippocrates, a Greek physician of that time, still highly respected for his professional competence and moral honesty, exploited the real or presumed real therapeutical powers of the mushrooms. Unfortunately, we do not know what mushrooms he used and what results he obtained.

Theophrastus, a Greek philosopher and naturalist of the fourth century B.C., who succeeded Aristotle as a teacher in the Athens Lyceum, faithfully following the empiric (experimental) methods of scientific research adopted by Aristotle, in his studies of nature, paid attention to the mushroom also; his conclusions might make us smile today: he concluded that mushrooms were plants, that truffles were not roots, but different plants, and that mushrooms do not form fruits. It would have been sufficient to add that the mushrooms themselves are the fruiting bodies of the fungi, but he did not arrive at this final conclusion. He also described mushrooms fossilized by the sun along the shores of the Red Sea. He was actually describing the *Polyporous tuberaster*, a live mushroom, not a fossilized one: when water is scarce, the mycelium of this mushroom contracts and becomes as hard and compact as stone; when water is available again, this mushroom starts growing and forming fruiting bodies again.

Pliny the Elder, Roman warrior and scholar of the first century A.D., wrote that the mushrooms grow in water-rich ground, and especially after rain; that some species will form from the root of certain trees; that the average life of the mushroom is about a week, but that truffles can live even for a year; that there are both edible and poisonous mushrooms and gave guidelines to distinguish one type from the other. The Romans loved mushrooms, truffles most of all, but also *Amanita caesarea* and *Suillus* (piglike, pertaining to pigs), which almost surely indicated *Boletus edulis*.

Still in the first century, Dioscorides, Greek physician in proconsular Asia, wrote that mushrooms were used mostly as food seasoning, and that, if eaten in large quantities, even the best edible mushrooms could be harmful; and that the remedy for a mushroom's indigestion was the administration, to the patient, of an enema of salted water.

There are no further reports about mushrooms until the time of Avicenna (980–1036), a Persian Aristotelian, a philosopher and naturalist as Aristotle was, and also a physician. In his works, written in Arabic he wrote, among other things, that the green mushrooms are poisonous. Surely he was referring to the green forms or varieties, *viridis* and *virescens*, of the deadly *Amanita phalloides*; he did not know that other green mushrooms, such as the *Russula virescens* and the *Clytocibe odora*, are edible.

Some time later the group of those interested in mushrooms was joined by Saint Albertus Magnus, of Cologne (1193? or 1206?–1280), philosopher, naturalist, and theologian. He showed that a housefly would die after sucking a little milk containing a small, macerated piece of *Amanita muscaria*; he also showed that this mushroom was poisonous to man, and indicated ways of reducing its toxicity.

The interest in mushrooms was present during the Renaissance, but the results were of little consequence. In the sixteenth century, Pierandrea Mattioli (1500–1577), physician and naturalist in Siena, collected all the botanical knowledge of his times in one corpus embellished with drawings of various species of mushrooms.

Andrea Cesalpino (1519–1603), physician and naturalist, born in Arezzo, laid the first serious foundations for a classification of the mushrooms, which he knew to be the fruiting bodies of fungi. The Florentine botanist Pier Antonio Micheli (1679–1737), in his work *Nova Plantarum genera*, described four thousand new species of plants, claimed that the mushrooms grow from seeds, as all other plants, and gave an experimental demonstration of this assertion of his, by cultivating several species of mushrooms. The Dutch Christian Person (1755–1837) perfected the classification of mushrooms, and established their scientific denominations, with such a care and skill, as to be considered, and with good reason, the founder of modern mycology.

Some time later the Swedish Elias Fries (1749–1878) further improved the classification of the mushroom, using, as a base for it, the color of the spores and various microscopic characteristics; the system which, with further improvements, is in use today. And so a way was open, a way that a large army of mycologists would follow with brilliant results. Space does not allow us to mention even the names and the titles of the most important works of these mycologists. We will just mention, among the modern Italian mycologists, Pier Andrea Saccardo (1845–1920), professor at the University of Padua, and author, among other works, of a *Sylloge fungorum omnium hucusque cognitorum* (anthology of all the mushrooms known up to this time), a work to which his pupils made further additions; and the Tridentine canon Giacomo Bresadola (1847–1929), a keen observer, discoverer of numerous species of mushrooms and author of the twenty-four-volumed *Iconographia mycologica*.

Peziza eximia

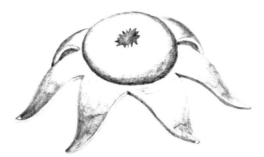

Astraeus hygrometricus

Geaster fimbriatus

Aleuria vesiculosa

Auriscalpium vulgare

Gloeophyllum saepiarum

Claudopus parasiticus

Clathrus cancellatus

Tremella mesenterica (1)
and *foliacea* (2)

Clavaria pistillaris

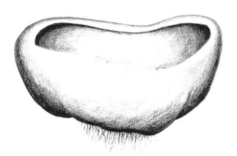

Daldinia concentrica

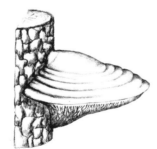

Daedalea quercina

Exidia glandulosa

Clavaria vermicularis

Ganoderma lucidum

Gomphidius glutinosus

Craterellus cornucopioides

Identification of the Most Common Genera

Ascomycetes

We will not deal here with the Protoascomycetidae (Hemi-ascomycetidae), a subclass of very primitive Ascomycetes with asci formed directly on the mycelium, without a differentiated hymenium, without ascocarps, and of microscopic dimensions (the yeasts belong to this subclass). We will deal here only with the mushrooms of the subclass Euascomycetidae, whose mycelium produces ascocarps (carpophores) with hymenium, asci, and spores inside the asci. Some genera of these ascomycetes are hypogean: they grow underground and remain so even when fully ripe; other genera are epigean and are found above ground, at least when fully ripe. We will give consideration to the most common genera.

Epigean Ascomycetes

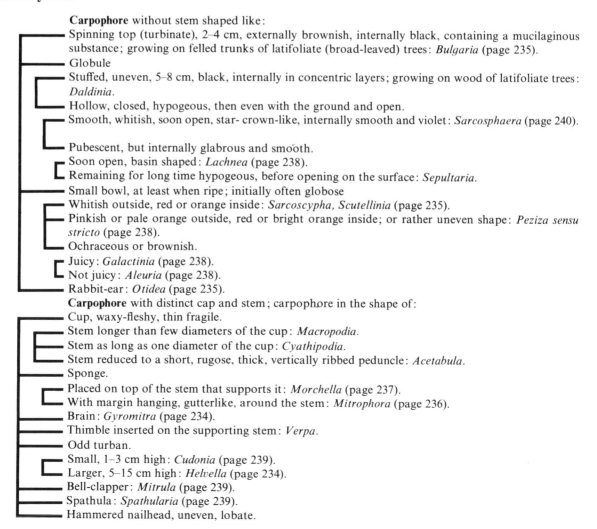

Carpophore without stem shaped like:
Spinning top (turbinate), 2–4 cm, externally brownish, internally black, containing a mucilaginous substance; growing on felled trunks of latifoliate (broad-leaved) trees: *Bulgaria* (page 235).
Globule
Stuffed, uneven, 5–8 cm, black, internally in concentric layers; growing on wood of latifoliate trees: *Daldinia*.
Hollow, closed, hypogeous, then even with the ground and open.
Smooth, whitish, soon open, star- crown-like, internally smooth and violet: *Sarcosphaera* (page 240).
Pubescent, but internally glabrous and smooth.
Soon open, basin shaped: *Lachnea* (page 238).
Remaining for long time hypogeous, before opening on the surface: *Sepultaria*.
Small bowl, at least when ripe; initially often globose
Whitish outside, red or orange inside: *Sarcoscypha, Scutellinia* (page 235).
Pinkish or pale orange outside, red or bright orange inside; or rather uneven shape: *Peziza sensu stricto* (page 238).
Ochraceous or brownish.
Juicy: *Galactinia* (page 238).
Not juicy: *Aleuria* (page 238).
Rabbit-ear: *Otidea* (page 235).
Carpophore with distinct cap and stem; carpophore in the shape of:
Cup, waxy-fleshy, thin fragile.
Stem longer than few diameters of the cup: *Macropodia*.
Stem as long as one diameter of the cup: *Cyathipodia*.
Stem reduced to a short, rugose, thick, vertically ribbed peduncle: *Acetabula*.
Sponge.
Placed on top of the stem that supports it: *Morchella* (page 237).
With margin hanging, gutterlike, around the stem: *Mitrophora* (page 236).
Brain: *Gyromitra* (page 234).
Thimble inserted on the supporting stem: *Verpa*.
Odd turban.
Small, 1–3 cm high: *Cudonia* (page 239).
Larger, 5–15 cm high: *Helvella* (page 234).
Bell-clapper: *Mitrula* (page 239).
Spathula: *Spathularia* (page 239).
Hammered nailhead, uneven, lobate.

With distinct groove, separating it from the stem: *Leotia* (page 239).

Without distinct, separating groove between the stem and the cap.

Carpophore smooth: *Geoglossum* (p. 239).

Carpophore velvety, pubescent: *Trichoglossum* (page 239).

Carpophore with stem sometimes filiform, long with terminal head; sometimes thick, with globose or cuspidate cap; fleshy, often brightly colored, from a few millimeters to a few centimeters high; on wood, on insects, larvae and chrysalises, on *Elaphomyces*, on humus: *Cordyceps*.

Carpophore club shaped, simple or branched, corky, brown or black, a few centimeters high, on wood: *Xylaria* (page 239).

Hypogean Ascomycetes

Receptacle globular, 1–5 cm, protected by a very thick tegument; flesh reddish, then brownish, finally turning into powder: *Elaphomyces* (page 240).

Receptacle of various shapes, 3–15 cm, without a tegument distinguishable from the flesh; flesh eventually becoming mushy.

Receptacle tuber shaped, more or less irregular; with external surface.

Smooth, verrucose, or rugose; blackish, ochraceous, or reddish; flesh soapy, whitish, ochraceous, reddish, brownish, or blackish; odor strong: *Tuber* (page 240).

Smooth, then cracked, reddish; flesh white, then yellowish with ochraceous streaks; odor agreeable: *Choeromyces*.

Smooth and silky, whitish; sometimes with few cracks; flesh has small veins: *Terfezia*; typical of warm Mediterranean climates.

Receptacle vaguely globose, often misshapen; external surface uneven, rusty; flesh soft, whitish, with winding streaks, soon yellowish, mushy and fetid: *Balsamia*.

N.B. The terms *carpophore* and *receptacle* are often used interchangeably to indicate the fruiting bodies (basidiocarp in the basidiomycetes and ascocarp in the ascomycetes) of mushrooms.

Basidiomycetes

Mushrooms whose spores are borne on the top of supporting structures called basidia constitute the class Basidiomycetes. Sometimes, in the hymenium, together with the fertile basidia, there are also long, sterile cells, sticking out of the hymenium: the cystidia. The examination of the cystidia, which are not always of microscopical size, is sometimes very useful for the identification of certain genera of Basidiomycetes, which cannot be easily identified just by the study of the characteristics easily visible to the naked eye. The typical basidium is formed by·a single cell bearing on top some peduncles, more often four, called sterigmata (pl., sing. = sterigma) bearing the basidiospores, one for each sterigma. The mushrooms with typical basidia compose the subclass of Autobasidiomycetes, or Homobasidiomycetes. Most of the macromycetes belong to this subclass, and we will deal with them in deeper details. But first we have to mention a few genera of basidiomycetes with atypical basidia: either with long arms, called epibasidia, terminating in a sterigma bearing the basidiospore: the Heterobasidiomycetes; or with pluricellular basidia, sometimes transversely septate, sometimes longitudinally septate. Some authors classify the basidiomycetes with septate basidia as Protobasidiomycetes; others include them in the subclass Heterobasidiomycetes.

Among the Heterobasidiomycetes is the genus *Calocera* (page 231); lignicolous with the basidiocarps resembling sea coral, yellow colored, gelatinous in humid weather and yet tenacious, and hard as bone when dried up.

Among the Protobasidiomycetes with transversely septate basidia is the genus *Auricularia* (page 231), lignicolous, with basidiocarp (carpophore), gelatinous in humid weather, coriaceous in dry weather, of varied shape, bowl-like, earlike, tuberculate, leaflike.

Among the Protobasidiomycetes with longitudinally septate basidia are the genera *Exidia, Tremella, Tremellodon, Gyrocephalus* (page 233): these are lignicolous fungi with gelatinous or waxy basidiocarps of varied shapes and texture.

Gasteromycetes, or Angiocarps

And now let us come back to the Homobasidiomycetes, that is, the basidiomycetes with typical basidia. The further subdivision of this subclass is based on the presence or absence of a tegument enveloping the carpophore (basidiocarp) from its initial stages of development, that is, the presence or absence of the universal veil.

Some Homobasidiomycetes have the basidiocarp enwrapped by a long-lasting veil; their hymenium is never exposed to air and is contained in some sort of cavity opening only after maturation of the spores. Since the hymenium is contained within the basidiocarp, these mushrooms are called Gasteromycetes, that is, fungi with cavity; since they have a permanent tegument they are also called Angiocarps, that is, covered fruits. In all other Homobasidiomycetes the hymenium is more or less exposed to air even before maturation of the spores, and is not enclosed within the basidiocarp; these mushroom are called Hymenomycetes, that is, fungi with hymenium particularly conspicuous.

Numerous Hymenomycetes possess a protective tegument, but less substantial than that of the Angiocarps and often evanescent (caducous, ephemeral). Because of this they are called Semiangiocarp (Hemiangiocarps), that is, half-covered fruits. They are also known as Agaricales.

The rest of the Hymenomycetes have no veil of any kind; hence sometimes they are called Gymnocarps, that is, naked fruits; and, since they hymenium is not borne on lamellae (gills), they are also called Aphyllophorales, that is, not-bearing gills. It might be worth noting that the developing Gymnocarps can enclose (inglobate, fill up with), without harm, grass, leaves, stems, twigs found in their growing path; and that the Gymnocarps with woody texture might have several seasons of active growth, during which a new hymenium is laid on top of the exhausted ones formed during previous seasons. A description of the Gasteromycetes, with particular attention to the shape of the basidiocarp, follows.

Hypogean Gasteromycetes

Carpophore globose or tuber shaped

- With bulky tegument; flesh black, divided into zones by whitish septa, firm, eventually gelatinous; diameter of the carpophore 1–4 cm: *Melanogaster.*
- With thin whitish tegument; flesh white, then reddish or violaceous, eventually gelatinous; diameter 1–2 cm: *Hymenogaster.*

Epigean Gasteromycetes

Carpophore of a porous tissue, fragile, fetid, eventually dissolving into a dense liquid; variously shaped, but globular when unripe and hidden by moss or humus, wrapped by a thick, but internally mucilaginous volva; volva eventually opening and carpophore developing on the surface of the ground

- With hymenium initially turned toward the inside of the carpophore
  - Carpophore similar to an upside-down octopus or to a star: *Anthurus* (page 224).
  - Carpophore similar to a fusiform net with few meshes: *Colus, Pseudocolus* (page 224).
  - Carpophore similar to a spheroidal net with wide meshes: *Clathrus* (page 229).
- With hymenium turned, since the beginning, toward the outside of the carpophore, which is shaped like a hollow candle
- Thin, terminating with a pointed or matchhead-like top: *Mutinus.*
- Larger, terminating in a hood-shaped top with externally alveolate surface (hymenium)

- With a net, more or less wide, hanging from the margin of the hood: *Dictyophora* (page 226).
- No net hanging from the margin of the hood: *Phallus* (page 226).

Carpophore small, about one centimeter high, of various and odd shapes, often nest shaped, initially close, then open; with thin peduncles, bearing egg-shaped bodies containing the spores (peridioles), protruding from the inside walls: *Crucibulum, Nidularia, Cyathus* (page 227).

Carpophore globular

- On a long, cylindrical, fibrous stem: *Tylostoma* (page 227).
- Without stem
- Tegument, at least initially, simple, generally thick (bulky)
- Flesh, to the naked eye, does not seem divided into nodules
  - Tegument opening unevenly at maturity, and dissolving: *Scleroderma* (page 227).
  - Tegument separating into two layers, the external one opening starlike
  - Central globule opening on top with an even orifice; points of the star folding back on the central bulb in dry weather: *Astraeus* (page 232).
  - Central globule opening irregularly (unevenly): *Sclerangium.*
- The flesh, to the naked eye, appears divided into pea-size nodules; carpophore supported by a thick, sterile, upside-down cone-shaped peduncle: *Pisolithus, Polysaccum.*
- Tegument two-layered from the beginning of its development

- External tegument opening starlike
- Central globule neatly pierced, here and there, and supported by several peduncles, arranged in a circle: *Myriostoma.*
- Central globule opening on top with a single, even orifice: *Geaster* (page 232).
- Central globule opening unevenly: *Trichaster.*
- External tegument not opening in the shape of a star, but instead dissolving into warts, scales, granules
- Carpophore stuffed with fertile tissue, without a spongy, sterile base
- Inner tegument thin, papery, opening evenly on top: *Bovista.*
- Inner tegument thick, coriaceous, fragmenting unevenly: *Mycenastrum.*
- Carpophore not completely stuffed with fertile tissue but with a spongy, sterile base, more or less voluminous
- External tegument dissolving into warts, granules, or sharp scales; and internal tegument opening on top with a roundish orifice: *Lycoperdon, sensu stricto* (page 230).
- External tegument, on top, dissolving together with the internal tegument, opening widely and unevenly; the remaining lower part cup shaped, brownish: *Calvatia* (page 230).

Carpophore with stem, cap, and gills; most of the tissue of the cap is reduced to the gills. In contrast to their exterior appearance, these mushrooms belong with the Angiocarps because of the structure of their tissues; they are typical of sandy grounds, in the Mediterranean regions

- Gracilent: cap disk shaped or conical, radially fissured; stem very long, hard, fibrous, rough; volva at the base; gills on the underside of the cap, black when the spores are ripe: *Montagnites.*

- Stout: cap small, thin; stem fairly developed, fibrous, rough, hard; gills close, intersecting, incomplete, brownish when the spores are ripe: *Gyrophragmium.*

Aphyllophorales, or Gymnocarps

The Gymnocarps are the Homobasidiomycetes without universal veil, even during the initial stages of development of the basidiocarp. They also have no partial (inner) veil, membrane protecting the hymenium. The hymenium is not formed by true gills; and therefore the Gymnocarps are also called Aphyllophorales, meaning "without gills". The primordium of the Aphyllophorales is shaped like a small tubercle, which becomes larger and larger, assuming various shapes, different not only from genus to genus or from species to species, but sometimes even from specimen to specimen within the same species.
The tissue of the basidiocarp can be bulky, fleshy, soft, or hard; corky or woody; thin and coriaceous. The hymenium is not limited to a well-defined zone, as it is in other mushrooms, but tends to expand gradually on all most recently formed parts. The structure of the hymenium is varied: smooth, granulose, rugose, tuberculate, with thorns, with teeth, with coarse pseudogills, with alveoli, with pores. It can be of such a varied structure even within the same genus: in the genera *Lenzites, Trametes,* and *Daedalea,* the hymenium, either in succession or at the same time, can be formed by pores, alveoli, and pseudogills. A description of the Aphyllophorales, with particular attention to the shape of the basidiocarp (carpophore) and to the structure of the hymenium, follows.

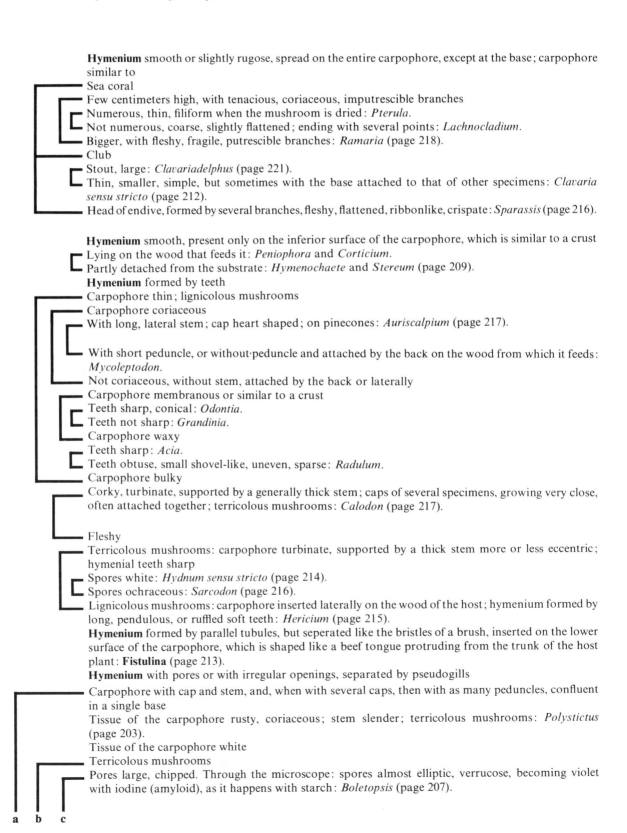

Hymenium smooth or slightly rugose, spread on the entire carpophore, except at the base; carpophore similar to
Sea coral
Few centimeters high, with tenacious, coriaceous, imputrescible branches
Numerous, thin, filiform when the mushroom is dried: *Pterula.*
Not numerous, coarse, slightly flattened; ending with several points: *Lachnocladium.*
Bigger, with fleshy, fragile, putrescible branches: *Ramaria* (page 218).
Club
Stout, large: *Clavariadelphus* (page 221).
Thin, smaller, simple, but sometimes with the base attached to that of other specimens: *Clavaria sensu stricto* (page 212).
Head of endive, formed by several branches, fleshy, flattened, ribbonlike, crispate: *Sparassis* (page 216).

Hymenium smooth, present only on the inferior surface of the carpophore, which is similar to a crust
Lying on the wood that feeds it: *Peniophora* and *Corticium.*
Partly detached from the substrate: *Hymenochaete* and *Stereum* (page 209).
Hymenium formed by teeth
Carpophore thin; lignicolous mushrooms
Carpophore coriaceous
With long, lateral stem; cap heart shaped; on pinecones: *Auriscalpium* (page 217).

With short peduncle, or without·peduncle and attached by the back on the wood from which it feeds: *Mycoleptodon.*
Not coriaceous, without stem, attached by the back or laterally
Carpophore membranous or similar to a crust
Teeth sharp, conical: *Odontia.*
Teeth not sharp: *Grandinia.*
Carpophore waxy
Teeth sharp: *Acia.*
Teeth obtuse, small shovel-like, uneven, sparse: *Radulum.*
Carpophore bulky
Corky, turbinate, supported by a generally thick stem; caps of several specimens, growing very close, often attached together; terricolous mushrooms: *Calodon* (page 217).

Fleshy
Terricolous mushrooms: carpophore turbinate, supported by a thick stem more or less eccentric; hymenial teeth sharp
Spores white: *Hydnum sensu stricto* (page 214).
Spores ochraceous: *Sarcodon* (page 216).
Lignicolous mushrooms: carpophore inserted laterally on the wood of the host; hymenium formed by long, pendulous, or ruffled soft teeth: *Hericium* (page 215).
Hymenium formed by parallel tubules, but seperated like the bristles of a brush, inserted on the lower surface of the carpophore, which is shaped like a beef tongue protruding from the trunk of the host plant: **Fistulina** (page 213).
Hymenium with pores or with irregular openings, separated by pseudogills
Carpophore with cap and stem, and, when with several caps, then with as many peduncles, confluent in a single base
Tissue of the carpophore rusty, coriaceous; stem slender; terricolous mushrooms: *Polystictus* (page 203).
Tissue of the carpophore white
Terricolous mushrooms
Pores large, chipped. Through the microscope: spores almost elliptic, verrucose, becoming violet with iodine (amyloid), as it happens with starch: *Boletopsis* (page 207).

a   b   c

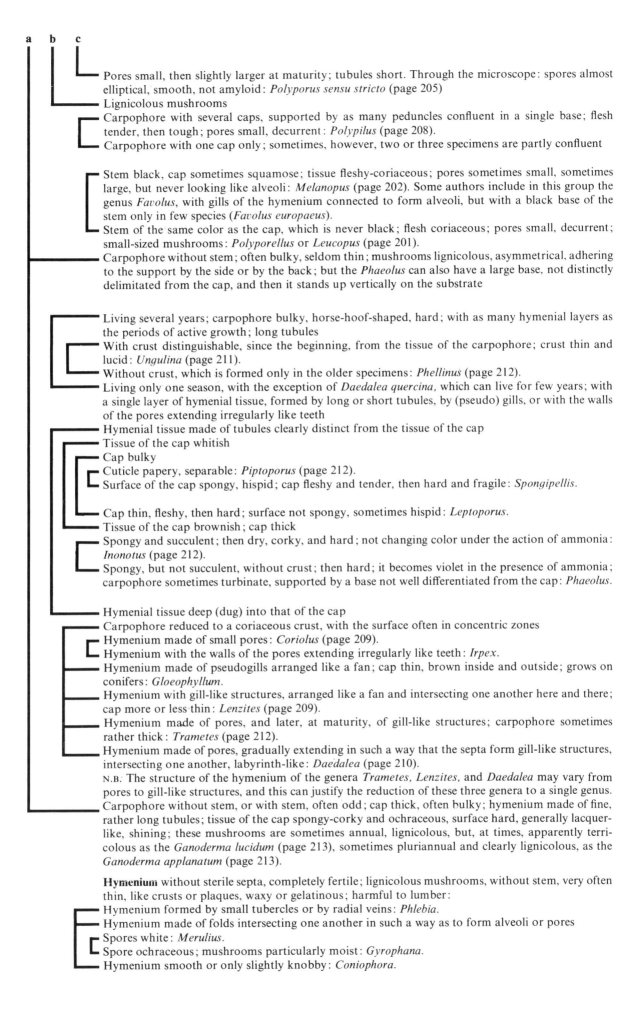

Pores small, then slightly larger at maturity; tubules short. Through the microscope: spores almost elliptical, smooth, not amyloid: *Polyporus sensu stricto* (page 205)

Lignicolous mushrooms

Carpophore with several caps, supported by as many peduncles confluent in a single base; flesh tender, then tough; pores small, decurrent: *Polypilus* (page 208).

Carpophore with one cap only; sometimes, however, two or three specimens are partly confluent

Stem black, cap sometimes squamose; tissue fleshy-coriaceous; pores sometimes small, sometimes large, but never looking like alveoli: *Melanopus* (page 202). Some authors include in this group the genus *Favolus*, with gills of the hymenium connected to form alveoli, but with a black base of the stem only in few species (*Favolus europaeus*).

Stem of the same color as the cap, which is never black; flesh coriaceous; pores small, decurrent; small-sized mushrooms: *Polyporellus* or *Leucopus* (page 201).

Carpophore without stem; often bulky, seldom thin; mushrooms lignicolous, asymmetrical, adhering to the support by the side or by the back; but the *Phaeolus* can also have a large base, not distinctly delimitated from the cap, and then it stands up vertically on the substrate

Living several years; carpophore bulky, horse-hoof-shaped, hard; with as many hymenial layers as the periods of active growth; long tubules

With crust distinguishable, since the beginning, from the tissue of the carpophore; crust thin and lucid: *Ungulina* (page 211).

Without crust, which is formed only in the older specimens: *Phellinus* (page 212).

Living only one season, with the exception of *Daedalea quercina,* which can live for few years; with a single layer of hymenial tissue, formed by long or short tubules, by (pseudo) gills, or with the walls of the pores extending irregularly like teeth

Hymenial tissue made of tubules clearly distinct from the tissue of the cap

Tissue of the cap whitish

Cap bulky

Cuticle papery, separable: *Piptoporus* (page 212).

Surface of the cap spongy, hispid; cap fleshy and tender, then hard and fragile: *Spongipellis.*

Cap thin, fleshy, then hard; surface not spongy, sometimes hispid: *Leptoporus.*

Tissue of the cap brownish; cap thick

Spongy and succulent; then dry, corky, and hard; not changing color under the action of ammonia: *Inonotus* (page 212).

Spongy, but not succulent, without crust; then hard; it becomes violet in the presence of ammonia; carpophore sometimes turbinate, supported by a base not well differentiated from the cap: *Phaeolus.*

Hymenial tissue deep (dug) into that of the cap

Carpophore reduced to a coriaceous crust, with the surface often in concentric zones

Hymenium made of small pores: *Coriolus* (page 209).

Hymenium with the walls of the pores extending irregularly like teeth: *Irpex.*

Hymenium made of pseudogills arranged like a fan; cap thin, brown inside and outside; grows on conifers: *Gloeophyllum.*

Hymenium with gill-like structures, arranged like a fan and intersecting one another here and there; cap more or less thin: *Lenzites* (page 209).

Hymenium made of pores, and later, at maturity, of gill-like structures; carpophore sometimes rather thick: *Trametes* (page 212).

Hymenium made of pores, gradually extending in such a way that the septa form gill-like structures, intersecting one another, labyrinth-like: *Daedalea* (page 210).

N.B. The structure of the hymenium of the genera *Trametes, Lenzites,* and *Daedalea* may vary from pores to gill-like structures, and this can justify the reduction of these three genera to a single genus.

Carpophore without stem, or with stem, often odd; cap thick, often bulky; hymenium made of fine, rather long tubules; tissue of the cap spongy-corky and ochraceous, surface hard, generally lacquer-like, shining; these mushrooms are sometimes annual, lignicolous, but, at times, apparently terricolous as the *Ganoderma lucidum* (page 213), sometimes pluriannual and clearly lignicolous, as the *Ganoderma applanatum* (page 213).

Hymenium without sterile septa, completely fertile; lignicolous mushrooms, without stem, very often thin, like crusts or plaques, waxy or gelatinous; harmful to lumber:

Hymenium formed by small tubercles or by radial veins: *Phlebia.*

Hymenium made of folds intersecting one another in such a way as to form alveoli or pores

Spores white: *Merulius.*

Spore ochraceous; mushrooms particularly moist: *Gyrophana.*

Hymenium smooth or only slightly knobby: *Coniophora.*

Agaricales, or Semiangiocarps

In these mushrooms the basidiocarp is enveloped, during the initial stages of development (button stage), by a protective membrane known as the universal veil; the hymenium is generally produced on the underside of the cap and is very often covered by a partial or inner veil that connects the margin of the cap to the stem. Sometimes these membranes disappear without leaving any trace; in some instances they seem to be completely absent, so that some genera of mushrooms are classified with the Semiangiocarps even though they are Gymnocarps; but this is due to the presence of other characteristics that make these mushrooms more like the Semiangiocarps than the Gymnocarps. The classification and subdivision into genera are based on the morphology of the hymenium, which is formed by gills or tubules, sometimes smooth, sometimes plicate, and on the color of the spores. Other important characteristics for the identification of these mushrooms is the presence or absence of the remains of the universal and inner veils: warts, volva, ring, cortina.

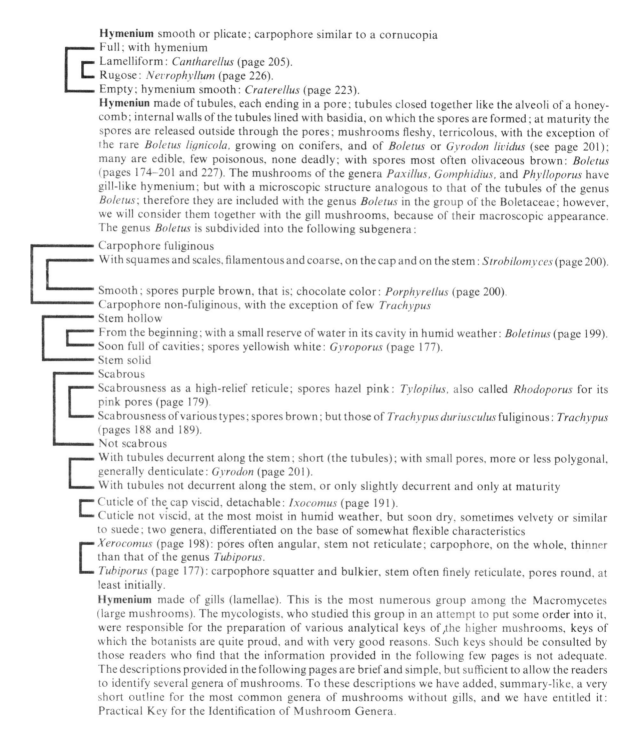

Hymenium smooth or plicate; carpophore similar to a cornucopia
Full; with hymenium
Lamelliform: *Cantharellus* (page 205).
Rugose: *Nevrophyllum* (page 226).
Empty; hymenium smooth: *Craterellus* (page 223).

Hymeniun made of tubules, each ending in a pore; tubules closed together like the alveoli of a honeycomb; internal walls of the tubules lined with basidia, on which the spores are formed; at maturity the spores are released outside through the pores; mushrooms fleshy, terricolous, with the exception of the rare *Boletus lignicola,* growing on conifers, and of *Boletus* or *Gyrodon lividus* (see page 201); many are edible, few poisonous, none deadly; with spores most often olivaceous brown: *Boletus* (pages 174–201 and 227). The mushrooms of the genera *Paxillus, Gomphidius,* and *Phylloporus* have gill-like hymenium; but with a microscopic structure analogous to that of the tubules of the genus *Boletus*; therefore they are included with the genus *Boletus* in the group of the Boletaceae; however, we will consider them together with the gill mushrooms, because of their macroscopic appearance. The genus *Boletus* is subdivided into the following subgenera:

Carpophore fuliginous
With squames and scales, filamentous and coarse, on the cap and on the stem: *Strobilomyces* (page 200).

Smooth; spores purple brown, that is; chocolate color: *Porphyrellus* (page 200).
Carpophore non-fuliginous, with the exception of few *Trachypus*
Stem hollow
From the beginning; with a small reserve of water in its cavity in humid weather: *Boletinus* (page 199).
Soon full of cavities; spores yellowish white: *Gyroporus* (page 177).
Stem solid
Scabrous
Scabrousness as a high-relief reticule; spores hazel pink: *Tylopilus,* also called *Rhodoporus* for its pink pores (page 179).
Scabrousness of various types; spores brown; but those of *Trachypus duriusculus* fuliginous: *Trachypus* (pages 188 and 189).
Not scabrous
With tubules decurrent along the stem; short (the tubules); with small pores, more or less polygonal, generally denticulate: *Gyrodon* (page 201).
With tubules not decurrent along the stem, or only slightly decurrent and only at maturity
Cuticle of the cap viscid, detachable: *Ixocomus* (page 191).
Cuticle not viscid, at the most moist in humid weather, but soon dry, sometimes velvety or similar to suede; two genera, differentiated on the base of somewhat flexible characteristics
Xerocomus (page 198): pores often angular, stem not reticulate; carpophore, on the whole, thinner than that of the genus *Tubiporus.*
Tubiporus (page 177): carpophore squatter and bulkier, stem often finely reticulate, pores round, at least initially.

Hymenium made of gills (lamellae). This is the most numerous group among the Macromycetes (large mushrooms). The mycologists, who studied this group in an attempt to put some order into it, were responsible for the preparation of various analytical keys of the higher mushrooms, keys of which the botanists are quite proud, and with very good reasons. Such keys should be consulted by those readers who find that the information provided in the following few pages is not adequate. The descriptions provided in the following pages are brief and simple, but sufficient to allow the readers to identify several genera of mushrooms. To these descriptions we have added, summary-like, a very short outline for the most common genera of mushrooms without gills, and we have entitled it: Practical Key for the Identification of Mushroom Genera.

Practical Key for the Identification of Mushroom Genera

1

Mushrooms with gills: (*go to number*) 2
mushrooms without gills: (*go to number*) 49

2

leucosporous, that is, with white spores: 3
rhodosporous, that is, with pink spores: 28
ochrosporous, that is, with ochraceous spores: 37
iantinosporous, that is, with violaceous spores: 44
melanosporous, that is, with black spores: 44

3

most often thin or gracilent: 4
most often bulky: 10

N.B. Although not absolute, these characteristics will allow, many a time, the identification of the genus of several of the mushrooms with white spores; however, one should try to further check this identification on the basis of other characteristics. See *Hygrocybe* at numbers 6 and 15, *Collybia* at numbers 9, 18, and 19, *Tricholoma* at numbers 9 and 20.

4

exsiccate easily: 5
rotting after ripening: 6

N.B. Together with the fresh specimens, one can also find the seasoned ones.

5

cap smooth: *Marasmius* (pages 88–92).
cap velvety: *Xerula* (page 84).

6

gills waxy or juicy; field mushrooms, brightly colored, moist, fragile: *Hygrocybe* (pages 170–172).
not like above: 7

7

gills decurrent: *Clitocybe* (minor, pages 111, 114, 115, 116, 118).
gills slightly decurrent, sparse: *Laccaria* (page 119).
gills not decurrent: 8

8

gills sparse: 9
gills close; granules on the cap and on the stem from the base to the ring: *Cystoderma* (page 40).

9

terricolous: *Mycena* (pages 92–93) and *Tricholoma* (minor, pages 98–99).
lignicolous: Collybia (pages 86–87, 90) and Mycena (lignicolous, pages 92–93).

10

flesh granular: 11
flesh not granular: 12

11

with latex: *Lactarius* (pages 130–144).
without latex: *Russula* (pages 144–164).

12

gills decurrent: 13
gills not decurrent: 16

13

lignicolous: 14
terricolous: 15

14

gills serrate: *Lentinus* and *Lentinellus* (pages 126–128).
gills not serrate: *Pleurotus* (pages 124–125).

15

gills waxy, sparse, fragile: *Hygrophorus* (pages 166–170): those of *Hygrocybe punicea* (page 170) soon detached from the stem, which we mention again because it can reach considerable size.
gills not waxy: *Clitocybe* (major, pages 112–114).

16

lignicolous: 17
terricolous: 19

17

glutinous; with ring on the stem: *Mucidula* (page 85).
not gluttinous: 18

18

cespitose: *Collybia* (pages 86, 88, 89–90); *Tricholomoposis edodes* (page 126) and *Tricholomopsis ornata* (page 97).
non-cespitose: *Tricholomopsis* (pages 87, 97, 126).

19

gills adhering to the stem little or not at all: *Collybia* (pages 86–88).
gills rounded or eroded near the stem, but adhering to it: 20

20

stout mushrooms: *Tricholoma* (major, pages 93–105).
thinner mushrooms, quite sensitive to humidity: *Melanoleuca* (pages 106–109).

21
cap and stem not clearly separable: 22
cap and stem clearly separable: 25
22
with two rings on the stem; carpophore squat, brown, half buried: *Biannularia* (page 109).
with one ring only; lignicolous mushrooms: 23
23
glutinous: *Mucidula* (page 85).
not glutinous: 24
24
gills decurrent: *Armillariella* (page 110).
gills not decurrent: *Tricholomopsis* (pages 87, 97, 126).
25
with volva at the base, at least initially: 26
without volva, but with ring on the stem: 27
26
with ring: *Amanita* (pages 17–31).
without ring: *Amanitopsis* (pages 30–33).
27
viscid mushrooms: *Limacella* (page 32).
dry mushrooms: *Lepiota* (pages 35–39).
28
with volva around the base: *Volvaria* (pages 40–42).
without volva: 29
29
stem easily separable from the cap: 30
stem not easily separable from the cap: 31
30
terricolous, ring ephermeral: *Lepiota naucina* (page 39); spores with pink shades, but more often white.
lignicolous, without ring: *Pluteus* (page 41).
31
lignicolous: 32
terricolous: 33
32
gracilent, stem eccentric, lateral or none: *Claudopus*.
stout, also in the grass, but more frequently on dead and buried shrubs, spores pale pink: *Pleurotus* (page 123–124).
33
gracilent: 34
stout: 35
34
gills not annexed to the stem: *Nolanea* (page 83).
gills annexed to the stem, but not decurrent along it: *Leptonia*.
gills decurrent: *Eccilia*.
35
gills not decurrent: 36
gills very decurrent: *Clitopilus* (page 122).
gills slightly decurrent and only at maturation, eroded near the stem: *Rhodopaxillus* (pages 120–121).
36
gills close *Rhodocollybia (Collybia) maculata* (page 86).
gills crowded only near the margin of the cap because of the presence of many intermediate gills; with eroded edges: *Entoloma* (pages 82–83).
37
lignicolous mushrooms: 38
terricolous mushrooms: 39
38
gills slightly decurrent: *Flammula* (page 58); some species of this genus are terricolous; cap smooth, stem almost always slender; bright colors, flavor often bitter, spores rusty.
gills not decurrent; squamose mushrooms: *Pholiota* (page 58–61).
39
with cortina: 40
with ring, although tenuous and evanescent: 42
without cortina and without ring; gills decurrent: 43
40
cortina glutinous or filamentous, more or less conspicuous: *Cortinarius* (pages 66–78).
cortina tenuous or filamentous: 41
41
cap rather fleshy, smooth, often viscid: *Hebeloma* (pages 65–67).
cap not too fleshy, fibrous, squamose; carpophore most often slender: *Inocybe* (pages 79–81).
42
cap initially with micaceous scurf, then with radial wrinkles; fibrous stem: *Rozites* (page 62).
cap and stem smooth; carpophore thinner; brownish spores: *Agrocybe* (pages 63–64).

43

gills thin, close, easily detachable in lumps: *Paxillus* (pages 175–176).

gills quite thick, sparse, connected together: *Phylloporus* (page 174).

44

gills deliquescent: *Coprinus* (pages 51–52); black or fuliginous spores.

gills not deliquescent: 45

45

speckled with small stains, because the spores ripen in different sections at different times: 46

not speckled: 47

not always speckled; ring on the stem: *Stropharia* (pages 54–55); brown violet or black violet spores.

46

small mushrooms, cap neither squamose nor fibrillar: *Panaeolus* (page 53); spores blackish or black.

bigger mushrooms, cap squamose-fibrillar: *Lacrymaria* (page 53); spores fuliginous.

47

gills decurrent along the stem, thick, sparse: *Gomphidius* (pages 173–174); blackish spores.

gills not decurrent: 48

48

mushrooms bulky, terricolous, with gills not adhering to the stem: *Psalliota* (major, pages 43–49); spores cocoa; some small species are also included in this genus. Mushrooms less bulky or also rather small, not too sensitive to humidity not too fragile, often cespitose and lignicolous, with adhering gills, filamentous cortina: *Hypholoma* (page 55); gray violet spores.

mushrooms slender, sensitive to humidity, fragile, often cespitose and lignicolous; cap thin, glabrous, flocculose, or micaceous, smooth or striate at least in humid weather, especially at the margin in transparency: *Drosophila*; cocoa-colored spores.

49

with tubules: 50

with teeth: 60

different from the two above: 64

50

adhering to the lower surface of the cap: 51

dug into the very tissue of the cap: 59

51

separated from one another like the bristles of a brush: *Fistulina* (page 213).

massed together: 52

52

short, not easily detachable: *Polyporus* (pages 201–209).

larger, more easily detachable: 53

53

carpophore with well-differentiated cap and stem: 54

carpophore hoof shaped, without stem; lignicolous mushrooms: 55

54

stem central, putrescible mushrooms: *Boletus* (pages 174–201).

stem eccentric; mushrooms lignicolous, sometimes apparently
terricolous, imputrescible: *Ganoderma lucidum* and *Tsugae*
(page 213).

55

with several layers of tubules: 56

with only one layer: 57

56

with distinct crust: *Ungulina* (page 211).

with crust only tardily distinct: *Phellinus* (page 212).

57

flesh pallid: *Piptoporus* (page 212).

flesh brownish: 58

58

putrescible mushrooms: *Inonotus* (page 212).

imputrescible mushrooms: *Ganoderma applanatum* (page 213).

59

with small, rounded pores; mushrooms thin and of the consistency of bark: *Coriolus* (page 209).

with polygonal, irregular pores, separated by pseudogills: *Trametes, Lenzites, Daedalea* (pages 209–212).

60

with gelatinous teeth: *Tremellodon* (page 233).

with teeth not gelatinous: 61

61

cap very thin, heart shaped, on a tall, lateral stem: *Auriscalpium* (page 217).

carpophore irregular, with very long teeth; lignicolous mushrooms: *Hericium* (page 215).

carpophore turbinate: 62

62

corky: *Calodon* (page 217).

fleshy: 63

63

with white spores: *Hydnum* (page 214).

with ochraceous spores: *Sarcodon* (page 216).

64

carpophore globular or tuberlike: 65

not like above: 71

65

epigeous mushrooms: 66

hypogeous mushrooms: 69

semihypogeous or facultative hypogeous mushrooms; with thin, whitish involucre with brownish filaments adhering to its base: *Rhizopogon*.

66

on a tall, fibrous cylindrical stem: *Tylostoma* (page 227).

without stem: 67

67

thick, hard involucre (tegument): *Scleroderma* (page 227).

soft involucre: 68

68

carpophore with sterile base: *Lycoperdon* (pages 228–231).

carpophore without sterile base: *Bovista* (page 231).

69

at maturity dissolving into brown or fuliginous powder: *Elaphomyces* (page 240).

not dissolving into powder at maturity: 70

70

flesh black, odor tenuous: *Melanogaster*.

flesh not black, soapy and marbled; odor sharp: *Tuber* (page 240).

flesh white or yellowish, soft, with meandering streaks, soon fetid: *Balsamia*.

71

carpophore shaped like a cornucopia: 72

carpophore shaped like sea coral: 73

carpophore of different shape: 74

72

full, with decurrent pseudogills, more or less prominent: *Nevrophyllum* and *Cantherellus* (pages 221–223).

without pseudogills: *Craterellus* (page 223).

73

fragile: *Ramaria* (pages 218–220).

gelatinous but tenacious: *Calocera* (page 233).

corky: *Xylaria* (page 239).

74

club: *Clavaria* (pages 220–221).

head of endive: *Sparassis* (page 216).

star with small onion in the center: *Geaster* and *Astraeus* (page 232).

bowl, ear, curled leaf: *Auricularia* (page 231), *Gyrocephala* (page 233), *Peziza* (pages 235–240).

small nest with small eggs: *Cyathus* and other genera (page 227).

hollow, colored sponge on a hollow, whitish stem: *Morchella* and *Mitrophora* (pages 236–237).

thimble inserted on a hollow stem: *Verpa*.

brain supported by a hollow stem: *Gyromitra* (page 234).

turban on a rugose or hollow stem: *Helvella* (page 235).

spathula or small nail: *Spathularia* and other genera (page 239).

spheroidal net, upside-down octopus, small hollow candle, with volva at the base; fragile, spongy, fetid mushrooms: *Dictyophora* and other genera (pages 223–224).

Etymology of Scientific Terms

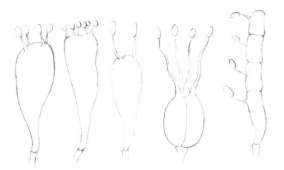

Asci with ascospores.

Basidium with four, six, two spores, vertically septate, transversely septate.

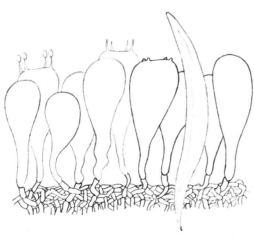

Hymenium of Basidiomycetes: basidium with mature spores (1), old, after the falling of the spores (2); unripe (3); sterile cystidium (4).

Angiocarps: fruits covered by a tegument (ἀγγεῖον = tegument, involucre; καρπός = fruit)

Aphyllophorales: not bearing gills (ἀ = without; φύλλον = gill; φέρω = to bear)

Ascomycetes: fungi with asci (ἀσκός = sac; μύκητες = fungi)

Ascus: sac (ἀσκός)

Basidiomycetes: fungi with basidia (βάσις = foot; βασιδίον = small foot; μύκητες = fungi)

Basidium: small foot (βάσις = foot; βασιδίον = small foot)

Carpophore: bearing fruits (sometimes used to mean the fruit body of the higher fungi) (καρπός = fruit; φέρω = to bear)

Cormophyte: plants with trunk (with stem, root, and leaf) (κόρμος = trunk; φυτόν = plant)

*Cryptogamae: with hidden nuptials (κρυπτός = hidden; γάμος = nuptials)

Cystidium: small sac (κύστις)

Gasteromycetes: fungi (mushrooms) with cavity, with the fruiting body closed at maturity (γαστος = stomach; μύκητες = fungi)

Gymnocarps: fruits without tegument (mushrooms with hymenium exposed at an early stage) (γυμνός = naked; καρπός = fruit)

Hymenomycetes: mushrooms (fungi) with hymenium (ὑμέναιος = hymenium; μύκητες = fungi)

Hyphae: tissue, filament (ὑφή = tissue, filament)

Iantinosporus: with violet seeds (spores) (ἰανθινος = violet; σπορά = seed, spore)

Leucosporous: with white seeds (spores) (λευκός = white; σπορά = seed)

Macromycetes: large fungi (μακρός = large)

Melanosporous: with black seeds (spores) (μέλας = black; σπορά = seed, spore)

Micromycetes: small fungi, microscopic (μικρός = small)

Mycelium: the tissue of which the mushrooms are made (μύκης = fungus)

Mycetes: fungi (μύκητες = fungi)

Mycorrhiza: root fungus (the association of a fungus with the root of a plant) (ῥίζα = root)

Ochrosporous: with ocher color seeds (spores) (όχρα = ocher; σπορα = seed, spore)

*Phanerogamae: with visible nuptials (φανερός = visible; γάμος = nuptials)

Rhodosporous: with pink seeds (spores) (ῥόδον = the rose; σπορα = seed, spore)

Semiangiocarp, Hemiangiocarps: fruits covered by half an involucre (mushrooms with hymenium enclosed at the beginning of development, but exposed at maturity) (ήμι = in half; ἀγγεῖον = involucre; καρπός = fruit)

Sterigma: support (στήριγμα)

Thallophyta: plants with thallus, that is, with a body not differentiated into stem, leaf, and root (θαλλός = thallus, shoot; φυτόν = plant)

* The terms *cryptogamae* and *phanerogamae*, respectively, refer to the absence and presence of plant reproductive organs, visible to the naked eye, such as flowers.

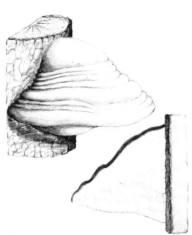

Ungulina fomentaria

Corticium roseo-carneum

Phlebia strigoso-zonata

Merulius tremellosus

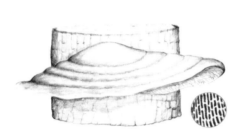

Lenzites: in the circle detail
of hymenium, magnified

Phellinus pomaceus

Crepidotus variabilis

Favolus europaeus

Schizophyllum comune and
section of the pseudogills

Tremetes cinnabarina: in the circle
detail of hymenium, magnified

Sparassis laminosa

Peziza venosa

Phaeolus Schweinitzii

Myriostoma coliforme

Sclerangium polirrhizon

Tuber melanosporum

Terfezia Leonis

Verpa digitaliformis (at left)
and *bohemica* (at right)

Macrocystidia cucumis

Omphalia (from the left)
integrella, crispula, fibula

Ramaria fennica

Ramaria condensata

Crinipellis stipitarius

Colus hirundinosus

Coprinus (from the left) *hiascens,
extinctorius, sterquilinus, fimentarius*

Boletus torosus

Xeromphalina cauticinalis

Cordyceps militaris

  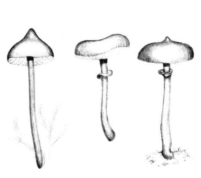 

Gyrophragmium Delilei

Alnicola

Galera or *Galerina* (at left) *sphagnorum;*
(in the middle): *unicolor var. muscigena;*
(at right): *unicolor*

Montagnites Candollei

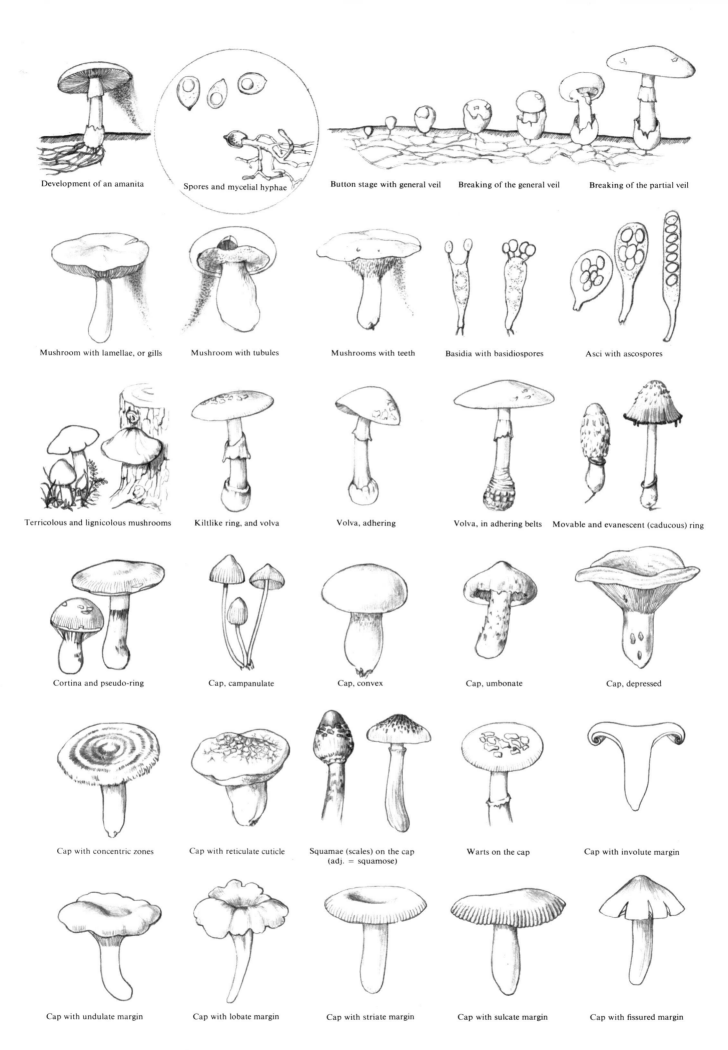

Development of an amanita

Spores and mycelial hyphae

Button stage with general veil

Breaking of the general veil

Breaking of the partial veil

Mushroom with lamellae, or gills

Mushroom with tubules

Mushrooms with teeth

Basidia with basidiospores

Asci with ascospores

Terricolous and lignicolous mushrooms

Kiltlike ring, and volva

Volva, adhering

Volva, in adhering belts

Movable and evanescent (caducous) ring

Cortina and pseudo-ring

Cap, campanulate

Cap, convex

Cap, umbonate

Cap, depressed

Cap with concentric zones

Cap with reticulate cuticle

Squamae (scales) on the cap
(adj. = squamose)

Warts on the cap

Cap with involute margin

Cap with undulate margin

Cap with lobate margin

Cap with striate margin

Cap with sulcate margin

Cap with fissured margin

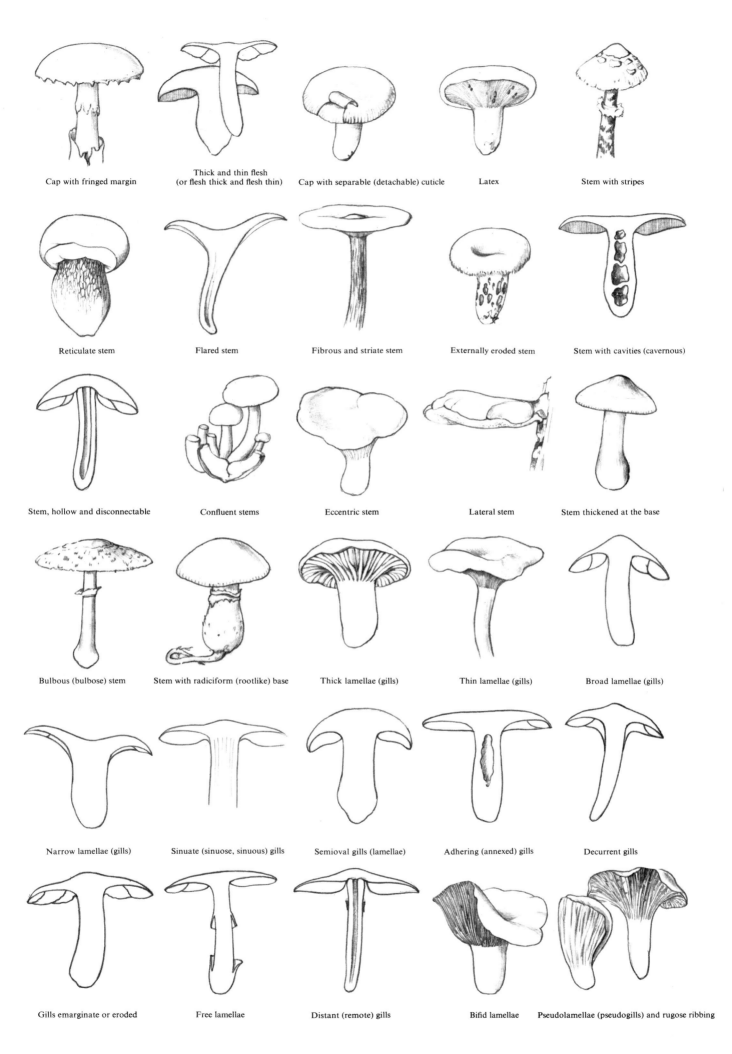

Cap with fringed margin

Thick and thin flesh
(or flesh thick and flesh thin)

Cap with separable (detachable) cuticle

Latex

Stem with stripes

Reticulate stem

Flared stem

Fibrous and striate stem

Externally eroded stem

Stem with cavities (cavernous)

Stem, hollow and disconnectable

Confluent stems

Eccentric stem

Lateral stem

Stem thickened at the base

Bulbous (bulbose) stem

Stem with radiciform (rootlike) base

Thick lamellae (gills)

Thin lamellae (gills)

Broad lamellae (gills)

Narrow lamellae (gills)

Sinuate (sinuose, sinuous) gills

Semioval gills (lamellae)

Adhering (annexed) gills

Decurrent gills

Gills emarginate or eroded

Free lamellae

Distant (remote) gills

Bifid lamellae

Pseudolamellae (pseudogills) and rugose ribbing

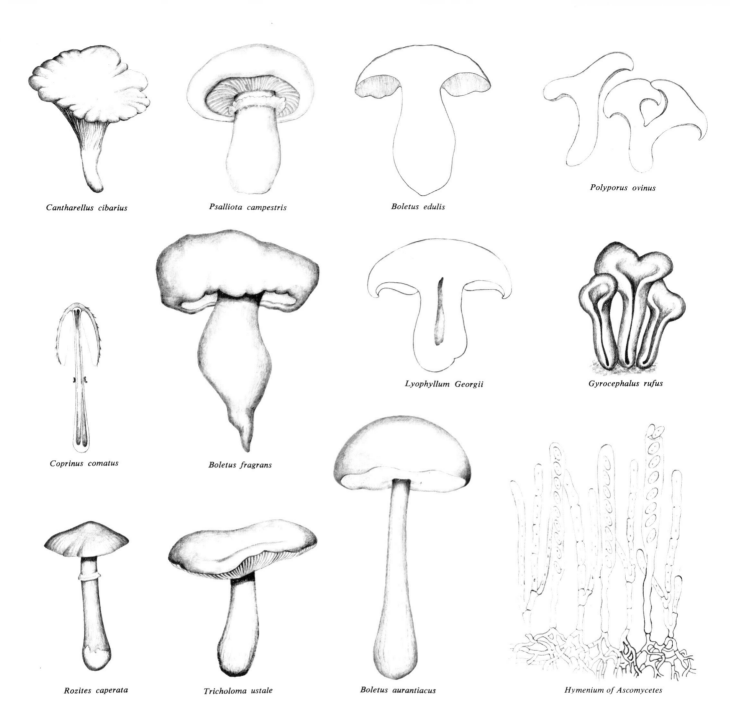

Cantharellus cibarius

Psalliota campestris

Boletus edulis

Polyporus ovinus

Coprinus comatus

Boletus fragrans

Lyophyllum Georgii

Gyrocephalus rufus

Rozites caperata

Tricholoma ustale

Boletus aurantiacus

Hymenium of Ascomycetes

A Short Dictionary of Scientific Terms

The official language of botany, and therefore of mycology, is Latin. The scientific names of the mushrooms are in Latin; in turn, many of these Latin scientific names were derived from the Greek language; the Greek words from which they are derived are written using the Greek alphabet. The derivation of a word from a language other than Greek is also indicated.

In Latin, *ae* = *i*, *æ* = *ae*, *oe* = *oi*, *œ* = *oe*, *y* = *i*, *ph* = *f*, *th* = *t*, *ti* = *shi*, *ti* = *ti*. In Greek α = a, β = b, γ = gh, γγ = ngh, δ = d, ε = short e, ζ = z, η = long e, θ = English th, ι = i, χ = ch, χχ = nch, λ = l, μ = m, ν = n, ξ = cs, o = short o, ου = u, π = p, ρ = r, σ/ς = s, τ = t, υ = French u, φ = f, χ = ch, soft, ψ = ps, ω = long o.

Sometimes, for those adjectives terminating with *a*, *us*, and *um*, respectively for the feminine, masculine, and neuter gender, we have given only the masculine form.

The initial letter of the names of animals and higher plants is in lower case to distinguish them from the genera of the mushrooms.

The word *Coprinoides*, terminating in -*ides* (from εἶδος, meaning similarity), means similar to *coprinus*. The word *Tricholomopsis*, terminating in -*opsis* (ὄψις = resemblance), means similar to *Tricholoma*. The word *tubaeformis*, terminating in -*formis* (from *forma* = shape), means shaped like a trumpet. The word *Euflammula*, beginning with *eu*- (from the Greek εὖ = beautiful), means beautiful *Flammula*. The word *Pseudocolus*, beginning with ψεῦδος (meaning lie in Greek), means false (likely to be confused with) *Colus*. The word *semiliber* beginning with *semi*- (the same as the Greek ἥμι, meaning half), means free for only one-half. The word *subtomentosus*, beginning with *sub*- (meaning under or almost), means slightly inferior to *tomentosus*, or almost like *tomentosus*. The explanation of the above words will not always be repeated for the names in which they are found.

Abiétinus: pertaining to fir trees (*ábies*)
Abíetum: of the fir trees (*abies* = fir tree)
Abruptibúlbus: with a prominent, abrupt bulb (*abruptus* = broken off; *bulbus* = bulb)
Acanthocýstis: with thorny, prickly cystidia (ἄκανθος = prickly, thorny; κύστις = sac, bladder)
Acanthoídes: pertaining to or resembling the acanthus (ἄκανθος)
Acérrimus: very acrid, sharp (superlative of *acer* = sharp)
Acérbus: sour, bitter, acerb
Acervátus: heaped
Acetábulum: a vinegar cruet
Ácia: thread, yarn
Ácris: acrid, sharp
Acuminátus: acuminate, ending in a sharp point
Acutesquamósus: with sharp, acute scales (*acutus* = sharpened, acute; *squamosus* = scaly, squamose)
Adhaérens: adherent, attached
Adipósus: adipose (*adeps* = fat)
Adústus: adust, burned, scorched
Aegeríta: pertaining to the poplar (αἴγειρος)
Aéreus: bronzy, of bronze
Aerugíneus: copper rust color, bluish green (*aerugo* = the rust of copper; verdigris)
Aeruginósus: same as *Aerugineus*
Aerumbonátus: without umbo (αἴρω = I take away; *umbo* = umbo; knob)
Aestívus: pertaining to summer
Agáricus: of the country, mushroom in general (ἀγαρικόν)
Agathósmus: perfumed (ἀγαθός = good; ὀσμή = smell)
Aggregátus: aggregate
Agrócybe: head of the field (ἀγρός = field; κύβη = head)
Albéllus: whitish (diminutive of *albus* = white)
Albídipes: with whitish foot (*albidus* = whitish; *pes* = foot)

Álbidus: whitish
Albobrúnneus: white and brown (*albus* = white; German *brun* = brown)
Albocýaneus: white and blue (*albus* = white; κυανός = azure blue)
Alboflávus: white and yellow (*albus* = white; *flavus* = yellow)
Albóniger: white and black (*albus* = white; *niger* = black)
Albovioláceus: white and violaceous (*albus* = white; *violaceus* = violaceous)
Albus: white
Alcálina: alkaline (Ar. *al-kali* = potash)
Alexándri: of Alexander (Alexander)
Aléuria: pertaining to wheat flour (ἄλευρον = flour)
Alnícola: living near alder trees (*alnus* = alder tree; *colo* = I live)
Alpínus: of or pertaining to the Alps
Alutáceus: resembling thin leather (*aluta*)
Alutárius: same as *alutaceus*
Amaníta: from Ἄμανος = a mountain between Cilicia and Syria; or from ἀμανῖται = mushrooms in general
Amanitópsis: similar to or resembling *Amanita*
Amárus: bitter
Amaréllus: somewhat bitter (diminutive of *amarus*)
Amaréscens: becoming bitter
Amarissímus: very bitter (superlative of *amarus*)
Ambíguus: ambiguous, uncertain
Ambrósii: of F. Ambrosi, Italian (ca. 1800–1900)
Americánus: American
Amethýsteus: the color of amethyst
Amethystinus: amethystine (ἀμεθύστινος)
Amiánthinus or *Amiántinus:* incorruptible, incontaminate (ἀμίαντος = incorruptible)
Amici: of G. B. Amici, Italian (ca. 1800–1900)
Ammóphilus: sand-loving (ἄμμος = sand; φίλος = friend)
Amoénus: pleasant, cheerful
Amoenátus: made pleasant or cheerful
Amoénolens: pleasant smelling (*amoene* = cheerfully; *oleo* = I smell)
Androsáceus: pertaining to or resembling an alpine, dwarf herb, called *androsaces*
Angústiceps: with a small head (*angustus* = small; *caput* = head)
Annulátus: furnished with rings, ringed
Anómalus: anomalous, irregular
Anserínus: pertaining to or resembling a goose
Anthúrus: flower of tails (ἄνθος = flower; οὐρά = tail)
Apícreus: not bitter, not acrid (ἀ = not; πικρός = bitter, acrid)
Appendiculátus: with small appendix (*appendicula*)
Applanátus: flattened
Aprílis: of or pertaining to the month of April
Aquósa: watery
Archéri: of W. Archeri, Irish
Arculárius: maker of small chests
Arenárius: sandy
Arbustívus: sustained by a tree
Argilláceus: argillaceous; pertaining to or consisting of clay
Argyráceus: silvery (ἄργυρος = silver)
Armeníacus: pertaining to the apricot (*Prunus armeniacus*)
Armillária: resembling or consisting of a bracelet or ring (*armilla*)
Armillariélla: diminutive of *Armillaria*
Armillátus: with bracelet
Arvénsis: of or pertaining to a tilled field (*arvum*)
Aséma: without sign (ἀ = without; σῆμα = sign)
Aseroifórmis: of unpleasant shape (ἀσηρός = unpleasant; *forma* = shape)
Áspera: rough, hard
Aspidéllus: small shield (diminutive of ασπίς = shield)
Asterophora: bearing stars (ἀστήρ = star; φέρω = I bear,

carry)

Asteróspora: with seeds similar to stars (ἀστήρ = star; σπορά = seed)

Astraeícola: living on "Astraeus" (*colo* = I live)

Astraeus: starry (αστραῖος)

Astragalínus: pertaining to the goldfinch (ἀστραγαῖνος)

Atramentárius: pertaining to ink (*atramentum*)

Atrátus: in mourning clothes

Atromarginátus: with dark margin (*ater* = dark; *marginatus* = margined)

Atropurpúreus: dark purple (*ater* = dark; *purpureus* = purple)

Atrorúbens: dark red (*ater* = dark; *rubens* = reddish, ruddy)

Atrosquamósus: with dark scales, or dark and scaly (*ater* = dark; *squamosus* = scaly, squamose)

Atrotomentósus: covered with dark pubescence (*ater* = dark; *tomentosus* = covered with hairs, pubescent)

Atróvirens: dark green (*ater* = dark; *virens* = verdant)

Augústus: of great dimension

Aurantíacus: pertaining to orange (*Malum aurantium* = orange)

Aurántio-turbinátus: cone or top shaped and golden as an orange (*Malum aurantium* = orange; *turbinatus* = turbinate)

Aurántipes: with orange-colored foot (*Malum aurántium* = orange; *pes* = foot)

Aurántium: the orange (*Malum aurántium*, or simply *aurantium*)

Aurátus: gilded

Áureus: golden

Auréolus: diminutive of *aureus*

Aurícula: small ear

Auriculária: pertaining to the small ear (*auricula* = small ear)

Auríporus: with golden pores (*aurum* = gold; *porus* = pore)

Auriscálpium: auriscalp (*auris* = ear; *scalpo* = I scrape)

Aurivélla: with golden fleece (*aurum* = gold; *vellum* = fleece)

Auróra: pertaining to the dawn

Azonítes: without zones (α = without; ζωνίτις = zonate)

Azúreus: blue (Ar. *azurd* = blue)

Badhámii: of C. Badham, English (1806–1857)

Badiorúfus: of red brown color (*badius* = reddish brown; *rufus* = red)

Badiosanguíneus: of blood-red brown color (*badius* = reddish brown; *sanguineus* = pertaining to blood)

Bádius: reddish brown

Balsámia: pertaining to balsam

Bárlae: of J. B. Barla, French (1817–1897)

Bernárdi: of G. Bernard, French (ca. 1800–1900)

Betulárum: of the birches (*betula* = birch tree)

Betúlinus: pertaining to the birch tree (*betula* = birch tree)

Biannulária: with two rings (*bis* = twice; *annulus* = ring)

Bícolor: of two colors

Bírrus: reddish brown

Bísporus: with two spores, for each basidium (*bis* = twice; σπορά = seed)

Bisporígenus: producing two spores, for each basidium (*bis* = twice; σπορά = seed; γεννάω = I generate)

Bitórquis: with two necklaces (*bis* = twice; *torquis* = necklace)

Blénnius: mucilaginous (βλέννα = mucilage)

Bohémicus: of or pertaining to Bohemia (*Bohemia*)

Boláris: pertaining to small clods (βωλάριον = small clod)

Bolbítius: pertaining to cattle excrement (βόλβιτον)

Boletínus: diminutive of *Boletus*

Boletópsis: similar to *Boletus*

Bolétus: from βῶλος = clod; from which βωλήτης = mushrooms in general, and βωλίτης = *Amanita caesarea*

in particular

Bombýcina: silken (*bombyx* = silkworm)

Botrýtes: pertaining to a bunch of grapes (βότρυς = a bunch of grapes)

Bovínus: bovine

Bovísta: puffball (German dialect *bofist*)

Bresádolae: of G. Bresadola, Italian (1847–1929)

Brévipes: with short foot (*brevis* = short, brief; *pes* = foot)

Broomeriánus: of Ch. E. Broome, English (1812–1886)

Brumális: of the winter solstice

Brúnneoincarnátus: of flesh brown color (French *brun* = brown; *incarnatus* = of flesh color)

Brúnneovioláceus: violaceous brown (French *brun* = brown; *violaceus* = violaceous)

Brunnéscens: becoming brown (French *brun* = brown)

Bryóphilus: moss-loving (βρύον = moss; φίλος = friend)

Bufónius: pertaining to the toad (*bufo*)

Buglossoídes: similar to a beef tongue (βοῦς = ox; γλῶσσα = tongue)

Búlbiger: bearing a bulb (*bulbus* = bulb; *gero* = I carry, bear)

Bulbósus: bulbous

Bulgária: pertaining to a wineskin (*bulgarus* = animal skin used for making wine containers)

Bulliardi: of P. Bulliard, French (1752–1793)

Butyráceus: pertaining to butter (*butyrum*)

Caelátus: chiseled

Caeruléipes: with ceruleous foot (*caeruleus* = ceruleous, blue; *pes* = foot)

Caeruléscens: becoming blue

Caesáreus: Caesarean, worthy of Caesar (*Caesar*)

Caésiocyáneus: glaucous blue (*caesius* = glaucous; κύανος = deep blue)

Caésius: glaucous, greenish blue

Caespitósus: growing in tufts (*caespes* = stem from which many others branch out)

Calamistrátus: curled

Calcéolus: boot

Califórnicus: of or pertaining to California

Caligátus: with boots

Caliginósus: caliginous, dark

Calócerus: with beautiful horns (καλός = beautiful; κέρας = horn)

Calóchrus: beautiful skin (καλός = beautiful; χρῶς = skin)

Calócybe: beautiful head (καλός = beautiful; κύβη = head)

Cálodon: beautiful tooth (καλός = beautiful; ὀδών = tooth)

Calólepis: beautiful covering (καλός = beautiful; λεπίς = covering)

Calóporus: beautiful pore (καλός = beautiful; πορος = pore)

Cálopus: beautiful foot (καλός = beautiful; πούς = foot)

Calvátia: pertaining to bald heads (*calvus* = bald)

Calyptrodérma: with the skin (δέρμα) shaped like a cap (καλύπτρα)

Camarophýllus: with curved gills (καμάρα = arch; φύλλον = lamella)

Campanulátus: with the shape of a small bell (*campanula*)

Campéster: of fields, country

Campéstris: campestral, pertaining to fields

Camphorátus: pertaining to camphor (Ar. *kafur*)

Cancellátus: shaped like a gate or lattice

Cándidus: snow white, bright white

Candolleánus: of A. P. De Candolle, French (1778–1841)

Candóllei: same as *Candolleanus*

Caninus: canine, pertaining to dogs

Cantharéllus: small cup (diminutive of κάνθαρος = cup)

Caperáta: corrugated, wrinkled

Capnoídes: smoky (καπνώδης)

Capreolárius: pertaining to a roebuck (*capreolus*)

Caprínus: caprine, like a goat

Cáput Medúsae: head of Medusa

Cáput ursi: bear's head

Carbonárius: pertaining to charcoal

Carchárias: rough, scabrous (κάρχαρος = rough)

Cardaréllus: small thistle (diminutive of *cardus* = thistle)

Carneifólia: with flesh-colored gills (*carneus* = flesh colored; *folium* = leaf, lamella)

Carnéipes: with flesh-colored foot (*carneus* = flesh colored; *pes* = foot)

Coroliniánus: of Carolina, North America

Cárpini: pertaining to the hornbeam (*cárpinus*, not *carpínus*)

Cartilagíneus: cartilaginous

Caruophýlleus: with walnut-colored gills (κάρυον = walnut; φύλλον = gill)

Castáneus: the color of chestnuts (*castanea*)

Catínus: basin

Caulicinális: pertaining to the stem of herbaceous plants (καυλικός)

Cávipes: with hollow foot (*cavus* = hollow; *pes* = foot)

Cepaéstipes: with onion-shaped foot (*cepa* = onion; *pes* = foot)

Ceráceus: ceraceous, waxy

Cerussátus: cerused (*obs.,* washed or painted with ceruse: white lead)

Cervínus: cervine, pertaining to deer

Chamaleontínus: changing into various colors like the chameleon (*chamaeleon*)

Chloroídes: greenish looking (χλωρός = greenish)

Chloróphanus: greenish looking (χλωρος = greenish; φαινω = I appear)

Choerómyces: sow's mushroom (χοίρα = the sow; μύκης = mushroom)

Chrysáspis: golden shield (χρυσός = gold; ασπίς = shield)

Chrysénteron: internally golden (χρυσός = gold; ἔντερον = internal)

Chrysodácryon: golden tear (χρυσός = gold; δάκρυον = tear)

Chrýsodon: golden tooth (χρυσός = gold; οδών = tooth)

Chrysórrheus: that which lets gold flow (χρυσός = gold; ῥέω = I flow)

Cibárius: edible

Ciliátus: with cilia and fringes (*cilium* = eyelid)

Cilicioídes: similar to a cilice (hairshirt) made of goat's hair (κίλικιον = garment made of goat's hair)

Cincinnátus: curled, curly

Cineráscens: tending or turning to cinereous, ash colored

Cinereofúscus: gray (*cinereus* = cinereous; *fúscus* = dark)

Cinéreus: cinereous, ashen, ash colored

Cingulátus: wearing a belt (*cingulum*)

Cinnabárinus: red as cinnabar (κινναβάρινος)

Cinnamómeus: pertaining to cinnamon (κινναμωνον)

Circellátus: rounded ringwise (*circellus* = small ring)

Círcinans: tending to become circle shaped

Cirrátus: curly

Cítrinus: pertaining to citron and lemon (*pómum cítreum*)

Claroflávus: light yellow (*clarus* = light, clear; *flávus* = yellow)

Cláthrus: pertaining to an iron grating (*cláthri*)

Clavária: pertaining to club (*cláva*)

Clavariadélphus: brother of Clavaria (ἀδελφός = brother)

Clavátus: club shaped (*clava*)

Cláviceps: with a club-shaped head (*clava* = club; *caput* = head)

Clávipes: with the base or foot thickened clublike (*clava* = club; *pes* = foot)

Clitócybe: depressed head (κλίτος = angle; κύβη = head)

Clitopílus: depressed cap (κλίτος = angle; πίλεος = cap)

Clypeátus: with a round shield

Clypeolária: pertaining to a round shield (*clypeus*)

Cnísta: scraped

Coccíneus: cochineal, scarlet red

Cochleátus: spiral shaped like the shell of a snail

Coelátus: chiseled

Coélopus: with hollow foot or base (κοῖλος = hollow; ποῦς = foot)

Coerúleus: cerulean, deep blue

Cóffeae: pertaining to coffee (*coffea*)

Cognátus: cognate, kindred, born together

Collínitus: viscous

Collínus: pertaining to hills

Collýbia: round coin-shaped pastries (κόλλυβος = a small coin; κόλλυβα = round pastry)

Colóssus: colossus

Columbétta: small dove (diminutive of *columba* = dove)

Columbínus: pertaining to doves

Cólus: distaff

Comátus: covered with hair

Comósus: covered with hair

Cómtulus: dressed up, adorned

Concéntricus: concentric, having a common center

Conchátus: shell shaped

Cónfluens: confluent

Confragósus: rough, scabrous

Confúsus: confused, untidy

Conglobátus: gathered into a ball or rounded mass

Cónicus: conical

Conígenus: growing on conifer cones (κῶνος = cone; γεννάω = I generate)

Conióphorus: powder bearer (κονία = powder, dust; φερω = I carry)

Connátus: born together

Conócybe: conical head (κῶνος = cone; κύβη = head)

Consobrínus: cousin

Controvérsus: controversial, turned in an opposite direction; as in a mushroom whose edibility is controversial

Cookei: of Cook

Cóprinus: pertaining to dung (κόπρος)

Coralloídes: similar to coral (κοράλλιον = coral)

Córdyceps: club-shaped head (κορδύλη = club; *caput* = head)

Coríolus: tender leather (diminutive of *corium* = leather)

Cornucópiae: of or pertaining to a cornucopia

Cornucopioídes: similar to a *cornucopia*

Coronárius: pertaining to a crown

Coronátus: crowned

Coronílla: small crown (diminutive of *corona*)

Corrugátus: corrugated, wrinkled

Corrúgis: with wrinkles

Corticátus: having a bark, cortex

Cortícium: pertaining to bark (*cortex*)

Cortinárius: pertaining to curtains (*cortina* = curtain, fringe)

Corvínus: black

Corydálina: pertaining to the plant called *Corydalis cáva* (because of its smell)

Cóssus: woodworm

Costátus: ribbed

Costifera: ribbed, having ribs (*costa* = rib; *fero* = I carry)

Cramesínus: bright red (Ar. *qirmiz* = bright red color)

Crássipes: big foot (*crassus* = fat, big; *pes* = foot)

Crateréllus: small cup (diminutive of *crater* = cup)

Crémor: mucilage

Crepidótus: with sandal-shaped ear, that is, cap without stem (*crepida* = sandal; οὖς = ear)

Cretáceus: cretaceous, chalky

Crinipéllis: filamentous skin (*crinis* = hair; *pellis* = skin)

Críspulus: curly (diminutive of *crispus* = curly)

Críspus: curly, curled, crisp

Cristátus: having a crest

Crocátus: yellow, like saffron

Cróceus: yellow, like saffron

Crocipódius: foot or base the color of saffron (*crocum* =

saffron; πούς = foot; πόδιον = small foot)

Crocodílinus: pertaining to crocodiles

Crucíbulum: crucible, lamp

Crustulinifórme: shaped like a bread crust (*crustulina* = a thin bread crust)

Crystállinus: crystalline

Cubénsis: of or pertaining to the island of Cuba

Cúcumis: cucumber

Cudónia: pertaining to a leather helmet (*cudo*)

Cumátilis: of glaucous color, like seawater

Cyanéscens: becoming deep blue (*cyanus* = deep blue)

Cyánopus: blue foot (κυανός = deep blue; πούς = foot)

Cyanoxánthus: blue and yellow (κυανός = deep blue; ξανθός = yellow)

Cyathifórmis: in the shape of a cup (κυανός = cup)

Cyathipódius: footed cup (κυανός = cup; πόδιον = small foot; πούς = foot)

Cyathoídes: similar to a cup (κυανός = cup)

Cyáthula: small cup (diminutive of κυανός = cup)

Cýathus: cup (κυανός)

Cylindrácea: pertaining to a cylinder (κύλινδρος)

Cyphélla: the hollow of the ear (κυφελλα)

Cystodérma: skin with blisters (κύστις = cyst, bladder; δέρμα = skin)

Cytídia: small box (κυτίς)

Daedáleus: artfully wrought, manufactured (δαιδάλεος)

Dealbátus: white, bleached

Decástes: by tens (*decas* = ten)

Deceptívus: deceiving, misleading

Decípiens: deceiving, misleading

Decolórans: fading

Decórus: becoming, befitting

Dégener: degenerate

Delibútus: greasy, smeary

Délicus: weaned

Delicátulus: delicate (diminutive of *delicatus* = delicate)

Deliciósus: delicious

Densifólia: with crowded gills, lamellae (*densus* = thick, close; *fólium* = leaf)

Densíssimus: very thick or dense

Depállens: becoming pale

Dermócybe: head of skin (δέρμα = skin; κύβη = head)

Déstruens: destroyer, destroying

Díbaphus: bicolor, dyed twice

Díchorus: bicolor (δίχροος)

Dícolor: bicolor

Dictyóphora: the bearer of a net (δίκτυον = net; φέρω = I bear, carry)

Dictyópus: with reticulate foot (δίκτυον = net; πούς = foot)

Diffórmis: deformed (*dis* = privative prefix; *forma* = form)

Digitalifórmis: having the form of a finger

Disciótis: with the ear in the form of a disk (δίσκος = disk; οὖς = ear)

Discoídeus: resembling a disk (δίσκος = disk; εἶδος = similitude)

Disseminátus: disseminate, scattered, diffuse

Dissipábilis: easily dissipatable

Distórtus: twisted, distorted

Dochmíopus: with oblique foot (δόχμιος = oblique; πούς = foot)

Doménsticus: domestic

Driméia: acrid (δριμεῖα)

Drosóphilus: friend of the oak tree (δρόσος = oak tree; φίλος = friend)

Dupainii: of M. Dupain, French

Du Portii: of J. du Port, English (1832–1899)

Duriúsculus: hard (diminutive of *durus* = hard)

Dúrus: hard, resistant

Ebúrneus: eburnean, made of ivory

Eccília: rolled up (ἐκκυλίω = I roll up)

Echináceus: pertaining to a hedgehog (ἐχῖνος)

Echinátus: prickly, like a hedgehog (ἐχῖνος)

Echinocéphalus: with the head prickly, like a hedgehog's (ἐχῖνος = hedgehog; κεφαλή = head)

Edódes: aliment (ἐδωδή)

Edúlis: edible

Elaphómyces: deer mushroom (ἔλαφος = deer; μύκης = mushroom)

Elasticus: elastic (ἐλαστής = pulling)

Elátus: raised, lifted up

Elátior: more raised (comparative of *elátus* = raised)

Elátius: same as *elatior*

Élegans: elegant, choice

Elegántior: more elegant (comparative of *elegans* = elegant)

Elegantíssimus: very elegant, the most elegant (superlative of *elegans* = elegant)

Emética: emetic, that which induces vomiting

Entolóma: with the margin rolled inward (ἐντός = inward; λῶμα = margin)

Epipterýgia: covered with membrane (ἐπί = over; πτερύγιον = membrane)

Epixanthus: of a color tending to blonde (ἐπίξανθος)

Equéstre: equestrian

Erébia: dark (ἔρεβος = darkness)

Ericáceus: pertaining to heaths (*érice* = heath)

Erináceus: hedgehog

Eriócoris: woollen helmet (ἔριον = wool; κόρυς = helmet)

Erubéscens: becoming red

Erumbonátus: see *Aerumbonatus*

Erýngii: of or pertaining to *Eryngium*

Erythrópodus: red foot (ερυθρός = red; πούς = foot)

Erýthropus: same as above

Esculéntus: edible

Eupáchypus: with very heavy foot (εὖ = well; παχύς = heavy; πούς = foot)

Eurýporus: with large pores (εὐρύς = large; πόρος = pore)

Evenósus: without veins (*ex* = without; *vena* = vein)

Exalbicans: becoming white (*ex* = particle indicating changing; *albesco* = I become white)

Excélsus: lofty, high

Excipulifórme: with the shape of a container (*excipulum* = container)

Excoriátus: excoriated, flayed

Exídia: staining or perspiring (ἐξιδίω = I stain, I perspire)

Exímius: extraordinary, excellent

Expállens: becoming pale

Exscissus: torn

Extinctórius: pertaining to the extinguisher (*extinctor* = extinguisher)

Fállax: fallacious

Farinipes: with floured, or farinaceous, foot (*farina* = flour; *pes* = foot)

Fasciculáre: pertaining to a fascicle (*fasciculus* = small bundle)

Fastigiátus: cuspidate, terminating in a point

Fávolus: small honeycomb (diminutive of *favus* = honeycomb)

Felinus: feline, sly, treacherous, stealthy like a cat (*felis*)

Félleus: pertaining to bile, gall; very bitter

Fénnicus: of Finland (in place of *Finnicus*; *Finnia* = Finland)

Férrii: of G. Ferri, Italian (ca. 1800–1900)

Ferrugíneus: rusty

Fértilis: fertile

Férulae: of or pertaining to an Umbellifera called *Ferula*

Fibrósus: fibrous

Fíbula: a clasp, buckle, pin

Ficoídes: similar to a fig (*ficus* = fig)

Fimbriátus: with fringes

Fimetárius: pertaining to a dunghill (*fimetum*)

Firmulus: firm (diminutive of *firmus* = firm)

Fischeri: of R. Fischer, German (1861–1939)

Fistulína: small tube (diminutive of *fistula* = tube)

Fistulósus: hollow as a tube

Flabellifórmis: fan shaped (*flabellum* = fan)

Fláccidus: flaccid

Flámmans: blazing

Flámmeus: flaming, blazing

Flámmula: small flame (diminutive of *flamma* = flame)

Flavéscens: becoming yellow

Flávidus: yellow

Flávipes: with yellow foot (*flavus* = yellow; *pes* = foot)

Flavobrúnneus: yellow brown, or yellow and brown (*flavus* = yellow; French *brun* = brown)

Flavocónia: with yellow dust (*flavus* = yellow; κόνις = dust, powder)

Flávus: yellow

Flóccopus: with flocculose foot (*floccus* = a flock or lock of wool; πούς = foot)

Flocculósus: flocculose, with flocci (*flocculus* = lock), woolly

Foétens: fetid, ill-smelling

Foliáceus: foliaceous, leafy

Fomentárius: of a substance that can be used as tinder to light a fire (*fomentum*)

Fómes: any substance that catches fire easily

Formósus: of beautiful form

Fornicátus: arched

Forquignoni: of L. Forquignon

Frágilis: fragile

Frágrans: fragrant

Fritillifórmis: shaped like a dice box (*fritillus* = dice box)

Frondósus: frondent, leafy, having fronds

Fróstii: of C. Frost

Fúlgens: fulgent, shining, bright

Fuligíneoálbus: white and fuliginous (*fuligineus* = fuliginous; *albus* = white)

Fuligíneovioláceus: fuliginous and violaceous, that is, smoky violet (*fuligineus* = fuliginous; *violaceus* = violaceous)

Fuliginósus: fuliginous

Fulmineus: fulminous, exploding

Fulvíssimus: very deep reddish blonde (superlative of *fulvus* = reddish blonde)

Fúlvus: fulvous, reddish blonde

Fumósus: smoky, smoked

Funiculáris: pertaining to a small cord (*funiculus* = a small rope)

Furcátus: bifurcate, that is, with bifid gills (*furca* = fork with two points)

Furfuráceus: pertaining to scurf (*furfura*), scaly

Fuscéscens: becoming black

Fúscopurpúreus: dark purple red (*fuscus* = dark; *purpureus* = purple)

Fuscóruber: dark red (*fúscus* = dark; *ruber* = red)

Fúscovináceus: dark vinous red (*fuscus* = dark; *vinaceus* = pertaining to wine)

Fúscus: dark

Fusifórmis: fusiform (*fusus* = a spindle)

Fúsipes: with fusiform foot (*fusus* = spindle; *pes* = foot)

Galactínia: pertaining to milk (γάλα)

Galéra: pertaining to fur cap called *galerus*

Galerína: diminutive of *galera*

Galericuláta: wearing a small fur cap called *galericulum*

Galóchroa: of the color of milk (γάλα = milk; χρόα = color) or skin as white as milk (γάλα = milk; χρώς = skin)

Gálopus: with foot containing latex (γάλα = milk; πούς = foot)

Gambósus: with well-developed hock (*gamba* = hock)

Ganodérma: with shining skin (γάνος = sheen; δέρμα = skin)

Geáster: star of the earth (γῆ = earth; ἀστήρ = star)

Geástrum: star of the earth (γῆ = earth; *astrum* = star)

Gelatinósus: gelatinous

Gemmátus: adorned with gems

Gentílis: kind, pretty

Geogénius: born from the earth, terricolous (γῆ = earth; γένος = birth)

Geoglóssum: tongue of the earth, or of earth (γῆ = earth; γλῶσσα = tongue)

Geopétalum: petal of the earth, or earthen (γῆ = earth; πέταλον = petal)

Geóphilus: friend of the earth (γῆ = earth; φίλος = friend)

Geophýllus: with earthen gills (γῆ = earth; φύλλον = lamella, gill)

Geórgii: of St. George, celebrated the 23rd of April

Geótropa: turned downward, vertically toward the ground (γῆ = earth; τροπή = turning toward)

Gibbósus: gibbous, humped

Gigánteus: gigantic (γιγάντιος)

Gigantéus: gigantic (γιγαντέιος)

Gigas: giant

Gilvus: light yellow, whitish

Glábrus: glabrous, hairless

Glandulósus: full of glands

Glaucéscens: becoming glaucous (γλαυκός)

Glaucocánus: glaucous and hoary (γλαυκός = glaucous; *canus* = hoary)

Glaucophýllus: with glaucous gills (γλαυκός = glaucous; φύλλον = gill)

Gláucopus: with glaucous foot (γλαυκός = glaucous; πούς = foot)

Gliodérma: with glutinous skin (γλία = glue; δέρμα = skin)

Gloeophýllus: with glutinous gills (γλοιός = gluten; φύλλον = lamella)

Gloiocéphalus: with glutinous head (γλοιός = gluten; κεφαλή = head)

Glutinósus: glutinous

Glycyósmus: with sweet odor (γλυκός = sweet; ὀδμή = odor)

Gomphídius: similar to a nail (γόμφος = nail; εἶδος = similar)

Gómphus: nail

Gongylóphora: bearer of small breads (γογγύλη = breads; φέρω = I carry)

Goniospérmus: with angular seed (γωνία = angle; σπέρμα = seed)

Gaciléntus: gracilent

Grácilus: gracile

Grammocéphalus: with signs on the head (γραμμή = sign; κεφαλή = head)

Grammopódius: with signs on the foot (γραμμή = sign; πούς = foot)

Granulátus: covered with granules

Gravéolens: with a strong odor (*gravis* = heavy, weighty; *oleo* = I smell)

Grevillei: of R. K. Greville, English (1794–1866)

Grifola or *Grifólia* or *Griphola:* braided (γρῖφος = net made of interwoven reeds)

Gríseus: gray (French *gris*)

Groanénse: of the *groane*, moors of Lombardy

Guepínia: of Guepin

Gummósus: gummous, gummy

Guttátus: with droplets

Gymnopilus: with a cap without tegument (γυμνός = naked; πίλευς = cap)

Gymnopódius: with foot lacking tegument (γυμνός = naked; πούς = foot)

Gyrocéphalus: round head (γυρός = round; κεφαλή = head)

Gýrodon: round and denticulate (γυρός = round; ὀδών = tooth)

Gyromítra: round miter (γυρός = round; μîτρα = miter)

Gyróphana: appearing round (if from γυρός = round; φαίνω = I appear), or round torch (if from γυρός = round; φανῆ = torch)

Gyrophrágmium: palisade with disk (γυρός = circle, ring; φράγμα = palisade)

Gyroporus: with round pores (γυρός = round; πόρος = pore)

Haematítes: of the color of blood

Haemátopus: with bloody foot (αîμα = blood; πούς = foot)

Haematospérmus: with blood-colored seed (αîμα = blood; σπέρμα = seed)

Haemorrhoidárius: pertaining to bleeding (αἱμορροîς = hemorrhage)

Hartigii: of R. Hartig, German (1839–1901)

Hatsudake: early mushroom (Jap. *hatsu* = beginning; *dake* = mushroom)

Hebelóma: with obtuse, not sharp, margin (*hebes* = obtuse; λῶμα = margin)

Helomórphus: shaped like a nail (ἧλος = nail; μορφή = form)

Helvélla: any kind of edible aromatic herb

Helvelloídes: resembling *Helvella*

Helvéolus: yellowish, blondish (diminutive of *helvus* = yellowish, blonde)

Helvéticus: of Switzerland (*Helvetia*)

Hélvolus: yellowish, blondish (diminutive of *helvus* = yellowish)

Helvus: yellowish blonde

Hemicyáneus: semiblue (ἥμι = a half; κυανός = deep blue)

Hemisphaéricus: hemispherical (ἥμι = a half; σφαîρα = sphere)

Hepáticus: pertaining to the liver

Herícium: pertaining to a hedgehog (*hericius*)

Heterophýllus: with irregular lamellae (ἕτερος = different; φύλλον = lamella)

Hexagonoídes: appearing hexagonal (εξαγονος = hexagon; εîδος = form)

Hiáscens: that which opens

Hiemális: of winter

Hinnúleus: a fawn

Hirnéola or *Hirníola*: small pitcher (diminutive of *hirnea* = pitcher for wine)

Hirsútus: hirsute, hairy

Hírtipes: with bristly foot (*hirtus* = bristly, shaggy; *pes* = foot)

Híspidus: hispid

Holoséricus: all silken (ὅλος = all, entire; σηρική = silken)

Hórdum: swollen, puffed up (either from *hordior* = I am full of barley, or *horda* = pregnant cow)

Hornemánnii: of Hornemann

Horténsis: pertaining to the gardens

Hyacínthinus: of or pertaining to the jasmine

Hýbridus: hybrid

Hýdnum: truffle (ὕδνον)

Hydrócybe: head of water (ὕδωρ = water; κυβή = head)

Hydróphilus: liking water (ὕδωρ = water; φίλος = friend)

Hygrocybe: moist, humid head (ὑγρός = humid; κύβη = head)

Hygrometricus: measuring humidity (ὑγρός = wet, moist; μετρικός = metric)

Hygróphanus: appearing wet, humid (ὑγρός = wet, humid; φαίνω = I appear)

Hygrophorópsis: similar to *Hygrophorus*

Hygróphorus: bearer of moisture (υγρός = moist, humid; φέρω = I carry)

Hymenochaéte: hymenium with bristles (ὑμέναιος = hymenium; χαίτη = hair)

Hypholóma: with fringed margin (ὕφος = tissue; λῶμα = margin)

Hypódrys: growing under oaks (ὑπο = under; δρῦς = oak)

Hypothéius: little less than yellow (ὑπο = under; θεîον = sulfur)

Hypóxylon: little less than wood (ὑπο = under; ξύλον = wood)

Ianthinoxánthus: violet and yellow (ἰάνθινος = violet; ξανθός = yellow)

Iaponicus: Japanese (*Iaponia* = Japan)

Ichorátus: intoxicated (ἰχώρ = blood of the gods, lymph of the plants, putrefaction, poison)

Igniarius: pertaining to the fire

Illinítus: greasy, smeary

Illótus: not washed, dirty

Illúdens: deceiving

Imbricátus: covered with tiles, imbricate

Impénnis: featherless

Imperiális: imperial

Impolítus: not clean

Impudícus: immodest

Inamoénus: not pleasant

Inaurátus: gilded

Incílis: ditch, brook

Inclinátus: sloping, slanting

Índigo: blue, indigo

Indusiátus: wearing an overall

Ínfula: the head covering of a priest in the early Christian church

Infundibulifórmis: funnel shaped (*infundibulum* = funnel)

Inócybe: fibrous head (ἴς = fiber; κύβη = head)

Ínolens: odorless or without perfume; hence ill-smelling

Inolóma: fibrous margin (ἴς = fiber; λῶμα = margin)

Inonótus: fibrous ear (ἴς = fiber; οὖς = ear)

Inornátus: unadorned

Ínquinans: polluting

Insígnis: with some distinctive sign, illustrious, remarkable

Íntegra: whole, entire, untouched

Integrélla: diminutive of *integra*

Intermédius: intermediate

Intybáceus: pertaining to the endive

Inúnctus: anointed

Invérsus: upside down, overturned

Involútus: rolled up

Inzéngae: of G. Inzenga, Italian (1815–1887)

Ionochlórus: violaceous and green, or violaceous and yellow (ἴον = violet; χλωρός = green or yellow)

Írinus: pertaining to the iris

Írpex: harrow

Irrorátus: moistened by dew

Iunquílleus: pertaining to the yellow narcissus (Sp. *junquillo*)

Iuránus: of the Jura Mountains, between France and Switzerland

Ixócomus: viscous hair (ἰξός = bird lime; κόμη = hair)

Karsténii: of P. A. Karsten, German (1834–1917)

Krombhólzia: of J. Krombholz, Czechoslovak (1782–1843)

Kymatódes: similar to a wave (κῦμα = wave; εîδος = form)

Laccária: pertaining to paint (Per. *lak* = paint)

Laccáta: painted (Per. *lak* = paint)

Lácerus: lacerated

Lachnea: woolly (λαχναῖα)

Lachnocládium: woolly twig (λαχναῖα = woolly; κλάδιον = twig)

Laciniáta: frayed, torn (*lacinia* = a hem; *laciniae* = rags)

Lacrymabúndus: weeping

Lacrymária: pertaining to the tears (*lacryma* = tear)

Lactárius: pertaining to milk, or giving milk

Lácteus: milky

Lactífluus: secreting milk (*lac* = milk; *fluo* = I let flow)

Lacunósus: with cavities

Laétus: glad

Laévis: smooth

Laminósus: lamellar, lamellate

Langeii: of J. E. Lange, German (1864–1941)

Laníger: bearer of wool

Lárgus: wide, large

Largusoides: similar to *largus*

Laricínus: pertaining to the larch tree (*larix*)

Lascívus: wanton

Laterális: pertaining to bricks

Laterítius: same as above

Latisporus: with large seeds (*latus* = large, wide; σπορά = seed)

Laurocérasi: of the *Prunus laurocerasus*

Lenticuláris: pertaining to small dewy droplets (*lenticula* = small lens)

Lentiginósus: freckled

Lentinéllus: diminutive of *Lentinus*

Lentínus: rather tenacious, rather pliable (*lentus* = tenacious, pliable)

Lenzítes: of H. O. Lenz, German botanist

Leonínus: pertaining to the lion

Leónis: of the lion (*leo*)

Leótia: smooth (λειότης = smoothness)

Lepídeus: scaly (λεπίς = scale, squama)

Lépidus: agreeable, amiable

Lepióta: squamose ear (λεπίς = squama; οὖς = ear)

Lepiotoides: similar to *Lepiota*

Lepísta: wine pitcher

Lepórinus: pretty (*lepos* = gracefulness)

Leporínus: leporine; of or pertaining to the hare (*lepus* = hare)

Leptónia: fine, delicate, or like a small coin (λεπτόν = small coin; λεπτή = fine, delicate)

Leptóporus: with not too conspicuous pores (λεπτός = fine, light; πόρος = pore)

Léptopus: with thin foot (λεπτός = thin, fine; πούς = foot)

Leucocéphalus: with white head (λευκός = white; κεφαλή = head)

Leucocortinarius: white *Cortinarius* (λευκός = white)

Leucogáster: with white entrails (λευκός = white; γαστήρ = entrails)

Leucomelas: white and black (λευκός = white; μέλας = black)

Leucophaéus: white and dark (λευκός = white; φαιός = dark)

Leucóporus: with white pores (λευκός = white; πόρος = pore)

Léucopus: with white foot (λευκός = white; πούς = foot)

Levigátus: smooth

Lévis: smooth

Lignícola: growing on wood (*lignum* = wood; *colo* = I live)

Lignyótus: with fuliginous ear (λιγνύς = soot; οὖς = ear)

Ligula: small tongue (same as *lingula*, diminutive of *lingua*)

Liláceus: of amethystine color (Per. *lilak*)

Lilacínus: same as above

Limacélla: small snail (diminutive of *limax* = snail)

Limacínus: pertaining to snails (*limax* = snail)

Limácium: same as *limacinus*

Linnaéi: of C. v. Linné, Swedish (1707–1778)

Lividoálbus: livid white (*lividus* = livid; *albus* = white)

Lividopalléscens: becoming livid pale (*lividus* = livid; *pallesco* = I become pale)

Lívidus: livid

Lóngipes: with long foot (*longus* = long; *pes* = foot)

Loricátus: armored

Lúbricus: slippery

Lúcidus: glossy, polished

Lucífer: bearer of light (*lux* = light; *fero* = I carry)

Lucórum: of the sacred woods (*lucus* = sacred wood)

Lúgubris: mournful

Lupínus: lupine, pertaining to a wolf

Lupuletórum: pertaining to hop plantations (if from *lupuletus* = hop plantation)

Lúridus: dirty, filthy

Lúscinus: with a blind eye

Lutéolus: yellowish (diminutive of *luteus* = yellow)

Lutéscens: turning to yellowish

Lúteus: yellow

Lycoperdoides: similar to *Lycoperdon*

Lycopérdon: flatulence of a wolf (λύκος = wolf; πέρδομαι = to send forth air from the intestines)

Lyophyllum: with loose, free lamellae (λύω = I undo, loose; φύλλον = gills, lamellae)

Macrocystídia: with huge cystidia (μακρός = big; κύστις = bladder)

Macropódia: with large foot (μακρός = big, tall; πόδιον = small foot; πούς = foot)

Mácropus: large foot (μακρός = large, tall; πούς = foot)

Maculátus: stained

Mádidus: soaked

Magnátum: of dignitaries (magnates)

Mágnus: great

Maiális: of or pertaining to the month of May (*Maius*)

Mairei: of R. Maire, French Algerian (1878–1949)

Malicórius: pertaining to the rind of the pomegranate (*malicorium*)

Mammósus: with mammary protuberances

Máppa: napkin

Marásmius: withered, emaciated (μαρασμός = a wasting away)

Marginátus: with margin

Mariae: of Maria

Marzúolus: of or pertaining to the month of March (*Mars*)

Mastoídeus: similar to a breast (μαστός = a breast; εἶδος = form)

Matsutake: pine mushroom (Jap. *matsu* = pine; *take* = mushroom)

Máximus: the greatest

Médius: medium, of intermediate size, between large and small

Melaléucus: black and white (μέλας = black; λευκός = white)

Melanocéphalus: with black head (μέλας = black; κεφαλή = head)

Melanogáster: with black entrails (μέλας = black; γαστήρ = entrails)

Melanoléuca: black and white (μέλας = black; λευκός = white)

Melánopus: black foot (μέλας = black; πούς = foot)

Melanósporus: with black seed (μέλας = black; σπορά = seed)

Melaspérma: with black seed (μέλας = black; σπέρμα = seed)

Meleagris: guinea hen (μελεαγρίς)

Melegróides: similar to *meleagris*

Melizeus: pertaining to honey (μέλι = honey)

Mélleus: pertaining to honey

Melliolens: with honey smell (*mel* = honey; *oleo* = I give off odor)

Mérisma: subdivision (μέρισμα)

Merúlius: dead drunk (if from *merulentus*)

Mesentéricus: pertaining to the circumvolutions of the mesentery (μεσεντέριον = membrane enfolding the small intestine)

Metátus: measured (*metor* = I measure, I am measured)

Metulaéspora: with cone- or pyramid-shaped seed (*metula* = small pyramid, or small cone; σπορά = seed)

Mexicánus: of or pertaining to Mexico (*Mexicum*)

Micáceus: pertaining to mica (*mica* = granule, crumb)

Microglóssum: small tongue (μικρός = small; γλῶσσα = tongue)

Miniátus: painted with minium, red lead

Mirábilis: wonderful

Mitis: mild, not acrid; or tender, not hard

Mitíssimus: very mild

Mitróphora: carrying a miter (μίτρα = miter; φέρω = I carry)

Mitrula: small miter (diminutive of *mitra*)

Móllis: soft, tender

Molybdites: pertaining to lead (μόλιβδος)

Monachélla: small nun (diminutive of μοναχή = nun, alone, isolated)

Montánus: growing in the mountains

Morchella: morel (Ger. *Morchel*)

Morgáni: of A. Morgan, American (1836–1907)

Mucídulus: slimy mucus running from the nose (diminutive of *múcidus* = slimy)

Mucífluus: secreting mucus (*mucus* = mucus; *fluo* = I let flow)

Mucósus: mucous

Múlticeps: with many heads (*multus* = much; *caput* = head)

Multífidus: divided in many parts

Multifórmis: multiform

Múndulus: rather clean (diminutive of *mundus* = clean)

Muricátus: pointed

Murícinus: purple (*murex* = a shell from which purple is extracted)

Murináceus: pertaining to gray mice (diminutive of *murinus* = of a gray mouse)

Murinéllus: rather gray (diminutive of *murinus* = of the gray mouse)

Murínus: of a gray mouse

Muscárius: pertaining to flies

Muscígenus: generated by the mosses (*muscus* = moss; γεννάω = I generate)

Mustelínus: pertaining to martens (*mustela* = marten)

Mutábilis: changeable

Mycéna: pertaining to mushrooms (μύκης = mushroom)

Mycenastrum: star mushroom (μύκης = mushroom; ἄστρον = star)

Mycoléptodon: mushroom with thin teeth (μύκης = mushroom; λεπτός = thin; ὀδών = tooth)

Myómyces: mouse mushroom (μυός = mouse; μύκης = mushroom)

Myrióstoma: thousand mouths (μυριός = countless; στόμα = mouth)

Myxácium: mucilaginous (μύξα = mucilage)

Myxcollýbia: mucilaginous *Collybia* (μύξα = mucilaginous)

Nánus: dwarf

Nápipes: with foot thickened like that of rape (*napus* = rape; *pes* = foot)

Nápus: rape

Naucínus: pertaining to the nut shell (*naucum* = nut shell)

Nauseósus: nauseating (ναυσία = nausea, seasickness)

Nebrodénsis: of the Nebrodi Mountains (*Nebrodes* = mountain range of Sicily)

Nebuláris: pertaining to fog (*nebula* = fog)

Necátor: killer

Negléctus: neglected

Nematolóma: with filament along the margin (νῆμα = thread; λῶμα = margin)

Nemóreus: woody, sylvan

Nevrophýllum: with nervations instead of gills (νεῦρον = nerve; φύλλον = lamella)

Nidorósus: with burnt smell

Nídulans: nesting

Nidulária: pertaining to the nests (*nidus* = nest)

Níger: black

Nigra: black (f.)

Nigrescens: becoming black

Nígripes: with black foot (*niger* = black; *pes* = foot)

Niǵritéllus: rather black (diminutive of *niger* = black)

Nigroflocculósus: with black flocci (*niger* = black; *flocculus* = flock)

Nígrum: black

Nimbátus: enveloped by a nimbus, cloudy

Niphoídes: similar to snow (νίφα = snow; εἶδος = form)

Nítidus: spotless, clean, shiny

Nivális: snow white

Nivéscens: becoming snow white

Níveus: white as snow

Nolánea: pertaining to a bell (*nola* = bell)

Núdus: naked, bare

Nýctalis: pertaining to night darkness

Obcónipes: with rather conical foot (*ob* = about, almost; *conus* = cone; *pes* = foot)

Obrússeus: yellow like fine gold (*obrussa* = gold refining)

Obscúrus: dark

Obsolétus: soiled, worn-out, obsolete

Ochráceovirens: of yellow ocher color, but becoming green (*ochraceus* = yellow ocher; *vireo* = I become green)

Ochráceus: yellow as ocher

Ochroléucus: yellowish and white (ὠχρος = yellowish; λευκός = white)

Odóntia: pertaining to the teeth (ὀδών = tooth)

Odorátus: perfumed

Odórifer: perfumed

Odórus: perfumed

Oedemátopus: with edematous foot (οἴδημα = edema; πούς = foot)

Officinális: usable in pharmaceutics and distillery

Oleárius: pertaining to the olive trees

Ólidus: giving off odor

Oliváceoálbus: olivaceous and white (*olivaceus* = olivaceous; *albus* = white)

Oliváceus: olivaceous

Oliváscens: turning to olivaceous

Omphália: pertaining to the navel, that is, with small depression at the center of the cap (ὀμφαλός = umbilicus, navel)

Omphalódes: similar to *Omphalia*

Omphalomýces: umbilicate mushroom, that is, with a small depression in the center of the cap (ομφαλός = umbilicus; μύκης = mushroom)

Omphalótus: umbilicate ear (ομφαλός = umbilicus; οὖς = ear)

Onóticus: pertaining to the donkey ear (ὄνος = donkey; οὖς = ear)

Orcélla: small vase (*orca* = a clay vase, dice box)

Oréades: mountain nymph

Oréinus: mountainous (ὀρεινός = of the mountains)

Orellánus: pertaining to mountains (ὄρος = mountain)

Orírubens: reddening in the mountains (ὄρος = mountains; *rubeo* = I redden)

Osmóporus: with perfumed pores (οσμή = odor, perfume; πόρος = pore)

Ostreátus: covered with oysters, like a mass of oysters

Otídea: similar to an ear (οὖς = ear; εἶδος = form)
Ovátus: oval
Overhóltsii: of L. O. Overholts, American (1890–1946)
Ovínus: pertaining to sheep
Ovoídea: similar to an egg (*ovum* = egg)
Oxidábilis: oxidizable

Páchypus: heavy, bulky foot (παχύς = thick; πούς = foot)
Pállens: paling
Palléscens: turning pale
Pállidus: pale
Palmátus: adorned with palm fronds, similar to a palm frond or the palm of the hand
Paludósus: pertaining to swamps
Palumbínus: pertaining to ringdoves
Panaéolus: dazzling (παναίολος)
Panéllus: diminutive of *Panus*
Pantherínus: pertaining to a panther
Panuoídes: similar to *Panus*
Pánus: tumor
Papilionáceus: pertaining to butterflies (*papilio* = butterfly)
Parasíticus: parasitic
Parazúrea: related to *azurea* (παρά = beside)
Pardínus: pertaining to leopards (*pardus* = leopard)
Parthenopéius: of the city of Naples (if from *Parthenope* = Naples); or virginal (if from παρθενοπήιος)
Párvulus: small
Páscuus: of the pastures
Patouillardi: of N. Patouillard, French (1854–1926)
Patricius: patrician
Paxillus: peg, stick
Pectinadoídes: similar to *Pectinata*
Pectinátus: combed
Peliánthinus: livid flower (πελιός = livid; ἄνθος = flower)
Pellítus: covered with skin or fur
Pellúcidus: very glossy, very polished
Peltereaui: of E. R. Peltereau, French (1842–1928)
Pénetrans: penetrating
Penióphara: bearer of fabric (πηνίον = fabric; φέρω = I carry)
Perénnis: lasting for several years
Pérforans: piercing
Pergaménus: pertaining to the parchment (περγαμηνὴ = skin of Pergamum)
Perlátus: adorned with pearls (if from Italian *perla*), or largely diffused, widespread (if from *perlate* = very widely)
Permágnus: very large
Permíxtus: mixed
Peronátus: booted
Perrárus: very rare
Personátus: masked
Pes cáprae: goat's foot
Pessúndatus: ruined
Petaloídes: similar to a petal (*petalum* = petal, lamina)
Petasátus: with wide-brimmed hat
Peziza: mushroom with very small, or completely without, (stem (πέζυζ)
Phaéocollýbia: dark *Collybia* (φαιός = dark)
Phaéolepióta: dark *Lepiota* (φαιός = dark, obscure)
Phaeóporus: with dark pores (φαιός = dark; πόρος = pore)
Phalloídes: similar to *Phallus*
Phállus: swollen, puffed up (φαλλόω = I inflate)
Phéllinus: corky (φέλλινος)
Phlébia: pertaining to the veins (φλεψ = vein)
Phlegmacium: mucous (φλέγμα = mucus)
Phlogiótis: flaming ear (φλοξ = flame; οὖς = ear)
Phoeníceus: purple
Pholídeus: squamose (φολίς = squama)
Pholióta: with squamose ear (φολίς = squama; οὖς = ear)

Phosphóreus: bearer of light
Phyllóporus: with the gills connected pore-wise (φύλλον = lamella; πόρος = pore)
Phyllotópsis: similar to (a mushroom with) lamellae (φύλλον = lamella; ὄψις = appearance, form)
Physomítra: similar to a miter (φύσις = nature, figure, form; μίτρα = miter)
Picáceus: pertaining to the magpie (*pica* = magpie)
Píceae: pertaining to the pine (*picea*)
Pícinus: pitch black
Pícipes: black foot (*pix* = pitch; *pes* = foot)
Píctus: painted
Pinícola: living among pines (*pinus* = pine; *colo* = I live)
Piperátus: peppery
Piptóporus: with easily detachable pores (πίπτω = I fall, I come off; πόρος = pore)
Pirifórme: pear shaped (*pirum* = a pear)
Piriodórus: smelling like a pear (*pirum* = a pear; *odorus* = fragrant)
Pisólithus: stone peas (πίσος = peas; λίθος = stone)
Pistilláris: pertaining to the pestle (*pistillum* = pestle)
Plácidus: pleasant
Placómyces: flat mushroom (πλαξ = flat surface; μύκης = mushroom)
Platyphýllus: with broad gills (πλατύς = large, broad; φύλλον = lamella)
Pláutus: flat, wide
Pleurotéllus: diminutive of *pleurotus*
Pleurótus: with the ear on the side (πλευρόν = on the side, beside; οὖς = ear)
Plicatúra: fold
Plórans: weeping
Plumolósa: with small feathers (*plumula* = small feather)
Plutéolus: diminutive of *Pluteus*
Plúteus: pluteus, bracket, console
Poëtarum: of the poets (*poëta*)
Polygrámma: with many signs, with many lines (πολύς = much; γράμμα = sign, line)
Polymórphus: assuming several forms (πολύς = much; μορφή = form)
Polýmyces: multiple or cespitose mushrooms (πολύς = much; μύκης = mushroom)
Polypílus: with many caps (πολύς = much; πίλεος = cap)
Polyporéllus: diminutive of *Polyporus*
Polýporus: with many pores (πολύς = much; πόρος = pore)
Polýrrhizon: with many roots (πολύς = much; ῥίζα = root)
Polysáccum: with multiple sack (πολύς = much; σάκκος = sack)
Polystíctus: with many marks, speckled (πολύς = much; στίκτης = mark)
Pomáceus: pertaining to fruit trees (*pomum* = fruit)
Pompósus: pompous, magnificently dressed
Ponderósus: heavy
Populínus: of or pertaining to the poplar (*populus* = poplar)
Porcellánus: pertaining to small pigs (*porcellus* = small pig)
Porninsis: of Pornin, French
Porothélium: pierced nipple, teat (πόρος = pore; θηλή = nipple, teat)
Porphyrius: purple (πορφύρεος)
Porphyrósporus: with purple seeds (πορφύρεος = purple; σπορά = seed)
Portentósus: prodigious
Potroni: of M. Potron, French
Praécox: precocious, premature, ripe before the time
Praéstans: imposing
Prasiósmus: with odor similar to that of the leek (πράσιον = leek; οσμή = odor)
Pratélla: of meadows (from the diminutive of *pratum* = meadow)
Praténsis: of meadows, fields
Procérus: tall

Próminens: prominent, standing out

Próximus: very near

Pruinósus: covered with hoarfrost or bloom

Prunuloídes: similar to *prunulus*

Prúnulus: diminutive of *prunus* = plum

Psallióta: with fringed ear (ψάλλιον = a curb; οὖς = ear)

Psámmopus: sandy foot (ψάμμος = sand; πούς = foot)

Psáthyra: fragile

Psathyrélla: diminutive of *Psathyra*

Pseudoacérbum: likely to be confused with *acerbum*

Pseudócolus: likely to be confused with *colus*

Pseudocónicus: likely to be confused with the *conicus*

Pseudodélica: likely to be confused with the *delica*

Pseudoíntegra: likely to be confused with the *integra*

Pseudoporphýria: likely to be confused with *porphyria*

Pseudorosácea: likely to be confused with *rosacea*

Pseudorubéscens: likely to be confused with *rubescens*

Pseudoscáber: likely to be confused with *scaber*

Psilócybe: uncovered head (ψίλος = uncovered, naked; κυβή = head)

Psittacinus: pertaining to parrot

Pterósporus: with winged seed (πτερόν = wing; σπορά = seed)

Ptérula: little wing (diminutive of πτερόν = wing)

Pubéscens: pubescent, becoming downy

Púbipes: downy foot (*pubes* = down; *pes* = foot)

Pudícus: modest

Pudorínus: modest, rosy (*pudor* = modesty)

Puelláris: of or pertaining to a girl

Pulchérrimus: very beautiful

Pulmonárius: of, like, or affecting the lungs

Púlverobóletus: pulverulent *Boletus*

Pulveruléntus: powdery

Punctátus: dotted

Puníceus: purple

Purpuráscens: becoming purple, or almost purple

Purpúreus: purple

Púrus: pure, clear

Pusíllus: small, little

Pustulátus: covered with pustules

Pyriodorus: smelling like fire (if from πύρ = fire), a pear (if from *pirum* = pear)

Pyrógalus: with burning latex (πύρ = fire; γάλα = milk)

Pyxidátus: shaped like a pyx or box

Quadrífidus: fissured or divided in four parts

Queletii: of L. Quelet, French (1832–1899)

Quercínus: of or pertaining to the oak tree

Quiétus: quiet, solitary

Rádians: shining, bright

Radicans: taking root, rooting

Radicátus: rooted

Radicosus: with many roots

Ratodinense: of the valley of Ratodin, near Prague

Rádulum: pertaining to scrapers (*radula* = scraper)

Ramária: pertaining to branches (*ramus* = branch)

Rameális: of the branches (*rameus* = of the branches)

Ramósipes: with branchy foot (*rámosus* = branchy, branched; *pes* = foot)

Ráncidus: rancid

Recutítus: flayed, ulcerated, circumcised

Regális: pertaining to king

Régius: pertaining to king

Rehmii: of H. Rehm, German (ca. 1800–1900)

Repándus: folded backward or upward

Repraesentáneus: representative

Resímus: folded upward or backward

Reticulátus: woven netlike

Rhacódes: ragged (ῥακώδης)

Rhizópogon: bearded root (ῥίζα = root; πώγων = beard)

Rhodocollýbia: pink *Collybia* (ῥόδον = a rose)

Rhodócybe: rosy head (ῥόδον = a rose; κυβή = head)

Rhododéndri: of the rhododendron (*rhododendron*)

Rhodopaxíllus: rosy *Paxillus* (ῥόδον = rose)

Rhodophýllus: with rosy lamellae (ῥόδον = rose; φύλλον = lamella)

Rhodopólius: of a bright, pale rosy color (ῥόδον = rose; πολιόν = whitish, shining)

Rhodóporus: with pinkish pores (ῥόδον = rose; πόρος = pore)

Rhódotus: rosy ear (ῥόδον = rose; οὖς = ear)

Rhodoxánthus: rosy and yellow (ῥόδον = rose; ξανθός = yellow)

Rimósipes: with fissured foot (*rimosus* = fissured; *pes* = foot)

Rimósus: fissured

Rivulósus: pertaining to brook (if from *rivulus* = brook)

Robústus: strong, stout

Roméllii: of L. Romell, Swedish (1854–1927)

Rosáceus: rosaceous, rosy

Rosáns: rosy

Roseocárneus: flesh pink (*roseus* = rosy; *carneus* = flesh color)

Róseus: rosy

Rótula: little wheel (diminutive of *rota* = wheel)

Rousselii: of L. Roussel, French (—1916)

Rozítes: from E. Roze, French (1833–1900)

Rubéllus: bright red

Rubeolárius: rather red (either from *rubeola* = red star, or *rubeolus* = rather red)

Rúber: red

Rubéscens: becoming reddish

Rubiginósus: rusty

Rúbrosanguíneus: blood red color (*ruber* = red; *sanguineus* = sanguineous)

Ruféscens: becoming blonde or reddish blonde

Rúfus: blonde or reddish blonde

Rugátus: corrugated

Rugósus: rugose, wrinkled

Rússula: reddish (diminutive of *russa* = red)

Rútilans: shining, glowing

Rútilus: of shining color like red gold

Saccátus: sack shaped (*saccus* = sack)

Sacchariolens: smelling of sugar (*saccharon* = sugar; *oleo* = I smell)

Saepiárius: pertaining to a hedge (if from *saepes* = hedge)

Saévus: cruel, horrible

Salicínus: pertaining to willow (*salix* = willow tree)

Salmonicolor: with same color as that of salmon meat (*salmo* = salmon; *color* = color)

Sandícinus: carmine or flesh color

Sanguífluus: flowing with blood (*sanguis* = blood; *fluo* = I let flow)

Sanguíneus: sanguineous, bloodred

Sanguinoléntus: sanguinolent, bloody

Saniósus: pertaining to pus, sanies (*sanies*)

Sapíneus: pertaining to fir tree (*sapinus*)

Saponáceus: saponaceous, soapy

Sarcocéphalus: fleshy head (σάρξ = flesh; κεφαλή = head)

Sárcodon: fleshy tooth (σάρξ = flesh; ὀδών = tooth)

Sarcóscypha: fleshy cup (σάρξ = flesh; σκύφος = cup)

Sarcosphaéra: fleshy sphere (σάρξ = flesh; σφαῖρα = sphere)

Sardónius: very acrid or bitter (σαρδόνιον = a plant whose flavor makes the lips contract)

Sátanas: Satan (Heb. *satan* = tempter)

Saundérsi: of W. Saunders, English (1809–1879)

Scáber: scabrous, scabby, rough

Scabrósus: scabrous, scabby, rough

Sculpturátus: sculptured, carved (*sculptura* = a sculpture)

Schellenbergiae: of Schellenberg

Schizophýllum: with the lamellae halving along the edges (σχίζω = I cleave; φύλλον = lamella, leaf)

Schweinitzii: of L. v. Schweinitz, German American (1780–1834)

Sciódes: similar to shadow or shade (σκία = a shadow; εἶδος = form)

Sclerángium: hard vase (σκληρός = hard; ἀγγεῖον = vase)

Sclerodérma: hard skin (σκληρός = hard; δέρμα = skin)

Scobináceus: pertaining to a rasp (*scobina*)

Scobinélla: little rasp (diminutive of *scobina* = rasp)

Scorodónius: pertaining to garlic (σκόροδον = garlic)

Scótioarrhágadus: dark and without cracking (σκότιος = dark; ἀ = without; ῥαγάς = a crack)

Scrobiculátus: with small erosions (*scrobiculus* = small erosion)

Scutellátus: bowl shaped (*scutella*)

Scutellina: little bowl (diminutive of *scutella* = bowl)

Scutulátus; shaped like a rhomb, checkered

Sebácina: pertaining to tallow (*sebum*, or *saebum*)

Seiúnctus: disjoined

Semiglobátus: hemispheric (*semi* = half; *globus* = ball)

Semilanceátus: shaped like a half lance (*semi* = half; *lanceatus* = in the form of a lance)

Semilíber: half free (*semi* = half; *liber* = free)

Semiovátus: shaped like a half egg (*semi* = half; *ovatus* = oval)

Semipileátus: half covered with felt (*semi* = half; *pileatus* = with a felt cap)

Semisanguífluus: bleeding less than *sanguifluus* (*semi* = half)

Semisanguíneus: less sanguineous than *sanguineus* (*semi* = half)

Semivestítus: only half covered (*semi* = half; *vestitus* = covered)

Semótus: removed, remote

Sempervívus: house leek

Sépium: of the hedge (*sepes* = hedge)

Sepultária: pertaining to something buried (*sepultus* = buried)

Serífluus: flowing with serum (*serum* = serum; *fluo* = I flow)

Serótinus: late, of evening

Shiitake: mushroom growing on *Q. hodoghi* (Jap. *shii* = hodoghi oak; Jap. *take* = mushroom)

Sibíricus or *Sibéricus:* of or pertaining to Siberia

Silvaticoídes: similar to *silvatica*

Silváticus: wild, of the woods

Silvéstris: sylvan, of the woods

Silvícola: living in the forests

Sinápizans: with the flavor of mustard

Sinuátus: bended, curved

Sinuósus: sinuous, curved

Sistotréma: with well-fixed pores (if from *sisto* = I make firm; τρῆμα = hole)

Smarágdinus: pertaining to emeralds

Solitárius: solitary

Sordídulus: dirty (diminutive of *sordidus* = dirty, soiled)

Sordídus: filthy, dirty

Sorórius: of or pertaining to sister

Spadíceus: with the color of a fresh date (*spadix* = frond of a palm tree with ripe dates)

Sparássis: dilaceration (σπάραξις)

Spathulária: pertaining to a spatula (*spathula* = spatula)

Speciósus: beautiful

Spectábilis: admirable, wonderful

Sphaeróbolus: sphere thrower (σφαῖρα = sphere; βόλος = throwing)

Sphaerocéphalus: with spheric head (σφαῖρα = sphere; κεφαλή = head)

Sphaerósporus: with spheric seeds (σφαῖρα = sphere; σπορά = seed)

Sphagnórum: of the sphagnum (*sphágnos*)

Sphinctrinus: with tightening (*sphincter* = string to tighten)

Spilómeus: pertaining to the soiling (σπίλομα = stain)

Spinulósus: with small thorns (*spinula* = little thorn)

Spíssus: thick

Spléndens: shining

Spodoléucus: cinereous (σποδός = ashes; λευκός = white)

Spongíola: little sponge

Squálidus: soiled

Squamátus: with scales

Squamósus: with scales, with squamae

Squamúlifer: bearer of little squamae (*squamula* = little squama; *fero* = I carry)

Squamulósipes: with the foot covered by squamules (*squamula* = squamule; *pes* = foot)

Squarrósoadipósa: covered with pustules and fat (*squarrosa* = covered with pustules; *adiposa* = fat)

Squarrosoídes: similar to *squarrosa*

Squarrósus: covered with pustules

Squarrulósus: covered with little pustules (diminutive of *squarrosus* = covered with pustules)

Stans: straight

Stellátus: starry

Stéreum: hard (στερεός)

Sterquilínus: pertaining to the dunghill (*sterquilinum*)

Stipatíssima: very close (superlative of *stipatus* = close, dense)

Stipitárius: pertaining to the stem (*stipes* = stem, stalk, trunk)

Stipitátus: with stem (*stipes* = stem, stalk, trunk)

Stípticus: astringent, tart

Strangulátus: throttled, strangled

Striátus: striate

Stríctipes: thin foot (*strictus* = narrow; *pes* = foot)

Stríctus: narrow

Strigósus: emaciated, lean

Strobiláceus: pertaining to pinecone (*strobilus* = pinecone)

Strobilifórmis: shaped like a pinecone (*strobilus* = pinecone)

Strobilómyces: pinecone-shaped mushroom (στρόβιλος = pinecone; μύκης = mushroom)

Strophária: pertaining to pectoral bands (*stróphium* = pectoral band)

Suavéolens: sweet smelling

Subannulátus: similar to *annulatus* (*sub* = almost; *annulatus* = with ring)

Subbalteátus: with a not too conspicuous belt (*sub* = almost; *balteum* = belt)

Subdúlcis: almost sweet (*sub* = almost; *dulcis* = sweet)

Subincarnátus: tending to flesh color (*sub* = almost; *incarnatus* = flesh colored)

Sublaterítius: almost the color of brick (*sub* = almost; *lateritium* = brick)

Sublúteus: almost yellow, or similar to *luteus* (*sub* = almost; *luteus* = yellow)

Subperonátus: with not too conspicuous boots (*sub* = almost; *peronatus* = with boots)

Subrutiláscens: almost rutilant (*sub* = almost; *rutilasco* = I become bright, I become red)

Subsquarrósa: similar to *squarrosa* (*sub* = almost)

Subtomentósus: similar to *tomentosus* (*sub* = almost)

Succósus: juicy, succulent

Súdus: dry, not wet

Sulfúreus or *Sulphureus:* sulfurous

Sulphuréscens: becoming sulfur (*sulphur* = sulfur)

Suspéctus: suspect

Tabéscens: decomposing

Tabácinus: of the tobacco plant

Tábidus: decomposed, corrupted

Telamónia: pertaining to belts ($\tau\epsilon\lambda\alpha\mu\omega\nu$ = belt)

Tenacélla: tenacious (from the diminutive of *tenax* = tenacious)

Tephrótricus: adorned with cinereous braids ($\tau\acute{\epsilon}\phi\rho\alpha$ = ashes; $\theta\rho\acute{\iota}\xi$ = braid)

Téner: tender

Terebrátus: pierced

Terfézia: a genus of hypogeal mushrooms, called in Arabic *terfez*

Térreus: ashen, pallid

Terrígena: born from, or springing from, the earth

Tesselátus or *Tessellatus:* mosaiclike

Theiógalus: with yellow latex ($\theta\epsilon\hat{\iota}o\nu$ = sulfur; $\gamma\acute{\alpha}\lambda\alpha$ = milk)

Thýinos: pertaining to citrus fruits ($\theta\acute{\upsilon}o\nu$ = the citrus plant)

Tigrínus: pertaining to tigers

Tinctórius: used for dyeing

Tintinnábulum: a little bell

Tomentósus: covered with pubescence (*tomentum*)

Torminósus: causing dysentery

Torósus: muscular

Tórtilis: twisted

Torulósus: muscular, bulky

Torúnda: stuffing for birds, chicken feed; material for dressing wounds

Tórvus: grim, surly

Tráchypus: with scabrous foot ($\tau\rho\alpha\chi\acute{\upsilon}s$ = scabrous, rough; $\pi o\acute{\upsilon}s$ = foot)

Tráganus: pertaining to goat ($\tau\rho\acute{\alpha}\gamma os$ = goat)

Tramétes: pertaining to footpaths (because of the large and sinous pores, like trails, if from *trames* = paths); or the perineum (if from $\tau\rho\acute{\alpha}\mu\iota s$)

Tremélla: trembling (*tremesco* = I tremble)

Treméllodon: with trembling teeth ($\tau\rho\acute{\epsilon}\mu\omega$ = I tremble; $\acute{o}\delta\acute{\omega}\nu$ = tooth)

Tremellósus: trembling (*tremo* = I tremble)

Tricháster: hairy star ($\theta\rho\acute{\iota}\xi$ = hair, braid; $\dot{\alpha}\sigma\tau\acute{\eta}\rho$ = star)

Trichoglóssum: hairy tongue ($\theta\rho\acute{\iota}\xi$ = hairs, bristles; $\gamma\lambda\hat{\omega}\sigma\sigma\alpha$ = tongue)

Tricholóma: with pubescence along the margin ($\theta\rho\acute{\iota}\xi$ = hairs, braid; $\lambda\hat{\omega}\mu\alpha$ = margin)

Tricholomópsis: similar to *Tricholoma*

Trícolor: tricolor

Tridentinus: of Trentino (*Tridéntum*)

Tríplex: triple

Tristis: sad

Triviális: vulgar

Trullisáta or *Trullissáta* or *Trullizáta:* plastered (*trullissátio* = plastering)

Truncátus: truncated, cut off

Truncórim: of the trunks (*truncus*)

Tsúgae: of Tsuga, opening word of Japanese sentence: *Tsuga no mannendake*, which means "mushroom of ten thousand years of Tsuga"

Tubaefórmis: trumpet shaped

Tubárius: maker of trumpets

Túber: tuber, bump

Tuberósus: tuberous, bumpy

Tubifórmis: shaped like a pipe (*tubus*)

Tubíporus: with tubules and pores (*tubus* = tube, pipe; *porus* = pore)

Túmidus: tumid, swollen

Túrci: of the baroness Turco-Lazzari, Italian (ca. 1800–1900)

Túrpis: base, vile

Tylopílus: with pulvinate cap ($\tau\acute{\upsilon}\lambda os$ = pillow; $\pi\acute{\iota}\lambda\epsilon\upsilon s$ = cap)

Tylóstoma: pillow with mouth ($\tau\acute{\upsilon}\lambda os$ = pillow; $\sigma\tau\acute{o}\mu\alpha$ = mouth)

Údus: wet, moist

Ulmárius: pertaining to elm tree (*úlmus*)

Umbellátus: furnished with umbrella (*umbélla*)

Ubilicátus: with umbilicus (*umbilicus*)

Umbonátus: umbonate, with a protuberance

Umbonatéscens: tending to become umbonate

Umbrinolúteus: dark yellow (*umbrinus* = dark; *luteus* = yellow)

Umbrínus: dark

Ungulína: pertaining to the hoof (*ungula* = hoof)

Unícolor: of only one color

Úrens: burning

Ustális: yellow red or golden red (*usta* = burnt cinnabar, a yellow red or golden red dye)

Ustaloídes: similar to *ustale*

Útilis: useful

Utrárius: bearer of wineskins

Utrifórmis: shaped like a wineskin (*uter* = wineskin)

Úvidus: damp, moist, humid

Vaccínus: pertaining to cow

Vaginátus: protected by a sheath

Válidus: valid, resistant

Vaporárius: of warm and humid places (*vaporarium* = a steam pipe)

Variátus: modified (*varius* = I modify, I make different)

Variegátus: variegated, painted in many ways

Variícolor: of various colors (*varius* = various; *color* = color)

Várius: various, varied, variegated

Velenóvskyi: of J. Velenovsky, Czechoslovak (1858–1949)

Velléreus: covered with fleece (*vellus* = fleece)

Velútinus: velvety (either from *velum* = veil or French *velu* = covered with hairs)

Velútipes: velvety foot (either from *velum* = veil or French *velu* = covered with hairs, and *pes* = foot)

Venenátus: poisoned

Venenósus: poisonous

Vénetus: with the color of seawater

Venósus: with prominent veins

Vermiculáris: pertaining to little worms (*vermiculus* = little worm)

Vernális: of spring

Vérnus: of spring

Verrucósus: full of warts

Versícolor: multicolored

Versipéllis: transforming, changing appearance

Véscus: emaciated

Vesciculósus: with blisters

Veternósus: affected by lethargy, weak

Vibecínus: pertaining to bruises (*livex* = bruise)

Viétus: wilted, wrinkled

Villáticus: rustic, rural

Villósus: hairy

Vinícolor: of the color of the wine (*vinum* = wine; *color* = color)

Violáceus: violaceous, violet

Violáscens: tending to become violaceous

Violéipes: violaceous foot

Viréscens: verdant

Virgátus: with striae, or stripes

Virgíneus: virginal

Víridis: green

Virósus: poisonous or fetid

Víscidus: viscid

Vitéllinus: yellow like an egg yolk (*vitéllus* = egg yolk)

Vítilis: twining, coiling

Vittadini: of C. Vittadini, Italian (1800–1865)

Volémus: big as a pear (*Volemum pirum* = pear that fills the hollow of the hand)

Volváceus: pertaining to the volva (enveloping the base of the stem)

Volvária: same as *volvaceus*

Volvariélla: diminutive of *Volvaria*

Volvátus: having *volva*

Vulgáris: common, known

Vulpínus: with the color of fox fur

Wassonii: of R. G. Wasson, American (living)

Xanthóchrous: with yellow skin ($\xi\alpha\nu\theta\delta_S$ = yellow; $\chi\rho\dot\omega_S$ = skin)

Xanthodérmus: with yellow skin ($\xi\alpha\nu\theta\delta_S$ = yellow; $\delta\acute\epsilon\rho\mu\alpha$ = skin)

Xerampélinus: with the color of a dry vine leaf ($\xi\eta\rho\alpha\mu\pi\acute\epsilon\lambda\iota\nu o_S$)

Xerócomus: with arid hair, not viscid ($\xi\eta\rho\acute o_S$ = arid; $\kappa\acute o\mu\eta$ = hair)

Xeromphálina: little dry *Omphalia* ($\xi\eta\rho\acute o_S$ = arid; *Omphalina* = diminutive of *Omphalia*)

Xérula: small dry (diminutive from $\xi\eta\rho\acute o_S$ = arid, dry)

Xylária: pertaining to the wood ($\xi\acute u\lambda o\nu$ = wood)

Zapotecorum: of the Zapotec, people of Mexico

Zelleri: of S. M. Zeller, American (1885–1948)

Zinziberátus: seasoned with ginger (*zingiber*)

Zonarioides: similar to *zonárius*

Zonárius: pertaining to zone (*zona* = zone)

Zonátus: with zones

Index

Remember that in Latin: *ae = i, æ = e, oe = oi, œ = oe,*
y = i, ph = f, ti = shi, ti = ti.

abiétina, Clavária 220, 221
abiétina, Lenzítes or *Tramétes* 209
abiétum, Amaníta pantherína variety 18
abiétum, Hýdnum 216
abruptibúlba, Psallióta 48
Acanthocýstis 127
acanthoídes, Polýporus = gigánteus, Polýporus 209
acérbum, Tricholóma 97
acérrimus, Lactárius 140
acerváta, Collýbia = Bresádolae, Marásmius 88
acervátus, Marásmius = Bresádolae, Marásmius 88
Acetábula = Peziza 235
acetábulum, Peziza 235
ácre, Hýdnum 216
ácris, Lactárius 139
acuminátus, Panaéolus 53
acutesquamósa, Lepióta 37
acutesquamósa variety *furcáta, Lepióta* 37
adhaérens, Lentínus 126
adipósa, Pholióta 58
adústa, Rússula 147
aegeríta, Agrócybe or *Pholióta* 64
aéreus, Bolétus or *Tubíporus* 180
aerumbonátus, Lactárius 140
aerutináscens, Bolétus = víscidus, Bolétus 191
aeruginea, Rússula 152
aeruginósa, Geóphila or *Strophária* 55
aestívum, Túber 240
Agáricus = Psallióta 43–49
agathósmum, Limácium = agathósmus, Hygróphorus 168
agathósmus, Hygróphorus 168
aggregáta, Clitócybe = aggregátum, Lyophýllum 106, 107
aggregátum, Lyophýllum or *Tricholóma* 106, 107
Agrócybe 64
álba, Amaníta citrína variety 26
álba, Amaníta phalloídes variety 26
álba, Amanitópsis vagináta variety *= nívea, Amanitópsis*
  vagináta variety 33
álba, Clitócybe odóra form 115
álba, Lepióta clypeolária variety 38
álba, Psallióta campéstris variety 45
albéllum, Lyophýllum Geórgii variety 105
albídipes, Bolétus 192
álbidum, Hýdnum repándum variety 214
álbidus, Bolétus 182
álbidus variety *eupáchypus, Bolétus* 182
albobrúnneum, Tricholóma 94
albocyánea, Strophária 55
albonígra, Rússula 146, 147
alboviláceum, Inolóma = alboviláceus, Cortinárius 74
alboviláceus, Cortinárius 74
álbum, Tricholóma 102
álbum variety *lascívum, Tricholóma* 102
álbus, Bolétus 215
álbus, Bolétus = plácidus, Bolétus 182
álbus, Bolétus calópus variety 182
álbus, Cantharéllus cibárius variety 224, 225
Aleúria = Peziza 238
alliáceus, Marásmius 92
alnícola, Pholióta 59
alpínum, Hebelóma 65
alutácea, Otídea 235
alutácea, Rússula 154, 155
Amaníta 17–32
Amanitópsis 30–33
amára, Rússula = caerúlea, Rússula 153
amaréllus, Bolétus 195
amaréscens, Hýdnum or *Sárcodon* 216

amaríssima, Rússula lépida variety 146
amárus, Bolétus = álbidus, Bolétus 182
ambígua, Strophária 55
Ambrósii, Cystodérma 40
americana, Lepióta = Badhámii, Lepióta 36
americánus, Bolétus 194
amethýsteus, Cantharéllus cibárius variety 224, 225
amethýstina, Gyróphila = saévus, Rhodopaxíllus 120
amethýstina, Laccária 119
amethýstina, Psallióta 48
amethýstina, Rússula = Túrci, Rússula 153
amethýstinum, Tricholóma = saévus, Rhodopaxíllus 120
amiánthina, Lepióta = amiánthinum, Cystodérma 40
amiánthinum, Cystodérma 40
amiánthinum variety *rugosoreticulatum, Cystodérma* 40
Amíci, Amanita 25
ammóphila, Psallióta 49
amoéna, Rússula 151
amoéna variety *cítrina, Rússula* 151
amoéna variety *violéipes, Rússula* 151
amoenáta, Rússula = caerúlea, Rússula 153
amoénolens, Cortinárius cyánopus variety 73
androsáceis, Marásmius 92
angústiceps, Morchélla 237
annulátus, Bolétus = lúteus, Bolétus 192
annulosulphúrea, Amaníta 20
anómalus, Cortinárius 74
anserínum, Tricholóma = saévus, Rhodopaxíllus 120
Anthúrus 224
apícrea, Pholióta 58
appendiculátus, Hypholóma = candolleána or *hydróphila,*
  Drosóphila 52
appendiculátus, Bolétus or *Tubíporus* 181
applanátum, Ganodérma 213
applanátus, Crepidótus 127
aprile or *aprílis Entolóma* 83
aquósa, Rússula 157
arbustívus, Hygróphorus 167
Archéri, Anthúrus = aseroifórmis, Anthúrus 224
arculárius, Polýporus 201
argéntea, Amanitópsis vagináta variety 33
argillácea, Clavária 222
argyráceum, Tricholóma = scalpturátum, Tricholóma 98, 99
armeníacus, Bolétus 196, 197
Armillária = Armillariélla 110, *Biannulária* 109, *Clitócybe*
  116, *Lentínus* 126, *Mucídula* 84, 85, *Tricholóma* 93
Armillariélla 110
armillátus, Cortinárius 77
arvénsis, Agáricus = arvénsis, Psallióta 46
arvénsis, Psallióta 46
arvénsis variety *nivéscens, Psallióta* 46
aséma, Collýbia 88
aseroifórmis, Anthúrus 224
áspera, Lepióta = acutesquamósa, Lepióta 37
Aspidélla 22, 32
aspídeus, Lactárius 136, 137
asteróphora, Nýctalis 108
asteróphora, Inócybe 80, 81
astraeícola, Bolétus 227
Astraéus 232
astragalína, Phóliota 59
atráta, Collýbia 86
atramentárius, Cóprinus 50
atromarginátus, Plúteus = nigroflocculósus, Plúteus 41
atropurpúrea, Rússula 157
atrórubens, Rússula 157
atrosquamósum, Tricholóma 100
atrotomentósus, Paxíllus 176
atrotomentósus form *hirsútus, Paxíllus* 176
atróvirens, Tricholóma saponáceum variety 102, 103
augústa, Psallióta 48

aurántia, Armillária = aurántium, Tricholóma 94, 95
aurántia, Pezíza 238
aurantíaca, Clavária = hélvola, Clavária 222
aurantíaca, Clitocybe = aurantíaca, Hygrophorópsis 118
aurantíaca, Hygrophorópsis 118
aurantíaca variety nígripes, Hygrophorópsis 118
aurantíaca variety pállida, Hygrophorópsis 118
aurantíacum, Cálodon 217
aurantíacum, Hýdnum = aurantíacum, Cálodon 217
aurantíacus, Bolétus 189
aurantíacus, Cantheréllus = aurantíaca, Hygrophorópsis 118
aurantíacus, Lactárius 142
aurantíacus, Tráchypus = aurantíacus, Bolétus 189
aurántio-turbinátus, Cortinárius 70
aurántipes, Leótia lúbrica variety 239
aurántium, Sclerodérma 227
aurántium, Tricholóma 94, 95
auráta, Rússula 156
áurea, Clavária 218
áurea, Phaeolepióta 62
áurea, Pholióta = áurea, Phaeolepióta 62
áurea, Ramária = áurea. Clavária 218
auréola, Amaníta muscária variety 18
áureus, Hygróphorus 167
aurícula Júdae, Auriculária or Hirnéola 231
aurícula, Otídea 235
Auriculária 231
auríporus, Bolétus = cramesínus, Bolétus 195
Auriscálpum 217
auriscálpium, Hýdnum = vulgáre, Auriscálpium 217
aurivélla, Dryóphila = aurivélla, Pholióta 58
aurivélla, Pholióta 58
auróra, Rússula 146
azonítes, Lactárius = fuliginósus, Lactárius 139
azúrea, Rússula 151

Badhámii, Lepióta 36
bádia, Pezíza 238
bádia, Rússula 160
badio-rúfus, Bolétus 198
badiosanguíneus, Lactárius 140
bádius, Bolétus or Xerócomus 198
Bárlae, Rússula 152
Bernárdi, Psallióta 46
Bertillónii, Lactárius velléreus variety 129
betulárum, Rússula emética variety 160
betúlina, Ungulína = betúlinus, Piptóporus 212
betúlinus, Piptóporus or Polýporus 212
Biannulária 109
bícolor, Laccária laccáta variety 119
bírrum, Hebelóma 65
bíspora, Psallióta 43–44
bíspora variety bitórquis, Psallióta 44
bíspora variety horténsis, Psallióta 44
bíspora variety úmbrina, Psallióta 44
bisporigena, Amaníta 28, 29
bitórquis, Psallióta bíspora variety 44
blénnius, Lactárius 136
blénnius form víridis, Lactárius 136
bohémica, Vérpa 237
boláris, Cortinárius 75
Bolbitius = Drosóphyla 52
Bolétinus = Bolétus 199
Boletópsis = Polýporus 206, 207
Bolétus 174–201, 227
bombýcina, Volvária or Volvariélla 41, 4
Bongárdii, Inócybe 80
botrýtes or botrýtis, Clavária or Ramária 218
botrýtis variety párvula, Clavária 218
botrýtis variety ruféscens, Clavária 218

bovinus, Bolétus or Ixócomus 174, 194
Bovísta 231
bovísta, Lycopérdon = coelátum, Lycopérdon 230
Bresádolae, Bolétus = Quelétii, Bolétus 186
Bresádolae, Bolétus víscidus variety 191
Bresádolae, Hygrócybe 170
Bresádolae, Marásmius 88
bresadoliánus, Lactárius = zonarioídes, Lactárius 132, 133, 140
brévipes, Bolétus 192
brévipes, Melanoléuca 109
brévipes, Rhodopaxíllus panaéolus variety 122
brumále, Túber 240
brumále, Tylóstoma 227
brumális, Clitócybe 118
brumális, Leucóporus or Polyporéllus or Polýporus 201
brúnneoincarnáta, Lepióta 38
brúnneoviolácea, Rússula 148
brunnéscens, Amaníta 18
brúnneus, Cortinárius 77
Bryóphila = (fasciculáre) Hyphológma 55
bufónium, Tricholóma sulphúreum variety 104
Bulgária 235
búlbiger, Cortinárius or Leucocortinárius 79
buglossóides, Fistulína = hepática, Fistulína 213
bulbósa, Amaníta = phalloídes, Amaníta 26–27
Bulliardi, Trámétes = rubéscens, Trámétes 212
butyrácea, Collýbia 88

caeláta, Utrária = caelátum, Lycopérdon 230
caelátum or coelátum, Lycopérdon 230
caerúlea, Rússula 153
caeruléipes, Cortinárius mucósus variety 68
caeruléscens, Cortinárius 71
caeruléscens, Hýdnum = caerúleum, Cálodon 217
caeruléscens, Phlegmácium = caeruléscens, Cortinárius 71
caerúleum, Cálodon 217
caesárea, Amaníta 17
caesiocyáneus, Cortinárius 71
caespitósus, Rhodopaxíllus 122
calcéolus, Polýporus = pícipes, Polýporus 202, 203
califórnica, Helvélla 234
caligáta, Armillária = caligátum, Tricholóma 93
caligátum, Tricholóma 93
caliginósa, Nýctalis = parasítica, Nýctalis 108
Calócera 233
calóchrous, Cortinárius 70
Calócybe = Lyophýllum 105
Cálodon 217
calólepis, Crepidotus móllis form 127
Calóporus = Boletópsis, Polypílus, Polýporus 206, 207
cálopus, Bolétus 182
cálopus variety álbus, Bolétus 182
cálopus, Tubíporus = cálopus, Bolétus 182
Calvátia = Lycopérdon 228–230
calyptrodérma, Amaníta 17
camarophýllus, Hygróphorus 168
campanulátus, Panaéolus 53
campéster, Agáricus = campéstris, Psallióta 45
campéstris, Pratélla or Psallióta 45
campéstris variety álba, Psallióta 45
camphorátus, Lactárius 144
cancellátus, Cláthrus 228, 229
cancellátus, Cláthrus form discancellátus 228
cándida, Clitócybe = gigantea, Clitócybe 112
cándidum, Lycopérdon = gemmátum, Lycopérdon 230
candolleána, Drosóphila 52
candolleánum, Hyphológma = candolleána, Drosóphila 52
caninus, Cortinárius 74
caninus, Mútinus 226, 9

elegántior, Cortinárius 70
elegantíssima, Clavária 218
Eliae, Amaníta 25
emética, Rússula 160
emética, Rússula variety betulárum 160
emética, Rússula variety silvéstris 160
Entolóma 82
epipterýgia, Mycéna 93
epixánthum, Hypholóma 56
equéstre, Tricholóma 100
erébia, Agrócybe 63
erináceus, Drýodon or Herícium 214, 215
erubéscens, Hygróphorus 165
erubéscens, Tricholóma = erubéscens, Hygróphorus 165
erumbonátus or aerumbonátus, Lactárius 140
erýngii, Pleurótus 123
erýngii, variety férulae, Pleurótus 123
erythrópoda, Rússula = xerampélina, Rússula variety erýthropus 152
erýthropus, Bolétus 184, 185
erýthropus, Marásmius = Bresádolae, Marásmius 88
erýthropus, Rússula xerampélina variety 152
erýthropus, Tubíporus = erýthropus, Bolétus 184, 185
esculénta, Collýbia 91
esculénta, Gyromítra 234
esculénta, Morchélla = Morchélla cónica 236 or rotúnda or vulgáris 236, 237
esculénta, Physomítra = esculénta, Gyromítra 234
esculénta, Volvária = volvácea, Volvária 42, 43
esculéntus, Bolétus = edúlis, Bolétus 177
eupáchypus, Bolétus álbidus variety 182
europaeus, Favolus 207
evenósa, Melanoléuca variety stríctipes 106
exálbicans, Rússula sanguínea variety 158
excélsa, Amaníta spíssa variety 20
excipulifórme, Lycopérdon = saccátum, Lycopérdon 230
excoriáta, Lepióta 37
exímia, Pezíza or Sarcosphaéra 240
Exobasídium 238
expállens, Clitócybe 118
expállens, Hygróphorus 168, 169
expállens, Rússula = sardónia, Rússula 158, 159
exscissa, Melanoléuca 109

fállax, Cystodérma 40
fállax, Geoglóssum 239
fállax, Rússula = frágilis, Rússula 161
família, Collýbia 88
farínipes, Rússula 162
fasciculáre, Hypholóma or Nematolóma 55
fasciculáris, Bryóphila or Geóphila = fasciculáre, Hypholóma 55
fastigiáta, Inócybe 80
felína, Lepióta 38
féllea, Rússula 162
félleus, Bolétus 178, 179
félleus, Rhodóporus = félleus, Bolétus 178, 179
félleus, Tylopílus = félleus, Bolétus 178, 179
fénnicum, Hýdnum or Sárcodon 216
Ferrii, Strophária 55
ferrugíneum, Cálodon or Hýdnum 217
ferrugíneus, Boletínus cávipes form 199
ferrugíneus, Bolétus = spadíceus, Bolétus 196
fértile, Entolóma = lívidum, Entolóma 82
férulae, Pleurótus erýngii variety 123
fibrósa, Inócybe 79
ficoídes, Hygróphorus = praténsis, Hygróphorus 170
fimbriátus, Geáster 232
fírmula, Rússula 151, 153
Fischeri, Limacélla 32

Fistulína 213
fistulósa, Clavária 222
flabellifórmis, Pánus = conchátus, Pánus 128
fláccida, Clavária 221
fláccida, Clitócybe = fláccida, Lepísta invérsa variety 119
fláccida, Lepísta invérsa variety 119
flámmans, Pholióta 59
flámmea, Calócera = viscósa, Calócera 233
Flámmula 58
fláva, Clavária 218
flavéscens, Clavária = áurea, Clavária 218
flavéscens, Pratélla = silvícola, Psallióta 48
flávida, Spathulária 239
flávidus, Bolétus 191
flávidus, Boletínus cávipes form 199
flávidus, Lactárius = aspídeus, Lactárius 136, 137
flávipes, Mycéna 93
flavobrúnneum, Tricholóma 94
flavocónia, Amaníta 18
flavus, Bolétus 191
flóccopus, Bolétus = strobiláceus, Bolétus var. flóccopus 200
floccósus, Cantharéllus 224, 225
focále, Tricholóma robústum variety 93
foétens, Rússula 164
fomentária, Ungulína 210, 211
fomentária, Ungulína variety Inzéngae 210, 211
fomentária, Ungulína variety nígricans 210
fomentárius, Fómes = fomentária, Ungulína 210, 211
Fómes = Ungulína 210–211
formósa, Amanita muscária form 19
formósa, Clavária or Ramária 218
fornicátus, Geáster 232
Forquignóni, Polýporus 202
frágile, Hebelóma 65
frágilis, Clavária vermiculáris variety 222
frágilis, Crepidótus 127
frágilis, Rússula 161
frágrans, Bolétus 181
frágrans, Clitócybe 111
Friesii, Cantharéllus 224
frondósa, Grífola = frondósus, Polýporus 208
frondósus, Calóporus or Polypílus or Polýporus 208
frondósus, Polýporus variety intybáceus 208
Fróstii, Bolétus 184
fúlgens, Cortinárius 70
fuligíneo-Hýdnum or Sárcodon 214
fuligíneo-violáceum, Hýdnum or Sárcodon 216
fuligíneus, Bolétus porphyrósporus variety 200
fuliginósa, Lepióta procéra variety 34
fuliginósus, Lactárius 139
fuliginósus variety pterósporus, Lactárius 139
fulmíneum, Phlegmácium = fulmíneus, Cortinárius 70
fulmíneus, Cortinárius 70
fúlva, Amaníta = fúlva, Amanitópsis vagináta variety 33
fúlva, Amanitópsis vagináta variety 33
fulvíssimus (Romagnesi), Lactárius = mitíssimus, Lactárius 142
fúlvum, Tricholóma = flavobrúnneum, Tricholóma 94
fumósa, Clavária 222
fumósum, Tricholóma = cineráscens, Lyophýllum 106, 107
funiculáris, Collýbia dryóphila variety 89
furcáta, Lepióta acutesquamósa variety 37
furfuráceum, Lycopérdon 230
fúsca, Collýbia lóngipes variety 84
fúsca, Morchélla = hýbrida, Morchélla 236
fúsca, Rússula xerampélina variety 152
fuscéscens, Cóprinus 50
fuscéscens, Hygróphorus níveus variety 166
fúscopurpúreus, Marásmius 92
fuscóruber, Bolétus edúlis variety 180
fúscovinácea, Lepióta 38

fúscus, Lactárius 140
fúscus, Omphalómyces or *Pleurótus* = *erýngii, Pleurótus* variety *férulae* 123
fusifórmis, Clavária 220, 221
fúsipes, Collýbia 86

Galactínia = *Pezíza* 238
Galéra 60
galericuláta, Mycéna 93
galóchroa, Rússula heterophýlla variety 148
gálopus, Mycéna 93
gambósum, Lyophýllum Geórgii variety 105
Ganodérma 213
Geáster or *Geástrum* 232
gelatinósa, Clavária 218
gelatinósum, Pseudohýdnum or *Treméllodon* 233
gemmáta, Amaníta = *junquíllea, Amaníta* 25
gemmáta, Utrária = *gemmátum, Lycopérdon* 230
gemmátum, Lycopérdon 230
gentílis, Bolétus = *cramesínus, Bolétus* 195
geogénius, Acanthocýstis or *Pleurótus* 127
Geoglóssum 239
Geóphila = *Strophária* 54–55
geophýlla, Inócybe 79
geophýlla, Inócybe variety *laterítia* 79
geophýlla, Inócybe variety *violácea* 79
Geórgii, Calócybe = *Geórgii, Lyophýllum* 105
Geórgii, Lyophýllum 105
Geórgii variety *albéllum, Lyophýllum* 105
Geórgii variety *gambósum, Lyophýllum* 105
Geórgii variety *gravéolens, Lyophýllum* 105
Geórgii variety *palumbínum, Lyophýllum* 105
Geórgii, Tricholóma = *Geórgii, Lyophýllum* 105
geótropa, Clitócybe 112
gibbósa, Daedálea or *Tramétes* 210
gigántea, Bovísta or *Calvátia* = *maxímum, Lycopérdon* 228
gigántea, Clitócybe 112
gigánteum, Lycopérdon = *maxímum, Lycopérdon* 228
gigánteus, Polýporus 209
gigas, Gyromítra 234
gílva, Clitócybe = *gílva, Lepísta* 119
gílva, Lepísta 119
glábra, Amaníta cítrina variety 26
glandulósus, Pleurótus ostreátus variety 125
glaucéscens, Lactárius = *piperátus, Lactárius* 130
glaucocánus, Rhodopaxíllus 120
glaucophýlla, Clitócybe = *marzúolus, Hygróphorus* 171
gláucopus, Cortinárius 72, 73
gliodérma, Limacélla 32
Gloeophýllum = *Lenzítes* 209
gloiocéphala, Volvária 40
gloiocéphala variety *speciósa, Volvária* 40
glutinósus, Gomphídius 173
glycyósmus, Lactárius = *impolítus, Lactárius* 136
Godéyi, Inócybe 80, 81
Gomphídius 173–176
Gómphus = *Nevrophýllum* 221
goniospérmum, Tricholóma 105
gracilénta, Lepióta = *puelláris, Lepióta* 34
gracilis, Gomphídius maculátus variety 173
grammocéphala, Collýbia = *platyphýlla, Collýbia* 87
grammopódia, Melanoléuca 109
grammopódium, Tricholóma = *grammopódia, Melanoléuca* 109
granulátus, Bolétus 192, 193
granulátus, Elaphómyces 240
granulátus, Ixócomus = *granulátus, Bolétus* 192, 193, 14
granulósum, Cystodérma 40
granulósum, Tylósoma 227
gravéolens, Cálodon or *Hýdnum* 217

gravéolens, Lyophýllum Geórgii variety 105
gravéolens, Tricholóma = *gravéolens, Lyophýllum Geórgii* variety 105
Grevíllei, Bolétus or *Ixócomus* = *élegans, Bolétus* 191
Grífola or *Grifólia* 206
grísea, Amaníta = *grísea, Amanitópsis vagináta* variety 33
grísea, Amanitópsis vagináta variety 33
grísea, Rússula 148
grísea, Rússula variety *ionochlóra* 148
grísea, Collýbia tenacélla variety 91
groanénse, Tricholóma 98
Guepinia = *Gyrocéphalus* 233
gummósa, Dryóphila or *Flámmula* 58
guttáta, Limacélla 32
Gymnopílus = *Pholióta* 59
gymnopódia, Clitócybe = *tabéscens, Clitócybe* 116
Gyrocéphalus 233
Gýrodon = *Bolétus* 201
Gyromítra 234
Gyróporus = *Bolétus* 174–177

haematítes, Cystodérma 40
haemátopus, Mycéna 93
haematospérma, Lepióta = *Badhámii, Lepióta* 36, 9
haemorrhoidária, Psallióta 46, 47
Hansénii, Cóprinus 50
Hartígii, Fómes or *Phéllinus* 212
hatsúdake, Lactárius 134
Hebelóma 65–67
helomórpha, Ripartítes tricholóma variety 79
Helvélla 234
helvelloídes, Guepínia or *Phlogiótis* or *Tremélla* = *rúfus, Gyrocéphalus* 233
helvéola, Lepióta 38
helvéticus, Bolétus sibíricus variety 191
helvéticus, Gomphídius 174
hélvola, Clavária 222
hélvus, Lactárius 140, 141
hemicyáneus, Lactárius 134
hemisphaérica, Pezíza 238
hepática, Fistulína or *Hypódrys* 213
hepáticus, Lactárius 140
Herícium 214, 215
heterophýlla, Rússula 148
heterophýlla, Rússula variety *galóchroa* 148
heterophýlla, Rússula variety *virgínea* 148
hexagonoídes, Tramétes 210
hiemále, Hebelóma 66
hinnúleus, Cortinárius 77
Hirnéola = *Auriculária* 231
hirsútum, Geoglóssum 239
hirsútum, Stéreum 209
hirsútum, Trichoglóssum = *hirsútum, Geoglóssum* 239
hirsútus, Coríolus 209
hirsútus, Cýathus = *striátus, Cýathus* 227
hirsútus, Paxíllus atrotomentósus form 176
híspida, Tramétes 210
híspidus, Inonótus or *Xanthóchrous* 212
holosérica, Lepióta 38
hórdum, Tricholóma 98
Hornemánnii, Strophária 55
horténsis, Lepióta rhacódes variety 36
horténsis, Morchélla 237
horténsis, Psallióta = *bíspora, Psallióta* 44
horténsis, Psallióta bíspora variety 44
hyacínthinus, Hygróphorus 168
hýbrida, Flámmula 58
hýbrida, Mitróphora or *Morchélla* 237
Hýdnum 14 and *Cálodon* 217, *Herícium* 214, 215, *Sárcodon* 216

virgíneus, Hygróphorus 166
víride, Geoglóssum or *Microglóssum* 239
víridis, Amaníta = Amaníta phalloídes 26–27
víridis, Amaníta phalloídes variety 27
víridis, Clitócybe odóra form 115
víridis, Lactárius = blénnius, Lactárius 136
víridis, Lactárius blénnius form 136
virósa, Amaníta 28, 29
víscida, Rússula 160
víscidus, Agáricus = glutinósus, Gomphídius 173
víscidus, Bolétus 191
víscidus variety *Bresádolae, Bolétus* 191
víscidus, Gomphídius 174
víscidus, Ixócomus = víscidus, Bolétus 191
viscósa, Calócera 233
vitéllina, Rússula = lútea, Rússula 156
vitéllina, Rússula chamaeleontína variety 156
vitéllinus, Bolétus = álbidus, Bolétus 182
Vittadíni, Amaníta or *Aspidélla* 22
volémus, Lactárius 135
volémus variety *oedemátopus, Lactárius* 135
volvácea, Volvária 42, 43
volvácea variety *nígricans, Volvária* 42, 43
volváceus, Cláthrus = cancellátus, Cláthrus 228, 229
Volvária 40–43, 4
Volvariélla = Volvária 41

volvátus, Bolétus = lúteus, Bolétus 192
vulgáre, Auriscálpium or *Léptodon* 217
vulgáre, Crucíbulum = crucíbulum, Cýathus 227
vulgáre, Sclerodérma = aurántium, Sclerodérma 227
vulgáris, Acetábula = acetábulum, Pezíza 235
vulgáris, Melanoléuca 106
vulgáris, Morchélla 236, 237
vulpínus, Bolétus 190
vulpínus, Lentínus 126

Xanthóchrous = Inonótus 212
xanthodérma, Psallióta 49
xerampélina variety *erýthropus, Rússula* 152
xerampélina variety *fúsca, Rússula* 152
xerampélina variety *olováscens, Rússula* 152
Xerócomus = Bolétus 196–198, 227
Xérula = Collýbia 84
Xylária 239

Zélleri, Armillária = imperiális, Biannulária 109
zinziberátus, Cortinárius 75
zonarioídes, Lactárius 132, 133, 140
zonárius, Lactárius 133
zonátus, Coríolus 209

Bibliography

The illustrations used in this volume were prepared on the base of original drawings and photographs, and, partly, on the base of various mycological iconographies, listed below:

Alessio C. L., *I boleti*, Ceva 1969.

Atkinson G. F., *Mushrooms edible, poisonous* etc., New York 1961.

Bettín A., *Le Amanite*, Verona 1971.

Bresadola G., *Iconographia mycologica*, Milano 1927.

Bresadola G. e Ceruti A., *Funghi mangerecci e velenosi*, Trento 1965.

Cetto B., *I funghi dal vero*, Trento 1971.

Dumée P., *Nouvel atlas de poche des champignons comestibles et vénéneux*, Paris 1905.

Engel F., *Pilzwanderungen*, Wittenberg Lutherstadt 1965.

Essette H., *Les psalliotes*, Paris 1964.

Frieden L. von, *I funghi di tutti i paesi*, Milano 1964.

Gramberg E., *Pilze der Heimat*, Leipzig 1939.

Heim R., *Les champignons d'Europe*, Paris 1957.

Heim R., *Les champignons toxiques et hallucinogènes*, Paris 1963.

Farlow, W. and G., *Icones Farlowianae*, Cambridge (Massachusetts) 1929.

Jaccottet J., *Les champignons dans la nature*, Neuchâtel 1925.

Kleijn J., *Mushrooms and other fungi*, Amsterdam 1961.

Konrad P. et Maublanc A., *Icones selectae fungorum*, 1924–1936.

Lange M., *Illustreret svamperflora*, Copenhagen 1961.

Lange J. E. und Lange M., *600 Pilze in Farben*, München 1964.

Maublanc A. et Viennot-Bourgin G., *Les champignons de France*, Paris 1959.

McKenny M., *The savory wild mushroom*, Washington 1926.

Michael-Schulz-Hennig-Schäffer, *Handbuch für Pilzfreunde*, Jena 1958.

Pilát A., *Mushrooms*, Amsterdam 1954.

Pilát A. and Ušák O., *Mushrooms and other fungi*, London 1961.

Rokuya Imazeki and Tsuguo Hongo, *Coloured illustrations of fungi of Japan*, Osaka 1957.

Rolland L., *Atlas des champignons de France, Suisse et Belgique*, 1910.

Romagnesi H., *Nouvel atlas des champignons*, Paris 1956.

Union des sociétés suisses de mycologie, *Planches suisses de champignons*, Zürich 1947.

Viola S., *I funghi come sono*, Milano 1963.

The translators (the editors) suggest the following books that American readers might also find useful:

Usher, G. *A Dictionary of Botany*. London: Constable, 1966.

Krieger, L. C. C. *A Popular Guide to the Higher Fungi Mushrooms) of New York State*. Albany: Lyon Co. 1935.

Alexopoulos, C. J. *Introductory Mycology*. New York: J. Wiley & Sons, 1962.

A Short List of Mushrooms Found in North America

Page reference is to page in present volume where the species is described. When no page is given, it means that no description for that mushroom appears in the present volume.

Contents